M W Banks

O LAUGHING RIVER

"STONEWALL" JACKSON – THE REALITY OF MILITARY GENIUS

novum ⬤ pro

This book is also
available as
e-book.

www.novum-publishing.co.uk

© 2019 novum publishing

ISBN 978-3-99064-554-3
Editing: Hugo Chandler, BA
Cover design created by:
Andrew Cachia, Malta
Layout & typesetting: novum publishing
Internal illustrations:
p. 122: © US National Archives
p. 123: © Photobulb | Dreamstime.com
p. 124–125: © David Rumsey Map
Collection, www.davidrumsey.com

www.novum-publishing.co.uk

Contents

"O LAUGHING RIVER"

....

*"Let us determine to die here and
we will conquer. Look! There is Jackson
standing like a stone wall.
Rally behind the Virginians"*
Bernard E. Bee[1]

....

IN the ballad of nostalgia and lament, the laughing river is the Shenandoah, *'Bright Daughter of the Stars'* in the enchanting tribal metaphor. Divine, to love her daughters; to long for her verdant pastures; her pine and beech-clad slopes, and tumbling cascading waters. Nature in all her glory, before the trampling of tarmac and rubber; the clank of engine and the stink of exhaust. Pre-cursed by the echoing crack and acrid whiff of gunpowder. Death-dealing harbingers of desecration. Humanity, plodding from a simple struggle for existence within nature, to an arrogant, uncaring divergence. In the days of the native tribe alone, what arcane and squalid rights were dreamt-up and enacted amid those sun-bright and shadowed glades? When Red disputed with encroaching White, what cruel and vulgar horrors were not perpetrated in a gloomy twilight, deep in the dripping forest?

Towards the close of that vicious struggle between the recently arrived in America, Phil Sheridan and his Union horsemen reduced 'Paradise Valley' to an arid desert of ragged starvation and wary hate. Not for the first time during the war had the Valley been desecrated as a battle ground; but two years previously there were differences. The tramping boot heels and clopping hooves were not those of the alien striving for domination; but those of

---

1 Shouted by General Bee when *"hard pressed by the enemy"* at the first battle of Manassas or Bull Run.

defensive locals. Virginian and Valley Confederate soldiers led by Virginia born and bred Thomas Jonathan Jackson, recently dubbed – and already recognised verbally, if not always visually in those fortunate days before the media became over-weaning – as 'Stonewall'. His Shenandoah Campaign, in the opening months of 1862, is a gem of the futile art of war, which the truly great captain of any era would be proud to include on their record. To have served with 'Old Jack' marked forever those who were involved with him, in a similar way to those who fought with 'Old Ironsides' in the New Model Army of England's Parliament.

Tucked away at the end of an early biography[2] of Jackson is a revealing anecdote, recorded for the Southern Historical Society by Mr W.P. St John, one-time president of the Mercantile Bank of New York. Long after the 'War between the States' had ended, Mr St John visited the great Shenandoah Valley of Virginia with Thomas Jordan, formerly General Jordan of the Confederate States Army. During the trip they had the occasion to seek refuge in the rustic hut of *"a 'track-walker' for the railroad. … The unprepossessing look of everything was completed when the host came in and took his seat at the head of the table. A bear out of the woods could hardly have been rougher, with his unshaven hair and unkempt beard. Imagine the astonishment of the travellers when this rough backwoodsman rapped on the table and bowed his head. "Never,"* recalled Mr St John, *"did I hear a petition that more evidently came from the heart. It was so simple, so reverent, so tender, so full of humility and penitence, as well as of thankfulness. We sat in silence, and as soon as we had recovered ourselves, I whispered to General Jordan 'Who can he be?' … 'I don't know',* he replied, *'but he must be one of Stonewall Jackson's old soldiers,' and he was. As we walked out in the open air, I accosted our new acquaintance, and after a few questions about the country, asked: 'Were you in the War?' 'O yes', he said with a smile, 'I was out with Old 'Stonewall'."*

2 Lieutenant-Colonel G.F.R. Henderson CB, *"Stonewall Jackson and the American Civil War"*, Longmans, Green and Co., London New York and Bombay, 1904.

Jackson's spirituality, his religious motivation, was a defining characteristic of his memory and contributed greatly to the enduring freshness and immediacy of that memory for those who had been involved with him. *'He lived by the New Testament,'* it was said of him, *'and fought by the Old.'* *"No one, when he had gone, ever left behind him among the ranks greater reverence or a more tender memory,"* wrote the youngest member of Jackson's wartime staff.[3] *"The morning after the unveiling of the Lee Statue in Richmond as the sun rose over the city, its first rays fell upon a row of figures, wrapped in grey blankets and sleeping on the grass around the Statue of Jackson in Capitol Square … 'Could you find no other beds in Richmond?' 'Oh yes,'* was the riposte … *'all Richmond was open to us … but we were his boys and wanted to sleep with the old man just once more'."*[4]. To recall Jackson's special brand of the winning art of command. To experience, however fleetingly, the unique satisfaction of life under the sun, rain and stars, with the trusted leader who, they believed, *"could do anything he wished"* and who, in return, believed that *"they could do anything he commanded."*[5] By then, his fame had spread far beyond their Valley, although nearly a Century would pass before this second Jackson name would be installed amongst the great of America's *'Hall of Fame'*. It is quite conceivable that the man who at a young age decided, *"his every thought and act was under the constant guidance and direction of the Maker, and all for his glory alone,"* would neither have approved of such a list, nor of his inclusion on it. *"You can,"* he would say, *"be whatever you choose to be,"* and all he achieved, he ascribed to God's will alone. In half the time it took his name to reach that list, Field Marshal Lord Roberts recognised his greatness and kept a likeness of the Virginian in his study at home, when he was Chief of England's Imperial General Staff. The CIGS, like the Lord Protector, the

---

3 Henry Kyd Douglas, *"I Rode with Stonewall"*, The University of North Carolina Press, Twelfth Printing 1940.

4 Ibid.

5 Henry Kyd Douglas.

Duke and Old Jack himself, demonstrated beyond doubt that Victory prefers intellectual finesse to bludgeoning muscle, for Defeat never dared show its face in Southern Lines when Jackson was present on the battlefield. After his death, Victory defected to the North, and no matter who was in charge, erstwhile and worsted colleagues in that renowned Army of Northern Virginia were heard to murmur, *"O for another Jackson."*

1. ORPHAN

....

"Maybe I ought to Ma'am,
but I am not going to."
Thomas Jackson

....

THE individual whose character, methods and achievements so lastingly captivated those with whom he came into contact, as well as those whose minds were made up from reputation and hearsay, was born into financial poverty and into a family circle rich in relations. His ancestry was Irish-Scotch. His family were immigrants to America in the Seventeenth Century, on both his mother's side – Neale (probably changed from O'Neill or O'Neal[6]) – and his father's – Jackson – all from Irish counties; she from County Limerick and he from around Derry. Many of their predecessors had reached Ireland from the border country of Scotland. It was said that of all the immigrants to America there were none tougher than the Irish-Scotch of Celtic origin, whose self-reliant and resolute courage largely populated the frontier, leaving it to those from other parts of the British Isles to provide the more prosaic and niggling trappings required to weld nascent communities. *"Taken all in all, they were generally men and women of whom posterity may be proud. We will find many things in the character of our early settlers to command our admiration … fearless of danger yet fearing their God … their word was their bond, its seal their honour."*[7]

The first quarter of the Nineteenth Century was ending when Thomas was born[8] into this community of enterprising border stock. The true frontier days of the 'pale', as it were, for incoming

---

6 Cook.
7 Arnold quoting from *"The Monongahela of Old"* by the Hon. James Veach.
8 21 January 1824.

settler groups had been extended inland beyond the western border of the Old Dominion of Virginia. The need to cultivate, export and import; to negotiate business, apply the law, and enjoy simple, boisterous moments of drinking and eating, live-music and dance, all within quick concentrating distance of a log and plank stockade, had passed. The last battle with the Redman, east of the Ohio River, had taken place some fifty years before, in 1744. No more did the Jackson's, the Neale's and others, established in the counties round about Thomas's birthplace of Clarksburg,[9] in Harrison County, need to keep an eye and ear ever-alert for the sting or thump of an arrow and the glint of metal heralding the rush of half-naked, fur and paint clad men. Participating Frenchmen had been thrust away north into a corner of Canada, and the Redman himself had been driven to a remote, more inland wilderness, there to renew the doomed contest with a chain of more militarily sophisticated forts, and men more trained, drilled and equipped for the purpose.

If Tom Jackson did not grow up under out-and-out frontier living conditions, everyday life still meant the unremitting hard work demanded by an implacable nature, and, in the face of harsh elements, a vigorous determination to survive. Death, if less from violence, was a familiar companion still, in his guise of disease, weakness or accident. Jackson was named Thomas after his mother's father. He himself added the Jonathan, when nearly an adult, in memory of his own, who was both lawyer and frontiersman. The family had been commended for their exertions in the Indian wars of the previous Century, and the practising lawyer and inland revenue agent was made first lieutenant of a troop of volunteer cavalry, which the family's home county of Harrison, offered to the president – fellow Virginian James Madison – for the conflict with an England whose struggle to

---

9 324–328 Main Street, Clarksburg. *"In August 1911, the Stonewall Jackson Chapter of the Daughters of the Confederacy attached a bronze tablet … commemorating … the birthplace of 'General Stonewall Jackson.'"* (Cook)

unseat Napoleon still had three years to run. There is no record of the Harrison County irregulars being called upon to confront an enemy. Having nursed his elder daughter, Elizabeth, through a terminal fever, father Jonathan died just three weeks after her, of that same fever, leaving his wife Julia, two boys; Warren the eldest, Thomas just two months into his third year, and their sister Laura, whose own son would write later; *"At that period a lawyer in practice did well if his profession yielded a support for himself and family. If he acquired anything in excess of this, it was almost invariably the result of speculation, … the little family was left in destitute circumstances."*[10] Father Jonathan had been a Freemason for more than the last ten years of his life, and the Order, with true concern for its own, supplied the family with a furnished, three-room cottage. Although reputedly of good looks, Julia Jackson was not strongly constituted. She started a private school to help make ends meet and took in sewing. She re-married, and the family moved to newly constituted Fayette County, where her second husband, Captain Blake Woodson, was appointed clerk of the county court in Mountain Cove, the seat of local government. But the strain of trying to survive with her young family, gradually asserted itself. Warren was sent to live with a maternal uncle and, when Thomas was six, it was decided that he and his sister Laura should be taken in by their father's grandmother, who lived alone with unmarried daughters and sons, in Lewis County. When the pair were told of the reason for the visit of their Jackson uncle, Thomas actively protested against being parted from his mother. He bolted for the surrounding woods and was not found until he chose to return at nightfall. It was two days before brother and sister were persuaded and the move completed. A courageous and selfless action by a mother who had glimpsed the end, and wished to see her surviving children at least secure, before she followed their father to the

---

10 *"Early Life and Letters of General Thomas J. Jackson"* By his nephew Thomas Jackson Arnold.

grave. Within a year, Laura and Thomas, in the care of a trusted slave-servant known as Uncle Robinson, returned in time to be at the bedside of their dying mother. Julia was a devout woman, and it was described as a *'happy death.'* Thereafter, neither she nor the circumstances of her death, were far from her son's thoughts. Given his very young age when father Jonathan died, mother Julia was the one true influence of their son's childish decade. Acknowledgement of his father came later, when Thomas met with men and women who had known him, and could recount their first hand memories, thus giving the son a vicarious image of which to be proud, and a relationship to acknowledge and to remember, rather than one by which to be influenced.

If those first ten years were years of insecurity and much grief, for a child capable of the determination and courage, which we are entitled to assume from the decades of manhood, they were years which brought an understanding of a harsh reality. He had the strength of character, independence of mind and everyday physical and moral courage, to deal effectively and well with every combination of circumstance. Having a fundamental strength and goodness he became accomplished at living under very challenging conditions. Thomas and sister Laura still suffered disruptive change, then, in addition, separation. A guardian was appointed for Laura, *"but for some reason this was rescinded the same day … shortly after this, Laura rode behind her Aunt Rebecca White to Parkersburg."*[11] After two years, Tom went to live with his uncle Isaac Brake; but soon left. Stopping for something to eat with a relative in Clarksburg, he discussed with her why he was leaving. She told him he should go back. *"Maybe I ought to, Ma'am,"* he replied, *"but I am not going to."* One can only wonder what line of thinking led to so absolute a decision and so firm a response by the youthful orphan. Elder brother Warren, meanwhile, continued to live in Parkersburg with Alfred Neale, a relation on his mother's side.

---

11 Cook.

His mother's position of influence in the earliest years, was assumed, in the main, during the teenage decade by the uncle, Cummins E Jackson, with support from maiden aunts and uncles and, for the first few years, a grandmother, the second wife of Edward Jackson, Tom's paternal grandfather. In all he would spend twelve years at the family home of Jackson's Mill, near Weston, on the West fork of the Monongahela River, in Lewis County, which uncle Cummins had enlarged by adding fresh holdings of land to the original homestead, inherited from Edward Jackson. Tom developed into a skilled, all-round countryman, contributing both to the family and to the wider community. For uncle Cummins, he was more of a colleague than a growing boy, who he would often task with overseeing the work force on tree-felling and logging, to feed the sawmill which supplied the surrounding area with seasoned and cut timber; then the material of choice for many trades, including builders, furniture-makers, and packagers of a wide variety of products.

A gristmill was housed in a separate building nearby. For Tom there were chickens to feed, and eggs to be retrieved, ahead of some furry denizen of the riverbank or nearby woodland burrow, and a collie dog for all occasions, be it quiet high-summer moments with a book beside the millstream, organising the sheep for shearing, or the local lads with their 'coon dogs', for a racoon hunt. Collie, the enthusiastic companion, ever eager for a dawn excursion to reset and relocate rabbit traps; but happy investigating his or her own agenda of scent trails during less active fishing trips. Young Tom turned skill at tickling or hooking fish into pocket money, by having a commercial arrangement with Conrad Kester, the Weston gunsmith. Seeing him early one morning with *"a three-foot pike"* slung over one shoulder, Colonel Talbott offered a dollar. *"... this fish is sold to Mr Kestler ... a dollar and a quarter, Tom, surely he will not give you more than that?... Colonel Talbott, I have an agreement with Mr Kestler to furnish him fish of a certain length for fifty cents each. He has taken some from me a little shorter than that; now he is going to get this big fish for fifty cents.*"[12] The gunsmith's dollar for the big, bony predator was refused also, and for the same reason. Like most boys, Tom could make *"corn stalk fiddles"* for himself; but when he came by a broken down violin, Conrad Kestler took care of the restoration. Practice and determination alone brought proficiency enough for the 'makee-learn' fiddle-player to lead a small band of would-be soldiers down farm tracks, and along the trails of a rapidly depleting forest. A keen interest in music probably went with that for mathematics, a chosen subject when he attended a local school. He had a repertoire of negro spirituals, both the words and the music. In the vicinity of the homestead, a magnificent chestnut tree had been spared the axe, and became the chosen refuge of a big raccoon on one hitherto fruitless, hunt. The animal got the better of the first boy sent aloft, who fell from the tree, declaring the animal to be a bear not a racoon. Tom Jackson climbed up and settled the matter with a club. One wonders about the pelt of the racoon, for he would wear clothes made from yarn spun from the wool of sheep he had sheared. Hunting then had a purpose more important than the kill. There is no record of Tom Jackson ever having affected Davey Crockett headgear. William Arnold, a distant cousin, writing years later in the *'Weston Democrat,'* described him as *"one of those untiring matter-of-fact persons who never would give up an undertaking until he accomplished his object … not quick to decide, but when he made up his mind to do a thing, he did it on short notice and in quick time."*[13] The same cousin Arnold recounted the somehow traditional tale of Tom pitching into a big school bully who was rude to two girls on the way to school, and was mistaken enough to be contemptuous of the smaller boy's invitation to apologize.

Elder brother Warren visited from nearby Upshur County *"in the fall of 1836, when Thomas was twelve years old,"*[14] and together,

---

12 Cook.

13 Ibid.

14 Cook.

they went to see Laura. Whilst with her, at the home of a Neale uncle, they heard that money could be made from chopping wood for sale as fuel for passing riverboats. The boys decided to give it a try and went south to a malarial island in the Mississippi. The venture was not a commercial success and within four months they were back with little to show for their effort and initiative but a trunk or chest each. Tom gave his to Laura.

Infrastructure planning was, seemingly, a tortuous process even in the comparatively people-sparse decade of 1830s Virginia; but after thirteen years, the main construction work got underway on the Parkersburg to Staunton section of the turnpike through Lewis County, in the summer of the brothers' return from the Mississippi. Tom proved a keen assistant to Major Bailey – owner of Bailey's Hotel in Weston – and commissioner for the sale of construction contracts. He showed a special interest and aptitude in the surveying problems involved, as well as gaining a reputation as a conscientious worker. Mrs Bailey provided him with a packed lunch each day.

During the Jackson's Mill years, Tom was developing the then essential skills of an accomplished horseman, and Uncle Cummins frequently mounted him in a race on the nearby track, from the age of twelve onwards. Perhaps not always to his liking. An unidentified friend of that period recalled being told that *"Uncle Cummins does not go to church but that he had always been good to him, and that he would stick to him through thick and thin, and, though he did not like his horse racing, he would ride any horse for him that he would bring out."*[15] The unknown diarist also noted that *"Tom knew how to make a horse walk. He kept tapping the whip with almost every step and my horse had to sometimes trot to keep up."* Years later, Henry Kyd Douglas said of the Confederate officer, *"Walking or riding the General was ungainly: his main object was to get over the ground. He rode boldly and well, but not with grace or ease; and 'Little Sorrel' –* his

---

15 Cook quoting *"Diary of a journey to Parkersburg on the Ohio" by Thomas Jackson and myself.*

celebrated Civil War charger – *was as little like a Pegasus as he was like an Apollo. He was not a man of style."*

Throughout these experiencing, teenage years, the innermost Tom Jackson was working out for himself his own, personal relationship with a supreme being. He revealed little of his inner journey, and it has often been written that the spirituality which was so strong an adult characteristic was largely absent – or at least barely remarkable – in the youth; hard to discern, surely, but absent surely not. Tom would have been set upon the path of religion by the person of his beloved mother. The true font of his belief was the nature and spirituality of his mother Julia, and the example which she set in her struggle to survive. The enquiring mind of the determined individual thinker did the rest. Whether the concept of one Almighty should be embraced as a buttress for his own precarious, and somewhat harsh existence, would be considered thoroughly and precisely by an inherently focused and very individual nature. It reflects well on the person of Julia Jackson that in many ways, her son became an ideal harbinger for the concept of religion, for he never had a shred of religious bigotry in him; acting always in the firm belief that there were many paths to God. Just as with Frederick the Great in Prussia, for whom *"everyone must find their own way to heaven."* In later life, Jackson would not support the idea of a country having an established religion; but encouraged everyone in the system they themselves had chosen. His own path to an outward, formal acceptance was unusually varied. A daughter of one of the elders of the Broad Run Baptist Church noted that *"on several occasions 'Thomas Jackson, a shy unobtrusive boy, sat with unabated interest in a long sermon, having walked three miles in order to attend.'"*[16] In Mexico City, following the successful fighting outcome of America's first warlike venture on foreign soil – and while the price for grabbing California and New Mexico was being haggled out – we know that the twenty-four year old Major Jackson

---

16 Cook.

discussed Catholicism with Mexican divines, and possibly religion in general with Colonel Taylor, who had the reputation for being concerned about the spiritual welfare of his men. Tom did not, however, pursue Catholicism on returning to the States; but on further research, was baptised Episcopalian and then, being transferred by the army to serve in Florida, completed his deliberations there, and was welcomed formally as a Presbyterian. Not long afterwards, in a letter to Aunt Clementine Neale, of Parkersburg, he wrote: *"The subject of becoming a herald of the Cross has often seriously engaged my attention, and I regard it as the most noble of all professions. It is the profession of our divine Redeemer, and I should not be surprised were I to die upon a foreign field, clad in ministerial armor, fighting under the banner of Jesus. What could be more glorious? But my conviction is that I am doing good here, and that for the present I am where God would have me."* (He was writing from Lexington, having left the army on being elected to the chair of Professor of Natural and Experimental Philosophy at the renowned VMI – the Virginia Military Institute). *"I do rejoice to walk in the love of God,"*[17] he added.

Major Jackson was always very happy and content to attend services conducted in the forms of other denominations, although his own stance on the Almighty was one of calm confidence, happiness and love, quite devoid of any vestige of hell-fire, brimstone and fear. During the last months of his life, when by then a Lieutenant-General commanding the Second Army of Corps of Lee's Army of Northern Virginia, he went to great lengths to secure a Roman Catholic priest for one of his brigades whose ranks were mostly Catholics. Earlier in the war, his then medical chief Dr Hunter McGuire, told of Jackson banning tents for one particular phase of operations; but relenting solely in the case of a catholic priest who, alone of the ministers of the command, threatened resignation on the grounds that without a tent he could not perform his religious duties.

17 Cook.

Along with religion, horsemanship and country skills, the teenage orphan not only gained some academic learning for himself during the Weston years; but also did a bit of teaching. One slave-servant, having received personal tuition from him in the basic skills of reading and writing, promptly and sensibly, wrote himself a pass for the *'Underground Railroad'* and lit out for a freer life in Canada. For a set piece in handwriting the young teacher chose the significant slogan *"A man of words and not of deeds is like a garden full of weeds."* One parent, Mr Smith Gibson, later wrote a confirming testimonial to his educational efforts, saying *"I sent my children to him"* ... at the school, and ..."*he is in my opinion well skilled in arithmetic and is quite a smart youth."*[18]

Tom landed his first real employment shortly after his seventeenth birthday. This was a surprising official appointment, given his youthful inexperience, to the post of Constable to the Justices of the Freeman Creek Rural District, designated 'District Two – West Fork'. The prime instigator in Tom securing the appointment was Colonel Alexander Scott Withers JP – a friend of the Jacksons, a classicist, and the widely acclaimed author of *"Chronicles of Border Warfare."* On a visit to the Jackson Mill, Withers had remarked that *"gentlemen worked their heads instead of their hands."* Tom had replied *"when one has money to go to William and Mary College, then he knows how to work his head."* As he rode away, the Colonel responded with *"someday I will get you a job so that you can earn some money."* Tom lost the ballot for Constable against a well-liked and local family man by five votes to twelve; but within three days Tom had been sworn in. The statutory bond of $2,000 was secured to the Lieutenant Governor of Virginia, by Uncle Cummins and the hotelier Major Minter Bailey. An absolute determination to fulfil the unpalatable tasks of writ-serving and debt-collection became the hallmark of the conscientious young constable, and one widow, at least, had cause to be thankful for it. After repeated visits had failed to recover money

---

18 Ibid.

from one debtor, Tom happened to be at the blacksmith's when the man rode up. He remained hidden while the man dismounted and tethered his horse, and then came out to seize the reins. The man quickly un-hitched and re-mounted, for the law decreed that a writ could not be levied upon a horse with the owner in the saddle. Young Jackson, hunched against a horse-whip's lashing to his head and shoulders, drew the horse through the blacksmith's door, forcing the exasperated debtor to leap off or be scraped off, the saddle. Having no option but to pay-up or lose the horse, the man repaid the widow, no doubt ungraciously.

2. CADET

....

*"Sir, you have a good name. Go to West Point,
and the first man who insults you, knock him '
down, and have it charged to my account."*

John C. Spencer (Secretary of War)

....

TOM had held the post of Constable for just twelve months or so, when the opportunity of a cadetship at the United States Military Academy, West Point, became available to a constituent of the congressional district of Samuel L. Hays, a prominent local politician and near neighbour of the Jackson's of Weston. The Jacksons were then *"the most prominent political faction in western Virginia"*[19] and had backed Hays for Congress in the fall elections of 1840. When the West Point place came up, Hays had been a member of Congress for some eighteen months. The coveted vacancy, however, was filled originally by Gibson Butcher, possibly following an informal, locally devised test in which he had shown a greater academic knowledge than Tom. However, after just one week of *"seeing the movements and learning the duties which I had to perform"*, Butcher, *"came to the conclusion that ... he ... never could consent to live the life."*[20] Tom Jackson eagerly took up the renewed opportunity, and packing his kit into a pair of well-used leather saddle-bags, caught up and boarded the stagecoach to Washington DC, where Congressman Hays took him in to see John C Spencer, the Secretary of War. Doubtless having in mind, also, former president Andrew Jackson – the victor of

---

19 Cook.

20 Ibid. From Butcher's resignation letter, addressed to Hon. Sam'l L Hays at the House of Representatives, and written from Weston just eleven days after he had first entered West Point.

New Orleans in the War of 1812 – and with an informed suspicion about the effect a country-boy dressed in homespun clothing would have on the culture of practical joking at the Academy, the Secretary endorsed Tom's candidacy with, *"Sir, you have a good name. Go to West Point, and the first man who insults you, knock him down, and have it charged to my account."*[21] The summer term was already underway, and eager to get to grips with the initial assessment exam, the would-be Cadet declined Hays' offer to stay with his family, and see something of the nation's capital. He did, however, spare the time to look briefly over the city, from the unfinished dome of the Capitol, and across the Potomac into Virginia, his spiritual home, which would be the setting for the greatest of his future battlefield victories.

The US Military Academy at West Point was far more than a military school, it was a university, with a strict, disciplined regime and demanding standards, which turned out men of broad education who, apart from their academic knowledge, had undergone a four year indoctrination into the qualities and personal habits that make useful citizens. Looking out to the demands of a still-expanding frontier, Congress had endorsed West Point for the benefit of all the States, and many graduates left to become the builders of roads and railroads; engineers, surveyors and architects, as well as garrison and frontier officers in the small standing army. The bar at the Academy was set high, and only the most able and determined obtained the coveted Certificate to proclaim their achievement. As Cook records, between *"1838 and 1917, four thousand nine hundred and sixty-six boys were rejected by the Academic Board, two thousand eight hundred and ninety failing to pass in grammar."* Securing a place was to do no more than stand on the threshold of an arduous upward path and if, to an observer, Tom

---

21 Henderson. Cook is sceptical that any such interview took place. Jackson's letter accepting *"a conditional appointment as Cadet in the service of the United States"*, is signed *"Thos. J. Jackson"*, indicating that he adopted the name Jonathan before entering West Point.

Jackson's credentials seemed barely to fit him for the climb, the man himself had no doubts of his fitness for the summit.

The 'Class of '42' initially totalled one hundred and nine aspirants, although the number would increase at one point, possibly due to the back-terming of stragglers. By the end of the first year, some thirty-seven had abandoned the attempt and the total was down to seventy-two. Tom was rated fifty-one. Fate, together with their own good fortune, natural ability and training, ensured that his intake would spawn some distinguished soldiers. Apart from himself, no less than twelve generals – six Confederate and six Federal. Three of the future Southern generals[22] happened to be together and witnessed the arrival of nineteen year old Tom Jackson at 'the Point,' to formally sign in on July the first. *"There was about him,"* said one, *"so sturdy an expression of purpose that I remarked; 'That fellow looks as if he had come to stay".*[23] Despite the determined visage, the homespun did, indeed, attract the jokers; but their attempts to disturb were quickly 'smoked'; and as they were *"apparently more productive of amusement to their victim than to themselves,"*[24] the would-be tormentors turned swiftly to other, more satisfyingly responsive prey. The surname too did not pass unnoticed, and Tom was speedily dubbed 'the General,' although, with his rudimentary arithmetic and no more than a few weeks cramming in algebra, *"It was all he could do to pass his first examination,"* the US general John Gibbon later told Henderson. When called out to solve mathematical problems on the blackboard, his perspiring efforts were such that it was said, *"he was certain to flood the classroom,"* – as well as cover his own uniform in chalk. Tom was ever quite open about this struggle to achieve the academic standard demanded, and in the early terms it was not unusual for him to be marked down as being un-prepared for the lesson of the day, having confessed to being still hard at

---

22 A.P. Hill, G.E. Pickett and Dabney H. Maury (Henderson).

23 Henderson.

24 Ibid.

work mastering the one set for the previous day. During his first winter at USMA, and before 'lights out' was sounded to end the cadet's day, *"he would pile up his grate with anthracite coal,"* a class-mate wrote to Henderson, *"and lying prone before it on the floor, would work away at his lessons by the glare of the fire,"* until the small hours. He was not only amenable to the unyielding code of the Academy, it mirrored in many ways the exacting standards that he had set for the conduct of his own life. He cared nothing for the opinion of others, as Henderson observed. He was *"tolerant of association rather than seeking it,"* and *"his self-contained nature asked neither sympathy nor affection."* The ability to concentrate on his studies, to the complete exclusion of all else, became ingrained, and was a habit of method he would take with him to the bat-tlefield, and employ throughout his thirty-nine year life. In the classroom, his ability to concentrate totally to the exclusion of all distractions, required him to sit bolt upright at his desk, be-cause he believed that to sit hunched forward was to stimulate internal disorders. In the opening months of the Civil War, an onlooker watching the, by then, 'Stonewall' Jackson writing a field report, was impressed to see neither the writer nor the pen so much as flinch or pause, when a cannon ball crashed through the upper branches of a nearby tree, showering the ground and the table below with leaves and twigs. In the following Century, a one-time student of the Virginia Military Academy – where Professor Jackson taught in the 1850s – George Scott Patton, America's most effective fighting general in the European Theatre of the Second World War, was disappointed with himself for be-ing unable to match the unruffled Stonewall calm, whilst under fire during the campaign in Sicily.

If Jackson himself was perfectly in sync with Academy reg-ulations demanding a high standard from cadets, he expected nothing less of his fellow students. During his room-mate's stint of orderly-sergeant duty, it was suggested to Tom that he could skip morning reveille roll-call. Never once did he avail himself of the offer. On the occasion of his musket being switched for a poorly maintained weapon, the authorities were immediately notified, and informed how his personal weapon could be identified. At evening muster, it was duly identified in the possession of another cadet on parade. Tom was adamant that the culprit was unfit to be a USMA member and should be court marshalled and ejected. Only after great pressure from staff and cadets did he agree not to press charges. *"The warm smile that revealed a warm heart,"* was quite absent from the incident. There was no trace of the customary concern for the comrade in need, *"either from misfortune or sickness,"* which invariably elicited *"a tenderness so womanly that it sometimes excited ridicule."*[25]

Tom made the West Point years, years of steady achievement and development, both intellectually and physically. Relentless and determined – dedicated even – would be equally appropriate. He lived a favourite maxim, *"Duty is ours; Consequences are God's."* The course itself fulfilled a long-held craving for knowledge which, during the first two years, involved a syllabus which included; Algebra, Geometry, Topographical Drawing, Engineering, French and English. The regulations of the Academy did not allow for an overly generous quota of leave. Just one furlough was permitted during the four years; and only granted if specifically requested by a recognised guardian. One Sunday, whilst enjoying his furlough at Weston during the summer of 1844, Tom rode to Broad Run Baptist Church in the company of Miss Caroline Norris. Decked out in the natty white and grey uniform of a West Point cadet, his horse stumbled mid-stream, pitching him head-foremost into the Broad Run. So trivial an unscheduled occurrence as total immersion disturbed neither his composure nor his resolve, and he attended divine service as planned, baptised by nature if not by priestly intervention. Back at College, his one physical recreation was a brisk walk, taken between classes. He did, however, allow himself one extra-curricular indulgence throughout the student years. A very personal correspondence as *"well-wisher, friend and brother"* with his *"Dear*

---

25 Henderson.

Sister" Laura. *"It is through a sense of duty and affection, and not because of any information that I have, which induces me to send you these few lines,"* he wrote on one occasion.[26] Yet he told Laura all he was experiencing, including a certain longing for home which outlasted the early days and weeks, before morphing into pleasurable anticipation, as the days of furlough approached. *"I am almost homesick and expect to continue so until I can have a view of my native mountains, and receive the greetings of my friends and relatives, when I shall have the opportunity of mingling with my schoolmates, and the companions of my earliest youth. It is the anticipation of one day realizing them that fills my heart with joy and causes me to urge forward and grasp that prize which will qualify me for spending my life with them in peace and honour."*[27] Despite his dedication to duty, Tom had a strong inclination towards family. As he told Laura a year or so later, *"... I hope that the same kind Providence, which has preserved us as a remnant of a family up to the present time, will again favour us with an interview, although in Its wisdom It has marked out for us, at least for a period, widely different spheres of action, and different places of abode. But I look forward with no small degree of satisfaction to the time when my circumstances will allow me to settle down near you, and among my relatives, in order to share with yourselves the ineffable pleasure of domestic circles."*[28] He often commented upon health – both his own and Laura's. He suffered some form of, a not especially disabling, digestive disorder, or dyspepsia, all his life, which may have accounted for his belief in the importance of desk posture. In this letter he reported that, *"My health is far better than it was when I parted from you, and indeed more flattering than it has been for the last two years; and I think by the time I graduate, if that should ever be* (this most logical of men was never given to assuming) *my health will be as good as ever. I hope in the meantime that no pains will*

26 Letter from USMA, May 17, 1845 (Arnold).
27 Letter from *Military Academy, West Point, NY, January 28, 1844* (Arnold).
28 Letter from *West Point, U.S.M.A., November 25, 1845* (Arnold).

be spared on your part, for the recovery of your health."[29] Tom wrote this letter in the winter before his mid-course furlough when he wrote, *"If no change takes place in the army, and I continue to progress in my class as I have so far, my pay when I leave the institution will be about one thousand dollars a year; though fate may decree that I shall graduate in the lower part of my class, in which case I shall have to go into the infantry and would receive only seven hundred and fifty dollars a year. But I feel confident that unless fortune frowns on me more than it has yet, I shall graduate in the upper half of my class, and high enough to enter the Dragoons. But be that as it may, I intend to remain in the Army no longer than I can get rid of it with honour, and the means to commence some professional business at home."* Before signing off, *"your true and well-wishing brother,"* he asked Laura to, *"Give my respects to Seely, if you should see her –* (Seely (nominally a slave) was head cook and housekeeper in the Cummins Jackson household) *– "and tell her that there is not a day that passes by without my thinking of her, and that I expect to see her in less than five months."*[30]

Tom returned from furlough to find that he *"was made an officer"* – a cadet officer, that is, and, as he wrote to Laura, *"consequently my duties are lighter than usual."* Clearly his qualities of leadership and command were becoming discernible to the directing staff, and he went on to encourage Laura with something from his own philosophy for living. *"Be not discouraged by disappointment and difficulties,"* he wrote, *"but on the contrary, let each stimulate you to greater exertions for attaining noble ends, and an approving conscience at least will be your reward. My health is as good as usual."*[31] Laura was married towards the end of that month; but, was not sure where she would be living. Tom did not write to congratulate her until the following February. *"My sincere desire is that you may both enjoy all the blessings which a bountiful Providence can bestow,"* he wrote. *"I think if happiness exists in this world, matrimony is one*

---

29 Letter from Military Academy, West Point, N.Y., *January 28, 1844* (Arnold).

30 Ibid.

31 Letter from *West Point Military Academy, September 8, 1844* (Arnold).

of its principal factors. … My studies for the approaching June exami-
nation," he continued, *"will include Optics, Mechanics, Astronomy,*
Magnetism and Chemistry, together with (topographical) *drawing. I*
expect to commence taking exercises in riding in a day or two. At the
last examination I rose in each department of my studies."[32] The sub-
jects he listed in this letter comprised the syllabus for the second
two years of the course, and also included Ethics – which would
certainly have pleased the persecutor of the musket-thief – together with Logic, in the study of which he went straight to the
top of the class.

That summer, with less than a year to go before graduation,
he was once more thinking of the future. *"I am enjoying myself*
very well, he told Laura, *"considering that I am deprived of the bless-*
ings of a home, the society of the friends of my childhood, the cordial wel-
come of relatives, and above all the presence of an only sister. Times are
far different from what they were when I was at my adopted home; none
to give their mandates; none for me to obey, but I chose arms; surround-
ed by my playmates and relatives, all apparently eager to promote my
happiness; but these were the days of my youth; they have been succeed-
ed by days of quite a different aspect; manhood with all its cares. I have
before me two courses, either of which I may choose. The first would be
to follow the profession of arms; the second, that of a civil pursuit, such
as law . If I should adopt the first, I could live independently and sur-
rounded by friends whom I have already made, have no fear of want. My
pay would be fixed; the principle thing I would have to attend to would
be futurity. If I adopt the latter course, I presume that I would still find
plenty of friends, but my exertions would have to be great in order to ac-
quire a name. This course is most congenial to my taste, and consequently
I expect to adopt it, after spending a few years in pursuing the former. …
There are sixty members in my class at present, nineteen above me and
forty below me. I propose coming to see you in July next,"[33] after having graduated and left West Point.

---

32 Letter from *U.S.M.A., February 10, 1845* (Arnold).
33 Letter from *West Point, August 2, 1845* (Arnold).

"It has been but a few moments since I had the pleasure of receiving your affectionate and sister-like letter" Tom wrote in the early winter of the last complete year of the course. "As to your health, it is my sincere wish that you may recover it. My constitution as well as your own have received a severe shock; but I believe I am gradually recovering. My exercises this year with the broadsword as well as the small, are well calculated to strengthen the chest and the muscles. So, I have some reason to believe that they will have the desired effect of restoring me to perfect health. For your kind advice and well wishes you have my hearty thanks. Since my last letter I have been transferred to the first section in ethics, and I think I probably have a mark in it, which will place me among the first five in my class in this science, and which I consider preferable to any other in the course. ... It is probable you think hard of me because of my not writing more frequently, but I hope the strict requirement of many duties (Tom's italics) as well as want of information, will prove a partial if not a complete excuse. Give my respects to Mr A_____ (Arnold), and rest assured of my unalterable attachment. Thos. J. Jackson."[34]

With little more than two months before Graduation Day, Cadet Jackson told his sister, "I am enjoying my usual state of health, and live in anticipation of shortly paying you a visit. Times are here nearly as usual. Of course, there is a little excitement owing to the proximity of furlough and graduation ..."Rumor (sic) appears to indicate a rupture between our government and the Mexican. If such should be the case the probability is that I will be ordered to join the army of occupation immediately, and, if so, will hardly see home until after my return, and the next letter that you will receive from me may be dated from Texas or Mexico ... I shall ever continue to love you with a brother's love. T.J. Jackson."[35]

Of the sixty whom Tom had told Laura were in his class in the Spring, all were passed as being "qualified for service of the United States," by the specially convened Board of Physicians. All graduated. Cadet Jackson was recommended for promotion on the

---

34 Letter from *West Point, U.S.M.A., November 25, 1845* (Arnold).

35 Letter from *West Point, U.S.M.A., April 23, 1846* (Postmarked *May 5, 1846* (Arnold).

twenty ninth of June; assigned to the Light Company of the Third Artillery and on graduating, on the first of July 1846, breveted Second Lieutenant of Artillery. His belief before entering West Point that he had the necessary intellectual capacity to succeed was triumphantly vindicated. He passed-out seventeenth. It has been recounted many times since, that had the course been a year longer, both staff and his fellow cadets believed, he would have finished first. He had proved beyond any doubt that, if nothing else, he had the most fundamental of all requirements for successful generalship, a superior intellect. Another graduate of the Academy, General F H Smith, wrote, *"The lesson which his academic career presents is that what he lacked in early previous preparation he made up by extra diligence and unceasing effort, while resolute determination to do his duty caused him to have but forty-eight demerits, notwithstanding the strict discipline of West Point, in the course of four years. It was scarcely possible for a young man to have entered upon a course of studies for which he was less prepared from want of early preparation than he was, but the resolute purpose to accomplish what he had undertaken, and thus to vindicate the confidence of his friends, animated him through all his difficulties …"*[36] The overall view of the staff was that the Jackson's mind *"was sound and strong but not quick,"* which may well have been true of the student. Victory herself would attest to the speed, strength and soundness of mind of the officer in action. Fellow graduate, and later colonel, P T Turnley, who clearly did not speak for the musket-thief, told Henderson *"that he went through the trying ordeal of four years at West Point without ever having a hard word or bad feeling from cadet or professor."* The Colonel, who seems also not to have registered the intellectual quality of the achievement, did say, *"there was no one of our class who more absolutely possessed the respect and confidence of all; and in the end, 'Old Jack', as he was always called, with his desperate earnestness, his unflinching straightforwardness, and his high sense of honour, came to be regarded by his comrades with something very like affection."*[37]

---

36 Arnold.

37 Henderson.

3. INVASION

"Blessed is the man who expects little,
and can gracefully accept less."
Winfield Scott

....

"One of the most unjust wars ever waged
by a stronger against a weaker nation."
Ulysses Simpson Grant

....

DURING the first week of March 1847, the ships of an American invasion fleet sailed south from New Orleans, and other ports along America's eastern seaboard, for an anchorage in the lee of the Lobos Islands, which would provide temporary shelter for assembly in the face of prevailing northerly gales. The triple task facing Major-General Winfield Scott, General-in-Chief of the United States Army and field commander for the expedition, was to affect a landing near Vera Cruz; to inflict defeat upon the forces of Mexico under their President-General Santa Anna, and to capture Mexico City.

The basic ingredients of the conflict, which had been bubbling briskly; but inconclusively, for the previous twelve months, and having been a decade or so in coming to the boil, was first and foremost Texas, which, amid the slaughter of Goliad and the Alamo, had parted from Mexico in 1836, and had been recognised by the administration of President Andrew Jackson as an independent republic in March 1837. Secondly, the United States was experiencing a renewal of the flood tide of immigration, which having receded after 1815, in the wake of the European Wars, was now accompanied by unprecedented expansion and exploitation of the continent. Settlers driven by powerful and primitive cravings, probed westwards for the ultimate boundaries of their burgeoning republic. Those taking the more northerly Oregon Trail were, by 1840, already in dispute with Canadian trappers on the west coast, largely because of the Ashburton Treaty of 1818, which had made provision for a US – Canadian boundary up to, but not beyond, the Rocky Mountains. Great Britain, under the largely benevolent umbrella of whose navy the United States was able both to develop and to trade without interference from lesser maritime powers, was sympathetic to the cause of her Canadian colonists.

Further south, settlers had swarmed across the vast tracts of Texas, and were embarking upon their final surge for California and the coast. In the process, they seemingly stirred up latent feelings of resentment in Santa Anna, who in the early 1840s renewed his fulminations against the former Mexican territory, by exuding dire threats against its inhabitants, and by meddling in their trading activities. As a result, Jackson's successor, President Tyler, felt constrained to prepare a Texas annexation treaty, which was finally thrown out by the US Senate, after the issue became mixed-up in the unsavoury politics of slavery. Here again, the British Government was against the USA, their viewpoint being that an independent Texas would be a more reliable supplier of cotton to the textile mills of Yorkshire and Lancashire, than one owing allegiance to the Stars & Stripes. Official views and policies notwithstanding, the men and women opening North America in the mid-Nineteenth Century were a very different breed from their descendants of today. Unimpeded by excessive legislation, and such absurdities as political correctness and human rights, stiffened by a total lack of welfare and their own self-reliance, and without the slightest dependence on a character degenerating materialism, their belief in individual liberty and initiative made them a hardy, independent and uncompromising lot. Although a prince of the species, Thomas J Jackson, with his *"absolute fearlessness, whether of danger or responsibility, the utter disregard of man, and the unquestioning faith in the Almighty,*[38] was also typical of the species overall. His take on life; his personal guidelines and the maxims he listed

---

38 Henderson.

for himself at West Point, such as *'All things work together for the good of God's children, Duty is ours consequences are God's, Sacrifice your life rather than your word, Resolve to perform what you ought; perform without fail what you resolve,'* were believed in and governed the lives of many. They too had strongly held personal codes of right and wrong, acknowledged no superiority save that of proven merit, and believed that even the topmost pinnacles in life could be reached by energy and perseverance.

In the year before Tom graduated from West Point, the voters of America sent a Democrat to the White House who had toured the hustings with the suitably uncompromising slogan of *"Fifty four Forty or Fight,"* 54° 40"N being the boundary claimed to keep Oregon in the United States. *"Humourless and unexciting"* a politician, who would stoop at nothing to do down an opponent he may have been, but James Knox Polk, with his uncommon ability to see the underlying realities of political situations, was in many ways, an ideal choice.

Together with a Nation to whom the enormities of the Napoleonic and 1812 Wars had receded to the point where war was looked upon once again, as being no more objectionable than any other political expedient, Polk had inherited a Texas Annexation Resolution, finally signed by his predecessor. With it and the Nation came an apparent commitment to wage war simultaneously against both Great Britain and Mexico. Unlike the future Confederate Government, for whom Britain's attitude to cotton would prove such a fatal fascination, President Polk realised from the outset that cotton would never make an actionable issue. In the meantime, yes, of course, the President understood the British point of view, and yes absolutely he agreed with those hand-wringing advisers advocating stringent preparations for a cross the pond war; but ... well ..., it seemed to James Polk that the softer option was both the easiest and the best. He would ignore the dogs of war baying about their fur and cotton interest. It was, after all, his personal belief that they were all bark and no bite, and that this was in marked contrast to their counterparts in Mexico, with their rekindled interest in Lone Star real estate. All that aside, the President was only too aware that the annexation of Texas represented an opportunity given to no US President since Thomas Jefferson had doubled the size of the then United States by the purchase of the Louisiana Territory, from the France of Bonaparte, some forty four years earlier. True, that crowning achievement of the Third Presidency had been purchased with money and not lives; but then it was equally true to say that even the supreme pacifist, Jefferson would not have stopped short of war to secure the prize.

Twelve months before the Class of '42 graduated from USMA, Texas agreed to its own annexation by the United States, and the Eleventh President ordered General Zachary Taylor and an army of fifteen hundred men – just three regiments of regulars – forward to Corpus Christi. Despite a national mood, rather endearingly referred to in the New York *'Morning News'* as one in which *"nine tenths of our people would rather have a little fighting than not"*, this Army still numbered less than four thousand all ranks; when, towards the end of 1845, it was ordered up to the Rio Grande. Less than three months before Jackson and his classmates left West Point to take up their various regimental appointments, the Mexicans crossed the river and pushed-in Taylor's outpost positions. The war was on, and even if to Grant, from a hindsight thirty years in the maturing, it did seem *'one of the most unjust'*, from the even more lifeless objectivity of some one hundred and eighty years, it hardly seems any more unjust than a good many contests between bellicose belligerents waged both before and since, and certainly would seem to have been less morally reprehensible – less of a crime against humanity – than the bombing interventions, invasions and occupations; the killing of local people, and ensuing economic exploitation, practised by America and, to a lesser extent Britain, in post-World War Two. In the more realistic view of Winfield Scott at the time, it was simply a war needing *"plainly to be made to march towards a successful conclusion, if the (US) was not to be bankrupted and dishonoured."*[39] Scott advocated the invasion solution at the outset,

---

39 *"Memoirs of Lieutenant-General Scott, LL.D" "Written by himself";* Sheldon and Company, Publishers, New York, 1864.

but instead, the first year had been spent in somewhat irrelevant grappling along the Rio Grande. Several US battlefield victories made Taylor a national hero but, in reality, achieved little beyond the butchering of combatants. It was in short, the prefect recipe for *"a war like a peace; a perpetual condition,"*[40] as both the Mexicans and Scott fully appreciated.

Although by 1847 the railroad was beginning to track across North America, the horse was the main motive of power for a general wishing to shift heavy weapons and supplies for the fighting arms; which meant that an advance into the heart of Mexico through the northern deserts and the Sierra Madre Mountains, was not a realistic option. On the other hand, Scott's proposed assault from seaward, whilst it would enable a direct thrust at the Mexican capital, was not without considerable difficulties. There was no harbour close enough to serve as a landing in the region of Vera Cruz, the first choice area from which to launch a fighting advance inland, which meant both the assault and the landing of essential supplies would be exposed to the open seas of the Gulf of Mexico. Plus, there was every likelihood that a landing would be vigorously contested. Indeed, since shortly after Christmas, the prospect of an opposed landing seemed more of a foregone conclusion, after an officer carrying operational documents to Taylor's headquarters in northern Mexico was killed at Villa Gran. The invasion plan was found and had been presented in its entirety to Santa Anna, even before Taylor had seen the duplicate. Such a breach of security notwithstanding however, the precedents for such belligerent water frolics of the Nineteenth Century were inauspicious to say the least. As recently as 1830, a well prepared French expedition, unopposed, and landing in a relatively sheltered North African bay, had been beset with confusion, slowness of execution and loss of life. Even England, the pre-eminent maritime power of the age, whose *"storm beaten ships,"* in US Admiral Mahan's emotive conclusion, had stood

---

40 Ibid.

between Napoleon and *"dominion of the World;"*[41] had a patchy record when tackling the complexities of 'Combined Operations.'

It was with some interest, therefore, that on the afternoon of March seventh, the observers of foreign powers, watched from the weather decks of their own ships, as Scott's invasion force of some twelve thousand, carried in a fleet of some eighty transports and warships, approached the Mexican coast near Vera Cruz. Throughout the hundred and twenty mile voyage from a Lobos Island anchorage, the sea state had caused the American transports to wallow sickeningly and, as the land loomed closer, a majestic swell marched relentlessly onward, to deflate in a rumble of froth and foam, and a final seething hiss, across shell-white sand. To the extended telescopes and rows of anxious eyes lining poop, waist and fo'c'sle rail, it became gradually apparent that to assault through so turbulent a coupling of land and water was to invite disaster. The would-be invaders stood away to the south, to anchor off Anton Lizardo; to reflect and reconnoitre, and to wait for the whim of wind and water to grant more favourable conditions. At last, the apparent turmoil of ships backing and filling, to drop anchor at close quarters, gave way to a general stillness and sense of overall relief. Embarked troops lounged against hatch covers, or on the upturned planking of boats, and either played cards, wrote letters, or simply chatted and listened. Sailors on duty furled sails, spliced ropes and tended paintwork and rigging, whilst those off-watch fished, washed clothes, whittled and listened for a shrill pipe to announce the welcome injunction *'hands to dinner.'*

Four days earlier; but yet unbeknown to him, Tom Jackson had been confirmed in the rank of Second Lieutenant. Since graduating the previous July, he had managed to visit Laura and spend three days at the old family home in Weston, before leaving at the end of the month, to report to Captain Taylor at Fort Columbus,

---

41 A.T. Mahan: *"The Influence of Sea Power Upon the French Revolution and Empire"*

Governor's Island, New York. On the twelfth of August, he swore allegiance to the United States of America before Justice of the Peace Charles Lott at New Utrecht, New York, and, although the War Department endorsed the standard instrument of oath with an order to report to Pensacola, Florida, a week later, he and Captain Taylor, together with some thirty men and forty horses, left Fort Hamilton, New York, to join the US Army on active service in Mexico. After a ride of some four hundred miles; a sail down the Ohio and the Mississippi, followed by *"a march of some thirty six days",* they reached Port Isabel in Texas. From there, he told Laura, he was *"in the hope of starting up the Rio Grande tomorrow."* His hopes were realised, and the detachment soon reached Taylor's *'Army of Occupation,'* lying spread out and inactive between the Mexican towns of Saltillo and Agua Nueva. Having been *"performing the duties of Acting Asst. Commissary –* for the previous five months, Tom filed a return for *"the necessary abstracts of provisions received and issued by me from Fort Hamilton,"* with the Commissary General of Subsistence in Washington DC, adding the request that *"I may be allowed the usual compensation in like cases."* Communications from the War Zone were tenuous at best, as experience with the invasion plan showed, and Tom, having written to Laura with a mailing address, also commented that a letter *"may reach me, but not with certainty."* While the acting assistant commissary's return was taking a whole month to reach its destination, the regular units serving with Zachary Taylor were reassigned to Scott's invasion force, and together with the First Regiment of Artillery, moved down to the mouth of the Rio Grande, where the invasion fleet was assembling at Brazos San Jago. Scott sailed from this assembly area on the fifteenth of February. Four days later, despite having to manoeuvre with some far from unflinching volunteers, Taylor defeated Santa Anna at Buena Vista, largely thanks to his 'flying artillery,' who finding themselves holding the front of the line, continued firing furiously over open sights to such good effect that the massed ranks of Mexican infantry were repulsed. Although the victory did nothing to progress the war, when he learnt how close he had been to participating in a battle, a wistful Jackson said to his future brother-in-law and fellow Confederate general, *"I envy you men who have been in battle. How I would like to be in one battle."*[42] Secure in his belief that *"duty is ours; consequences are God's,"* it would have been hard to discern either frustration or impatience in the young officer of 'K' Company, First Artillery, as he concentrated on his rounds of the regiment's twenty-four and four-pounder guns, the eight-inch howitzers, and the limbers, together with the first-line ammunition, dispersed through the crowded transport. Stooping below beams in the deck-head – during his student years, Tom put on two inches to reach six feet – he and a battery sergeant, headed for the horse boxes; the foetid air of the damp and crowded compartments giving way to a cloying stench of straw, dung and stinging ammonia. Up companion ways to 'tween-deck' spaces employed as embarked troop mess decks and, finally, back to the upper deck, to exchange a parting salute, and to gulp fresh air in the slackening wind of approaching sunset. Over to the west, the masses of white and grey clouds, which throughout the afternoon had piled into the sky above Mexico, were as swiftly diminishing, and when warships in the vicinity of the transport served warning of the onset of night, by lowering flags and ensigns to the shrilling of a Bosun's call and the sombre notes of a bugle, only some final reconnoitring remained to be done, in the improving weather of next day, before the fulfilment of a desire for action by the immortality of youth.

As the invasion fleet sailed north under a cloudless sky, to anchor in allotted launch positions, and before the troops clambered down into the sixty-seven surfboats specially designed and ordered by Scott, the *Massachusetts*[43], flying the broad pen-

---

42 D.H. Hill; *"The Real Stonewall Jackson"* for the February 1894 edition of *"Century Magazine."*

43 Sister ship to the USS *Princeton*, the first single-screw warship, introduced into the US Navy six years earlier, in 1841. At this time USN comprised ships using engines and propellers for auxiliary propulsion, as well as sail only ships and paddle steamers.

nant of the Commander-in-Chief, steamed slowly through the fleet. As if to recognise this exact anniversary of his having been no less than thirty years a general, the army packed the decks and cheered Scott's progress. *"… the shouts and cheers"*, he would write later, *"gave me assurance of victory, whatever might be the force prepared to receive us."* Packed seventy or eighty to a boat, the assault wave of five and a half thousand men gave their chief another cheer and were rowed towards the now lightest of surfs lapping the endless sandy beach. By evening all were safely landed, *"… without opposition other than a few whizzing shells that did no harm …"* Apart from some understandable hyperbole and emphasis to ensure comprehension on the home front, the report of the New Orleans *'Bulletin'* some eighteen days later on twenty-nine March, was no more than the truth. *"The landing of the American army at Vera Cruz has been accomplished in a manner that reflects the highest credit on all concerned, and the regularity, precision and promptness with which it was effected, has probably not been surpassed, if it has been equalled, in modern warfare.*

"The removal of a large body of troops from numerous transports into boats in an open sea – their subsequent disembarkation on the seabeach, on an enemy's coast, through surf, with all their arms and accoutrements, without a single error or accident, requires great exertion, skill and sound judgement.

"… twelve thousand men were landed in one day, without, so far as we have heard, the slightest accident, or the loss of a single life."

The landing by the Royal Navy of a British Army, of some fifteen thousand all arms, to begin the mopping-up of the deserted residue of Bonaparte's ill-starred Egyptian escapade, albeit totalling nearly twenty-four thousand, at Aboukir Bay on the eighth of February, 1801, could certainly be sited as comparable. The assault wave, also numbering some five thousand faced fierce French artillery and small arms fire. Nelson, who had destroyed the French fleet of escorting warships in the same bay two years earlier, wrote of the landing, *"I have always said, and I do think, that the landing of the British Army was the very finest act even a British Army could achieve."* For the Twentieth Century, even that supreme exponent of the combined operation, Douglas MacArthur, would hardly have quibbled with the *'Bulletin'*, or with the achievement of the man who was America's ranking general from 1841 to 1861, and whose active service career reflected the growing pains of his country for over half a Century. A time span matched by MacArthur.

Winfield Scott was born in 1786, just forty years after his grandfather had eluded the victors of Culloden Moor, and emigrated to Virginia by way of Bristol. His father, a successful farmer and captain in the Independence War, died when he was six, and his mother, from whom he claimed the inspiration for any worthy achievements, followed her husband eleven years later. A natural talent, aided by a retentive memory and access to a rich man's library, made the youthful Scott a believer in approaching life in the manner paraphrased by Samuel Johnson as, *"If idle, be not solitary; if solitary, be not idle."* He professed a lifelong preoccupation with fine literature, and became a lawyer, as much perhaps for the political associations of the American Bar, as from any personal satisfaction to be gained from legal disputation. In June 1807, however, an abrupt career change was brought on by the clash between HMS *Leopard* and the US Frigate *Chesapeake,* off the Capes of Virginia. With all America in a state of indignation, Scott joined the ranks of volunteers called forward by President Jefferson to enforce an interdict denying landing rights to ships of the Royal Navy. Almost at once, Scott assisted at the capture of a small party put ashore from a Battle Squadron commanded by Sir Thomas Hardy, onetime Flag Captain to Admiral Lord Nelson. When an order was later received from Washington to restore the prisoners, Lance-Corporal Scott was unimpressed, commenting that it came, *"… with the imbecile admonition usual in such cases; 'Take care not to do so again.'"*[44]

As relations between England and America fluctuated, so Scott's career alternated between war and the law. In 1808 he

---

44 Scott.

was commissioned a captain of 'flying' (light) artillery, and the following year was suspended for twelve months, the victim of a politically motivated court martial. It was the first of several unfortunate political interludes in a military career already remarkably familiar with presidents and legal councillors. In 1812, on the very day war was declared against England, Scott survived, not only two up-endings in a gig driven by a fellow officer *"either drunk with the sentiment of the occasion, or the potations of the sylvan barbecue,"*[45] but also, on reaching his Baltimore destination, the information that no less than two promotions awaited him in Washington. A lieutenant-colonel at twenty-six, Scott finally set aside all aspirations to a life at the Bar of either South Carolina or New Orleans. The legacy of this intention, however, remained in a vigorous intellect – well able to divine and collate all the nuances of a problem – and to disseminate them with an instinct for tidy legal solutions, and a soldierly determination to bring about their realisation. The most significant examples of this were his implementation of his own plan for bringing the Mexican War to a conclusion, and, later, his grasp of the problems posed by the formation of the Southern Confederacy; including the options open to President Lincoln at the beginning of his first presidential term. His appreciation of the situation blossomed into the military plan for Union victory, which, although derided when first postulated, was essentially the blueprint which, when adopted, brought about victory in 1865. Possibly because his military training was more akin to his original choice of profession, in its blend of empirical experience and of knowledge gleaned from books by acknowledged protagonists, that Scott was unusually successful, for a soldier, in combining a feeling for academic controversy with the need to reach practical solutions. Between 1812 and 1814 he was continuously in action against the British along America's northern frontier, leading his regiment in sorties typical of both partisan and regular warfare. He also acted as

---

45 Ibid.

chief-of-staff to the Army, and still found time to reorganise the army staff. He finished the war a seriously injured major-general, with an honorary MA from Princeton College, and the thanks of Congress for *"his uniform gallantry and good conduct in sustaining the reputation of the arms of the United States."*

In the summer of 1815, Scott sailed for Europe, where he stayed for one year, visiting both England and France. At Lord Holland's table he became reacquainted with a Captain Fox, Royal Navy, one of two midshipmen captured by the lance-corporal in 1807. True to the manner of an age which could take the rabid aggression out of warring, he also came to count among his friends a Colonel Pearson, whose prisoner Scott had been for one night in 1813. Returning home, Scott conceived and executed the first set of *'General Regulations'* for the US Army; wrote a treatise on infantry rifle tactics, and a plan for the organisation and the instruction for the whole United States Militia. In a society sensible to what it could gain from the experience, ability and loyalty of an able and successful general, the Philadelphia *'National Gazette'* published an essay which led to the formation of the American Temperance Societies. The essay had been written by Scott as an active member of the societies, for the prevention of pauperism and the suppression of vice and immorality.

Involved in the Black Hawk War of 1832, Scott's humane treatment of the Sacs and Foxe tribes, together with his selflessness in overcoming *'Asiatic cholera'* in the ranks of his own men, were more worthy achievements than could have been won with sword and revolver under such circumstances. In the same year he played a semi-political, and at times almost clandestine, role in containing the belligerent secessionist sympathisers of South Carolina. A policy of *'humility and forbearance,'* undertaken almost as much with the pen as by his presence as the military personification of Federal power, was completely vindicated in a situation where the least indiscretion could have precipitated a blood-letting civil war between the Union and a single state. Command in the Seminole and Creek Indian War was abruptly terminated by the long nurtured rancour of President Andrew Jackson. A

Board, appointed to enquire into the supposed inactivity of the Army Commander, found completely in Scott's favour. In his absence, the war dragged on for another seven years. The years of the Mexican War were also beset by politicking. This time, the president was not a captious military rival emeritus, but Polk, who thought of Scott more as the recent opposition minority candidate for the vice-presidency, rather than as General-in-Chief of the Army. Yet another Board of Enquiry followed. This time it foundered against the proven record of an outstandingly successful field commander.

As the United States entered the second half of the Nineteenth Century, Scott retained his position as General-in-Chief; and was promoted to Lieutenant-General, the first man since fellow-Virginian George Washington to hold the rank and failed dismally in the presidential election of 1852. In 1861, with the Civil War still only a nascent horror, Scott retired, the ravages of vertigo and dropsy becoming increasingly manifest in his now overweight and literally almost worn out body. Not, perhaps, the most fitting exit for a soldier whose passing was mourned by governors, judges and professors but, above all, by Abraham Lincoln, who in presenting his first Annual Message to both Houses of Congress, called to mind " ... *how faithfully, and ably, and brilliantly* (Scott) *had served his country, from a time far back in our history, when few now living had been born, and thence forward continually. I cannot but think we are still his debtors."*

Throughout the Mexican Campaign of Invasion in 1847, it was Scott's sheer competence, vigour and determination; lively leadership and moral courage which provided the mainspring of the American success. For the alert among those professional young officers of the expeditionary force – who were later to become famous as Confederate or Union generals – Scott began an object lesson in active field command from the moment he stepped ashore on to the beach at Vera Cruz.

4. THREE FIERY STRIDES TO MAJOR

Promotion *"will give me more rank, which is of the greatest importance in the army."*
Second Lieutenant Jackson

4/1. Vera Cruz

"... a cannonball came within five steps of me."
Tom to Laura

SCOTT had come ashore believing that the twelve thousand men he had landed with were no more than half the number required to complete the campaign and bring the war to a successful conclusion. He would be economical with their lives for tactical as well as humanitarian reasons. As he reported to Washington, San Juan De Ulloa, the enceinte of the walled city of Vera Cruz – rebuilt after capture by the French nearly ten years earlier – had *"the capacity to sink the entire American navy,"* so when the more gung-ho of his headquarters staff volunteered to lead forlorn hope assaults, Scott thanked them gravely and went ahead with preparations for a bombardment and formal siege. Not that he was without his concerns. Zachary Taylor's blood-soaked victories were lauded to the point where Scott believed *"Americans were quite indifferent to head work ... and ... hardly acknowledged a victory unaccompanied by a long butchers bill."*[46]

---

46 Scott.

The ever-present threat of the *'vomito'*[47] on the hot, humid coastal plain was mitigated by the return of gales sweeping in from the Gulf of Mexico; but they disrupted the unloading of stores and equipment. It was nearly two weeks before the national representatives declined Scott's offer to withdraw their women and children, and his heavy guns joined the field artillery in taking-out gun positions and the targeting of selected breach-points. His opponent, meanwhile, had seriously misread the strategic situation. Believing that the Americans could only attack from the sea by seriously weakening Taylor's army, Santa Anna had rushed into unnecessary defeat at Buena Vista. In so doing, he was unable either to disrupt the landing or support the Vera Cruz garrison, and gave himself the additional task of having to raise a fresh army, if he were to oppose any march inland.

The civilian population of Vera Cruz were largely impervious to the bombardment in the stone cellars of their stone houses; but when the inevitable over-trained rounds began crumbling the upper stories and lighting fires, foreign diplomats hastily recanted and asked to accept the earlier offer to withdraw. The plea was sternly rejected, and the consuls told, that only an application for complete surrender on the part of the Governor himself would now be allowed. To Scott's well developed social conscience, it was always agreeable when *"policy concurred with humanity;"* but he understood more clearly than many – then and since – that victory demands a single-minded devotion to her cause, and that when confronting the enemy, the overall objective of country, government and cause comes before the privations of the army and the more everyday interests of humanity. Faced with a similar diversion, in the winter of 1862, while the muzzles of his unlimbered guns glowered across the icy waters of the Potomac, Major-General Jackson would reveal the same stern understanding of where his military duty lay.

---

47 Yellow fever.

Within one week, the *'vomito'* had broken out within the city limits, and prisoners, brought in by patrols of cavalry and dragoons operating inland, told of a rumour that a large relief force was gathering in the mountains to the west. For Scott the priorities were clear. He needed to be free of the siege, whilst keeping his army intact, and to move off the fever-ridden plain. The very morning after his put down of the foreign diplomats, the Governor of Vera Cruz sent General Landero across the siege lines with the message that the Governor was ready to parley. Peace commissioners were appointed to discuss terms and eighteen days after the landing Vera Cruz was signed over to the Americans. Scott's good fortune extended to getting the castle as well, because the Mexicans had assumed it would bear the brunt of the attack and had organised for it to be supplied daily from the city. When the city surrendered, it effectively emasculated the strength of its own citadel. Five thousand Mexican soldiers laid down their arms; were paroled and sent home. Four hundred cannons, of varying calibre, together with quantities of ammunition and small arms were taken over by the Americans. Scott reported that of the civilian inhabitants, *"not three were slain."* sixty-four Americans were either killed or wounded. Colonel Totten, who bore the official report to Washington, was duly promoted to Brigadier-General, as was traditional for such couriers, and of the two officers killed, Captain Vinton of the Artillery was awarded the posthumous distinction of being *"perhaps the most accomplished officer in the army,"* – also a traditional, if dubious, award; the fleeting glare of death suggesting qualities that would probably have remained dormant in a Century of living through war and peace. Jackson's citation for promotion to First Lieutenant of Artillery read simply, *"For gallant and meritorious conduct at the siege of Vera Cruz."* Tom was careful not to divulge any hair-raising details to Laura, beyond the close-ish approach of a solitary cannon ball, *"While I was at the advanced batteries … and … one who esteems you above all … prompted her to … take particular care that neither this nor any subsequent letter gets into a newspaper."* In later years, despite an active operational career, he would describe the landing as *"one of the most thrilling spectacles he had ever witnessed"*. He possibly played-up the siege which *"must in my opinion excel any military operations known in the history of our country,"* whilst being less complimentary about the paroling of prisoners *"that I cannot approve of, inasmuch* (sic) *as we had them secure, and could have taken them prisoners of war unconditionally … I expect to remain in Mexico for the rest of the war, and to move forward with the leading brigade."*[48] In his first, if relatively insignificant act of war, Tom had made the most of the opportunities as he discerned and developed them, and clearly intended to continue doing so.

4/2. Cerro Gordo

....

"If the enemy advance one step more,
the national independence will be buried
in the abyss of the past"
Antonio Lopez de Santa Anna

....

HAVING learnt of Santa Anna's colourful, if militarily useless, assessment of the effect created by the American seaborne invasion, Scott, somewhat primly, informed Washington, *"We have taken that step."* He did indeed take it; but by no means as quickly as he would have wished. The speed with which Vera Cruz had been conquered created the opportunity to reach and to seize Cerro Gordo – the first and most rugged of the mountain passes between the port and the plateau of Mexico City – without

---

48 Letter, undated, *"written from camp near Vera Cruz"* (Arnold).

a fight. Contrary to rumour, during the siege, Santa Anna had not secured the pass; but the opportunity to achieve a second, relatively bloodless, strategic success, slipped away, for want of transport. Parties of US Dragoons scoured the plain, relieving the wretched 'contadino' population of the mules and wagons by which they ground out their life-sapping subsistence struggle. Payment for the requisitioning would have been at best a temporary palliative. Probably they could, in time, build new wagons; but only those fortunate enough to have animals too small for the army's purpose could, eventually, replace the vital, all-purpose 'work-horses'.

It was some ten days after the fall of Vera Cruz before a Division of regular troops began the fifty mile march over the plain, to Plan del Rio, at the foot of the eastern Sierra Madres. A further six days and a volunteer Division, under the second-in-command, Major-General Patterson followed, carrying cooked rations for six days in their haversacks, and three days' worth of oats for the horses, packed in the recently acquired wagons. Two days after them, and shortly after Scott learnt that the enemy had occupied the Pass of Cerro Gordo, a small siege train of six guns began the march, accompanied by the regulars of locally promoted Major-General Worth. Patterson had assumed command of the vanguard, pending Scott's reaching the front, *"according to the universal wish of the troops."* It is just possible that this surprising display of the popular will was the would-be politico in Scott getting the better of his military alter ego; but more likely, the expression exemplified what practice had made customary in the ranks of the regular army. To the generations immediately following the migrants who left Europe *"... in an age when subordination was broken; awe was hissed away, and when any unsettled innovator who could hatch a half-formed notion produced it to the public."* When the approach of a native man meant a fight, in which one consequence of defeat, and not being instantly killed, was to be held witness, while the ligaments were windlassed from the palpitating bodies of women and children. More recently, settlements had cohered sufficiently for professionals to be employed to bear the brunt of the unceasing cultural friction. In the years surrounding the Mexican War, the regular American Army had been kept continuously employed skirmishing with Plains Indians. From Canada to Texas, this eight and a half thousand man force waged a dual war, for survival against nature, and for dominion over the savage inhabitants, whose interests naturally clashed with the more advanced society represented by thrusting, aggressive settlers. Individual soldiers became invested with all the low cunning of the 'mountain man' and 'the brave,' and relied less upon orders, regulations and manuals, than on their own initiative, ability and willingness to accept responsibility. Circumstances crafted an ideal type of military fighter. Resolute and self-reliant, skilled in the use of personal weapons, comfortable with rough, outdoor living; with killing and in the presence of death, whilst themselves having a willingness to die. A type which America since the Second World War, with its ill-conceived obsession with ever-more sophisticated hardware, is no longer able to produce. Or, at least, does not do so, seemingly out of a failure to appreciate that in all acceptable types of warfare, the man is a greater factor than the equipment, for any successful outcome. By making their collective view known at Cerro Gordo, the regulars were merely following a practice which, despite strict discipline, had become commonplace during years of detachment duty on the western plains. Pleased to be able to grant the universal wish a rapid and popular relief, and escorted by the light dragoons of Captain Philip Kearney, Scott rode swiftly to an enthusiastic welcome from his *"wildly cheering"* vanguard. Feeling another strong premonition of victory, inspired by the obviously high morale of his men, he sent forward Lieutenant (later Confederate General) P.G.T. Beauregard and the pioneers, – part of whose statutory function was to undertake reconnaissance duties on behalf of the army – with orders to define the extremities of the enemy's mountain lair.

Believing that the towering promontories and rugged defiles of the Eastern Sierras made a frontal attack along the axis of the Vera Cruz – Jalapa – Mexico City road the only conceivable option, Santa Anna had deployed thirteen thousand men astride the road, in a position of narrow frontage but with considerable strength in depth. On the Mexican right, the ground dropped away steeply to a stream bed, in a jumble of sheer scarps and steep, rocky ravines. Their left was located on the lower slopes of Cerro Gordo itself – the dominant hill feature, in the rear of which was sited a battery of five heavy calibre guns. On the relatively flatter ground between these two extremities was entrenched the bulk of the Mexican infantry. Wherever the road doubled back on itself in the course of its tortuous approach to the heart of the pass, pits had been dug for the remaining thirty-seven artillery pieces. Santa Anna posted his reserve some two miles to the rear, in the direction of Jalapa. Superficially, he may have been justified in believing that a *"mountain goat"*[49] could not take him in flank; but after three days of diligent reconnaissance, Captain of Engineers, Robert E Lee, discovered a possible way to approach the Mexican redoubt. A further three days of surreptitious grading and the route was considered suitable for the manhandling of the guns forward to where they could enfilade some of the defensive works. Deciding that *"the time for aggression had arrived,"* Scott issued General Order Number Three to his subordinate commanders, which also included comprehensive instructions for a pursuit, clearly expressed in the best West Point fashion. *"The enemy's batteries being carried or abandoned, all our Divisions and corps will pursue with vigour. This pursuit may be continued many miles, until stopped by darkness or fortified positions towards Jalapa."* Distant some twenty-five miles. Scott's medical arrangements were equally precise. Ambulance wagons and medical officers were to follow each and every regiment and battery, as well as the cavalry. The disabled were to be transported back to a general hospital. All involved in the attack and the pursuit were to carry *"ammunition and subsistence for at least two days."*[50]

---

49 Scott.
50 Scott.

The battle for the Pass of Cerro Gordo began in the afternoon, with a tussle for a point of dominating high ground occupied by a Mexican outpost position. Both sides had killed and wounded before the defenders were dislodged. During the night, a gun and three heavy howitzers were dragged into a position to lob shells into the main Mexican emplacements, and soon after dawn the fighting became general. The doubtlessly expected frontal attack was carried out, to pin-down and divert, by just one brigade of volunteers, while two regular Divisions, accompanied by two further volunteer regiments, undertook the decision-making attack designed to turn the Mexican left flank. The frontal attack was initially driven-off; but by the time the volunteers had re-grouped for a second attempt, the main, infantry, attack had cleared the shot swept slopes of Cerro Gordo and continued on to carry the summit with the bayonet. Captured guns were immediately turned on their previous owners, and the enfilading fire from a hitherto friendly direction, so discomfited the Mexican centre – under the personal command of Santa Anna – that the whole position was abandoned in panic. Some eight thousand men fled back up the road towards Jalapa, before the blocking position, planned by Scott for just such an eventuality, was in place. The heavy battery in the rear of Cerro Gordo surrendered by negotiation, and by early afternoon the pursuit – led by cavalry and the flying artillery batteries of captains Taylor ('K') and Wall – was under way.

"On the seventeenth instant (April), *we attacked the Mexicans, but did not succeed in routing them completely until the eighteenth, when we took some thousands of prisoners.[51] ... We followed close on the retreating column until night and came near enough to give them a few shots from the battery, but they succeeded in effecting their escape for want of our dragoons,"* 'K' Battery's lieutenant wrote to his sister. *"General*

---

51 Mexican loss: one thousand two hundred killed and wounded, three thousand prisoners. American loss: sixty-three killed and three hundred and sixty-eight wounded.

Scott, after disarming the prisoners, allowed them to retire and released the officers on parole. But General La Vega, who is again our prisoner, refused to accept this, and I presume will be sent back to the United States. (Scott did not have the means to feed, or the manpower to escort prisoners to Vera Cruz, and he believed there was a *"ten to one"* chance of them escaping anyway. His practical parole policy lessened the chance of individuals reappearing in the ranks later on and was intended to encourage garrisons in the future to surrender, knowing they would be sent home to their families.) *"General Santa Anna escaped,"* Tom continued, *"but in his haste left us his carriage and wooden leg, together with some thousands of dollars in specie. … Captain Taylor, in his report to General Twiggs, has spoken of me in very flattering terms. I am now in Jalapa, which is situated about sixty miles from Vera Cruz and one hundred and ninety five from the city of Mexico. It is rumoured here that the Mexicans are fortifying their capital. If so, then we may have the grand battle there."* In the same letter,[52] Tom also gave Laura some impressions of the country he was passing through. *"A person passing through this sterile portion of the country would not suppose the inhabitants would be able to pay their taxes. In the cities it is different; there, wealth is frequently found. … You often see elegant buildings. The country General Santa Anna owns between this place and Vera Cruz contains three beautiful houses and a tract of land about fifty-five miles in length. The country in the south is very similar to our own. Whilst I was in Monterey, my quarters were in the outskirts of the city, having a large back-lot attached, which contained a beautiful orange orchard. Also, in this lot was a fine bathing establishment, the pool being about twenty-five by thirty feet … the houses are generally built of sun-dried brick … the church is the most highly ornamented in the interior of any edifice which has ever come under my observation. … Upon entering … we are struck with the gaudy appearance … but most especially the opposite end from the entrance, which appears to be gilded. At the base is a magnificent silver altar, and on each side statues which cannot fail to attract the attention of the*

---

52 Letter from, Jalapa, Mexico, April 22, 1847.

astonished beholder. ... I can say no more", he ended hurriedly, *"... the escort by which I wish to send this has just started and I must mount my horse and overtake it or miss a good opportunity."*

Tom was rather more downbeat, though resigned, when he wrote again from Jalapa, just over a month later: *"Lovely Sister: I have the mortification of being left to garrison the town of Jalapa. Captain Taylor used his influence to keep me with him, in which event I should have gone forward. But Colonel Childs, who was made Military Governor of this place, got General Scott to issue an order requiring me to join my company, which was under the command of the Governor. Notwithstanding my present situation, I have some hope of getting forward by and by, when more troops get in from the States. ... I throw myself into the hands of an all wise God, and hope that it may yet be for the better. It may have been one of His means of diminishing my excessive ambition; and after having accomplished His purpose, whatever it may be, He then, in His infinite wisdom, may gratify my desire."[53]*

On arriving at Jalapa, Scott too faced an irritating setback. His advanced units had gone on to take the next important pass of La Hoya, together with the town of Perote and the city of La Puebla, all without a fight, which left them within eighty-five miles of Mexico City. He had decided to garrison Jalapa to strengthen his already extended communications with Washington, through the port of Vera Cruz. However, no less than four thousand volunteers were coming to the end of their service, and a straw poll revealed that whilst all were prepared to serve loyally to the last day, none were prepared to 'soldier on,' for a day longer. Scott decided the lesser of two evils was to let them go during this quiet period, rather than risk being embarrassed by their downing tools when he was committed to a fight. The part-time soldier had presented practical problems ever since colonial times. Scott's dilemma was one which added to the awesome burdens of George Washington during the War of Independence and would return to plague Abraham Lincoln in the struggle between the States.

---

53 Letter from *Jalapa, May 25, 1847* (Arnold).

In 1862, it would briefly attempt to interfere with the plans of 'Stonewall' Jackson in the Shenandoah Valley; but his uniquely brusque way with volunteers in the service of the Southern Confederacy meant that his experience failed to achieve either the dignity of a dilemma, or the status of a plague. The problem stemmed from a comprehensive militia system, which was designed for the mass mobilization of citizens for the paltry period of three months only, in recognition of their essential peacetime tasks of crop planting, growing and harvesting. When, because of the Mexico situation, Congress decreed that volunteers should serve *"for twelve months or until the end of the war,"* President Polk chose to interpret that as meaning no longer than twelve months, no matter what. But Polk was playing politics, and was anti-Scott – who, unlike himself, was a Whig or Democrat. He had already proposed to Congress that Senator Benton, a junior major-general, should be promoted to lieutenant-general and appointed to command the invasion force, with Scott as his second-in-command. It was the hope of Polk that Benton would be credited with Scott's victories, which would benefit the presidential party at the polls. Congress was unimpressed with such shabby tactics and threw out the proposal. Unfortunately for Scott they also delayed legislation authorising the country to raise ten further regular regiments, by some three months. With everything still on hold at the end of May, due to the manpower shortage, Scott moved on to La Puebla. Only Santa Anna was benefiting from the enforced lack of action, although Tom also mentioned in his letter to Laura from Jalapa, (postmarked *New Orleans, June* the eighth) that he was *"in fine quarters, and making rapid progress in the Spanish language, and have an idea of making some lady acquaintances shortly,"* ending; *"I think of you often, and my heart has more than once upbraided me of my neglect of you. But I feared to inform you of things as they were. … Your brother always, T.J. Jackson."*

With the departure of the volunteers, Scott was reduced to just five thousand effectives. He none the less remained inactive, believing this the best policy whilst waiting for reinforcements. He *"played for big stakes. Keeping the army and the mind fixed upon the capital ... being morally sure that all smaller objects would follow that crowning event."[54]* The enemy had recently taken to flaunting his superior numbers and tried to draw the Americans into irrelevant and wasting skirmishes. Scott was too accustomed to the mantle of generalship to be either tempted or overawed. He had accurately assessed Santa Anna as a man of considerable energy and vigilance, and a president with exceptional ability as an administrator and organiser, but as a general, Scott felt, he failed at both *"quickness of perception and rapidity of combination."[55]* Secure in his own judgement, Scott sent his men sightseeing. By Divisions they visited the nearby remains of the ancient civilisation of Cholula, overpowered by Montezuma when in the later stages of decay, and subsequently dealt typically barbaric blows by Cortez. Meanwhile, the regular rump of the invasion force turned the fortress city of Puebla, with its cathedral and one hundred crafted spires, into a hive of professional military activity. Amid trees of apple and apricot, peach and pear – which, for Scott, was so redolent of the countryside around Frederick in Maryland – squadrons, batteries and companies practised battlefield manoeuvres and evolutions. Experienced men drilled, to put an even keener edge on an already ingrained discipline, in an effort to further ensure that even under the most withering of fusillades, orders would be precisely obeyed and screaming base instincts contemptuously ignored. In that fertile valley of Puebla, seven thousand feet above mean sea level; surrounded by lush grasses, clover and lucerne, in fields where two crops of barley, wheat, maize and rye were harvested each year, they also relaxed and rested. Beneath the massive mountain of Malinche, and with the snow-capped tips of Orizaba and Popocatepetl glittering in the hazy distance, they gathered and sang the bawdy, sentimental and patriotic songs of the trail and the bivouac fire. Growing

---

54 Scott.
55 Ibid.

familiar with boisterous renditions of *"Green Grows the Laurel,"* a diffident, ever-lurking enemy dubbed them *'Gringoes.'*

With July about to give way to August, Scott's patience, and his decision to remain faithful to his ultimate aim, were vindicated. Eight hundred reinforcements under Lieutenant-Colonel McIntosh, together with elements of a fresh brigade and field battery under Brigadier-General Cadwallader, having been checked by a Mexican force east of Jalapa as they escorted up an important supply train, finally brushed aside the opposition, and joined the main body at Puebla. Major-General Pillow then brought in a further thousand men, and they were followed on the sixth of August by a fresh brigade of two thousand five hundred men under Brigadier-General Pierce. With the capability of putting a force of some eleven thousand five hundred into the field, the time for a return to boldness had arrived. Scott decided to abandon his supply lines with Vera Cruz and to stake all on his long held belief that in Mexico City lay the key to outright victory and, as he termed it, a *"just and honourable peace."* When the news of this decision finally reached no less an authority than the victor of Waterloo – who had been following the campaign closely from the newspapers in London, and with whom Scott was slightly acquainted – commented, *"Scott is lost. He has been carried away by success. He cannot take the city, and he cannot fall back upon his base,"* which only goes to show that even such a genius for success in war as the Duke of Wellington is fallible when reliant upon the media for his intelligence. In the thick of things, and with no such reliance upon journalists, Tom Jackson, like his commanding general, was buoyant, having worked his escape from garrison duty. One of the novel features of American tactics throughout the Mexican Campaign, was the imaginative use made of light artillery. That Zachary Taylor's winning reputation was still intact after Buena Vista was entirely due to his 'flying' gunners.' The situations created by their tactics, however, demanded soldiers – and more especially officers – of extreme courage and an abiding determination. Captain John Bankhead Magruder of the First Artillery had proved himself the quintessence of a leader of light batteries, and as much with an eye to future employment, as a reward for past bravery, Scott had given him command of a battery of captured Mexican field guns. The only snag was that the same fiery, demanding nature, and exacting application of leadership, that so deterred hostile hordes, struck a similar chord in the ranks of friendly subalterns. Such was the reputation of this restless Virginian, that nobody wanted to be his Battery Lieutenant. Nobody, that is, except Brevet Lieutenant Jackson, who only needed the most fleeting glimpse of an opportunity to realise its full potential. As he would admit later, *"I wanted to see active service, to be the enemy in the fight, and when I heard that John Magruder had got his battery, I bent all my energies to be with him, for I knew if any fighting was to be done Magruder would be on hand."*[56]

In the best tradition of the Spanish *guerrilleros*, all American movement beyond the ranks of a major unit, the army itself, or the garrison of an occupied town, was carefully monitored. Scott himself wrote that he could hardly turn round, *"causing several citizens to fly off at full speed, on fine Andalusian horses, to report the fact to detachments of cavalry lurking in the vicinity."* Moving up from Jalapa, to join the main body at Puebla, Tom's group were jumped-on at the Pass of La Hoya, and in the ensuing scuffle, four Mexicans were killed and three captured, he told Laura, before the remainder fled, leaving behind *"a beautiful sabre and some other equipment."* Colonel Childs and his garrison also moved up, to hold Puebla as the base camp for the final advance; a force of some six hundred able-bodied men and a further six hundred sick and wounded.

---

56 Quoted by Professor R.L. Dabney DD in his *"Life & Campaigns of Lt-Gen Thomas J Jackson"*, and extensively resorted to thereafter.

4/3. Contreras – San Antonio – Churubusco

*"My greatest delight is in this
fine body of troops . . ."*
Winfield Scott

SCOTT's tactical march on the Mexican capital was conducted in four Divisions, a minimum of three always being able to unite within two hours. Throughout the approach, Santa Anna made no aggressive move. He had had nearly four months to raise an army of thirty thousand men, and to entrench them to his satisfaction about the very heart of his distracted country. Moving with his leading Division, Scott crossed the watershed between the Atlantic and Pacific Oceans on the tenth of August, and began moving down the western slopes of the Rio Frio Mountains. Clearly visible on that long descent from ten thousand feet were the glittering lakes, the peaks and volcanic scoria, the marshes, mule-tracks and arterial highways, radiating from the *'Halls of Montezuma.'* The sight, Scott would write later, filled his mind *"… with religious awe;"* but asked to join the brisk debate going on around him as to the most striking feature – the plain of Tenochtitlan, with its ripening harvest glowing beneath snow-capped peaks; the forests and lakes; the muscular, geometric strength of the city, or the 'pyramid of Cholula', ever the soldier's leader – he replied, *"I differ from you all. My greatest delight is in this fine body of troops, without whom, we can never sleep in the halls of Montezuma, or in our own homes."* Riding forward with a strong recce group to the mound of El Penon, a mere eight miles from the City, the great strength of the triple tier of fortifications, set amid flooding from rain and the sluiced waters of Lake Tezcoco, his mind was quickly made up. To attack head-on from the East would result in heavy casualties. *"Anxious to save the lives of this gallant army,"* he instigated further diligent reconnaissance, with the aim of once again turning the flank of the enemy and making a fighting approach from the South. Even for one who had grown to manhood amid the glories of the Virginia countryside – and who had glimpsed Washington – it was a memorable panorama; but for Tom Jackson, intent on putting a fresh dint in the pock-marked carapace of war, " ... *the only anxiety of which I was conscious ...* (was) ... *a fear lest I should not meet danger enough to make my conduct conspicuous."*[57] It has often been written that Jackson was an avid reader of Napoleon's 'Maxims', and we know he borrowed Walter Scott's biography of Napoleon from the Academy library on the twenty fifth of February 1843,[58] but it has to be said that he was tactically more imaginative than the Corsican on the battlefield. One cannot help feeling that the seed Jackson nurtured to the point where he became reckoned among the very greatest of the *'flankers and rearers,'* was not in fact planted originally by Winfield Scott in Mexico, good though Scott's tactics were. It would have been instinctive, and Scott's tactical acumen confirmed practical confirmation.

The natural obstacles in the way of moving the army – with its support wagons and artillery – off to a flank anywhere in the quadrant south-east of Mexico City, were prodigious, and it was several days before Scott had everything arranged to his satisfaction. Then, on the fifth morning after having first sighted the city of Mexico, three US Divisions moved across the foothills of the Sierras, rounded the east and southern shores of Lake Chalco, and after a march of some twenty-seven miles – which included tracks the Mexicans, once again, considered impassable to an army – emerged on the great southern approach road, just seven miles from the Mexican capital. It was at once apparent that the 'fire' had been substituted for the 'frying pan.' To the right of the highway was an impassable bog, and stretching away to the left, a deeply fissured volcanic outcrop known as the

---

57 Henderson.

58 Cook.

Pedregal. Several lines of fortifications had been readied astride the road, in conjunction with *San Antonio*, a now heavily fortified and well garrisoned *hacienda*. As if all this were not enough, the Mexicans had not been fooled for one moment, despite the fourth Division having been left behind to divert some attention form the flank march, and to inject an element of surprise. Having the advantage of interior lines, the bulk of the Mexican Army had simply moved across, from their positions facing east, to positions south of the City. Moving to re-join the main body, the fourth Division was forced to deploy, at one point, against a force twice its strength; but after a brief opening barrage from Captain Taylor's 'K' Battery, the Mexicans withdrew. Three days after starting the flanking manoeuvre, Scott's force was at least re-united, if not noticeably better placed.

A subsequent decision to slip still further left, and to move in from the south west, was made feasible by Scott's talented band of engineer officers, who first discovered – and then made passable for artillery and wagons; a narrow mule track spanning the Pedregal. The resulting move successfully by-passed *San Antonio*; but seemed only to substitute one set of obstacles for others equally formidable. Debouching from the Pedregal, on to an expanse of cultivated land, the would-be attackers found themselves confronted by some six thousand Mexicans in prepared positions along a dominant ridge-line, with ever-steepening scarps and crests at their backs. Apparently without waiting for further orders, the leading infantry brigade, closely supported by Magruder's Battery, now having Tom Jackson as second subaltern, moved forward on to a stretch of higher ground within one thousand yards of the prepared positions of the enemy. Shortly after noon, the light battery unlimbered and began firing. The first rounds of the battle for Mexico City had begun, with all the advantages, seemingly, in favour of the defence.

By three o'clock in the afternoon, the entire two Divisions of generals Pillow and Twiggs were deployed, and a battery of mountain howitzers and rocket launchers had been manhandled across broken ground, to support the twelve and six-pounder field guns commanded by Magruder. With their right flank secure on the line of a deep ravine, and with a joint force of infantry and cavalry clearly massed as reserve, in rear of the entrenched positions, the Mexicans responded with vigorous and effective fire from twenty-two guns, mostly of heavy calibre. The difficult terrain prevented any move forward by any heavy guns of the US Artillery in support of their infantry which, in turn, *"... could not advance in column without being mowed down by the grape and canister of the (Mexican) batteries, nor advance in line without being ridden over by the enemy's numerous cavalry."*[59] The destructive Mexican artillery disposed of Lieutenant Johnstone, Magruder's second-in-command, together with fifteen gunners and a like number of battery horses. On finding that death had placed him in command of the second section of the battery, Tom Jackson came quickly into his own, and proceeded to fight the three guns with considerable courage and ability. As the hot and dusty afternoon drew on, Jackson heard the guns of the first section being directed by Magruder from a position even further forward than his own, on the American right, and *"advanced in handsome style, to keep up the fire with equal briskness and effect."* The infantry, supported by Magruder and Jackson, managed to force their way, with considerable difficulty, across a scrub covered angle of the Pedrugal, to occupy the village of Contreras (which later gave its name to the whole engagement). The Mexicans mounted several counter-attacks, both by infantry and cavalry, in their attempts to drive the Americans back across the Pedregal; but, the line held, and they continued to occupy Contreras. Late in the day, before darkness brought obscurity, a final counter assault was undertaken by a single Mexican infantry battalion. It also failed – possibly, the whole Mexican effort had been too piecemeal – but with further reinforcements seen approaching from the direction of the capital – the Divisional commander[60]

59 Scott.
60 Major-General Pillow.

ordered Magruder to pull back from his exposed, forward position on the right, to an area of relative safety further to the rear. The two American Divisions which had been engaged throughout the afternoon could expect no reinforcements. The rest of Scott's Army was five miles back in the area of San Antonio, and with the order to retire came the rain; in torrential quantities. It lashed across the weary survivors of the battery as they slipped and struggled to manhandle the cumbersome cannons from the boulder-strewn slopes, and drenched the resting riflemen, whose dispirited huddles stood intermittently revealed in jagged flashes of flickering lightning. All around, the thunder rolled and echoed against dark, invisible mountains.

Magruder would report on his dead second-in-command as *"… a young officer of the highest praise"* and of the man who took his place at the height of the action, *"His conduct was equally conspicuous during the whole day, and I cannot too highly commend him to the Major-General's favourable consideration."* The star turn during the intense preparations of the soaking, dispiriting night that followed was captain of engineers, Robert Edward Lee, the future Confederate Commander-in-Chief. Closeted in the comparative calm of Contreras church, a council of war had come up with a bold plan to turn the Mexican left flank, by means of an immediate night march along a deep, secluded ravine which the defenders had failed to patrol. Either Lee or Brigadier-General Smith made the original suggestion; but certainly, Lee closed the discussion – so unusual in not having come-up with some half-baked, tentative proposal more typical of such councils – saying, he needed to clear the decision with Scott, who was back with the Divisions confronting the hacienda of San Antonio. Lee's ride through the pitch black and pouring rain of that eventful night, without either a single guide or escort, to Army Headquarters five miles away across the bandit infested Pedregal, Scott later described as being *"gallant and indefatigable."* Scott had sent forward no less than seven officer/despatch riders with orders for his leading units, and all had returned, their messages undelivered. When Lee appeared, Scott described his effort as *"… the greatest feat of physical and moral courage performed by any individual during the entire campaign,"* which may be considered a touch over-the-top, if only because the two engineers Tower and Brooke undertook the equally hazardous task of reconnoitring a route for the flank march under exactly similar conditions. For the alert, conscientious and brave, along with the unimaginative, unthinking and brave, many more desperate opportunities were about to unfold in that magnificent natural cockpit, surrounding the disinterested colossus of Mexico City.

During the remaining hours of darkness, on what was now the eleventh morning since the Americans had first sighted the Mexican capital, the four and a half thousand survivors of the encounter – which would turn out to be the first phase of the first of two pairs of battles, which ultimately decided the outcome of both the campaign and the war – began their tortuous night march to flank the Mexican defences. So bad were conditions underfoot, following the rain, that one company took two hours to cover a mere four hundred yards. With the coming of daylight, things speeded up considerably. Debauching from the Pedregal, no more than five hundred yards from the entrenchments, the leading battalions turned into line, and without the benefit of either artillery fire, or cavalry, went in with the bayonet, and no more than a distracting ripple of a volley from their own rifles. In a mere quarter of an hour, some seven hundred of the defenders had been killed; eight hundred and thirteen captured, including four generals, together with seven hundred pack mules, some horses, and a variety of weapons and ammunition. As the oriflamme of America fluttered in the dawn above the newly captured earthworks, some five thousand five hundred erstwhile defenders, plus a would-be reinforcing column of a further twelve thousand, fled in demoralised disarray. Reaching the objective closely behind his attacking units, Scott was able to share in the special pleasure of a company of the Fourth Artillery which had gleefully repossessed two brass six pounder cannons, which the Mexicans had taken from another company of the same regiment during the two days of fluctuating fortune at Buena Vista. He was also able to turn his immediate attention back to the fortified hacienda of *San Antonio*, the capture of which would open a shorter and clearer approach to the capital.

The two rear Divisions, which Scott ordered up in support of the dawn attack did not arrive in time. These he turned back to the hacienda. After some last moment reconnoitring and a few defining orders, one brigade of Major-General Worth's Division speedily prodded the Mexicans from *San Antonio*, *"… it's garrison, no doubt, much shaken by our decisive victory at Contreras."[61]* During the successful frontal assault, a second brigade manoeuvred to disrupt the Mexican retreat. This was also successful and had the effect of splitting the fugitives into two groups, one of which poured towards the fortified hamlet of Churubusco – the fourth of Scott's objectives for that morning. The third objective was the church cum convent of *San Pablo*, a second strongpoint associated with the hamlet, which was also being reconnoitred for an attack. In the first two or three hours of the day, Scott had all his Divisions moving at once, in different directions and with differing objectives. At one point his somewhat attenuated order of battle was ablaze from end-to-end, with the smoke and flame of firing. With *San Antonio* neutralised, Scott detailed-off the Second Pennsylvania Volunteers and a detachment of US Marines to guard *"… our sick and wounded, the siege, supply and baggage trains,"[62]* and concentrated his entire force, of something over eight thousand men, against the twin strongpoints of Churubusco. With Santa Anna's twenty seven thousand strong army of infantry, artillery and cavalry either directly involved in the defence of the hamlet, or within close supporting distance, a confrontation of decisive importance was clearly imminent.

First a sustained fire was directed against *San Pablo* for an hour or so, before two brigades led-off against the second *tête de pont* nearby. This was a fairly formidable fieldwork, employing regular

---

61 Scott.

62 Ibid.

bastions and curtains in the manner of more sophisticated military structures. Although the double nature of the attack prevented the two positions from being mutually supporting, the attacking battalions were severely treated, both by the defenders of the objective, as well as from a lengthy infantry position away to their left. Reaching the first obstacle – a deep, water-filled ditch – the attackers splashed through it without hesitation, to take both the curtain and a linking bridge with the bayonet. Immediately a captured four-pounder was directed against *San Pablo*, and from further back on the road to *San Antonio*. Two of the guns which had been supporting the assault, switched their fire to the tower of *San Pablo* church, which the Mexicans had been keeping well stocked with sharpshooters. Twenty minutes after taking the bridgehead, the Americans worked their bayonets into *San Pablo*, to end an engagement which had lasted for some two and a half hours. Its fall marked the end of any Mexican attempt to hold the line of the Churubusco waterway, and the defenders streamed away towards Mexico City, just four miles distant. Two brigades moving in rear of *San Pablo*, to foil a withdrawal, routed a reserve of four thousand infantry and cavalry, drawn up in some wet meadows beside the road to the capital. This fifth, local, victory of the day meant that for the time being the Mexican Army had ceased to be a cohesive, tactically useable entity, and was almost everywhere in disorganised retreat. Whilst virtually the entire army was wheeling and marching its way to this string of unbroken tactical successes, Magruder's Battery had been held largely in reserve. But although lacking the action he continued to crave, this day – the twentieth of August 1847 – was still a memorable date in the US Army career of Tom Jackson. The brevet promotion to First Lieutenant, earned at the siege of Vera Cruz, was confirmed, and, *"For gallant and meritorious conduct in the battles of Contreras and Churubusco,"* he was awarded the rank of Brevet Captain of Artillery. Any further, immediate, chance for distinguished active service looked unlikely.

4/4. Chapultepec

....

*"I was ordered to hold my position,
and I had no right to abandon it."*
Brevet Captain Jackson

....

DESPITE having defeated and demoralised the larger part of the Mexican Army, and as a consequence spread consternation amongst the hundred and eighty thousand inhabitants living at the heart of the Republic, Scott opted not to continue his vigorous offensive; but to try for an armistice. Failing to finally press home his hard-won advantage – and despite no army being too tired to win the last victory – was the charge that was made against him, despite the soundness of his reasoning for attempting to adopt a more peaceable course.

In the first instance, the great disparity in numbers was still a factor to be reckoned with, especially for a commander in the isolated position into which Scott had put himself. If the civilian population could be roused sufficiently to fight alongside the defending army then the meagre invading force might still be overwhelmed, amid the solid strength of the Spanish-style fortifications protecting the city. At Contreras and Churubusco, the cost of capturing three thousand prisoners, including two ex-presidents, and either killing or wounding a further four thousand, was the incapacitation – either by death or wounds – of one thousand and fifty-two Americans. Allowing for the detachments of Colonel Childs and those protecting the baggage train, the number which Scott had available to *"… conquer a peace,"* in the face of whatever the *"… climate, ground, fortifications and numbers"*[63] could combine to hold against him, had already dwindled

---

63 Scott.

to some seven thousand four hundred and forty-five all ranks. Both wishing and having to spare the lives of his men, Scott was against assaulting the city in broad daylight. To his credit, he was equally reluctant to adopt the night alternative because of the possibility that a massacre of the women and children might result from neither side being able to distinguish the armed from the unarmed, in the dark.

To his further credit, Scott felt that the actual process of victory should not include driving the Mexican people, their government and army, over the brink of despair. He wanted them to retain a real, if tarnished, degree of honour and national pride. Neutrals and ex-patriot Americans agreed with him in this, saying that to force an abject surrender, *"… might scatter the elements of peace, excite a spirit of national desperation, and thus indefinitely postpone the hope of accommodation."*[64] Scott was genuinely concerned with the dilemma of preserving the nation he was defeating in battle. Quite apart from theoretically eliminating certain problems before they arose, Scott also wanted the practical advantages of a negotiated settlement; an end to the fighting and no more 'butcher's bills.' With these considerations and the recent experience of Vera Cruz very much in mind, Scott billeted his men in the villages clustered about Mexico City, and prepared to take up *"… battering and assault positions,"* from where he could summon the capital to surrender.

Unfortunately for the cause of peace, the politician in Winfield Scott was no more a match for the tortuous wiles of a Mexican president than he had been for the home-grown American variety. In a country constantly shaken by war since 1789, Santa Anna had been a feared and evil genius in public life, ever since he led successful revolts against the presidencies of Iturbide, Guerrero and Gomes Pedraza, before going on to blow away the tattered remnant of external Spanish influence at the battle of Barradas, in September 1829. A vast landowner, his agricultural interests

---

64 Scott.

rose no higher than the breeding of roosters for the barbarities of cock fighting. An untutored soldier since early youth, he showed no real ability as a field commander, yet, when in power, he lived out an endless military charade, carrying the role of imperious general into the conduct of all his affairs. It was said that his battlefield victories were due entirely to the mistakes of his opponents, and that being *"… personally timid, he seldom meditated an advance without planning a retreat."*[65] His attitude to money fluctuated between the instincts of the compulsive gambler, and those of the insatiable miser. For women he was the rampant, selfish sensualist; wilful, haughty, boastful and bombastic, he carried avarice well beyond the incipient stages of amorality and malfeasance. Santa Anna could, on the other hand, reveal himself to be patient and observant, a skilled dialectician, and a master of the dramatic gesture. It was, however, eloquence which was the glittering jewel in the coronet of his turbulent talent. Either verbally or on paper, he wielded it with the ease of the natural sleight of hand artiste, to rise, seemingly untarnished from every disgrace, and to glide, apparently blameless, through every reverse. A most consummate *"…sophistry…changed defeat into victory or converted criminal faults into philanthropy"*. Assured of a fundamental unpopularity from his despotic wielding of the deliberately mingled strengths of army and church, the abilities which enabled Santa Anna to ride the revolutionary waves, were utilised on various occasions, by widely divergent factions. Although this led to enough curtain calls to satisfy the most ardent old trouper, stability never followed his return to power. The selflessness necessary to steer Mexico into the calmer waters of prosperity was simply not in his make-up. Like Robespierre, Trotsky, or the mullahs of a latter-day Iran, the creative initiative of a Washington, a Cromwell or an Ataturk, was beyond him. For the inveterate schemer of mid-Nineteenth Century Mexico, statesmanship was little more than an extension of the belief that all men are either

---

65 Ibid.

corrupt or candidates for corruption. In the desperate straits occasioned by American military success, it was doubtless due to some such venal philosophy – which had served him so well in local politics – that Santa Anna was instinctively turning; when he sent a truce mission to Scott on the morning of the twenty first of August. When the American, for his part, rejected the terms; but kept the door open with a counter proposal – which purposely omitted any summons to surrender, the Mexican surely felt a momentary surge of cynical optimism. Perhaps for the first time since Vera Cruz, Scott would allow himself to be confronted from a direction not of his own choosing. Commissioners appointed by both sides met on the twenty-third, reached a level of agreement on the following day and were exchanging ratification terms by the twenty fourth. With the purely military considerations taken care of, and the over-bearing problems of inter-governmental dispute placed in the hands of plenipotentiaries, Scott felt hopeful that a full-blown treaty could result. It was not to be. The fine and laudable intentions were all on one side. In 'Field Report No: 33' – written from his headquarters at Tacubaya on eleven September , Scott reported to 'Honourable William. L. Marcy,' Secretary of War, on both the continuance of the negotiations and their final demise. There had been *"… some prospect of a successful result up to the second instant, when our commissioner handed in his ultimatum …* (on boundaries) and … *some infractions of the truce … followed by apologies on the part of the enemy. These vexations I was willing to put down to the imbecility of the government and waived any pointed demands of reparation while any hope remained of a satisfactory termination of the war. But on the fifth, … I learned that as soon as the ultimatum had been considered in a grand council of ministers … President Santa Anna, … without giving me the slightest notice, actively recommenced strengthening the military defences of the city, in gross violation of the third article of the armistice."*[66] It only remained for Scott to send across a note of protest, and receive a

---

66 Scott.

reply, virtually by return, which *"... was absolutely and notoriously false, both in recrimination and explanation."*[67]

By late on the seventh of September, engineers were reconnoitring several of the formal approaches to the city, and at dawn the following day, an attack was launched on the outlying position of *Molinos del Rey*. Due to their losses in action, it had become apparent that the Mexicans no longer had sufficient artillery to defend all eight gates of the city and had resorted to removing church bells for casting into guns. The purpose of this swiftly mounted assault was to deny them the use of the foundry and iron mill at *Molinos del Rey*, together with a large supply of gunpowder stored in the *Casa Mata* nearby. The subsequent success of the operation also had the effect of removing the first hurdle on the approach to the south western, *San Cosme,* gate. However, the relatively high number of American casualties provided critics of the peace attempt with a substantial, if retrospective, cudgel with which to belabour the Commander-in-Chief.

From their position securing the open, right flank of the attack on *Molinos del Rey,* the section of Magruder's Battery commanded by Tom Jackson was not directly involved, apart from dispersing a body of cavalry which threatened at one point to intervene. Otherwise, they were virtual spectators to the killing and wounding of some eight hundred Americans amid the trenches and earthworks linking the small cluster of solid stone buildings. After losing yet another pair of generals, as well as a further three thousand lesser lights, the Mexicans made an orderly withdrawal to the mound of Chapultapec, about half a mile in rear of the *Molinos del Rey* position. Bowed and bloodied once more, their spirit was still not broken. The abortive days of the armistice had been used to some advantage.

Finally, up against Mexico City's extensive collection of in-depth defences, Scott called on the considerable reconnoitring talent of his ubiquitous engineer officers for the final time. On

---

67 Ibid.

this occasion, however, there could be no question of a deft out-flanking of prepared positions. The ancient capital of the Incas was so positioned and so clad that she would submit only to the most boisterous of full frontal assaults. The solitary question facing Lee, Beauregard and the others was – from which direction would she prove most susceptible?

Extensive marshes capable of inhibiting the deployment of cavalry and prohibiting all but the most restricted use of the vital artillery arm, ruled out assaults from both the western and eastern approaches. The nature of this terrain also put an end to any thoughts there may have been of a hooking movement planned to end in an attack from the north, where, in any case, the city was protected by an arc of linked salients. For two days, the engineers concentrated their energies in that sector south and south-west of the capital, which had come under threat from the moment the Americans had struggled free of the Pedregal, over three weeks earlier. Scott also scrutinised the defences of the four most southerly gates for himself. Behind a broad screen of troops he saw that each gate *"… had a system of strong works that seemed to require nothing but some men and guns to be impregnable."* The defensive ditch or moat was *"… a navigable canal of great breadth and depth"* and would, he decided, be *"very difficult to bridge in the presence of an enemy."*[68] This left a wide area of flat meadowland – between the American positions and the canal – in which all the elevated causeways, and numerous twisting link roads, had long since been comprehensively breached. Notwithstanding the relative dryness of the 1848 rainy season, these breaches had been flooded automatically by a general seepage of water from nearby lakes, into what was a very low-lying area beyond the city walls. Scott finally decided on a brief, diversionary build-up of men in front of the southern gates, followed by a longer period of bombardment, during which time his men would concentrate and initiate the final assault from a south-westerly point some two

---

68 Scott.

miles from the diversion. Although this meant fighting for the mound of Chapultepec it was preferable to negotiating all that water. Chapultepec, with its tiered defences reminiscent of *El Penon* in the eastern sector, was fortified at its base; around the sloping sides, and on the summit, where the National Military Academy – once a palace both to Montezuma and the Spanish viceroys – was now manned by would-be officers under training, together with a strong garrison force. The final arguments for assaulting from this direction were; the artillery would be able to deploy on reasonably firm ground, and once dislodged, the Mexicans would be hard put to re-organize on the long, narrow causeways which carried the roads – over more marshy ground – to the *San Cosme* and *Belen* gates three miles distant. Furthermore, a congested retreat would, in addition, turn the gates into bottlenecks, which would render them extremely vulnerable to a vigorous pursuit conducted in the style of Cerro Gordo.

The feints and diversions went much as planned, and the following day, one Division advanced against the south-east face of Chapultepec, while a second moved in from the north. An infantry brigade was tasked with linking the two attacks, with artillery support from the Second Section of Magruder's Battery, commanded by Brevet Captain of Artillery, Tom Jackson. As this combined column of guns and infantry moved into position along a cross track which skirted the face of the mound, it came under fire from some heavy calibre guns in emplacements around the summit. Almost simultaneously, they were subjected to particularly effective fire from a solitary field-gun, which had been skilfully sighted behind a breast-work at the very bottom of the slope, from where it could rake great tracts of the road selected for the approach. The land beside the road, where it had become the killing ground for the Mexican artillery, was too soft and marshy for Jackson to move his guns off to a flank and return the fire. The infantry colonel ordered him to deploy at the head of the column. By now the infantry had come to a stop, and with their casualties mounting by the minute, it was with some difficulty that the gunners struggled past them on the narrow pathway. Having done so, they were immediately halted in their turn by a deep ditch dug across the road. Pausing only to reload, the Mexican gunners began to scythe swathes in the now stationary men and battery horses of their counterparts. Jackson quickly appreciated that if he was to make any sort of effective response, he would have to establish his gun line beyond the ditch, and in the face of the lethal fire sweeping across them, he ordered his men to unhitch the guns from the dead or dying horses, and to manhandle one of the six-pounders across the gap. The sacrifice of doing so proved almost too great, and with the exception of Jackson, the survivors of the effort gave up all attempts at further offensive action and sought only their own safety. As befitting a West Point graduate, Jackson attempted to imbue his men with something of his own unquenchable determination to win through. For a time, it seemed that he had failed. *"The example of their lieutenant*(sic)*walking up and down on the shot swept road and exclaiming calmly, 'There is no danger: See! I am not hit', failed to inspire them with confidence."*[69] Already their spirits were well cowed, and the ditch, where dead men mingled with the mentally and physically scarred, was already too full. Suddenly, a solitary and now unremembered sergeant found a courage to match that of his young superior and joined Captain Jackson at the gun. Alone amid the murderous fire, officer and non-commissioned officer together plied their basic trade as artillerymen in a furious attempt to dominate their numerous enemies.

Later Jackson would come to rationalise his personal response to the excesses of the battlefield into a comprehensive religious philosophy, developed for the governance of his whole life. Mexico would have contributed memorable experiences to the process as independent thoughts at large in the subconscious. Those first experiences of battle with Scott's Expeditionary Force reveal the essential hallmarks of the soldier he both wished to be, and instinctively was, and the general, which his actions suggested he

---

69 Henderson.

was capable of becoming. The award of two brevets for his actions at both Vera Cruz and Contreras are simply pointers to what certain of Jackson's superiors thought of his conduct at the time. It is likely that his actions were early evidence of a talent equal to the task of fulfilling his extensive military ambitions – and thereby, for him, living up to the achievements of his ancestors and rehabilitating the honour of the family – but posterity has been left with no hard evidence. From Chapultepec the evidence is more comprehensive. For the first time we see the un-flurried, totally focused, thinking response in the face of extreme personal danger, which was entirely in keeping with his avowed intention to *"perform conspicuously,"* whenever he was in a position to grasp the moment. It was in the contemplation of such opportunities that D.H. Hill tells us, *"His face lighted up, and his eyes sparkled as he spoke, and the shy hesitating manner gave way to the frank enthusiasm of the soldier".* Possibly some measure of his enthusiasm for the action itself, when it came, would have been discernible beneath that calm exterior. Henderson detected something of the 'Old Berserker' in Stonewall Jackson, and he was surely right. To be involved in the clash of armies 'turned him on,' without a doubt; but never to any addictive extent, even as a twenty-two year old. Rather there was just sufficient of the unflinching ability to walk the path of duty – which others might fear to tread – to complement the absolute determination to succeed. At all times the instinctive talent for how to achieve at war was controlled by a cool, creative and perspicacious intellect, leavened by an instinct for appreciating exactly what was and what was not feasible amidst the chaos, with the whole under-pinned by a matching moral courage to achieve. Even as early in his career as Chapultepec it was not simply the physical attributes which were on display. Scott also provided valuable early lessons in combating superior numbers, as well as in his regard both for the lives of his own men, and in his consideration for those of the opposition.

The commander of the northerly attack on the mound of Chapultepec – Major-General Worth – had become aware of the plight of the linking column on his flank, and to him their situation had become untenable, and was no longer necessary. He ordered the gunners, and the remnant of Colonel Trousdale's infantry battalion, to withdraw, despite their being nominally under the operational command of General Pillow, leading the attack from the south-west. The response to what was, if nothing else, a most humane consideration would have both surprised and intrigued the general. Strictly speaking, the young Jackson did not obey the general's command; but neither did he disobey or ignore it. Whereas others fired in a similar kiln, might have resorted to a 'Nelson-touch,' when embroiled in the lethal uncertainties of battle, and simply either not seen or not heard the order to dis-engage, Jackson blithely suggested a more positive expedient. It was, he informed Worth, more dangerous for him to retire than to hold on; but if the General would send him *"one company of regulars as support ... (he) ... could carry the work."*

One of the most fundamental of all the attributes of military leadership – at every level – must be the ability to create a winning result from the volatile complexity of a fire-fight. In demonstrating such an ability, the twenty-two year old Jackson received the most open-handed support from his superiors. Mugruder struggled on to the scene, having had his horse shot under him in the murderous fire still sweeping the elevated road and, immediately organising a second gun across the ditch, brought its fire to bear on the stubborn Mexicans. Worth, who seems to have been fairly close in rear of Jackson's position at the time the reply to his order was received, moved, not a company but an infantry brigade, in support of what was now, a pair of isolated artillery pieces. Trousdale, despite having been twice wounded, had managed to rally the remnant of his fourteenth Infantry Regiment and with continuing close support from the two artillery pieces, they charged alongside the regular brigade of Colonel Garnet, to put an end to all resistance from the hitherto lethal breastwork.

Away to the right, the assault from the south-west was proving equally irresistible, despite the commander – Major-General Pillow – being wounded by sniper fire as he rode from the cover of some trees and having to relinquish control. Largely oblivious to any individual fluctuations of fortune but their own, the attackers forged on across the rocks and chasms that lumped and rent the lower slopes of the Mound. Up through the antique grace of a cypress grove named for the renowned Montezuma; on with barely a check across a redoubt set mid-way up the slope, before heading, amid a persistently heavy small arms fire, for the palace on the summit. So rapidly was the attack being pressed, that the defenders felt unable to disrupt it, by firing mines specially dug into the hillside for the purpose, for fear of killing their own. Snap shooting quickly dropped anyone attempting to light the remote, trailing fuses. After crossing an outer ditch, scaling ladders – which had been carried well forward throughout the attack – were raised against the palace walls. The momentary pause which this entailed was only briefly extended when the leading climbers were hurled back amidst those crowding below. In a matter of moments, an initial *"… lodgement was … made. Streams of heroes followed; all opposition was overcome, and several of our regimental colours were flung out from the upper walls, amid long-continued shouts and cheers, which sent dismay into the capital."*[70] For Scott, *"No scene could have been more animating or glorious"*, as he rode to join his men on the topmost battlement, with the shouts of victory ringing in his ears. Looking down on the two causeways snaking away to the north-west, he could see nothing but a twin stream of fugitives between himself and the *San Cosme* and *Balen* gates into the city. It was a crucial moment in the campaign. Delay could still bring disaster. For an isolated and outnumbered army, the requirement for a vigorous pursuit was paramount. The need to keep the enemy on the run and to make final victory the true outcome of this twin attack was imperative.

In his immediate vicinity, the chances of a brisk follow-through may have seemed unlikely to Scott, as units depleted by a continuous sniping fire and already disorganised and inter-mingled by rough going, dispersed through the palace, at least some of the

---

70 Scott.

men intent on nothing more constructive than plunder. In the event, individual initiative which so characterised the American soldier throughout the Mexican War, was already at work, in a pure example of why wars can only be won by men and not machines. Men with an unquenchable determination to win-through and a sure understanding that the cause for which they fight is of greater importance than any individual life. While he looked down, the Commander-in-Chief felt his immediate concern begin to fade, as his West Point trained junior officers led off along the causeways.

Having disposed of the Mexican breastwork, Worth had left Trousdale to join the attack on the summit, while he led his own Division north around the base of the Mound. They reached the twin-tracked causeway leading to the *San Cosme* gate shortly after the remnant of the Chapultepec garrison had passed on its precipitous retreat; but, with lieutenants Daniel H. Hill and Bernard E. Bee well to the fore, the pursuit was immediately underway, and progressed briskly in the dry conditions of the elevated tracks. Almost immediately, the pair were overtaken by Jackson's horse artillery, their two guns, only loosely shackled to wagon limbers, leaping and bounding wildly over the rutted, uneven surface of the causeway. Seeing the infantry heading off on Worth's flanking manoeuvre, Jackson had persuaded Magruder that extricating gun limbers from dead horses; sorting out the traces and awaiting fresh horses would all waste too much time; better, he suggested, simply to attach the guns to wagon limbers and drive on. Magruder agreed, and Jackson was soon galloping after the infantry. With Hill and Bee behind him, Jackson's guns were virtually the point of the American advance in that sector. Certainly, he was far enough ahead to cause concern to his immediate superior. When Magruder, in turn, caught up with the men from South Carolina, he expressed concern for the safety of his guns and his wish to have them pulled back. Pleading with him not to interfere, the young infantry officers, both of whom received two brevets each for their conduct in Mexico, hurried after their artillery support. If they found it strange to be the champions of boldness when the dashing Magruder was for caution, it has not been recorded. Jackson's future brother-in-law recounted later that he remarked to Bee: *"If all turns out well today, the Old State will remember us."*[71] It did, and it did! The legislature of South Carolina later presented each of them with gold-mounted swords of honour in recognition of their outstanding bravery. Tom Jackson meanwhile did have his headlong advance halted, not by the Battery Commander; but by the threatened charge of a brigade of Mexican Cavalry under General Amphidia. He speedily wheeled the cumbersome wagon limbers and a brief, brisk fire soon sent the horsemen scuttling for the shelter of stone walls.

Throughout the campaign, Jackson had made it a strict personal, rule to sight his own guns, and these shots fired to discourage the horsemen were among the last he aimed on Mexican soil. Effective resistance in the open country outside the capital was virtually at an end. The advancing Americans found the embrasures set at inter-sections on the *San Cosme* road devoid of both guns and men. By last light they had infiltrated the suburbs next both the *San Cosme* and *Balen* gates; but despite such imaginative efforts as that of Lieutenant Ulysses S Grant, who hoisted a mountain howitzer into the spire of a church to engage the nearby enemy over open sights, no further progress was made beyond the initial salient. Before dawn, a deputation of the beleaguered City Council – the *Ayuntamiento* – obtained an audience with Scott, and, informing him that both the army and the national government had absconded, asked for surrender terms. They demanded only that these should be in favour of the church, the citizens and the corporate authority. Scott was in no mood to be denied and, claiming that the city had been virtually in his possession since the lodgements of the previous afternoon, *"…regretted the silent escape of the Mexican Army"*, and terminated the interview by informing the deputation of elders that *"… the American Army should come under no terms not self-imposed,"*

---

71 Arnold.

adding with a touch of theatre, and the merest suspicion of a nod in the direction of posterity, that terms would be *"…such only as its own honour, the dignity of the United States, and the spirit of the age, should, in my opinion, imperiously demand and impose."* Captain Magruder, in his official report of the final action, wrote, *"I beg leave to call the attention of the major-general commanding the Division to the conduct of Lt. Jackson of the First Artillery. If devotion, industry, talent and gallantry are the highest qualities of a soldier, then he is entitled to the distinction which their possession confers."* On September 13, 1847, Tom Jackson was commissioned a Brevet Major on the US Army Register for *"gallant and meritorious conduct in the battle of Chapultepec…"* No other West Point graduate achieved as big an advancement in rank for his conduct in America's war against Mexico. It might be added, how much more beneficial to the army, as well as to the individual, was the system of awarding brevets to achieving officers, as opposed to the modern system of bits of coloured ribbon, stemming from a too literal embracing of the adage *"men are led by toys"*, a flashy Napoleonic banality, typically, containing no more than a pinch of truth.

5. GARRISON SOLDIER

....

"In New York may be found almost anything
which the inclination may desire; but peace and
quiet. Everything is in motion, everything alive
with animation."
Major T J Jackson

....

BACK in the States Tom kept up the intimate correspondence
with his sister. From time to time duty allowed a furlough to
visit Laura and her family; their relatives, as well as friends from
the haunts of their youth. Whilst continuing to progress his religious studies, he turned to history. *"I propose with blessings of*
Providence to be a hard student, and to make myself not only acquainted
with the Military Art and Science; but with politics, and of course, must
be well versed in history. My historical studies I have arranged in the fol-
lowing order: first a general history, ancient and modern, and then, spe-
cial histories of important events, countries, etc."[72] He asked Laura's
husband to box-up some of his books, and send them to Captain
T J Jackson, c/o the Quartermaster, New York. It was a full ten
months after leaving Mexico before he could tell Laura *"I have*
received my commission as brevet major".[73] It was in the rank of major
that *"Thomas Jefferson*(sic) *Jackson of the US Army* was baptised in
St John's Episcopal Church. *"Across the road from Fort Hamilton …*
and frequently called the Church of the Generals − on Sunday 29ᵗʰ. Day
of April 1849 − with *Sponsors Cols. Dimick and Taylor also of the*
US Army". He wished there to be no doubt of his having been

---

72 Letter to *Colonel Samuel L. Hayes* from *Fort Hamilton, Long Island, N.Y.*
   February. 2ⁿᵈ 1849 (Cook).
73 Letter to Mrs L.A. Arnold from Fort Hamilton, New York Harbor,
   June 12, 1849 (Arnold).

properly inducted into the Christian Religion. Mrs Jackson corrected the naming error when she visited the church in 1868. The font, which became a named memorial to 'Stonewall' Jackson, was restored in 1934.[74]

Laura had earlier sought to learn something of city society from his posting to Fort Hamilton, *"which is on Long Island, about ten miles below the city of New York, and on the East Bank of the Hudson River. … your request to write you and give you the fashions … would be a difficult thing for me to do, as I do not know even so much as the names of the different parts of a lady's apparel"*. Ever positive and considered, he continued *"I, in the matter of dress, agree perfectly with the Parisians, who not only give the fashions for New York but for the civilized world, that a person ought to adopt such a style of dress as is most becoming the particular individual; and not that which is adopted by the greater portion of mankind, unless it should be at least reasonably suited to your complexion, height, figure, etc."*[75] He would visit Britain and Europe in the decade that remained before the Civil War; but whether from reading widely, or his experience of Mexican City society, Paris was already something of a yardstick. *"I recalled to mind, and applied to New York, what the Frenchman asserted of Paris when he said that when a man had seen Paris, that he had seen all the world. In New York may be found almost anything which the inclination may desire but peaceful quiet. Everything is in motion, everything alive with animation. In its busy throng none feel the long and tedious hour; even the invalid for the time forgets his infirmities and, with wondering admiration, contemplates the surrounding scenes."*[76] The distracted invalid he envisaged may well have been himself, for health, against the background of his constitutional dyspepsia – not hypochondria – was an ever-present concern. *"I believe that my infirmity is dyspepsia, not of a dangerous character, but of a nervous"*, he wrote to

---

74 Cook.

75 Letter from *Fort Hamilton, February 1, 1849* (Arnold).

76 Letter from *Fort Hamilton, New York Harbor, April 7, 1849* (Arnold).

Laura,[77] *I told you that I believed God would restore me to perfect health, and such continues to be my belief."* He became very particular about food and shared his findings with his sister.

"My health is improving and my strength is returning. I have so strictly adhered to my wholesome diet of stale bread and plainly dressed meat (having nothing on it but salt) that I prefer it now to almost anything else. The other evening I tasted a piece of bread with butter on it, and then the bread without it, and rather gave my preference to the unbuttered bread; and hence I may never taste any more this once much relished seasoning. And I think if you would adopt for your breakfast a cup of moderately strong black tea, stale wheat bread (wheat bread raised, and not less than twenty four hours old), fresh meat – broiled or roasted is best – the yolk of one or two eggs – the white is hardly worth eating as it requires diges- tion and affords but little nutrition. For dinner the same kind of bread and meat, one vegetable only, say peas, beans or this year's potatoes, and for drink plain water. For tea the same kind of bread and drink as for break- fast, and nothing else unless you choose a little butter. The great beauty of the foregoing is that it furnishes all the nutrition which food can give, and at the same time does not interfere in the digestive process like other substances, such as salt meats, cabbage, lettuce, desserts, such as pies, pre- serves, nuts and all kinds of sweetmeats. Of what I have recommended, you can eat as much as your appetite craves, provided that you take regu- lar meals and plenty of exercise, say, not less than three hours per day. ... Salt meats may be eaten but fresh is preferable. And I regard green tea and coffee so injurious to the nerves that you should always prefer water to either. Now if you can make up your mind to adopt the foregoing for one year, I think that you will probably never wish to change it; and that, after using such diet for two or three months, you may experience marked advantage from it. But you must bear in mind that your meals must be at fixed hours. If you arise at five or six o'clock, and go to bed at nine or ten, then seven would be a good hour for breakfast, one for dinner, and seven for tea. And you ought always to retire to bed before eleven. If you should conclude to adopt the foregoing, do not taste other things of which

---

77 Letter from *Fort Hamilton, New York Harbor, Monday, July 2, 1849* (Arnold).

you are fond, unless it be fruits, and they should be ripe. I think that a small quantity of fruit, eaten when ripe, and in the fore part of the day, is advantageous. You should try and forget that you are infirm, and pay no attention to your symptoms, as most any person can, by being too attentive to every little pain. Remember that good wholesome food taken at proper times is one of the best medicines."

Advice, much of which is still as sound in the 21st Century as in the 19th. Many in western countries have far worse diets and eating habits today, as the high incidence of cancer, heart disease and the gross distortions of fat bear all too frequent witness. In giving such priority to bread and meat, Jackson had the then unrealised advantage that such were not being rendered harmful by inorganic farming practises and the extensive adulterations of food processing. Being less blindly arrogant and more realistic about the value of human life, his age – by and large – made a more common sense use of self-discipline. His belief in salt – unrefined salt, that is – never refined, which is nothing more than sodium and chloride and should not be allowed to be marketed as salt, continued to hold good in the 21st Century.

Tom was concerned also about sight and the use of the eyes – his own and Laura's. *"I feel much concern about your eyes, for fear that you will strain them. Remember that the best physicians are opposed to straining that important organ; and when it fails, or begins to fail, naturally, that they recommend spectacles. But this should be the last resort, and should only be used when necessary. ... The great objection to spectacles is that when their use is once commenced, it must be generally continued through life. A person in purchasing a pair should select the lowest number which will answer the proposed end; and then, as circumstances require, increase it. But I would advise you not to use them as long as you can do without them, at the same time avoiding pain.*

"My eyes were so weak some months since that I could not look at objects through the window; and to look out-of-doors was frequently painful, though but for a moment; and I was reduced to the necessity of masking my looking glass, on account of its reflection. I could not look at a candle, not even for a second, without pain. I consulted my physician, and he told me not to use them, and at the same time to avoid spectacles.

I did so, and at present I can read a letter of three or four pages without any inconvenience of consequence."[78] Possibly concern for his eyesight was the reason that during the War Jackson habitually wore his campaign kepi with the peak pulled low on his forehead.

From the security of his absolute belief in an *"All Ruling Being"* he wrote *"Yes, my dear sister, rather than wilfully violate the known will of God I would forfeit my life; it may seem strange to you, yet nevertheless such a resolution I have taken, and I will by it abide"* — and, ever *"thankful to Omnipotent God, from whom every blessing cometh"*, Jackson utilised all available means to maintain health. *"My exercises are of a violent character, when the chilblains on my feet do not prevent it"*, this after having written a month earlier *"When circumstances admit of it, my exercise partakes of the most active kind, such as running, leaping, swinging etc."* He tried celebrated cures. *"I am to commence staying at a water cure establishment this evening, where I expect to remain during my stay here. I have great faith in them for such infirmities as mine"*, he wrote from Fort Ontario during the summer of 1850, *"I have been for some months adopting it to a certain extent, and with advantage"*. Acknowledged experts were consulted. Most notably the renowned Dr Lowry Barney of Henderson, in Jefferson County, New York State, with whom Major Jackson spent several weeks *'on leave of absence'*[79] from the War Department, and with whom he long after remained in touch as with a friend who was also a professional advisor. The doctor's daughter Elva, barely three at the time of Jackson's visit, long remembered his greeting her with a *"cheery 'howdy'"* and when three of her brothers left for the War, each carried a letter to their father, from the Stonewall Jackson they well remembered, as a wishful passport in the event of capture.

None the less, health was seen as an unpredictable and fluctuating state, and Tom described his life at this time as *"… one of privation … I enjoy the pleasures of the World, but endeavor to restrict*

78 Ibid.
79 Cook.

them within the limits which Nature's God has assigned them." A month or two later, he felt *"My health is still improving, but is as yet so delicate as to render much regularity necessary, and it is probable that I am more particular in my rules than any person of your acquaintance".* Even writing took its toll, *"as I may have told you, it gives me pain in the right side, and which I am by no means free from at this moment."[80]* Would that it were only in the right side!

Despite privation and the need for regularity, he had very soon upon coming to New York, taken up a social pattern along the lines of his days in Mexico City. *"I have lately commenced visiting more frequently, and every few evenings receive an invitation to some social party. Yesterday, whilst walking through the city, I thought of the pleasure which I would derive from sharing the contemplation of its beauties and wonders with you."[81]*

Garrison duty comprised of training and administering his company and seeing to the health and welfare of his gunners. To this Tom added the *"duties of quartermaster and commissary"*, but duty also kept him on the move. *"You are probably surprised at hearing from me so frequently at different points as a member of Courts Martial. I am now about twelve hours' travel from Niagara Falls, and consequently intend visiting there before returning home. I will leave here* (Fort Ontario, New York) *in the evening, and be at the Falls next morning".* The Board also convened at West Point, and at Carlisle Barracks in Pennsylvania, from where after a third visit, Tom noted he *"had a pleasant week among its amiable and I might say lovely ladies".*

Two years or so after Mexico, Major Jackson was posted to Fort Meade, Florida, situated some fifty miles from Tampa. On his way south he spent several weeks with his sister in western Virginia, and Arnold recalls amongst his possessions *"a large tablespoon ... (with) ... a small oblong block of some metallic composition,*

---

80 Letter from *Fort Hamilton, New York Harbour, March 1, 1849* (Arnold).

81 Letter to *Dear Sister* from *Fort Hamilton, New York Harbor, April 7, 1849* (Arnold).

soldered to the centre of the bowl, about one-fourth by one-half inch in size. It was claimed that ... one would be enabled to detect any poison ... in food by its appearance on this metal block". Presumably, given his unflinching resolve to leave death-related arrangements in the hands of an all-wise God, the spoon was relevant to the pursuit of good health rather than a bulwark against attempted murder. In response to a *"very sister-like letter ... received ... with much pleasure",* he described Florida as *"a vast plain with occasional slight elevations ... filled with lakes and swamps"* which produced *"most excellent sugar and cotton",* where *"the sweet potato ... sometimes grows more than two feet in length and eighteen inches in circumference. ... a cow and calf will cost ten dollars. All that is necessary is to buy a sufficient number, and turn them into the woods, hunt them up every year, mark and brand them. ... when the steers become three, four, five, six and seven years old they are sold at from seven to sixteen dollars. ... I have just returned from an eight days' scout",* he continued, *"I travelled more than one hundred miles without seeing a house. I like scouting very much, as it gives me a relish for everything; but it would be still more desirable if I could have an occasional encounter with Indian parties. I have been on several sugar plantations."* In his homespun vein, he noted that *"Eatables here are very dear; eggs are from thirty-seven to fifty cents per dozen; corn between one and two dollars per bushel; hens fifty cents each",* before winding up with *"I wish that I could not only see you every year but every day".*[82]

The following month he told Laura that he had *"... received a letter from Colonel Smith, the superintendent of the Virginia Military Institute at Lexington (Va.), in which he kindly offers to present my name to the Board of Visitors, in June next, as a candidate for ... Professorship ..."* Just three weeks later he wrote *"Good news. I have been elected Professor of Natural and Experimental Philosophy in the Virginia Military Institute, and you may expect me home in the latter part of June. Your Brother."*[83]

---

82 Letter from *Fort Meade, Fla., March 1, 1851* (Arnold).
83 Letter from *Fort Meade, Florida, April 22, 1851* (Arnold).

6. PROFESSOR

....

"I am anxious to devote myself to study
until I shall become master of my profession"
Thomas J Jackson

....

"TIME as it passes brings me to the renewal of the pleasant duty of writing to my sister", Tom reflected on the first of April, 1853, just eighteen months after joining the staff of the Virginia Military Institute. *"Though there is nothing here of which I am aware that can be of interest to you, beyond what may be felt in an only brother, yet pleasure results from the mere act of writing to you. Our lives have been checkered(sic) in a most marked manner, and we are still notwithstanding all the ill omens of our youth, living even beyond the usual period of human life, and I trust that before us are the brightest of our days."*[84] He was 29 and single. Home in the sense of where he slept at night was the Lexington Hotel, some three quarters of a mile from his class or section room, on the first floor of the then two-storied, twin-turreted Institute building. Mexico had confirmed what four years at West Point had suggested, that Thomas J Jackson had an inherent and highly individual talent for the prosecution of war. Despite the genuine self-effacing nature, performing under fire, with all its potential for maiming, death or glory, clearly thrilled, both for itself and for the satisfaction of his own skill and competence. *"I think that he loved danger for its own sake"* said his future brother-in-law D H Hill. It is conceivable that he suspected that America would descend into civil war as early as ten years before the opening rounds were fired in the Spring of 1861. A northern historian has written *"as early as 1844, the contest between the abolitionists on one side, and the slave-holders*

---

84 Letter from *Lexington, Va., April 1, 1853* (Arnold).

on the other hand had become a mortal duel"[85] Well before the outbreak, however, in a letter to Dr Barney, he professed to being
*"… much worried over the state of our country; but if war comes, I must
go with my mother State, Virginia … which ever way the State should
go".* Certainly he was aware of a north-south rift developing by
June 1856, when in writing to Laura, he made reference to the
"… idea of locating some land (for investment) *in a Northern State, …
that I am a little afraid to put much there for fear that in the event of a
dissolution of the Union that the property of Southerners may be confis-
cated."*[86] Probably at the time of his joining VMI, it was as much
as anything a general realisation that warring was so imbedded
in the fabric of the species as to make a future occurrence likely
during his lifetime. None of which is to say that he welcomed,
liked, or approved the futile business, and although he went un-
complainingly to war when it came, he would described the life
of all those cursed with the undertaking, as *"a sacrifice".* As civil war became more and more inevitable, he would remark *"It is
painful enough to discover with what unconcern they* (the Government)
*speak of war, and threaten it. They do not know its horrors. I have seen
enough of it to make me look upon it as the sum of all evils."* On the
other hand, less than three years of peace-time soldiering had
brought him to a conviction, no less true today, that *"A man who
had turned with a good military reputation, to pursuits of a semi-civilian
character, and had vigorously prosecuted his mental improvement, would
have more chance of success in war, than those who had remained in the
treadmill of the garrison."* Not surprising then that he was pleased
to be given a job which so perfectly combined his objectives of
preparing himself as soldier and general, whilst at the same time
relieving him of the tedium of the garrison. At least four other
West Point old boys, who also went on to be generals, put themselves forward for the VMI professorship; but Jackson had been
elected unanimously. His conduct in Mexico, both on and off

---

85 Draper quoted by Henderson.
86 Letter from Lexington dated *June 6, 1856* (Arnold).

the battlefield, counted strongly in his favour, together with the remembrance of it having been widely agreed he would have finished first, had the West Point Course been one year longer.

Bvt. Maj. Jackson's resignation from the US Army was only formally *"Approved and respectfully recommended to the Secretary of War,"* by Winfield Scott, as Commander-in-Chief, on the twenty fifth of February, 1852, after no less than seven departments had reported to the Office of the Adjutant General, that all relating to his service record was in order. By then, he was in his second term of his professorship, having reported for the start of the academic year 1851-'52, on the thirteenth of August 1851. He was soon *"delighted with my duties, the place and the people,"* he told uncle Alfred Neale, the following month. To Laura he said, *"My health has through the blessings of Providence been so much improved as to enable me to enter on my duties, with which I am delighted."*[87] These duties, as a junior professor, were to drill the Cadet Battalion; instruct on the theory of gunnery, and to teach Astronomy, Mechanics and Optics on the academic syllabus. Virginia's famed Military Institute, for all its uniform, marching and strict military discipline, provided a solid grounding and a first class education for life in general. Its only direct military concern was for those going on to join the State Militia. West Point was the sole provider of officers for the national army.

"In taking a retrospective view of my own life", he continued, in his letter of April 1853, *"each year has opened, as I consider, with increased promise. And with my present views, the future is holding richer stores in reserve."* Although he did not say so, he was probably contemplating marriage and his engagement was imminent, if it had not already taken place. He wrote more or less monthly to Laura, and during the previous year had made regular reference to female cousins either living in or moving around nearby States. Arnold notes on his alluding to an *"Aunt Nancy: "Some maiden acquaintance about whom the family had been teasing him."*

---

87 Letter *8 October 1851* (Arnold).

The Professor, like the subaltern in Mexico, had a mind to make *"life more natural by sharing it with some amiable señorita."* Less than two weeks short of two years after arriving in Lexington, he was married to *"Miss Eleanor Junkin, the attractive and highly cultured* (younger) *daughter of the Reverend Dr George Junkin, president of Washington College,"* in Lexington, whom Arnold also describes as *"a most lovely, amiable and accomplished lady",* and remembered, when the couple visited his parental home a year after their marriage, *"how all the family were delighted and charmed with the uncle's bride."* It was not so from the outset, for prior notice of the marriage had been kept a secret from Arnold's mother Laura, Tom, having promised to abide by Elli's wish that it should be a surprise to all but her immediate family. *"...in his strict conception of the sanctity of his word he extended the obligation to include his sister, and,"* says Arnold, adding not in the least surprisingly, *"the failure to inform her ... proved a sore wound to her feelings, and one that was slow in the healing."*[88]

From the time, both his eldest sister Elizabeth and his father died – when he was just three years old – death intruded continuously throughout the thirty-nine year life of Thomas Jonathan Jackson, both off and on the battlefield. For him, as for the majority in the Nineteenth Century, death was an everyday factor in life. No matter how close or how personal the intrusion may have been, that supremely resolute nature was ever-able to see in tragedy the benign hand of God working for *"His Glory; the good of the deceased, and those immediately effected."* Jackson had researched and evolved his relationship with his Maker, and his faith in a benevolent deity and the superior nature of an after-life, was never shaken.

Less than one year after his marriage, Tom was expressing *"the hope that* (Laura's) *little Tom is free from that dreadful disease, the*

88 *"Early Life and Letters of General Thomas J. Jackson (Stonewall Jackson)"* by his Nephew Thomas Jackson Arnold, Reprinted, 1957, by The Dietz Press Inc. Richmond, VA.

scrofula. I trust that your apprehension may prove groundless," he wrote, going on to counsel his sister, *"it is always best to be wide awake and not permit ourselves to be taken by surprise;"*[89] two prominent characteristics of his prowess as a general. Within one month, he was commiserating with her over the death of her youngest baby. *"Your loss is one which I have never been called upon to bear up under; I can well conceive of the tender union which is thus sundered."*[90] On July the first he wrote, saying, *"Ellie and myself hope to be with you* (in Beverley) *this day week Saturday."* His work load at the Institute demanded that Ellie write the postscript, which she ended with *"... the weather is so extremely warm just now that we quite fear the ride in the stage,* (to Beverley) *but we hope to find it cooler further among the mountains. Yours affectionately, Ellie J. Jackson."* They stayed on into August. However, by the middle of November he was writing from Lexington *"My dear Ellie ... has now gone on a glorious visit though through a gloomy portal. Her companions are the Glorified Host. I look forward to the day when I shall join <u>her.</u> Religion is all that I desire it to be. I am reconciled for my loss and have joy and hope of a future reunion where the wicked cease from troubling and the weary are at rest."* Ellie had died suddenly upon their return. Tom's agony, as the one remaining, was intense. The swift, straightforward way in which he was able to resolve issues, and his total resolution and dedication to the fulfilment of a decision once reached, ensured that love when it came, would be absolute. Total commitment was as much the hallmark of the lover as the general. His future Chief-of-Staff[91] during the tense weeks of the Valley Campaign, would write later of these months, *"...his taste for secular occupations and pleasures was lost, and his only aspirations pointed to the other world."* In February, he wrote to his sister-in-law – Margaret, often Maggie, – *"My dear sister, from my heart I thank God that though he has left me to mourn in human desolation He has taken dear*

---

89 Letter from *Lexington, Va., May 2, 1854* (Arnold).

90 Letter from *Lexington, Va., June 12, 1854* (Arnold).

91 Reverend Dr Dabney (Major, CSA).

Ellie to Himself. I am well assured that He left her with us to the latest moment, consistent with His glory, hers, yours and my happiness. For no good thing will he withhold from His children."[92] He had gone on to say in the April of 1853 letter to Laura, *"I too have crosses, and am at times deeply afflicted, but however sore may be the trials, they lose their poignancy, and instead of producing injury, I feel that I am but improved by the ordeal. But how is this accomplished? By throwing myself upon the protection of Him whose law book is the wonderful Bible. My* dear sister, *I would not part with this book for countless universes. I feel ready to make every sacrifice to carry out the will of Him who so loved us as to give His only begotten son to die for me. How exceeding great must have been that love. The more I learn, the more dear does the precious volume appear to be to me ..."* Letters to Laura from her self-contained, but far from unsympathetic brother, continued to reflect his strong feeling for family, in the months immediately following Ellie's death. Their half-brother Wirt, in whom *"I think I can observe a likeness to* (late brother) *Warren,"* was an endless source of concern and brought to the fore Tom the Intellectual, that most fundamental and essential strand in the make-up of Jackson the General. *"If Wirt will study Latin, I will give him lessons during the Summer, and put him in the way of learning it ... I will also, if he will consent to do so, give him instruction in the different sciences of algebra, geometry, and in engineering, and other branches of education, and bring with me the necessary books."*[93] Tom continued *"My eyes are improving, but still I have to be careful with them; the spots continue to float before them,"* – (which sounds very much like a dietary or liver problem!). Certainly, he was back on butter during the Lexington years, and as he eschewed alcohol, and had not yet developed the reputation for sucking on lemons, which he gained during the War, then the Jackson liver may well have needed a good flushing through. A month later he was suggesting to Laura,

---

92 Arnold quoting from the *'Life and Letters of Margaret Junkin Preston"*, poet, and Ellie's elder sister.

93 Letter from *Lexington, Va., March 20, 1855* (Arnold).

"try and get him (Wirt) *to stay with you until I come. And get him to study arithmetic, geography and history."*[94] Farming was suggested. Jackson himself was especially into real estate investment, which was typical of the embryonic nation, and America in particular. *"I desire to employ all my spare funds in the purchase of lands."*[95] On land purchasing, Wirt took his own line. *"...he has gone beyond what I authorized him to do by purchasing a farm at eight dollars per acre. I restricted him to seven at most. ... I have determined to advance eleven hundred dollars. I well know there is a risk, but it appears to me that I ought to run this risk for him,"* Tom told Laura. Wirt eventually had reasonable success as a businessman in California; but died comparatively young, possibly due to having been severely poisoned by eating conkers (buckeyes), as a child.

Whilst the Professor refers to his being kept busy at the Institute, he made few mentions of teaching experiences, beyond such exceptional or peripheral occurrences as when he took the Cadet Battalion to Virginia Springs for some two weeks; the time of an up-coming faculty meeting, or that he had *"fired ten guns from the battery of artillery, in commemoration of the origin of the Institute. This day is thirteen years after it went into operation, and it is now in a very flourishing condition; so much so that we cannot accommodate all the applicants."*[96] One cadet was expelled at Jackson's instigation, and let it be known he was arming with intent to shoot the Professor. On being warned, Jackson refused to take precautions or to alter his walking routine. *"For my daily exercise, I have to walk about a mile and a half for each meal — three quarters to and three quarters from it — and in the morning I usually walk a mile and a half before breakfast, and in the afternoon about two miles or more before tea.".*[97] He duly met with the would-be assassin who, presumably, was familiar with the routes and routine of the Professor, who had

94 Ibid.

95 Letter dated *June 6th, 1856* (Arnold).

96 Letter from *Lexington, Va., November 11, 1852* (Arnold).

97 Letter from *Virginia Military Institute, Lexington, Va., May 14, 1852* (Arnold).

the reputation of being as *'regular as a metronome.'* The unflinching Jackson gaze was enough. As they approached one another, the young man turned away. Sometime later, to the lasting admiration of his young nephew, Thomas Jackson Arnold, Uncle Tom had deployed the technique, with equal success, against a particularly savage dog, when the pair were out walking together. Health was rarely, if ever, omitted from letters – certainly to Laura, – with whom he discussed such matters in some detail. An aspect of this were the endless vocational visits to experience some *'hydrotherapeutic cure'* or other. *"In that day,"* says Cook, *"even the best of medical men were firm in the view that the 'water treatment' was the last word in every obscure complaint."* A colleague commented on one occasion, that *"Jackson had returned to the institution not improved in health, but worse for the new system of treatment."*[98]

---

98 Cook.

7. EUROPE

....

"I could talk to you with much pleasure
About very many things of great interest"
Your affectionate brother

....

WITH no prior warning, Laura received a letter in mid-July headed New York City.[99] *"My dear Sister, I sail in the steamship 'Asia' for Europe at twelve o'clock today for Liverpool. The reasons for doing so I will give in my next"*, a couple more lines concerning *"thirty dollars … You can apply … towards father's and sister's graves,* and he signed off, *"With much love to all, Your affectionate brother, T.J. Jackson."* With the ship far out in the Atlantic some ten days later, his *'next'* began, *"You have doubtless been surprised at my sudden leaving for Europe instead of going West to purchase or locate land. You may remember that in 1851 I had a nine months' leave of absence for the purpose of visiting Europe, but that Colonel Smith induced me to relinquish the idea for the time, holding out to me an opportunity at some future time, and that I accordingly did postpone my contemplated trip."* It had been his intention to go West to seek land for investment; but two friends had *"discouraged"* him. One did not think *"investing money in such distant lands … a safe and profitable investment"*, and the other *"had come very near to losing a part of his money, in consequence of his being so far off as to interfere with his giving sufficient attention to it … I have rather concluded to keep my money invested in stocks of different kinds,"* he went on, *"and trust to the blessing of Providence for gradually increasing my worldly wealth."* Faced with potentially empty weeks before the start of the VMI Autumn Term, grief prompted a possible therapeutic move. *"Thus circumstanced, I, in a few days before starting, concluded that an opportunity*

---

99 Letter from *New York City, July 9, 1856* (Arnold).

was now offered of going to Europe … You are a very kind and affec-
tionate Sister, yet even with you I would be reminded of the loss of that
happiness which I once enjoyed with dear 'Ellie.' So, I have to some ex-
tent torn myself away from that state of mind which I feared, should my
summer have been passed at home, or in the United States."[100]

He wrote to Laura next from Naples, three weeks later, beginning; *"You must excuse my long silence, as I have been pressed for*
time,"[101] which was an understatement, if nothing else. His itin-
erary would have left even the most superficial American tourist
of the Twenty-First Century gasping. *"Since landing at Liverpool, I*
have been at Glasgow, Stirling Castle and Edinburgh in Scotland; York,
London and other places in England; Antwerp, Brussels, Waterloo and
other places in Belgium. Since then I have passed through Aix la Chapelle,
Bonn, Frankfort on the Main, having ascended the Rhine. From Frankfort,
I proceeded to Heidelberg and thence on to Baden Baden in Germany,
Strasburg, Basle, Lakes Lucerne, Brienz and Thum, Berne, Freiburg
and the city of Geneva in Switzerland, and so on, to the great Glacier
called Mer de Glace, that is, sea of ice. I continued in Switzerland for
about a week and crossed the Alps by the Simplon Pass, as it is called,
through which Napoleon entered Italy. The scenery of Switzerland is
very grand. After entering Italy, I visited the cities of Milan, Venice,
Mantua, Modena, Florence, Pisa, Leghorn, and finally to this place.
With Venice, Florence and Naples I have been much gratified. I was at
the volcano of Vesuvius last Friday and went about half-way down one
of the active craters. The scene was truly grand. This evening I leave for
Rome. Much love. Your attached brother, Thomas."

When Laura next heard, it was the last week in October and
Tom was back at the Institute. *"I was unable to come through Beverley*
and see you. I was several days later in returning home than I had de-
signed."[102] The return voyage had taken longer than scheduled
and the Professor had missed the first few days of Term. This

---

100 Letter from *Ship "Asia" at sea, July 18, 1856* (Arnold).

101 Letter from *Naples, September 9, 1856* (Arnold).

102 Letter from *Lexington, October 25, 1856* (Arnold).

prompted someone to ask afterwards if being late had caused him any anxiety. Typically, it had not. His programming allowed for his returning before the start of the Autumn Term. The ship not sailing to schedule was completely beyond his control. He was satisfied that he had done all in his power to avoid the occurrence, and so was quite at ease with himself over the adverse outcome. In this and subsequent letters to Laura, he added to the places he had visited in Europe. *"Leaving Liverpool, the same day of my landing, I proceeded to the city of Chester, which is about eighteen miles from Liverpool, and on entering the hotel, was met by a lady instead of a landlord, as I had been accustomed to at home. After having secured my quarters I proceeded to the cathedral ... a large edifice formerly occupied by the Roman Catholics... It was about the hour of evening service. ... the sexton showed me to a seat ... and ... after service was over, he showed me through the building, which was quite interesting. Among other things were the seats for the friars or monks, which were so constructed that, should they become drowsy and forgetful of their duty, their seats suddenly dropped them on the floor and recalled their wandering thoughts.* (The comment prompted nephew Arnold to wonder about his thoughts on seeing this *"ingenious arrangement of seats"*, given that during the Civil War, Jackson had the reputation for dozing off during church sermons, and Henry Kyd Douglas – the youngest member of the General's staff – recorded later that if Jackson halted for five minutes, on the march, he could sleep for three of them. Both are probably indications of the relentless pressure on an individual conducting a military campaign from the back of a horse).

I walked around the (city) *wall,"* he told Laura, *"and saw the* (Phoenix) *tower on which King Charles the First stood and saw the defeat of his army at Rowton Moor."*[103] (Following the comprehensive Royalist defeat by Fairfax and Cromwell at Naseby in June, 1645, and that of the king's un-cooperative subordinate, Goring, at Langport in July, Charles, eventually returned to his base at Oxford, then departed in

---

103 Letter from *Lexington, Va., December 6, 1856* (Arnold).

a forlorn, second attempt to join the 'Royal Champion,' Montrose, in Scotland. What the king did not know, however, was that following the brilliant, summer victories of Alford and Kilsyth, was that the Great Marquis had himself been surprised at Philiphaugh, and received a drubbing from which his fortunes never recovered. Getting only as far north as Chester, Charles did no more than spectate at the final destruction of his cavalry, by Parliamentary forces under Major-General Poyntz, in the three-day action of Rowton Moor – or Heath – as it is more generally known).

From Chester, Major Jackson went the four miles or so to *"the residence of the Marquis of Westminster; his house is called Eaton Hall".* (Despite Eaton Hall having been the training centre for Royal Navy officers for three years – following the bombing of Britannia Royal Naval College in 1943 – and going on to see the training of some fifteen thousand National Service officer cadets between 1946 and 1958, the great palace, now home to the Cheshire Military Museum; as well as being the principal residence of the Duke of Westminster, probably never opened its doors to a greater exponent of the Art of War than the future Confederate General, in August 1856). *"After ringing the bell, a servant, of quite a gentlemanly appearance, came to the door and admitted me by my giving him my ticket of admission, which I had procured before leaving Chester,"* Tom told Laura later. *"The interior of the building is magnificent. One of the rooms is copied from the celebrated Alhambra of Grenada, which was built by the Moors."*

Continuing south towards London, Jackson saw *"the residence of Oliver Cromwell",* with whom he has been compared. Such religious comparisons usually included comment unfavourable to the great Englishman, revealing a failed appreciation of Cromwell, as well as the era in which he lived. *"He that ventures his life for the liberty of his country, I wish he trust God for the liberty of his conscience, and you for the liberty he fights for."*[104] And later, *"I had rather*

---

104 Oliver reporting on victory, from the battlefield of Naseby, to the Speaker of the Commons.

Mahometanism (sic) were permitted amongst us, than that one of God's children should be persecuted."[105] Writings and speeches consistently show Oliver, the man, to have been no less a believer in religious toleration than was Tom Jackson. Both fought for liberty and freedom. Both held strong religious convictions and ascribed their actions and their outcomes to Divine Providence. In his official persona, however, Cromwell had no option but to forcefully uphold and implement Puritan ideals. Religion was a dominant, everyday political issue in the English Civil War. In stating the subject of his *'quarrel'* Charles The First lists it even before crown and friends. In the American Civil war religion was of no official concern whatsoever. As generals, the two were consistent winners. Both made major contributions towards victory in battles nominally under the direction of others and, most importantly of all and what is far rarer still, when in command themselves, both were able to deliver, not merely victory; but victory appropriate to the overall situation. That is to say they fully understood the strategic dimension of war, without which no general may be considered great. In choosing to visit Huntingdon, and not the homes of the English generals of Blenheim Palace or Stratfield Saye, Jackson was very possibly revealing his recognition of a kindred spirit; even if the brilliant demonstration of his own military genius was still five years away.

From Cadet Jackson's use of the West Point library we know that he had read widely on the theory of war, including the comments of Napoleon, and when he crossed the English Channel, Major Jackson went to the battle ground of Waterloo. It is unlikely that he would have overlooked the military achievements of the less voluble victor. Nearly three years after returning from Europe, he received a request for information from a VMI graduate planning a tour of his own. *"I fear that* (my notes) *would be of but little service to you ... Even with my recollection of places etc. to aid me, I am not always able to make out the sense. ... I would recommend*

---

105 Oliver in debate, May 1652.

you … keep a satisfactory journal, beginning with the first day, and clos-ing with the returning one of your tour. … As soon as you reach Liverpool purchase guide books … If you have time to see things leisurely don't employ guides." After recommending Chester and Eaton Hall, he advised Smith to *"take the cars and visit the great Tubular bridge … Dunbarton(sic) Castle and Lochs Lomond and Catreine. … In York observe the organ especially … in Antwerp note Reubens's paintings … (and the museum), in Heidelberg observe the castle, in Strasburg is a won-derful clock, in Freiburg one of the best organs in the world. In Verona is the most perfect amphitheatre in the world. … Stop for at least one day at Interlaken. … Study the original works of art … in Antwerp, Florence, Rome etc. and, when you reach Paris, … visit the neighbouring Royal residences."*[106] He would tell his second wife, *"Well do I remem-ber the influence of sculpture upon me during my short stay in Florence, and how there I began to realise the sentiment of the Florentine:* "Take from me my liberty, take what you will, but leave me my statu-ary, leave me these entrancing productions of art." *And similar to this is the influence of painting."*[107]

---

106 Letter *to J. Jaquelin Smith Esq* from *Lexington Va. April 11ᵗʰ, 1859* (Cook).
107 Anna Morrison Jackson quoted by Henderson.

8. APPROACHING WAR

....

*"It is not often that I am authorized to send
you invitations, and especially pressing ones."*
Tom to Laura[108]

....

SOME seven months after returning from Europe, Tom wrote his sister a gently waggish letter. *"… I will begin by stating I have an invitation for you; and what do you think it is? And from whom? … I suppose you begin to think … what does he mean? … why doesn't he tell me … and be done with it? … having cultivated your patience a little, as all women are said to have curiosity … Miss Mary Anna Morrison, a friend of mine, in the western part of North Carolina … is engaged to be married to an acquaintance of yours in this village … to use her own words, she says,* "I hope your sister will come. You must urge her to do so. I should be very glad if she could come"*… if you can't, just let me know in your next, and transfer the invitation to your humble servant, and he will not decline … he is much interested in the ceremony and the occasion, and the young lady is a very special friend of mine."* Professor Jackson was married to Miss Morrison at her father's home in Mecklenburg County, North Carolina, on sixteenth July 1857.

The honeymoon couple went to Richmond and on into the Northern States. En-route to his wedding Tom had visited Laura and her family in Beverley, and delivered *"the truly beautiful presents he had brought from Italy the previous Autumn"*[109] for his nephew and niece; but was unable to return with Anna because *"an enlargement of one of the glands of Anna's neck induced me to consult a physician, and my concern was so great as to induce me to take her to*

---

108 Letter from *Lexington, Va.* (un–dated, Arnold).
109 Arnold.

Philadelphia, where she consulted Dr Jackson of the University, and he was unable to decide as to the true character of the case. ... I regret that we have been unable to visit you this summer; but I felt that under the circumstances it was my duty to make Anna's health the first object of concern."[110]

When he wrote again in December; his own health had taken a turn for the worse *"... an inflammation of the tube leading to the ear, and also inflammation of the throat (chronic), and very painful neuralgia ... I never remember having suffered so much as within the last three weeks; and now I am compelled to use a vial of chloroform liniment per day externally and am also using internally a preparation of ammonia. The hearing of my right ear is impaired, but I trust not permanently. I have continued to attend to my recitations, notwithstanding my sufferings. In a few days I hope to be free from pain. The eye medicine helped me for a while, I think, but I can't say that I have been permanently benefitted, and I would advise you not to try the medicine. Anna is quite robust again."* he continued. *"She joins me in love to you all."[111]*

Ear and throat were still a problem two months later. *"I have nearly, if not entirely, lost the use of one ear, and my throat has to be cauterized twice weekly, but it is improving."* Nephew Arnold adds the footnote to this letter[112] *"Fortunately he was later greatly relieved of this deafness. Though for the remainder of his life he was partially deaf, so much so that he was unable to locate the direction of sound."* One cannot help but think of Wellington saying, a few years previous to this, *"All doctors are more or less quacks"*, after the attempt to cure his deafness by pouring carbolic acid into the ear, had nearly killed him. Although mid-Nineteenth Century firearms lacked the penetrating crack of high velocity rifles of the past sixty years, probably gunfire initiated deafness in both their cases. Especially as, in Jackson's case, the right ear was said to be worst affected. However, in this February letter the main topic was

---

110 Letter from *Rockbridge Alum Springs, August 11, 1857* (Arnold).

111 Letter from *Lexington, Va., December 19, 1857* (Arnold).

112 Letter from *Lexington, Va., February 8, 1858* (Arnold).

spiritual. *"He that believeth and is baptized shall be saved,"*[113] he told Laura, *"We must not depend on making ourselves holy, but just come to the Father ... and rely entirely on the merits of Christ for our prayer being answered ... Do not trouble yourself too much about not having repented enough of your sins"*, he advised, *"for your letter shows that you have much concern on the subject. ... resolve to spend the remaining part of life in His service, to obey the teachings of the Bible until death, and to rely entirely on the mercy of God for being saved. ... Never despair ...Never omit to pray at regular times. For years your salvation has been my daily prayer and shall continue so. Write to me often, and tell me all your trials, that I may be able as an instrument in the hands of God of doing something for your eternal welfare."*

The decision to by-pass Beverley, and not visit Laura, caused disappointment all round and prompted a lengthy and friendly letter from Anna to her newly acquired sister – as such an 'in-law' relationship was known at the time, saying: *"It was quite a disappointment to both Mr Jackson and myself that we could not carry out our intention of visiting you, and we have felt very sorry to learn from your letters that you feel so hurt at being disappointed by us. ... My husband thought it was his duty to follow the physician's advice and you know he always makes every pleasure give way to duty. I hope that I shall be housekeeping next summer ... we are very pleasantly situated at the hotel here ... and have not decided yet when we shall leave it to assume the cares and responsibilities of housekeeping. I am anxious, however, to have a house so that friends can visit us. Mr Jackson has improved very much in health this summer and is now looking better than I have ever seen him. He has been very busy ... and is rather more studious than I would like him to be as, I see nothing of him in his study hours. ... Mr Jackson sends much love. I shall always be glad to hear from you. Your affectionate sister, Anna M Jackson."*[114]

It was November of the following year before the Jacksons bought the house, they made their home, and Anna could begin

---

113 St Mark's Gospel Ch.16 v.16.

114 Anna's letter from *Lexington, Virginia, September 27, 1857 To Mrs Laura Arnold* (Cook).

housekeeping. (In 1904 the house was bought by the United Daughters of the Confederacy – enlarged – and turned into the Jackson Memorial Hospital). The couple had only been in their new home for some two months, when, in January, Major Jackson marched the VMI Cadet Battalion to Charlestown, for the trial and hanging of John Brown, alias Isaac Smith, together with six others, following their capture by United States Marines, under Lieutenant Israel Green, at Harper's Ferry, for what a Senate Committee later described as *"… simply an act of lawless ruffians, under the sanction of no public or political authority …"*

Jackson's *"… early training upon his uncle's farm had instilled in him a love for rural pursuits,"* and a year later they bought a small farm for $500 *"which embraced twenty acres near town. Here with the aid of his negroes, he raised wheat, corn and other products, and every year his crops and land improved under his diligent care; the farm he sold during the war and invested the proceeds in Confederate bonds to assist the government.*[115]

In 1860, Jackson and three other VMI Professors – including his brother-in-law, Colonel Preston (the husband of Ellie's sister Maggie) – bought a plot of land for $1,050 which was developed as a tannery. The business lasted for not quite ten years and, after the war, went into receivership, and was wound-up without liability to the Jackson Estate. A financial stake in a Building Association was more profitable, and when terminated early in 1863 – very shortly before his death – Jackson's share was $1,644 (Confederate).

Although they had black household slaves, the Jackson's were not large slaveholders. Neither was their State of Virginia a holder on the scale of the large plantation states further south. In the mid-Nineteenth Century, there were some four million black slaves in the fifteen States comprising 'the South' – that is the States south of the Mason's and Dixon's Line – together with eight million three hundred thousand whites. Of these three hundred and forty six thousand were slave-holders, and of those,

---

115 Anna quoted by Cook.

sixty-nine thousand owned just one black slave.[116] Brought up in households worked by black slave-servants, Jackson did not look upon slavery as being 'a sin of the fathers visited upon the children' but, *"He found the institution a responsible and troublesome one, and I have heard him say that he would prefer to see the negroes set free, but he believed that the Bible taught that slavery was sanctioned by the Creator Himself, who maketh all men to differ, and instituted laws for the bond and free. He therefore accepted slavery, as it existed in the South, not as a thing desirable in itself, but as allowed by Providence for ends which it was not his business to determine."*[117] Tom and Anna set up and ran a Christian Sunday School to which all their friends were encouraged to send their black servants. His consideration for individuals and slaves in general earned him the reputation of being the 'black man's friend,' as indeed, he was also, to widows and poor people. His black manservant, Jim, was a valued member of his wartime headquarters family.

The home-life routine established by Jackson the husband and intellectual soldier – during the mere handful of years of married, domestic pleasure granted him – would have reduced even the most stringent of management gurus to a state of awed homage.

"His life at home was perfectly regular and systematic. He rose at six o'clock, and first knelt in secret prayer; then he took a cold bath, which was never omitted even in the coldest days of winter. This was followed by a brisk walk, in rain or shine. Seven o'clock was the hour for family prayers, which he required all his servants to attend promptly and regularly. He never waited for anyone, not even his wife. Breakfast followed prayers, after which he left immediately for the Institute, his classes opening at eight o'clock and continuing to eleven.

"Upon his return home, … he devoted himself to study until one. The first book he took up daily was his Bible, which he read with a commentary, and the many pencil marks upon it showed with what care he bent over its pages. From his bible lesson he turned to his textbooks. During

---

116 Henderson.

117 Anna quoted by Henderson.

these hours of study, he would permit no interruption, and stood all the time in front of a high desk. After dinner, he gave himself up for half an hour or more to leisure and conversation, and this was one of the brightest periods in his home life.

"He then went into his garden, or out to his farm to superintend his servants, and frequently joined them in manual labour. He would often drive me to the farm and find a shady spot for me under the trees, while he attended to the work of the field. When this was not the case, he always returned in time to take me, if the weather permitted, for an evening walk or drive. In summer we often took our drives in moonlight, and in the beautiful Valley of Virginia, the queen of night seemed to shine with more brightness than elsewhere.

"When at home, he would indulge himself in a session of rest and recreation after supper, thinking it was injurious to health to go to work immediately. As it was a rule with him never to use his eyes by artificial light, he formed the habit of studying mentally for an hour or so without a book. After going over his lessons in the morning, he thus reviewed them at night, and in order to abstract his thoughts from surrounding objects – a habit he had cultivated to a remarkable degree – he would, if alone with his wife, ask that he might not be disturbed by any conversation; he would then take his seat with his face to the wall, and remain in perfect abstraction until he finished his mental task.

"He was very fond of being read to, and much of our time in the evening was passed in my ministering to him in this way. He had a library, which, though small, was select, composed chiefly of scientific, historical and religious books, with some of a lighter character, and some in Spanish and French. Nearly all of them were full of his pencil marks, made with a view to future reference."[118] The love of history put Plutarch and Macaulay high amongst most favoured authors, with Shakespeare being an especial favourite. Novels, however, he gave up as being too time-wasting. The formidable Jackson powers of concentration meant that he became too engrossed in plot and story!

---

118 Anna quoted by Henderson.

The couple enjoyed entertaining in the three years that remained for a life together in their own home, before an all too human cocktail of idealistic emancipationist, diehard unionist and rabid secessionist; grasping estate-holder and overweening industrialist; stimulated by the, inevitable, self-serving politician, hounded a complacent majority into the havoc of self-destructive war. With true, Virginia hospitality the couple enjoyed entertaining; but despite his country roots and equestrian skill, Jackson did not share Virginia's love of hunting and field sports. In vacation time they travelled beyond the Potomac, to experience the glories of landscape in the northern States, the grandeur of big cities, and to undergo suspect treatment from numerous 'hydrotherapeutic spring spas,' peddling the elusive grail of better health.

After returning from one such trip, Tom wrote to his Aunt, Mrs Neale, *"I am living in my own house, I am thankful to say, as, after trying both public and private boarding, I have learnt from experience that true comfort is only to be found in a house under your own control. I wish you could pay me a visit during some of your leisure intervals, if you ever have such. ... Viewing things at Washington from human appearances, I think we have great reason for alarm, but my trust is in God; and I cannot think that He will permit the madness of men to interfere so materially with the Christian labours of this country at home and abroad."*[119] Writing to Laura, early the following month, he was *"much gratified to see a strong Union feeling in my portion of the state ... For my own part I intend to vote for the Union candidates for the* (Virginia) *Convention and I desire to see every honourable* (sic) *means used for peace, and I believe that Providence will bless such means with the fruits of peace. ... But if after we have done all that we can do for an honourable preservation of the Union, there shall be a determination on the part of the Free States* (i.e. non-slave owning) *to deprive us of our right which the fair interpretation of the Constitution, as already decided by the Federal Court, guarantees to us, I am in favour of secession."*[120]

119 Letter from *Lexington, Va., January 21st. 1861* (Cook).
120 Letter from *Lexington, Va. February 2nd, 1861* (Cook).

Anna wrote of her husband, *"He never was a Secessionist, and maintained that it was better for the South to fight for her place in the Union than out of it. ... he was strongly for the Union. At the same time, he was a firm States rights man."*[121]

121 Anna quoted by Cook.

9. PROFESSOR'S CHAIR TO GENERAL'S SADDLE

*"I do not want to make an appointment
to my staff except of such as are
early risers"*
Brigadier General T.J. Jackson

AS in all things worldly, the *"madness of men,"* rode roughshod over any faith in a Deity, and a bitterly divided United States – which by 1861 had outgrown the genius of the Founding Fathers' Constitution – progressed towards a constitutionally illegal and dictatorial act by one of her greatest Presidents, and so on into four years of bloodshed and misery.

On Wednesday, April the seventeenth, Governor John Letcher denied the illegal mobilisation order from Republican President Abraham Lincoln – to recruit troops to save the Union by force of arms – and Jackson's home State of Virginia switched allegiance to the already confederated states of South Carolina, Mississippi, Alabama, Florida, Georgia, Louisiana and Texas, and to the Provisional Government of President Jefferson Davis in Montgomery, Alabama. The task of building a military capability was begun at once, and a training camp was set up in the state capital, Richmond. On Sunday, the twenty first of April, cadets from the VMI left Lexington, under the command of Major Jackson, to report for duty at the camp, as student drill instructors for the numerous volunteers responding to the Governor's appeal to join up. At a loose end in Richmond, the Professor got an unsuitable job drawing plans in the Topographical Department which, as it was a military engineering responsibility, led to his being 'gazetted' a Major of Engineers.

The Virginia State Auditor, Jonathan M Bennett, was also in Richmond, and after a wholesome rather than memorable meal, took his local newspaper from the foyer table, and eased himself into the depths of an all-enveloping armchair to digest and scan the 'Officer's Appointments' columns. Noting with pleasure and a grunt of approval that fellow-Virginian Robert Edward Lee, of Arlington, had followed his conscience in the interests of his home state, he read on down the, thereafter, alphabetical list. Many of the names triggered memories, some personal and enjoyable, others no more than hearsay. Reaching the name Jackson, Thomas Jonathan, Mr Bennett glanced up with a smile, remembering a pleasant evening over whiskey, in their home territory of Weston, being regaled about Contreras and Churubusco by two visitors from South Carolina. With Jackson himself, Bennett had never got further than his most alarming moment in Mexico having been the night in the National Palace, when, having placed a strong-box containing pay for the First Artillery beneath his bed, he was wakened later in the night by the bed being violently shaken. Assuming a burglar to have been after the gold and silver, he went for his sword, only to realise he was experiencing an earthquake. Reading on to: 'Major of Engineers' in the Appointments column, Mr Bennett stopped smiling; discarded the paper, and headed for his hat and the Capitol. The Governor agreed with his Auditor and instructed the Secretary of the War Council accordingly. When a Member demurred with; *"Who is this Major Jackson, that we are asked to commit to him so responsible a post?"* The representative from Rockbridge County replied, *"He is one who, if you order him to hold a post, will never leave it alive to be occupied by the enemy."*[122] Seven days after leaving Lexington, the Professor was under orders to shape the Army of the Shenandoah, and on his way to command at Harper's Ferry. His rank of Colonel of Volunteers effective: the twenty seventh of April. From Harper's Ferry, just fifty-three miles upstream, and across the Potomac from Washington, Auditor Bennett had written two days previously to a resident of Clarksburg, *"Rapid arrangements are being made for actual operations. Gen'l Lee is a great acquisition. He won't*

---

122 Cook.

fight until he is ready and is sure to whip when he fights. Tom Jackson and Col Magruder both of whom so distinguished themselves in command of Flying Artillery are here in command."[123]

For the militia units of the Harper's Ferry Garrison, the unobtrusive arrival of their new commander, with no more than two aides, and all in the sombre, un-gilded uniforms of the VMI, was less than inspiring. They were exponents of glitter and dash, accustomed to frivolous movement rather than focused action. For them the merit of a uniform lay more with its ability to melt feminine resolve than as a clear system of identification amid the smoke and chaos of battle. They were, nonetheless, enthusiastic, energetic and determined patriots, dedicated to their home state. The Colonel was not only personally inconspicuous, he was also uncommunicative, not overly given to jollification, and unflinchingly determined to turn a collection of civilians in matching fancy dress, into a disciplined, well-drilled fighting entity, imbued with a collective enthusiasm to overcome or die. He was a patient instructor, forgiving of well-intentioned mistakes, and no stickler for military etiquette. His tent flap was never a barrier for those seeking clarification and understanding of orders, means, and the ways of soldiers. He instigated grinding, seven hour, training day schedules, and told no one of his intentions. On his frequent rounds of the outposts overlooking the Potomac and the Shenandoah junction, he took only one aide and issued strict orders that his passing was not to be acknowledged in any way. A visiting delegation, from the still non-aligned, slave-holding State of Maryland, was received with civility, but told nothing of the least military value. Exasperated, one finally posed the blunt question of how many men comprised the Colonel's Harper's Ferry Command. Colonel Jackson merely smiled and replied quietly *"Sir, I would be pleased if President Lincoln thought I had fifty thousand."*[124] To Anna, complaining that he never told

---

123 Ibid.
124 Henderson and others.

her any hard news, he wrote that it was un-soldierly for an officer to divulge information about his post – something which, surely, she would not want for him. He went on to describe the roses growing around his quarters; *"but my sweet little sunny face is what I want to see most of all."*[125]

Whatever the Northern President and his military advisers may have guessed at – or spies reported – in reality, the Harper's Ferry Command comprised no more than a collection of independent infantry companies; a few companies of light cavalry, and fifteen small calibre, smooth-bore cannons; in all, some four and a half thousand all ranks, of whom some four thousand hailed from Virginia. The high percentage of general and field officers, together with numerous staffs, made colourful pageants of the frequent parades, to the extent that Napoleon would not have looked out of place on the saluting platform. When the Virginia Governor and State Legislature reduced all above the rank of captain, it was considered a serious insult to worthy yeomen and volunteers. Companies formed convocations for formal protest. However, the Colonel's quiet, unrelenting dedication brought realisation of the serious task ahead, and when many of the volunteer officers returned to their units in less exalted positions, protest died away, and the Army of the Shenandoah began to take on a military bearing. Jackson held his independent command for a few days less than four weeks, Time enough for one offensive act amid the drilling and the weapon training. The Federal Government was stocking up on coal and sending it west in the trucks of the Baltimore and Ohio Railroad, which crossed the Potomac River, into Virginia, at Harper's Ferry. Day and night, the chains of laden wagons clanked westwards past the camps, and the strings of emptied freight carts bounced and rattled their way eastwards for re-loading on the coast. It disturbed his men's rest, Colonel Jackson told the President of the Baltimore and Ohio, and he would be grateful if all the load bearing traffic could be

---

125 Ibid.

scheduled to pass through Harper's Ferry between eleven in the morning and one in the afternoon. The Colonel had calculated that there was enough traffic over twenty four hours to fill a two hour period. The railroad duly obliged, and when the new schedule was established, it was requested that the eastbound trains should work to the same timings, which was quite feasible, as this section of the line was twin-tracked. The railroad agreed, and when the schedule was working smoothly, the Colonel sent two blocking detachments of the Fifth Virginia Infantry to points east and west of the Ferry, and some fifteen miles apart. When both sections of track were filled with the empty and the laden, Jackson requisitioned the engines and wagons, and had them shunted south to Winchester; a useful windfall for a Confederacy short of rolling stock.

General Joseph E Johnston arrived to relieve Jackson in command of the Army of the Shenandoah on the twenty third of May; but as he arrived ahead of his letter of appointment, the Colonel refused to step down, before reading a letter from General Lee referring to Johnston as commanding at Harper's Ferry. In the re-organisation which followed, Jackson was appointed commander of the First Brigade, comprising the Second, Fourth, Fifth, Twenty-Seventh and Thirty-Third Virginia Regiments, all of which recruited among the hardy forest and mountain dwellers of the Shenandoah Valley. Some who had joined-up were of such a vintage that their grizzled beards reached to their waistbands, while others were too young to need a razor. Some came from wealth – the *"ranks were filled with the best blood of Virginia."*[126] – and others from modest means and smallholdings; but *"Nothing was serious yet; everything much like a joke. When George Flagg, cleaning barracks, was seen carrying two buckets of scrubbings ...and was guyed for carrying slops, he responded with assumed dignity, "Slops! This is*

126 Henry Kyd Douglas, *"I Rode with Stonewall"*, The University of North Carolina Press, 1940.

not slops. It is patriotism!"[127] The Brigade's attached artillery battery had recruited mainly in Rockbridge County and from the-
ological colleges, and was commanded by the Reverend Doctor
Pendleton, formerly vicar of Lexington, and himself a graduate of
West Point, who ended the war as Lee's Chief of Artillery. *"Their
four guns were at once christened Matthew, Mark, Luke and John ...
and when ... at Harper's Ferry it was quartered in a church, ... occupied by the 'Grayson Dare-devils' ... they ... assigned the pulpit to
Captain Pendleton as an appropriate lodging."*[128]

With Spring giving way to Summer, all was about to change.
Abraham Lincoln was preparing to take the offensive, and to
begin the painful process of learning by bitter personal experience that even the ablest of politicians and statesmen invariably
make hopeless generals. The main line of his advance would
be from Washington, striking directly at Richmond, now the
opposing capital, down a southerly arc bordered, initially, by
the Alexandra to Fredericksburg road and the Alexandra to
Culpepper Courthouse railroad. A smaller force of some fourteen thousand, under General Robert Patterson would move
west through Maryland and cross the Potomac into Virginia at
Williamsport, some twenty miles upstream of Harper's Ferry, to
contain Johnston and prevent him from reinforcing a Confederate
Army of some twenty-thousand, under General Pierre Beauregard,
which would deploy around Manassas Junction to oppose the
main Federal force, totalling some fifty-thousand, under General
Irvin McDowell. Colonel Jackson took it upon himself to secure the tactically important ground of the Maryland Heights,
overlooking Harper's Ferry. *"... this place should be defended with
the spirit which actuated the defenders of Thermopylae,"* he wrote to
Lee, *"and if left to myself such is my determination."* Lee agreed
with Jackson's assessment of the moral imperative, *"The fall of
this place would, I fear, result in the loss of the north-western part of*

127 Ibid.
128 Henderson.

the State," Jackson had written, *"and who can estimate the moral power thus gained to the enemy, and lost to ourselves?"*[129] Johnston, seemingly neither a classicist nor a reader of Shakespeare, was allowed to abandon the Ferry in favour of Winchester, some thirty miles distant. He assumed, so it has been said, that his men, despite nearly a month of drilling by Colonel Jackson, could not manoeuvre. Regardless of the military merits of holding on to Harper's Ferry, if such was his reasoning, then it was second-rate generalship, in the 'bad workmen blame their tools' school of thinking. Potentially disastrous in war, and, possibly, indicative of a lack of determination, even of courage. Victory treats with disdain the timorous who miss the point.

Patterson was having problems of his own with ill-equipped, ill-clad, and ill-trained volunteer levies. He dithered, crossing and re-crossing the Potomac. Johnston ordered the destruction of the river bridge at Shepherdstown, mid-way between Williamsport and the Ferry. In the ranks of 'B' Company, Second Virginia – the regiment's Shepherdstown Company – was a local boy, Private Henry Kyd Douglas. The task of destroying the bridge was causing Douglas to vandalise his birthplace, *"and when, in the glare of the burning timbers, I saw the glowing windows in my home on the hill beyond the river and knew my father was a stockholder in the property I was helping to destroy, I realized that war had begun."* Years later, he would publish what he had felt when his *"hair was as black as his coat is now, and whose coat was as grey as his hair is now. But long after, "when the wounds had healed and left no hurt"*[130] he wrote *"I knew that I was severing all connection between me and my family ... and ... when I saw the heavens lighted up over in Maryland one dark night, and knew that the gorgeous bonfire was made from the material and contents of my father's barn, I saw that I was advancing rapidly in a knowledge of the meaning of war; and my soul was filled with revengeful bitterness."* Days later, on suffering a severe attack of neuralgia,

---

129 Henderson.
130 Douglas.

however, *"I was received in the house and family of a Union Man, Mr Lemon, and had the fullest hospitality without."*[131]

The First Brigade, alone, opposed Patterson's first crossing into Virginia. *"I immediately advanced with one regiment of infantry and a battery of artillery, but it amounted to nothing, as the enemy re-crossed the river into Maryland. They are evidently afraid to advance."*[132]

Jackson was strongly in favour of a proposal by the Auditor, Colonel Bennett, that he should be promoted to Brigadier-General, and wrote, *"I am in command of a promising brigade, ... and ... Providence has greatly blessed me in securing good staff officers in the quartermaster, commissary and ordnance departments, which are so essential to the efficiency of the troops."* The First was the only brigade still commanded by a colonel. Although the news had not yet reached him, he had already got his promotion when he halted Patterson's next attempt to advance near the rural chapel of Falling Waters, set amid the rolling fields and forested slopes of a northern Virginia sparkling in the fresh-green of early summer. Union skirmishers recoiled from the accurate firing of country-men born to hunting and shooting, and carefully sited amidst the hedges and ridges. Riding alone between his cavalry vedettes Lieutenant-Colonel J.E.B. 'Jeb' Stuart, overawed by the power of command alone, some fifty individuals; but recently classified as soldiers, who were taking a break from the invasion in a shady field. Disarmed of the weapons none had used against so confident a horseman, they were enabled to continue their advance as escorted prisoners. After the Fifth Virginia had eagerly swarmed forward to firing positions around a solitary house and barn nearer to the enemy, Jackson calmly withdrew the regiment back to the main body of the Brigade. Riding well forward, the brigadier had observed Patterson's regiments concentrating on the next hillside. Unthinking Federal cavalry rushed to pursue the move back; but one or two well-aimed rounds from the 'Apostles', in

---

131 Ibid.

132 Letter from *Headquarters 1ˢᵗ Brigade, Camp Stevens, June 24, 1861* (Cook).

close support of the Fifth, sent horses back upon their haunches; wheeling and plunging; struggling and straggling to reverse their untidy rush. Jackson, like Stuart at Falling Waters, achieved his first anecdote in what was to become a personal legend, when during the action, he paused to write an update for his superior. A cannon ball crashed through the tree-tops overhead, and a nearby observer was amazed to see that amid the cascading leaves and twigs, the pen never hesitated and the writer never so much as flinched until the brief despatch was finished. At the end of it all, few were hurt on either side. The uninvolved Johnston dismissed the engagement as the mere *"affair at Falling Waters."* For Private Douglas, however, *"... it was of memorable importance; for there, for the first time, I heard the whiz of a musket ball and the shriek of a cannon shot."* A single infantry regiment and a supporting artillery battery, together with Stuart's three-hundred horsemen had, alone, caused the uneasy General Patterson's fourteen thousand to veer from the cautious advance, and the general to report that he had been confronted in the field by a force of no less than three thousand five hundred.

Jackson's promotion came through within days of Falling Waters. Dated some three weeks earlier, it came with a cover letter from Lee in Richmond. *"My dear General, I have the pleasure of sending you a commission in the Provincial Army; and to feel that you merit it. May your advancement increase your usefulness to the State. Very Truly, R E Lee."*[133] With all anxiety over being superseded removed, Tom wrote to Anna *"My promotion was beyond what I had anticipated, as I only expected it to be in the Volunteer forces of the State. One of my greatest desires for advancement is the gratification it will give my Darling, and for serving my country more efficiently. ... I should be very ungrateful if I were not contented, and exceedingly thankful to our kind Heavenly Father."*[134]

---

133 Cook.

134 Henderson.

The period of inaction following Falling Waters caused grumbling in the Confederate ranks. Jackson commented *"I want my brigade to feel it can whip Patterson's whole army, and I believe we can do it."* Johnston, his strength increased to around ten thousand, brought his remaining brigades to Jackson's location where he drew out the Army of the Shenandoah, as if in preparation to fight a static, defensive battle. But he was opposing a general as lacking in initiative as himself. Patterson, in Henderson's phrase *"crawled on to Martinsburg"* and there halted. Neither side made any attempt at an offensive move, and after four days or so, Johnston pulled back to Winchester. It is impossible to believe that had Jackson been in overall command there would not have been some positive action, resulting in gain for the South, no matter how local. Morale, 'the greatest single factor in war' seems not to have entered the reckoning for Johnston. His primary task was to remain available to reinforce Beauregard when the main Federal invasion force advanced. Meanwhile he could think of nothing better to do than nothing. Lee had a concern that if Johnston moved too soon, in Beauregard's direction, it might deter the main invasion altogether. Patterson too seemed to think he could detain Johnston by nothing more active than his mere presence. In the wings was a third Federal Army of some twenty thousand, away to Patterson's right, moving through the Alleghenies, threatening the southern end of the Shenandoah Valley, more or less due west of Richmond. So, in the face of an advancing threat more than twice the strength of its entire 'Provisional Army', the Confederacy doomed itself in advance, by remaining inactive and, as it were, mentally, on the back foot.

P1: An 1862 photograph of Jackson in the uniform of a Lieutenant General, CSA, by the renowned Civil War photographer Matthew Brady. Although inherently strong, his features reflect the strain of running a campaign from the back of a horse.

P2: Equestrian statue of Jackson at Manassas, Virginia.

P3: *The State of Virginia, 1862*

10. "STANDING LIKE A STONE WALL"

....

"Then, Sir, we will give them the bayonet."
'Stonewall' Jackson

....

WHETHER he marched on reading Beauregard's message *"If you will help me, now is the time"*[135] or on receipt of *"a telegram from the President … received at one a.m. on the morning of the eighteenth of July, … to the effect that McDowell was marching on Manassas,"* Johnston immediately left Winchester heading south, by way of a diversion, and with the move masked by Stuart's cavalry screen. Marching with their backs to the enemy, the rank and file were listless and dragged their heels. After a few miles, however, the column swung eastwards and halted to hear a proclamation. *"Our gallant army under General Beauregard is now attacked by overwhelming numbers. The Commanding General hopes that his troops will step out like men and make a forced march to save the country."* The response was immediate. *"The soldiers rent the air with shouts of joy, and all was eagerness and animation."*[136] *"Jackson's brigade took the lead, as it was to do ever after."*[137] and, by two a.m. the following morning, had covered a further seventeen miles, crossing the rock and forested slopes of the Blue Ridge at Ashby's Gap, and wading waist deep through a ford where the road crossed the Shenandoah. Near the village of Paris, they dropped to the ground, and slept wherever they happened to be when the order to halt reached them. Told that no pickets had been posted, Jackson replied *"Let the poor fellows sleep, I will guard the camp*

---

135 Douglas.
136 Henderson quoting Jackson.
137 Douglas.

myself."[138] In the first half light of dawn he had them back on their feet and tramping the six or so miles down to Piedmont Station on the Manassas Gap Railroad, where the infantry entrained for Manassas Junction, leaving the cavalry and artillery to continue by road. The First Brigade reached Beauregard's lines on the evening of the Nineteenth. By the morning of Sunday, twenty-first July, three brigades of the Army of the Shenandoah, together with Stuart's cavalry, had reinforced Beauregard. The fourth was still on the way by rail. The enemy, seemingly, were none the wiser.

The Federal advance had developed something of a carnival air, with numerous men and women, press and politicians, walking, riding or being driven out from Washington, to swarm around the armed and the uniformed, to the general cry of *"on to Richmond!"* The part-army-cum-circus had reached Centreville, within six miles of Beauregard, on the Eighteenth. Beauregard had fortified six miles of the Bull Run – a naturally formidable obstacle of steep, over-grown banks – with twenty-six thousand men and fifty-five guns. McDowell, commanding thirty-five thousand men and forty-four guns, after some laborious reconnoitring, decided to turn the left flank of this position. This sound enough plan, opened at around six thirty a.m. on that sunny, summer morning, with direct musket and artillery fire as the precursor of a diversionary attack in full Division strength against the Brigade of Colonel Nathan Evans, holding the extreme left of the Confederate line.

McDowell began loading the dice against himself on his approach march, by disregarding the sound military principle of concentration and maintaining the aim. He left one entire Division seven miles back, before reaching Centreville, to defend his line of communication and the approach to Washington, thus weakening his means for achieving the essential victory. A second Division he marched through Centreville, for use as an immediate

---

138 Henderson.

reserve, leaving him with just two Divisions with which to carry out the flank attack. Seeing a rising pall of dust way out to his left Colonel Evans quickly rumbled what McDowell was about and was equally quick to respond. Leaving four rifle companies to hold the bridge, against what he had rightly decided was a diversion, Evans led six of his companies, plus *"a battalion called the Louisiana Tigers, and two six-pounder howitzers"* out across the turnpike and on to the Matthews Hill, a long ridge running at right angles to Bull Run, where he drew-up his men, without fully appreciating at this stage, the numbers he was facing. At the same time as altering his dispositions, he sent word back along the line to warn Johnston and Beauregard. Fortunately for them both, there was some confusion on the Federal right. Overnight camps had been taken up with no thought for the requirements of the morning attack, and units moving to take part in one attack crossed the routes of those heading for the other. The start of the flank march took some three hours to make progress, having been balked by those marching straight ahead for the Stone Bridge.

The integrity of the original Confederate position was for a time maintained by the quick and decisive action of a second brigade commander, Brigadier-General Bee. Leading his Brigade westwards, behind the line of the Bull Run to reinforce the Stone Bridge, Bee was informed, *"that the whole Federal army seemed to be moving to the north-west."*[139] He promptly wheeled left out on to the Henry Hill – a similar feature running parallel to the Matthews Hill – and deployed about a mile behind Evans. But by now, Evans, having fought off two assaults in the space of an hour, was being overwhelmed and was calling for support. Bee responded at once, hastening forward to the Matthews Hill; but his brigade could do no more than inflict a momentary pause on the Federal onslaught. Briskly handled, and well supplied with ammunition, the horse artillery McDowell had committed in some strength to his flank attack, galloped forward into action. Bee and Evans

---

139 Henderson.

were both forced from the Matthews Hill. Cannon balls tore into the panting ranks, as they splashed back through Young's Branch, to scramble back up the forward slope of the Henry Hill. Those retiring on the left – nearest the Bull Run – came under small arms fire from the brigade of Brigadier-General Sherman which, having discovered an upstream ford was, at the same time, flanking the defenders of Stone Bridge, in the original Confederate line-up. His twin attacks now beginning to fight in unison, and everywhere pressing forward, McDowell began to sense victory.

For Jackson's First Virginia Brigade the day of battle started before first light. *"About four A.M., on the Twenty-First, by request of General Longstreet, I sent first a reinforcement of two regiments. Subsequently, I received an order from General Beauregard to reinforce*(sic) *General Cocke. Finally, I was instructed by him to take up such a position as would enable me to reinforce either General Bonham or General Cocke. These instructions were executed in the order in which they were given,"* Jackson recounted, after the battle, in a letter to Colonel Bennett. For Henry Kyd Douglas – recently rated Orderly Sergeant in the Second Virginia, – it had seemed a tedious morning of *"meaningless"* marching. *"The hours passed slowly for men who had never tasted battle."*

At long last, they emerged from the flickering gloom and swirling dust of the forest shortly before Noon. Out into the hot July sun, four-abreast, a sinuous column some seven hundred and fifty files long. Five Regiments of Virginia; three thousand men in all, the First Brigade of the Confederate States Army. Sharp, silvered bayonets, glinting back the sun in gleaming anticipation, glistened above the weather-worn cloth of uniforms in every shade from iron grey to creamy, butternut-brown. At their head, a small cluster of mounted officers led by the Brigade-Commander, Thomas Jonathan Jackson, born and bred in Virginia, like his men. From the treeline, the dry-mud farm trail pointed upwards to the grass-bare, round back summit of the Henry House Hill. To left and right, a scattering of men descending; some furtive; straggling, others dragging wounds, heading painfully for the three hospitals established behind the battle line.

Out in front, the General was intent on reading the swirling, ever changing situation opening before him. He would have been too absorbed to recall – even fleetingly – that fourteen years ago, the twenty-three year old Substantive Lieutenant, Brevet Captain Jackson, United States Army, in command of a single section of 'Flying' Artillery, had headed an entire American Army in a final, fighting, approach to the storming of Mexico City. Nearing the summit of the Henry House Hill, the air became increasingly burdened with screeching metal. The bigger bits fleetingly visible for the all too naked eye. Shouts and cries too, got louder, amid the dispassionate, unfeeling grunt of guns, and the frantic stutter of musketry. A short way below the summit, the General wheeled the Brigade into line, and ordered the men to lie down on the reverse slope, just below the summit. An ideal position both for shelter, and from which to bayonet charge an approaching enemy disorganised by the success of his own attack. *"All the regiments had instructions to charge the enemy with the bayonet as soon as he should appear over the crest, and within about fifty yards."* Jackson wrote later.

Coming back along the winding track, their guns bounding over the uneven ground, a Confederate Battery galloped from the front, a cursing Battery Command riding up to the General, to complain of being abandoned by the infantry. *"Unlimber right here, I'll support you,"* Captain Imboden was told. Probably he did not notice the scowl of displeasure at his cursing. Jackson, a devout but in no way bigoted Christian, wore the peak of his campaign kepi so low over the bridge of his nose that little of his face was visible above the thick brown beard. Through the smoke and the crowd fellow Brigade-Commander, General Bernard E. Bee, then galloped up *"covered with dust and sweat, his sword in his hand and his horse foaming, 'General', he yelled, 'they are beating us back'!"* *"Very well, General."* *"But how do you expect to stop them?"*

"We will give them the bayonet," was the calm, determined reply. Bee looked at Jackson in silence for a moment, before spurring away. Pointing back with his sword, he shouted to his disrupted, depleted companies *"Look! There is Jackson standing like a stone wall! Rally behind the Virginians!"*

"Apprehensive lest my flank should be turned, I sent orders to the colonels of cavalry to secure them." Jackson then rode slowly along the front of his line, with the calming injunction, *"Steady men! Steady! All is Well!"* He neared Imboden, now checking the alignment of his guns, and that the fuses for shells were being cut to the required length. The General raised his hand, palm outwards, towards the Battery Commander, in a gesture he used frequently in conversation. Abruptly he jerked the hand down, blood flowing across hand and wrist. *"General, you are wounded!"*

"A scratch, a mere scratch." Wrapping a handkerchief around what was a smashed finger, Jackson continued on along his line, reassuring the inexperienced ranks.

To the boyish Sergeant Henry Kyd Douglas of the Second Virginia, the approach march up the Henry House Hill *"through wounded and stragglers hurrying to the rear … was … not an encouraging sight to brand-new troops. It seemed, as a looker-on, that the day was lost to us."* It had been that tedious morning of seemingly *"meaningless"* marching, which had begun around four a.m. *"The hours passed slowly for men who had never tasted battle."* Sergeant Douglas had been *"quite sick during the night and was horrified"* at the very thought of missing the action. However, *"the distant sound of musketry coming nearer and nearer made me forget my bodily ills and acted as a bracer."*[140]

Jackson noted that *"the enemy continued to advance, but not being able to force our centre, its batteries inclined to the right, evidently for the purpose of securing an oblique fire upon my front; but in so doing, one of them approached so near my left regiment – the thirty-third – that the colonel, by charging with the bayonet captured the guns."* The Thirty Third were then forced to abandon the captured guns, *"… in consequence of the severe small-arms fire of the enemy … but the battery was of no further service during the action; in consequence of the cannoneers having been driven off and the horses killed."* But the respite was

---

140 Henry Kyd Douglas, *"I Rode with Stonewall"*, The University of North Carolina Press, 1940.

no more than momentary. Fresh Federal regiments were pushing forward across the slope. A Confederate officer among the wounded and dispirited straggling to the rear, told Jackson, as he dragged past, *"General, the day is going against us." "If you think so, Sir,"* came the curt reply *"you had better not say anything about it."*

(It was at this point – around two-forty-five p.m. – that the Union Commander would write afterwards, *"all were certain that the day was ours."*[141])

The counterstroke, however, was imminent. Jackson rode to the centre of his Brigade, where lay the Second and the Fourth Virginia Regiments. Henderson records his order to the tense, expectant men, as, *"Reserve your fire till they come within fifty yards, then fire and give them the bayonet; and when you charge, yell like furies!"* Jackson himself reported afterwards *"Finally, the onward movement of the enemy brought them so near my battery and central regiments as to call for the free use of the bayonet, and I accordingly ordered the charge to be made, which cut the enemy's centre, and thus separated his wings. ...* he summed-up. *... A few moments more, and the field was essentially in the possession of the brigade, and of other troops; though both my flanks were turned by Federal force, ... by re-posting the artillery in rear, and giving a few shots, taken in connection with the small-arms fire of other troops on my left, the victory was made complete."*

Sergeant Douglas remembered the order for *'free use of the bayonet,'* reaching the Colonel of the Second Virginia, William Allan, as, *"Tell the colonels of this brigade that the enemy are advancing; when their heads are seen above the hill, let the whole line rise, move forward with a shout, and trust to the bayonet. I am tired of this long-range work. I confess,* Douglas wrote *"that I remember very little; my observation was confined to my own company, and I am sure my vision was not particularly clear. General Jackson said the Second and Fourth Regiments pierced the enemy's centre. I have no doubt he knew. I have been surprised that I cannot remember any of my sensations during that*

---

141 Lieutenant-Colonel G.F.R. Henderson, C.B., *"Stonewall Jackson and the American Civil War" (Vol.1)* Longmans, Green, and Co., London, 1904.

turmoil, but I have a vague recollection of personal discomfort and apprehension, followed by intense anxiety for the result of the battle. ... I know we went in. My part of the line was driven back at first; then we went in again and fought it through, and found, when the smoke cleared, and the roar of artillery died away, and the rattle of musketry decreased into scattering shots, that we had won the field, and were pursuing the enemy." The memories and emotions of Douglas were surely typical of many who survived the charge.

Such Confederate cavalry as was available, immediately followed up the victory; but soon became overloaded and bogged-down with prisoners. The victors took some fifteen hundred in the course of the long summer evening, as well as twenty-five guns and several thousand rifles. There was no panic in the retreat; the Union soldiers, mostly inexperienced as they were, had fought, in the main, bravely and resolutely. It had been a long, hot day and they had simply had enough.

Military discipline was not yet engrained, which was partly why Lincoln had been told by his generals that it was too soon to risk a major battle. The survivors simply wanted to get back and drink off the experience in the bars and shebeens of Washington. Inexperience aside, responsibility for defeat lay with the commanding general. McDowell had left one entire Division behind at Centreville, to secure his communications with Washington. Apparently, failing to appreciate that to destroy the Confederate Army was the best way of defending his lines of communication, and to achieve that he needed to be at full strength. His reserve Division could well have been sufficient to turn the tide of battle. But not, perhaps, if he had continued to commit his brigades to the attack in succession – the second major blunder – instead of in one concerted, overwhelming hammer-blow, intent on rolling up the Confederate line from left to right. To distract the enemy frontally, in conjunction with an overall turning movement, as the main attack, was certainly a sound enough plan.

The Confederates too had fought bravely and resolutely, and, in the aftermath, poor generalship too cost them the fruits of their efforts. Many excuses have been put forward for Johnston's failure to fling the army forward in pursuit from first light on Monday morning. The reality is there can be no excuses, his failure was a failure in generalship of the first magnitude, and it cost the South its only real opportunity to bring the War to an end with the Confederacy intact. If President Davis did intervene to prevent an immediate follow-up, it was Johnston's duty either to ignore the intervention or resign his command. He failed to do either.

Convinced that the proper course of action was an immediate advance upon Washington, Jackson held the First Virginia Brigade in readiness, from first light on the morning after the battle, *"with three days cooked rations in their haversacks."* He had said while having his smashed finger dressed, *"Give me ten thousand fresh troops and I will be in Washington tomorrow."* Presumably, in an attempt to exonerate himself, Johnston wrote *"Our army was more disorganised by victory than that of the United States by defeat."* In itself, a pathetic enough comment from a supposedly victorious general; but which, in the final analysis, is simply not true. *"Before twenty-four hours had passed, reinforcements had increased the strength of Johnston's army to forty-thousand."*[142] Douglas wrote *"It was remarkable how little Jackson's brigade was demoralized or disorganised by the battle ...* despite sustaining more deaths and wounds than any other Confederate brigade involved in turning defeat into victory – *the next morning it seemed ready for another."*

Lincoln's Secretary of War, Edwin Stanton wrote *"The capture of Washington now seems inevitable; during the whole of Monday and Tuesday (July the twenty second and the twenty third) it might have been taken without resistance. The rout, overthrow, and demoralisation of the whole army was complete."*[143] McClellan – the general with whom Lincoln replaced McDowell, and who passed-out top of Jackson's term at West Point – wrote, *"If the Secessionists attached any value to the possession of Washington, they committed their greatest*

---

142 Henderson.

143 Henderson quoting McClellan.

error in not following up the victory of Bull Run."[144] Jackson clear-ly did attach value to such possession, so it is not surprising that Douglas could write: *"Jackson afterwards was never enthusiastic over the results of that battle;. On the contrary, he said to me once in the Valley that he believed a defeat of our army then had been less disastrous to us."*

---

144 McClellan.

11. "SEVERAL TIRESOME WEEKS"

....

"I hope by your future deeds and
bearing you will be handed down to
posterity as the First Brigade in our
second War of Independence."
'Stonewall' Jackson

....

JOHNSTON's Army remained inert in the region where the battle had been fought, for what Douglas described as *"several tiresome weeks."* The man who, forever after, would be universally remembered as 'Stonewall' Jackson, kept the First Virginia Brigade continuously in training; drilling, weapon training, and patrolling. Little leave was granted, unlike other units of the army in which *"Furloughs were freely granted."*[145] Jackson himself took no leave. Neither the officers nor the men of the First Brigade complained or grumbled when their leave requests were denied. *"His brigade"* said Douglas, *"was a good school of war."*

Visiting Jackson's headquarters, in the early days when the finger wound was still healing, Captain Imboden took the opportunity of asking *"… how is it that you can … appear so utterly insensible to danger in such a storm of shell and bullets as rained about you when your hand was hit?"* Jackson's reply was in line with Platonic injunction that *"…a man who is good for anything ought not to calculate the chance of living or dying; he ought only to consider whether in doing anything he is doing right or wrong."*[146] He replied earnestly, looking directly at Imboden, *"Captain, my religious belief teaches me to feel as safe in battle as in bed. God has fixed the time for my death. I do not concern myself about that, but to be always ready, no matter when*

---

145 Douglas.
146 Plato, *"The Trial and Death of Socrates."*

it may overtake me. That is the way all men should live, and then all would be equally brave.[147]

Mrs Anna Jackson visited the headquarters for a few days in September, and shortly afterwards the Rev. William S. White, *"an intimate friend and correspondent of General Jackson. who was pastor from 1848 to 1867 of the Lexington Presbyterian Church of which Jackson was a member,"* was invited to headquarters and to minister to the Brigade. In the days immediately following the battle of Manassas, when all Lexington was waiting anxiously for news, the Pastor received an envelope and *"recognising the handwriting, exclaimed to the eager group about him, 'Now we shall know the facts."* The letter was very much to the point; but did little to relieve their anxieties: *"My dear Pastor, – In my tent last night, after a fatiguing day's service, I remembered that I had failed to send you my contribution to our coloured Sunday school. Enclosed you will find my check* (sic) *for that object, which please acknowledge at your earliest convenience, and oblige yours faithfully, T.J. Jackson."*[148] Jackson divulged military information on a very strict 'need to know basis.' Subordinate generals were often far from amused when, in response to a request for directions, they were told no more than 'follow those in front.' To requests for information he would sometimes respond with 'Can you keep a secret?' – 'Yes' – Well, so can I.'

On the fourth of October 1861, Jackson was promoted to Major-General, and was appointed to the Valley District in command. Although the appointment was welcome, his one regret was not being able to retain command of the First Brigade. He had trained, instructed and led them with care and consideration. He was meticulous in seeing to their wants and needs. In action they had already achieved much together. As a fighting entity, they had developed something of his – *"what I can I will"* mentality. Their esprit de corps was built around their regard for his ability and determination, as well as their affection for his individuality. To them all,

---

147 Henderson quoting from *"Battles and Leaders of the Civil War".*
148 Henderson.

he was either their 'Old Jack' or, since Manassas, 'Stonewall.' The habit of raising his left hand, palm out, they liked to say, *"was an appeal to Heaven."* He told the Rev. Dr White when his appointment to the Valley came through, that had it *"not come as an order, I should instantly have declined it and continued in command of my brave old brigade."*[149] Of a deputation of officers who called on the Brigade Commander to say farewell, Douglas, *"being the youngest in years and rank ... was the last to shake hands ... and ... ventured to remark that having lately been in the ranks ... wished to express the general grief among the soldiers at parting with him; while he had all their good wishes for his success in the future; they hoped that he would not forget that the old brigade he left behind would be ready to march at a moment's notice to his assistance, when he needed them. As I said this,"* Douglas noticed *"a strange brightness came into his eyes and his mouth closed with more than its usual tightness. ... He held my hand to the door and then said in his quick way, 'I am much obliged to you, Mr Douglas, for what you say of the soldiers; and I believe it. I want to take the brigade with me but cannot. I shall never forget them. In battle I shall always want them ... Goodbye."*[150]

Major-General 'Stonewall' Jackson bid a formal farewell to the First Virginia Brigade on the fourth of November, 1861, before leaving to take command of the Valley District three days later. The five regiments paraded in rear of the camp of the Second Virginia, *"in column of regiments closed en masse."* Accompanied by some of his staff, and mounted on *'Little Sorrel'*, he rode to the front of the dense columns. A moment or two of silence, as each looked at the other — *"silent as if in church"* Douglas recalled, — before he removed the campaign cap *"and in his sharp earnest voice,"* said;

"Officers and men of the First Brigade, I am not here to make a speech, but simply to say farewell. I first met you at Harper's Ferry in the commencement of the war, and I cannot take leave of you without giving expression to my admiration of your conduct from that day to this, whether on the march, in the bivouac, the tented field, or on the bloody plains of

---

149 Douglas.
150 Ibid.

Manassas, where you gained the well-deserved reputation of having decided the fate of the battle. Throughout the broad extent of the country over which you have marched, by your respect for the rights and property of citizens, you have shown that you were soldiers not only to defend, but able and willing both to defend and protect. You have already gained a brilliant and deservedly high reputation, throughout the army of the whole Confederacy, and I trust in the future by your own deeds on the field, and by the assistance of the same kind Providence who has heretofore favoured our cause, that you will gain more victories, and add additional lustre to the reputation you now enjoy. You have already gained a proud position in the history of this our second War of Independence. I shall look with great anxiety to your future movements, and I trust whenever I shall hear of the First Brigade on the field of battle, it will be of still nobler deeds achieved and higher reputation won."

This is probably as close to Jackson's words of farewell as it is possible to get. Douglas was joined in his tent by Sergeant T Harris Towner, of his Company, and *"within fifteen minutes,"* the pair had written down the address from memory *"comparing our recollection of every word until we thought it absolutely accurate."* Their version was published by the Richmond *'Despatch'* on the eighth of November.

Finally, Douglas remembered, Jackson *"paused for an instant. He then rose in his stirrups, threw the reins upon the neck of his horse, and stretching out his gauntleted right hand he concluded in a voice that sent a thrill through all that presence: "In the army of the Shenandoah you were the First Brigade; in the army of the Potomac you were the First Brigade; in the Second Corps of this army you are the First Brigade; you are the First Brigade in the affections of your General; and I hope by your future deeds and bearing you will be handed down to posterity as the Frist Brigade in our second War of Independence. Farewell!"* A moment of silence followed. Jackson settled back in the saddle, gathering *"up the reins slowly with his left hand."* As he wheeled *'Little Sorrel'* to ride away, the whole Brigade broke the silence *"with one of those wild discordant yells ... which he once pronounced 'The sweetest music I have ever heard."* An emotional General galloped from the parade, his cap held aloft in salute.

12. WINCHESTER, VA.

....

*"With one voice have they made
constant and urgent appeals that to
you, in whom they have confidence,
their defence should be assigned."*
Hon. J.P. Benjamin, Secretary of War

....

IF the loyal people of the Valley of Virginia and of the Shenandoah had *"with one voice"* expressed their *"urgent"* desire for fellow-countryman, 'Stonewall' Jackson, to be placed in charge of their defence, the feeling was mutual. Sometime earlier, in a note to Virginia State Auditor, Jonathan M. Bennett, the now Major-General Jackson wrote,*"… it is my duty to serve wherever I may be placed, and I desire to be always where most needed. But it is natural for one's affections to turn to the home of one's boyhood and family."*[151]

'Old Jack' – so often to his soldiers, as he had been to fellow students at West Point – was a little over one month short of his thirty eighth birthday when he established his operational headquarters in Winchester, the county-town of Frederick. *"The Winchester ladies were amongst the most famous of Virginia housekeepers,"* wrote his wife Anna, who joined her husband from her father's home in North Carolina, *"and lived in a good deal of old-fashioned elegance and profusion. … It seemed to me that no people could have been more cultivated, attractive, and noble-hearted. … The extreme kindness and appreciation shown to General Jackson by all, bound us to them so closely and warmly, that ever after that winter he called the place our 'war home.'"*[152]

---

151 Cook.
152 Henderson quoting Mrs Jackson.

12/1. The Arena

....

*"If this Valley is lost,
then Virginia is lost."*
Stonewall Jackson

....

MANKIND has never desecrated a more magnificent setting in which to indulge in the 'Art of War', than Virginia's Shenandoah Valley, the valley of the *'Laughing River'*. No great captain ever had a more beautiful, yet unyielding, arena in which to deliver a master class in the 'Futile Art,' than did Stonewall Jackson, nor yet one better suited for an incomparable demonstration of this most difficult of all the Arts.

The arena of conflict was a hundred and fifty miles, north to south, and some hundred and thirty miles east to west. An arena comprising some nineteen and a half square miles of serried mountain ridges, of which the peaks of the Blue Ridge – the most easterly, unbroken, ridge line – reach to six thousand feet, and were crossable by artillery and wagons, only through passes – known as Gaps – of which there are eleven. The ridges – behind which armies could march and counter-march unseen – were covered by dense, first-degree forest, ideal for concealing movement, and for applying the essential ingredient of surprise. The whole area was intersected by a network of rivers and streams, flowing amidst fertile pastures and meadows, albeit the rivers were significant barriers which, apart from a few fords, were crossable only by properly constructed bridges, and even then, with difficulty in times of spate. Matching the arteries and veins of the waterways, was a system of tracks and roads – some tarmac, many dirt only, which became bottomless ribbons of mud, in cold and wet weather, and generators of choking clouds of revealing dust in the heat and dry of summer. An uncompromising battleground of endless potential for the enterprising and

141

the active; neutral in its ruggedness, unlike the local people, who were, in the main, fiercely loyal to Virginia. None more so than the womenfolk, as uncompromising as the land itself, in a population, driven by private enterprise, spread out in villages and on isolated farms, tending to administration, grievance and justice in their court-houses, and working their smithies, their saw and grist mills.

Curving around the northern head of the Valley, flowed the all-absorbing Potomac, possibly, the *'River of Swans'* to American natives. For those four, bitter years, both a boundary and a barrier between Union and Secession. The Blue Ridge, the Shenandoah, and the arterial Valley Turnpike, or Valley Pike, all reached the Potomac at the strategically important crossing place of Harper's Ferry, at the northern end of the Valley. From there, after marching some twenty-five miles, south by west on the Valley Pike, an invader would reach the important town of Winchester, with its roads and tracks straggling off to all corners of the Valley, and including two which led eastwards through Snicker's and Ashby's Gaps; before uniting to end in Alexandria, immediately across the Potomac from Washington D.C. A further twenty miles along the Valley Pike, and the invader reached Strasburg, in another twelve, Woodstock, and New Market in another seventeen. These last two were situated in the shadow of the Massanutton, a thirty-seven mile long mountain bulk in the very centre of the Valley, with only a single road crossing, at New Market, halfway along its length. At the northern end, near Front Royal, the Shenandoah divided and passed either side of the Massanutton, as the North and South Forks. The Valley Pike followed the North Fork. Some nineteen miles after New Market, and the invader reached Harrisonburg, in another twenty-five, Staunton, and finally Lexington, thirty-five miles away, at the southern end of the Valley.

By 1862, several railroads pierced the Valley from the east and north and were useful – especially to the well-stocked North for transporting supplies and equipment – but were only of occasional use tactically. The main ways to get about were on foot, horseback, or in wagons.

12/2. State of Play

....

*"It is always best to be wide awake
and not permit ourselves to be
taken by surprise."*
Stonewall Jackson

....

PRIOR to the arrival of Stonewall Jackson at Winchester, the Confederates had had the worst of a series very much of not very major clashes with Union initiatives, emanating from across the Potomac in Maryland. The first, significant, Confederate force in this very northwest region of Virginia, had been outmanoeuvred by General George B McClellan, and its commander, General Robert Garnett, killed. McClellan's report of a minor action lost nothing in the telling and caught the imagination of the press and people of the North. He was dubbed the 'Young Napoleon,' and appointed, by Lincoln, to succeed McDowell, the General who had had victory snatched from him at the first battle of Manassas, by the stand and then the bayonet-charge of the First Virginia Brigade. Two other Confederate generals, commanding forces of no more than brigade strength, failed to co-operate, and did not succeed in redeeming any of the lost territory. General Robert E Lee was then sent to the area; but failed to recover the ground lost by Garnett. Lee was soon re-appointed and, with the Fall beginning to give way to Winter, operations ceased in this rugged, inhospitable region.

As Christmas approached, the Unionists held *"the greater part of the State of Virginia, west of the Alleghenies."*[153] They had patrolled

---

153 William Allan, *"Stonewall Jackson's Campaign in the Shenandoah Valley of Virginia",* re-issued by Hugh Rees Ltd, London, 1912. (Lieutenant-Colonel Allan commanded 2nd Virginia Regiment and was Chief Ordnance Officer, 2 Corps, Army of Northern Virginia).

and established footholds in the forested and mountainous terrain immediately west of the Shenandoah Valley, and General Kelly, commanding five thousand men under the District Commander, General Rosecrans, had secured Romney – the county-seat of Hampshire in the valley of the South Fork of the Potomac – no more than thirty four miles northwest of Winchester. A second force had crossed the Potomac and occupied Bath, the county-seat of Morgan – at most just thirty miles due north of Winchester. Near Leesburg, due east of Winchester, some thirty-four miles by road through Snicker's Gap, the Confederates had their one success in the region, at Ball's Bluff, on the south bank of the Potomac. Just over a fortnight before Jackson arrived in Winchester, a Federal recce patrol was upgraded to the dignity of a raid – against the standing orders of General McClellan – and, having crossed the river, was severely mauled by a similar strength Confederate force of less than two thousand. Over five hundred Federals were captured and some half that number killed and wounded. For the Confederates it was no more than a reactive strike, which would have stiffened the morale of the troops involved; but in keeping with the self-defeating, generally inactive, strategy of the Davis Confederate Government, achieved nothing of overall value; across the river in Maryland, the whole north bank of the Potomac was under Federal control.

For the defence of his District, Jackson had *"but three fragmentary brigades of State Militia and a few detached companies of cavalry. ... These troops were poorly armed, and the militia was almost entirely without discipline or experience."*[154] From the moment he took over responsibility for the Valley, Jackson's purposeful and vigorous activity is in stark contrast to the overall stagnation. He recruited; he drilled and trained; he planned and sought active solutions for the inert situation he had inherited. He appreciated unerringly the failings of the previous months, as well as the overall do-nothing folly. He recognised instantly that he had

---

154 Allan.

one ace in a hand, otherwise unburdened by a single trump. The cavalry. loose, uncoordinated groupings of accomplished horse masters – some as young as fifteen – all agile exponents of the Virginia hunting field, superbly mounted; reckless possibly; but adventurous and brimming with active initiative. They made as free with Federal camps and outposts as with each other's farms. One Union cavalry leader moaned to his chief *"I can't catch them, sir; they leap fences and walls like deer; neither our men nor our horses are so trained."*[155] Furthermore, among the carefree, hard-riding bands was a born leader of light cavalry, Turner Ashby. A landowner and businessman of Fauquier County, Ashby was just four years younger than Jackson, and had recruited the 'Ashby Rangers,' at the outset of war. Jackson took to him immediately, upon learning of his having gleaned intelligence by entering an enemy camp in the guise of a horse doctoring veterinary. The disparate squadrons he consolidated under *'the Colonel.'* and despatched them to the frontier, to ferret out and report back on every Federal ploy and gimmick. If the task was after their own hearts, he was the general for their talents, every bit as much as they were the troopers for his needs. They lived at the enemy's elbow and provided much raw-material for that fertile and focused mind to concoct and carry-through the shocks and surprises that curtailed and crippled the less understanding and imaginative generals opposing him in the field.

---

155 Henderson.

12/3. Mission

....

*"To move swiftly, strike vigorously,
and secure all the fruits of victory
is the secret of successful war."*
Stonewall Jackson

....

ON being appointed to command in the Valley, Jackson had been asked to *"forward suggestions as to the means of rendering his measures of defence effectual."* He responded: *"Deeply impressed with the importance of absolute secrecy respecting military operations, I have made it a point to say but little, respecting my proposed movements in the event of sufficient reinforcements arriving ...* he responded, further, in a letter to Secretary of War Benjamin, saying: ... *I deem it of very great importance that North-western Virginia be occupied by Confederate troops this winter. At present it is to be presumed that the enemy are not expecting an attack there, and the resources of that region, necessary for the subsistence of our troops, are in greater abundance than in almost any other season of the year. ... I venture to respectfully urge that after concentrating all ... troops here, an attempt should be made to capture the Federal forces at Romney. ... this ... would probably induce McClellan to believe that General Johnston's army had been so weakened as to justify him in making an advance on Centreville; but should this not induce him to advance, I do not believe anything will, during this winter."*[156] Confederate General Joseph E. Johnston commanded the military district east of the Blue Ridge, in which was the main Confederate Army under General Beauregard which had lain inactive in the area ever since the Manassas battle.

For Jackson, as for all the great commanders, defining the military situation meant to appreciate how it should be resolved.

---

156 Henderson.

Definition and resolution were but two stages in a single, simultaneous process. Jackson had been sent his 'old' First Brigade, at the end of November, and by early December commanded a force of nearly four thousand, all arms. General Loring commanded nearly twice that number, further west beyond the Shenandoah Mountains, and Colonel Edward Johnson another brigade, further on still, beyond the Alleghenies. It was these troops Jackson was proposing should be concentrated at Winchester. In his proposals, which were endorsed by General Johnston, Jackson kept the overall strategic situation ever in mind. *"Should General Johnston be attacked, I would be at once prepared to reinforce him with my present force, increased by General Loring's,"* Jackson informed Benjamin. In an attempt to urge the policy makers from their supine inertia, he added *"Postpone the occupation of that area until spring, and we may expect to find the enemy prepared for us, and the resources to which I have referred greatly exhausted. I know that what I have proposed will be an arduous undertaking and cannot be accomplished without the sacrifice of much personal comfort; but I feel that the troops will be prepared to make the sacrifice when animated by the prospects of important results to our cause and distinction to themselves."*[157]

Some twenty-seven thousand Federals, spread across two hundred miles, faced the Confederates in northwest Virginia. Apart from the five thousand at Romney, eighteen thousand seven hundred were based on Clarksburg and had sent units forward to occupy the western passes into the Valley. Nine thousand were stationed on the Ohio, and a further four thousand guarded the lines of communication. Jackson had earlier said that he required a force of fifteen thousand to recover northwest Virginia, and that to do so could result in as many as twenty thousand new recruits from amongst the loyal population. At the same time, he proposed that *"While the enemy was under the impression that* (the) *only intention was to recover North-west Virginia, he should ... march down upon Pittsburg,* (sic) *destroy the United States arsenal and then,*

---

157 Henderson.

in conjunction with Johnston's army ... advance upon Harrisonburg, the capital of Pennsylvania ... and from there continue the advance, ... upon Philadelphia."[158] His active strategy found no favour amid the do-nothing unreality of the Confederate hierarchy. How frustrating this must have been to the man of Jackson's ability and comprehension of war. To be compelled to fritter away time – to an 'Alexander' of war that most valuable of allies – whilst just across the river, the Federal war machine was being made ever more effective and powerful. Jackson would have been frustrated, not only from the overall failure to go on the offensive. In the course of corresponding with Colonel Alexander R. Boteler, representative from the Winchester District in the Confederate Congress, Jackson posed a question as postscript to one letter, saying, *"I do not understand why it is, that when I ask for an officer whose services are much needed and go so far as to name the person to be commissioned, that it is not <u>done at once.</u> The enemy are active and industrious. We must be so too if we are to expect success."* Davis endorsed the foot of the letter in pencil. *"To appoint an officer, after the person has been selected, requires a nomination and confirmation, and therefore cannot be <u>done at once. J.D."</u>*[159] Reading the endorsement would not have shaken the rock-like Jackson belief in Divine Providence; but it may have caused the reflection that wars are not won with such diffuse priorities, a continuing commitment to peace-time bureaucracy, and by a failure to understand the total commitment that victory exacts. On first meeting President Davis, General Jackson was said not to have proffered a companionable handshake; but simply to have stood to attention and saluted. An example both of Jackson's strict, formal views on hierarchy, as well as his strongly held belief that it is the leaders that have the potential to fail a cause, not the loyal rank and file. In much the same way, he would not attend a church service conducted by a divorced priest, or patronise a store owned by a trader of proven

---

158 Ibid.
159 Letter to *Hon. A.R. Boteler* from *Winchester, March 3rd, 1862* (Douglas).

dishonesty. Davis was said to have adversely criticised Jackson's campaign in the Valley, which, if true, probably makes him the only person ever to have done so, either north or south of the Potomac; then or thereafter!

By early December 1861, recruiting and basic training in the Winchester area, had produced three Militia brigades of one thousand men each.[160] The Valley Command now included Jackson's old First Brigade, referred to as the Stonewall Brigade; but not formally designated as such until after his death, and, as a result of his request that he should be joined by General Loring's Army of the North-West, one brigade had already reached him. The remaining two brigades, together with Loring himself – who was to be subordinate to Jackson, whilst commanding his own units – would arrive by Christmas. At that point Jackson could count on some eleven thousand, all arms. Meanwhile, he needed to temper the largely untried and slender instrument he was forging; to blood new recruits; to begin fostering a belief in victory – already part of the fabric of the Stonewall Brigade – and to instil the habit of hard, fast marching, which is so much more important for an individual than brute strength. In addition, he needed to put something of a dent in the complacent confidence of an enemy, well on the way to believing that only they called the shots. Although he would not have the means for heavy blows until Loring joined him, Jackson wasted no time in taking the offensive with unsettling, nuisance raids against Federal supply lines. For the past two weeks or so, Ashby's cavalry had been active along the river line west of Harper's Ferry, and on the afternoon of the sixth of December, a force of militia, with a battery of guns in support, arrived in the area of Dam Number Five, after marching the thirty-seven miles from Winchester. The infantry immediately began exchanging fire with enemy positions across the river. The objective was to obstruct maintenance work on the

---

160 Allan.

Baltimore and Ohio railroad – the track at this point running on the south, Virginia, side of the river – and to damage Number Five in the dam system, which supplied the Chesapeake and Ohio canal, here running along the north bank of the river. Attempts to break the wood framework of the dam, after dark on the seventh, *"effected little or no damage."*[161] The raiding party withdrew the next day. On the Sixteenth, leading a stronger force comprising cavalry, militia, and the Stonewall Brigade, Jackson returned to the river, which he neared at Falling Waters. Dam Number Five was some six miles upstream to his left. Williamsport, also upstream to his left, distant some five miles, was just three miles from Number five. Downstream to his right was Dam Number four, distant some five miles. (All distances being direct, rather than as rivers wriggle). Decoy parties were sent as feints against Williamsport and Dam Four, maintaining his flank guard out to the northwest, he moved against Number Five, keeping his main body on the high ground overlooking the river, from where the enemy on the far bank was subjected to constant small arms and artillery fire. Working parties were sent down to try and break the structure of the Dam from the Virginia bank. They too suffered a constant sniping fire and little, at first, was achieved *"until Capt. Holliday, of the Thirty-Third Virginia and Capt. Robinson, of the Twenty-Seventh Virginia, volunteered to go down by night with their companies, and cut out the cribs ...* (forming the wooden framework of the dam). *Standing waist-deep in the cold water, and under constant fire of the enemy ... a partial breach was effected, and the cribs so loosened that the next freshet made a wide gap in the dam, and rendered useless, for the time, a long stretch of the canal."*[162] Jackson's constant seeking after intelligence of enemy intentions and movements, by means of his cavalry, local people, or prisoners, enabled him to get wind of the fact that three regiments of infantry, a company of the

---

161 Ibid.
162 Allan.

Fourth United States artillery and two companies of Maryland cavalry were on their way to support the two regiments opposing his dam-busting efforts, and *"Having done all the damage he could to the canal from the south side, he withdrew on the Twenty-First, and returned to Winchester."*[163]

12/4. "Threatening Serious Consequences"

....

*"Through the blessing of God
I regard this district as essentially
in our possession."*
Stonewall Jackson

....

IN the first year of the Civil War, winter campaigning had not become, what Henry Kyd Douglas termed a *"common amusement."* and for considering a strike at Romney early in the new year, Jackson was considered *"mad,"* and was much criticised by ordinary people, the press, and fellow officers. Nonetheless, after Loring reached him on the twenty sixth of December, he forged ahead to complete preparations by the end of the month. The weather between Christmas and New Year was comparatively mild, and Jackson was determined upon action to clear the Federals from that part of the country in his care; which is bordered by the Blue Ridge and the Alleghenies – to the east and the west, respectively – and by the Potomac to the north. He would continue to interdict Federal supply lines when and where possible. Above all,

---

163 Ibid.

Stonewall Jackson would not lie idle and allow the enemy free rein. To seize the initiative, and usually in ways totally unforeseen by the opposition, was ever a characteristic of his vigorous generalship. On the first of January, the Column, comprising some ten thousand infantry, six hundred and forty-eight cavalry and twenty-six guns – both rifled and smooth-bore, departed Winchester. Opposing them were sixteen-thousand Federals guarding the line of the Potomac, under General Nathaniel Banks, whose headquarters, as commander of McClellan's Fifth Corps, was at Frederic in Maryland. In the 'Department of Virginia' itself were twenty-two thousand Federals, whom their commander, General Rosecrans, was concentrating on the Baltimore and Ohio railroad, whilst maintaining the five thousand at Romney under General Kelly, with whom he was planning to *"suddenly seize, fortify, and hold Winchester, whereby I should at once more effectually cover the north-eastern and central parts of Western Virginia, (while) at the same time threatening the left of the enemy's position at Manassas."*[164] i.e. Johnston's District and Beauregard's Army of Northern Virginia. Rosecrans had ridden to discuss his designs on Winchester with the Federal Army Commander; but McClellan had contracted typhoid fever, and before they could meet *"Stonewall Jackson, with a column of ten thousand men, began an advance in the direction of Cumberland, which threatened such serious consequences that … I was obliged to return to Wheeling."*[165] General Lander, to whom Rosecrans had been ordered to turn-over his troops, equipment and supplies, would also tell the Committee on the Conduct of the War *"… I would engage to penetrate the Blue Ridge mountains, and endeavour to take the town of Winchester."* So, even if Federal commanders were not aware of his precise intentions, by activity alone, Jackson was forcing them to scale back their freewheeling designs, and surrender the initiative, something which a passive stance could never have achieved.

---

164 Allan quoting *"Report on Conduct of the War"*, *1865* (Rosecrans's campaigns).

165 Ibid.

Ideally, Jackson would have wished for a second week of the *"bright and unusually mild"* weather; but on the very first evening, the weather broke. With the onset of darkness, a violent storm of sleet and snow swept across the Valley and over the forested ridges of Little North Mountain. It would remain appropriately foul for the time of year, throughout the next three weeks.

The storm continued the next day. Douglas recalled that night as *"the most dismal and trying night of this terrible expedition. It ... was still snowing lightly ... a squad of soldiers in the Stonewall Brigade had built a large fire ... some were lying about it wrapped up in their thin and inadequate blankets. The sharp wind was blowing over the hills and through the trees with a mocking whistle, whirling the sparks and smoke in eyes and over prostrate bodies. ... The small army was in uncomfortable bivouac,"*[166] scattered amongst the exposed fences and hedgerows surrounding Unger's Store, and many, doubtless, lying face down to counter an empty stomach. They had covered twenty miles in two days, since leaving Winchester, but during the second day, the supply wagons had failed to keep pace with the plodding columns on the tortuous, but more secretive, mountain back-roads, rendered ever more greasy by slush and freezing sleet. When the wagons caught up the next morning, Jackson allowed a short time for cooking and eating, before they trudged the next thirteen miles through Sleepy Creek Valley and crossed the final ridges to Bath. A Federal patrol was engaged in the course of the afternoon, and a few men captured. As darkness approached, Jackson halted for the night, four miles short of the town. Next morning, a diversionary force swung away to the left of the line of advance, to come in on Bath from the west, whilst the main body, with a regiment thrown out to either flank, closed in from the south. It was slow going in the icy conditions. Continuous exposure to the freezing weather was sapping the resilience of the men, and the short winter afternoon was well advanced before Colonel Baylor, Jackson's Inspector-General, led a final rush,

---

166 Douglas.

and the defenders abandoned Bath, after having exchanged fire for several hours.

Across the river in Hancock, reinforcements were being hastily organised. However, the local, overall, Federal Commander, Colonel Murray of the Eighty Fourth Pennsylvania, decided that the reinforcements would be insufficient, and withdrew his men back across the river. *"Finding the enemy gone, Jackson ordered an immediate pursuit. ... the main body ... pushed on towards Hancock, driving the retreating enemy over the river."*[167] A brigade headed east in pursuit of the retreating Federals; but was checked by a few men holding a narrow defile. *"After dark, the Federals retreated over the river."* After a stiff fight the next morning, the Confederate Third Arkansas and the Thirty-Seventh Virginia, with a pair of guns, demolished the railroad station and the rail bridge over the Great Cacapon River – six miles west of Bath – and ripped-out the telegraph installation.

Jackson, with the bulk of his force, spent the night opposite Hancock, on the Virginia side of the river, and the next morning, Colonel Ashby was sent to demand the surrender of the town, and *"in the event of refusal, to give notice that two hours would be allowed for the removal of non-combatants, before the Confederate batteries would open fire."* General Lander, with the Federal reinforcements, had just reached Hancock, and reckoning that he could speedily be further reinforced, refused to comply. Jackson, *"placed several pieces of artillery in position, and kept up a brisk cannonade during the remainder of the day."*[168] The bombardment was continued as soon as the gunners had enough light the next morning. On a night following, Douglas was on picket duty *"in the direction of Hancock ... to guard against any curiosity of the Yankee cavalry ... It was cloudy but not cold for the season,"* he recalled, *"in the middle of the night, I felt moisture on my face, and covering myself from head to foot in a blanket, I slept soundly. In the early light, I awoke and found myself oppressed*

167 Allan.
168 Ibid.

with heat. Rising up ... I scattered ... perhaps five inches of snow that had fallen on me. The scene ... was a weird one. Great logs of men lying in all directions, covered with snow and quiet as graves. Now and then, one would break out and look about him with amazement. ... After that night I knew what the Bible means when it speaks of snow as wool. – I often wished we could make durable blankets out of it. ..." That morning, Douglas breakfasted on a piece of beef spitted on the point of his sword and roasted over a campfire, plus *"hard tack, a tin cup of coffee, and dessert, furnished by a Sutler's wagon, captured by the cavalry. It consisted of a can of peaches into which I poured a small can of condensed milk and stirred it up with the point of my useful sword. ... this in January, and furnished by the enemy, too!"* At the same time, Jackson was exploring the possibility of bridging the Potomac a short distance upstream, to advance into Maryland; but deciding that Lander could be reinforced before a bridge could be completed, he broke camp and headed west for *"Romney, the head of his column reaching Unger's Store the same evening."*

On the day that Jackson's men left the Potomac area, a strong Federal detachment comprising elements of six infantry regiments, five cavalry squadrons and six guns – some two thousand men in all, – successfully routed a Confederate militia outpost at Hanging Rock pass, situated roughly halfway between Romney and Winchester, and some fifteen miles southwest of the position Jackson had reached at Unger's Store. The detachment commander, Colonel Dunning, moved fast and effectively, surprising the Confederate pickets, and seizing the tactical high ground, ahead of the militia, whom they volleyed and scattered. Dunning *"burnt their huts, captured two pieces of artillery (one a four-pounder rifled piece, the other a four-pounder smooth-bore) ... As soon as they had accomplished this and burnt the buildings of Colonel Charles Blue, nearby, and killed his livestock, leaving it on the ground, they returned to Romney."*[169]

---

169 Jackson's report to General Johnson dated: Unger's Store, January 11, 1862 (Allan).

A small, insignificant incident; but one which illustrates two very different approaches to the conduct of war itself, and of this internecine war in particular. Dunning wrote in his report *"seven prisoners were taken, and seven dead found."* he personally ordered the destruction of Colonel Blue's property and livestock and adds *"I am sorry to say that some straggling soldiers burnt other unoccupied houses on their return march."*[170] A tacit admission, either of the commander's inability to control his men, or a sham apology for his own connivance. Either way a fraudulent stance for a commander. One of which Sherman was the arch-exponent of, on his campaign in Georgia and South Carolina. In this first, small example of the war being taken beyond the uniformed line, and into the homes and hearths; stables and barns. Dunning was, in this also, the precursor of a form of warfare of which, to a far greater degree, Sherman was the evillest offender – or most capable exponent – in the 1864-'65 war, depending on where you stand with the antinomian processes of war. It was a way of waging war for which President Davis dubbed him *"the Attila of the American continent,"* and looking less far back in history, puts Sherman on a par with the Mongol hordes, and the scouring leaders of Europe's Thirty Years War. Napoleonic-style warfare, certainly in Spain, exacted a similar savagery. Looking forward from his own time, however, is to make Sherman the forerunner of several generals who prosecuted war around the world, throughout the Twentieth Century. If we project on into the Twenty-First Century, he would be more likely to be awarded the dock in a war crimes tribunal than a statue in Washington bearing *"the noble words he once uttered:* 'The legitimate object of war is a more perfect peace.' *Yet, apparently, he could not see that plunder and arson are not legitimate means to attain it,* ... and then, the most important end-consideration on the issue of how war should be fought ... *Unfortunately, the ruthlessness he relied on was carried into the peace which*

---

170 Allan quoting *Federal official reports, Adjutant-General's office.*

followed the war."[171] At least the 'American Attila' finally found conscience enough, to draw the line at running for president.

Stonewall Jackson had been dead for a year or more before Sherman 'marched through Georgia', but his feelings regarding the Dunning incident are unequivocally clear. *"I do not feel at liberty to close this report without alluding to the conduct of the reprobate Federal commanders, who, in Hampshire county, have not only burned valuable mill property, but also many private houses. The track from Romney to Hanging Rock, a distance of fifteen miles, was one of desolation. The number of dead animals lying along the roadside, where they had been shot by the enemy, exemplified the spirit of that part of the Northern Army."*[172] Like the truly great leaders of every era, up to and including the Twentieth Century, Jackson was not savage or barbarous in directing the sword. He, like them, reserved the ruthless element in the genius – without which a resolution to conflict cannot be achieved – for the armed opponent. This, he had made clear on saying farewell as Brigade Commander of the Stonewall Brigade, before leaving for Winchester: *"...by your respect for the rights and property of citizens, you have shown that you are soldiers, not only to defend, but able and willing both to defend and protect."* At the time of the Dunning affair, the dual to the death nature of the Civil War was not yet being widely realised, and *"A Northern Correspondent, writing from Romney at the time ...* reported ... *"The burning of dwellings along the road was a piece of vandalism which should be punished with death, not only of the men who did it, but of the officers who countenanced and encouraged it."*[173]

The going under foot, hoof and wheel, forced Jackson to remain at Unger's Store for three days whilst the horses were roughshod, *"for better service on the ice."* Douglas remembered a difficult march from the Potomac *"fearful weather ... sometimes it was impossible for the*

171 Major-General J.F.C. Fuller, *"The Conduct of War 1789–1961"*, University Paperback edition, 1975 & 1977.

172 Jackson's report to Johnston from Unger's Store (Allan).

173 Allan.

men of a regiment to move together over the smooth roads, and limbs were broken, as well as guns and swords, when a dozen soldiers went down at the same time. Horses fell and were killed. Sometimes, a team of four would be struggling on the ice, while the wagon or artillery to which they were attached was pressing upon them, slipping over the glassy surface." Ready to move after three days, he sent out two diversionary columns. "two hundred infantry and twenty-five mounted militia," north to Bath, and "five hundred and forty five infantry for Moorefield", a road and river junction, where the South Fork joined the South Branch of the Potomac, some forty-five miles southwest, and where he had already positioned a small garrison of four hundred infantry. He himself left Unger's with the main body of some eight thousand infantry and three hundred and seventy five cavalry, and within two days, was entering Romney with his advanced guard. The Federals had pulled back to the Baltimore and Ohio railroad, without engaging, and leaving a quantity of stores and equipment to fall into Confederate hands.

12/5. Resignation

....

"A sense of duty brought me into the field, and has thus far kept me. It now appears my duty to return to the Institute, and I hope that you will leave no stone unturned to get me there."

T.J. Jackson, Major-General

....

"THOUGH the enemy have retreated to the Potomac," Jackson told the Secretary of War, *"yet they continue in possession of the frontiers of this district. ... On last Friday night I designed moving rapidly, with*

my old brigade and one of Loring's, for the purpose of destroying one of the railroad bridges across the North Branch of the Potomac, … thus cutting off their supplies from the west, and consequently forcing them to reduce their army in front of me; but as General Loring's leading brigade, commanded by Colonel Taliaferro, was not in a condition to move, the enterprise had to be abandoned."[174] The conditions had so reduced the fitness of Loring's command, that Jackson was forced to suspend all further offensive action, and disperse the units into winter quarters.

Rarely, if ever, can those towards the bottom of the command chain fully appreciate the intentions of their commander, especially in the case of so security minded a general as Stonewall Jackson, who was renowned for keeping even his subordinate generals in the dark; a reticence not always appreciated.

Junior Lieutenant Douglas was not overly impressed by what their privations had achieved. *"Some stores and a few prisoners were taken, but the fruits of the expedition did not compensate for the sickness and suffering in our army."* The strategic reality was that *"In two weeks, and with trifling loss, he had placed the troops opposed to him, while preparing for an aggressive movement, upon the defensive; had expelled them virtually from his whole district; had liberated three counties from their rule and secured the supplies in them for the subsistence of his own troops."*[175]

Jackson quartered Loring and his three brigades around Romney where, in the fertile south Branch Valley, they could be well supplied. A militia brigade was sent southwest to Moorfield, and two others northeast to Bath and Martinsburg. Ashby and the cavalry patrolled the Potomac. The Stonewall Brigade, Jackson took with him to Winchester. He needed his most effective unit to face the potentially heaviest threat – from Maryland, south through Harper's Ferry – and to be poised to concentrate in the event of a lesser attack against Loring or the militia brigades. His dispositions

---

174 Letter to *Secretary of War, Hon. J.P. Benjamin, dated January 20, 1862* (Allan).

175 Allan.

complete, Jackson rode back to Winchester, which he reached well before both his staff and the tramping brigade, thanks to the powers of endurance of the *'Little Sorrel,'* and his childhood knack of continuous rhythmic tapping on the neck of his mount, to keep its stride at full reach. Jackson had obtained his most celebrated war-horse when he impounded the Baltimore and Ohio Company's rolling stock, whilst in command at Harper's Ferry. The horse *"was one of a dozen taken from a train of cars at Harper's Ferry, en-route for Washington. Little Sorrel was a plebeian-looking little beast, not a chestnut; he was stocky and well made, round-barrelled, close coupled, good shoulder, excellent legs and feet, not fourteen hands high, of boundless endurance, good appetite, good but heavy head and neck, a natural pacer with little action and no style. It would have been impossible to have found another horse that would have suited his new owner so exactly. …The endurance of the little animal was marvellous, and the General was apt to forget it was exceptional. He never seemed to change in looks or condition; his gait, except when the yells of the soldiers warmed him into a gallop, was always the same, an amble; he could eat a ton of hay or live on cobs."*[176]

In Winchester, having washed off the mud and grime which clung to skin and clothing after three weeks in the field, Jackson went around to the Graham house, where he and Anna were guests. He had no hesitation in pronouncing the doctor's home *"the very essence of comfort,"* and was, no doubt, looking forward to a few home comforts. Within the week a peaceful interlude was destroyed, and all that had been so sorely won thrown away, by a telegrammed order direct from the Secretary of War, which read: *"Our news indicates that a movement is making to cut off General Loring's command, and order him back to Winchester immediately."* Johnston, the overall commander in Virginia, was not consulted. Jackson responded at once, adjusting the dispositions of his men, and penning a quick reply to Secretary Benjamin *"SIR – Your order, requiring me to direct General Loring to return with his command to*

---

176 Douglas.

Winchester immediately, has been received and promptly complied with. With such interference in my command, I cannot expect to be of much service in the field, and, accordingly, respectfully request to be ordered to report for duty to the Superintendent of the Virginia Military Institute at Lexington. Should this application not be granted, I respectfully request that the President accept my resignation from the army. Respectfully, etc., your obed't servant, T.J. Jackson." The quartering at Romney "was exceedingly distasteful" to Brigadier General Loring, "and he made known his complaints, both personally and through his officers, in a most reprehensible manner."[177] Furloughs were freely dispensed, and Loring's officers visiting Richmond, forming a committee, through which they lobbied the Administration, to the point where the Secretary of War decided on the telegram.

Jackson notified Johnston, his immediate superior, on all that had taken place, including the claim of the Secretary of State to have been "informed the command (Loring's) was in danger of being cut off. Such danger ... he continued ... I am well satisfied, does not exist, nor did it, in my opinion, exist at the time the order was given, and I therefore respectfully recommend that the order be countermanded, and that General Loring be required to return with his command to the neighbourhood of Romney."[178] Despite concurring (to use Allan's word) with Jackson, Johnston, rather typically, avoided the responsibility of implementing the recommendation. He, furthermore, retained the letter of resignation, and himself wrote to his subordinate a letter which, in the main, chose to ignore the point which Jackson was so aptly making, and the important blow he was striking for the effective furtherance of the war by the Confederacy. Beginning "My dear Friend" Johnston included such phrases as: "a due sense of one's own dignity ... care for professional character and official rights ... requires sacrifices from us all ... as great an official wrong to me as the order itself to you, ... this appeal to your patriotism,"[179] This

177 Ibid.
178 Allan.
179 Allan/Henderson.

was all quite irrelevant, even if Johnston did not know that the Secretary's decision was driven by widespread insubordination; a failure to adapt to personal discomfort, and imagined favouring of the Stonewall Brigade. (At Romney, Loring's brigades were in hutted accommodation whilst the Stonewall Brigade was under canvas outside Winchester). Jackson was not about to compromise on the point he was making. *"Sacrifices! he exclaimed; have I not made them? What is my life here but a daily sacrifice? Nor shall I ever withhold sacrifices for my country, where they will avail anything. I intend to serve here, anywhere, in any way I can, even if it be as a private soldier. But if this method of making war is to prevail, the country is ruined. My duty to Virginia requires that I shall utter my protest against it in the most energetic form in my power, and that is to resign. The authorities at Richmond must be taught a lesson, or the next victims of their meddling will be Johnston and Lee."*[180]

That the men of the Stonewall Brigade were able to absorb the harsh, January campaign, and come through with reputation and fighting capability unimpaired, whilst Loring and his men were completely broken down by it, was due to several factors unconnected with corrosive weather and the rugged going under-foot. Jackson had been tireless in helping up and down the line throughout the march, literally 'putting shoulder to the wheel,' in aid of gun or wagon floundering amid the slush and ice. But with him it was all on … on … on; relentless. No obstacle which could not be overcome – in itself an important lesson for men in war, and one which, probably, he was intent on teaching. He was sparing with encouragement, except by example. Lycurgus with his unflinching endurance of hardship; obedience to authority, and victory or death in battle, would have recognised a kindred spirit in Stonewall Jackson, and the Spartan Ephors would surely have sacrificed bulls to the god *Ares* for Jackson the General. For the Brigade it was simply the way of the man and the leader. Garnet had so far proved a sound brigade commander, of whom

---

180 Henderson.

the men were proud and willing to follow; but – for the original majority still – Jackson was their general, from the training days at Harper's Ferry to the firing line at Manassas. Many of the rank and file would have become imbued with something of his absolute determination to overcome; be it against the enemy or the environment. They knew of his attention to their wants and needs, both out of action and off the line of march. They knew his worth. They knew too that their reputation as a fighting unit was founded on his skill as a general. After Romney, Jackson wrote of the Brigade, *"I am well assured, that had an order been issued for its march, even through the depth of winter and in any direction, it would have sustained its reputation. The alacrity with which it responded to the call of duty and overcame obstacles showed that it was still animated by the same spirit that characterised it at Manassas."[181]*

Loring's untried soldiers, on the other hand, saw only the unfamiliar, heartless taskmaster, who brought a harshness to their lives and was seemingly oblivious to all suffering. The pitiless overseer cracking the whip, regardless of life or limb, in the stern cause of duty and country. For Loring himself, it was a continuous, conscious-pricking lesson on what might have been achieved with 'his' men, by a younger man who had been his junior in the old United States Army. Seemingly he was not enough of a man, and a disciplined trained soldier, to enter into the spirit of Jackson as leader, even for the cause of duty and country.

Jackson summed-up the whole affair in a succinct and straightforward letter to *"His Excellency John Letcher, Gov. of Va."* beginning *"Governor: This morning I received an order from the Secretary of War to order General Loring and his command to fall back from Romney to this place immediately. The order was promptly complied with; but as the order was given without consulting me, and is abandoning to the enemy what has cost much preparation, expense and exposure to secure, and is in direct conflict with my military plans, and implies a want of confidence in my capacity to judge when General Loring's troops should fall*

---

181 Henderson.

back, and is an attempt to control military operations in detail from the Secretary's desk at a distance, I have requested to be ordered back to the Institute, and if this is denied me, then to have my resignation accepted. I ask as a special favour that you will have me ordered back to the Institute.

"As a single order like that of the Secretary may destroy the entire fruits of a campaign, I cannot reasonably expect, if my operations are thus to be interfered with, to be of much service in the field. A sense of duty brought me into the field and has thus far kept me. It now appears my duty to return to the Institute, and I hope that you will leave no stone unturned to get me there. If I have ever acquired, through the blessing of Providence, any influence over troops, this undoing of my work by the Secretary may greatly diminish that influence.

"I regard this recent expedition as a great success. Before our troops left here on the First instant, there was not, as far as I have been able to ascertain, a single loyal man in Morgan county who could remain at home in safety. In four days, that county was entirely evacuated by the enemy. Romney and the most valuable portion of Hampshire county was recovered without firing a gun, and before we had even entered the county.

"I desire to say nothing against the Secretary of War. I take it for granted that he has done what he believed to be best, but I regard such a policy as ruinous. Very truly, your friend, T.J. Jackson."[182]

When the Federals moved back into areas closed to them by the Jackson initiative, he was blunt and uncompromising in putting his views to the Honourable Alexander Boteler; Representative from the Winchester District in the Confederate Congress, and also colonel, and part-time volunteer aide-de-camp[183] on his staff –
"An official despatch received this morning informs me that the enemy are in possession of Moorefield. Such is the fruit of evacuating Romney. Genl. Loring should be cashiered for his course."[184]

182 Letter from *Winchester, January 31, 1862* (Allan).

183 Douglas.

184 Letter from *Winchester, February 12, 1862* (Douglas).

12/6. Fleeting Happiness

....

"We spent as happy a winter
as ever falls to the lot of
mortals upon earth."[185]
Anna Jackson

....

THE general public, as well as the prominent in Virginia, wrote supporting Jackson, and so were against his resigning, and against Benjamin. The General himself refused to criticise the Secretary – *"I take it for granted that he has done what he believes to be best"*. Neither would he allow the least criticism of the Secretary in his presence. Quite unperturbed, the General went about the duties of command, and enjoyed his personal and married life to the full. For him, the matter was in the hands of an omnipotent and benign Providence, which could be implicitly relied upon for the best outcome.

Governor Letcher, meeting with the Secretary and the Confederate Government received an assurance that the principle and practise of political meddling in field operations would cease. He therefore withdrew the resignation, with Jackson's concurrence. It was not a question of a victory for the military over the politicians; but a most valuable contribution to the way in which the war should be conducted, and a point which took considerable moral courage to make, so whole heartedly, from Jackson's position in the command structure. It was a lesson which the North had as great a need of at that time – and, given the personalities concerned, would have, probably, been put to better use – than did the South. Lincoln finally came to the realisation for himself; but not until 1864, when he handed complete operational control to Grant. Davis, on the other hand, reneged

---

185 Henderson quoting Mrs. Jackson.

within a year, and as Henderson has it *"once more assumed supreme control, retaining it until it was too late to stave off ruin."*

Jackson's frame of mind throughout the affair, was of a piece with his views on the threat of dissolution, as expressed to a clerical friend two years earlier. *"Why should Christians be disturbed about the dissolution of the Union? It can only come about by God's permission and will only be permitted if for his people's good. I cannot see why we should be distressed about such things, whatever be their consequence."*[186] Anyone expressing gloomy forebodings on either issue, in the glebe house at Winchester that February of 1862, would have been told by the guest-General *"Ah, now that is not the way to be happy."* Whilst both General and Parson enjoyed serious philosophical discussion – religious and lay – and the learned tomes on Dr Graham's well-filled library shelves were often referred to, the vicarage constantly rang to the sound of childish laughter, and was filled with eager young men in uniform, attracted to flashing eyes and warm, feminine smiles. The image of a light-hearted general, at large about the house, actively involved in child-inspired creation, is to visualize an aspect of enthusiasm driving greatness. So too, the image of the tall, strongly-built, uniformed figure, bounding down the stairs, urged on by his own happy laughter, mingling with the excited squeaks and squeals of the infant clamped around his shoulders. Images reminiscent of another instinctive master of the Art of War, the then Captain, Horatio Nelson, of His Majesty's Ship *Boreas* lying off Nevis, a little over half a Century earlier. On the youthful commanding officer having paid an unsociably early morning call on the Governor of Nevis; not an early riser, unlike both the future Admiral and the Confederate General – the Governor later remarked, *"Good God! If I did not find that great little man ... playing in the next room, under the dining-table, with Mrs Nisbet's child."*[187]

---

186 Henderson.
187 Carola Oman, *"Nelson"* Hodder and Stoughton Limited, London, June 1947.

Despite his complete control over his ability to relax, the truth is that the war was never far away for the commander of the Army of the Valley. Throughout the weeks of winter, Jackson kept himself constantly and comprehensively informed by various means, such as; Ashby's roving light cavalry and locals from villages and farms, on both sides of the Potomac, in Virginia and Maryland, an unwary Union soldier plucked from picket duty, or complacent, unsuspecting sutler, pounced upon in the half-light of dawn, by cavalry troopers, as active as their general. Conferring on the up-to-the-minute situation, on one occasion he told Johnston, *"I'll see what can be had from the Catholic fathers in Martinsburg"*. (twenty-one miles due north of Winchester on the Valley Turnpike). As winter loosened his grip, Virginia's tracks and trails began to dissolve from stark, iron-bound ribbons of ice, into bloated puddles of mud; impractical for use by horse-drawn wagons and gun limbers. In the wet transition towards Spring, the Potomac, achieved her highest level for twenty years, and together, mud and river delayed the renewal of hostilities.

12/7. Preliminary Evolutions

"A kind Providence may enable us to inflict a terrible wound and effect a safe retreat in the event of having to fall back."

Jackson to Johnston

THE sodden countryside dried out as February progressed, and by the end of the month, both sides were stirring. Johnston attempted no positive initiatives, simply reacting to the potential threat posed by the number of armed men gathering around Washington. Their number would reach two hundred and forty thousand by mid-March. He recoiled behind the Rappahannock, abandoning the ground he had allowed his army to sit idle upon since the previous summer. With the river in front of him, he apparently believed his never more than fifty thousand could block any one of three route options, which, if they could agree, Lincoln and McClellan might select, for advancing against Richmond. It is doubtful if the Federals had felt under any real pressure from Johnston's prolonged inability to show the slightest spark of aggression. By leaving what had effectively become his fortified prison, with never the merest glimmer of a hostile gesture, Johnston handed the Federal high command carte blanche to pursue the war's end in their own way.

Lincoln ordered McClellan, *"to advance with all the disposable force of the Army of the Potomac, after providing safely for the defence of Washington."*[188] That the proviso clause was fundamental to the Yankee President's thinking, few fully understood. Crucially, Stonewall Jackson was one of the few. McClellan ordered General Banks, at Frederick, Maryland, to advance the remainder of his fifth Corps forward into Virginia. A bridge of boats was constructed at Harper's Ferry, and by the end of the first week in March, the invasion was complete. Banks re-established his headquarters at Charlestown, with his three Divisions, numbering thirty-eight thousand – say thirty-thousand effective fighting men, after allowing for railway guard duties – poised to swarm down the northern mouth of the Valley like predatory locusts. Carefully monitoring developments from back down the throat of the Valley at Winchester, just eighteen miles from Charlestown, Jackson cleared for action, sending surplus baggage and the sick down the Valley by train to Staunton, accompanied by Anna Jackson, returning to the home of her parents. He stiffened discipline after the weeks in camp, ordering a ban on alcohol. *"Every*

---

188 Allan.

wagon that came into camp should be searched, and if any liquor was found, it was to be spilled out, and the wagon and horses turned over to the quartermaster."[189]

To oppose Banks and his three Divisions, Jackson had four thousand two hundred and ninety seven infantry soldiers, six hundred and one cavalrymen, and three hundred and sixty–nine gunners; a total of five thousand two hundred and sixty seven.[190] Allowing for the sick and those on leave – although he had by now stopped the practise of furloughs, which had recently been liberally given as inducements to Volunteers, to sign–on for the duration – the Army of the Valley totalled at most four thousand six hundred all ranks, organised into three brigades, and all made up of Virginia Regiments, apart from General Burke's Second Brigade, where the men of the First Regiment were Irish regular soldiers. Banks informed McClellan that: *"the enemy is weak, demoralised, and depressed"[191];* but the Corps Commander was a Lincoln political appointee, with no experience of either soldiering or war. An intelligent and successful civilian, Banks had been a youthful Governor of Massachusetts and Speaker of the House of Representatives; but he was no student of war. For their commander, on the other hand, the Valley Army few were, *"in fine spirits."*

Jackson had been instructed by Johnston, *"to endeavour to employ the invaders in the Valley, but without exposing himself to the danger of defeat, by keeping so near the enemy as to prevent him from making any considerable detachment to reinforce McClellan; but not so near that he might be compelled to fight."[192]* This was a broad-brush, uninspired and uninspiring directive, indicative of an originator blind to the demands of initiative, wary of moral responsibility,

---

189 Allan quoting the *"Diary"* of Major Jed. Hotchkiss, Jackson's Topographical Engineer officer.

190 Johnston's field return of February 28, 1862 (Allan).

191 Henderson.

192 Allan.

and primarily intent on avoiding the risk upon which success in war depends.

Fortunately for the Confederate cause, the recipient was altogether different, and well able to demonstrate how much can be achieved by the ability and vigour of a single individual. One who *"never took counsel of his fears ... and who set out to ... inflict a terrible wound,"* whilst being very much alive to the risks involved, and fully understanding that 'not to try is a greater risk than to fail.' Jackson already had the measure of the man in the White House, fearful for his capital, together with his political general, such in name only, unfamiliar with the application of initiative in wartime, and without any true understanding of who and what he was up against. When the well-equipped, well turned-out might of the Fifth Corps advanced into the throat of the Valley, intent on the strategically important communications hub of Winchester, Jackson's lightly accoutred and home-spun clad locals 'retreated,' straight at the approaching horde, and drew-out in line of battle. Banks, his plodding reconnoitring patrols largely unable to penetrate Ashby's lively cavalry screen, hesitated. Suddenly, the politically successful commander was less sure about the military *'weakness'* he had ascribed to his opponent from the cosy security of a desk, and pulled-back to Charlestown, thence to insinuate his way forward once more. When the Federal left reached Berryville, just ten miles east of Winchester – and so within striking distance of his rear – Jackson once more deployed for battle north of the town; but although the centre column of the Fifth Corps got to within four miles of his position, Banks declined to engage. Having remained in position all day, Jackson packed-up towards evening and, reluctantly, left Winchester, to suffer the first of many changes of occupation, which led to the town being dubbed the *'bandy ball,'* during the War. If Jackson permitted himself a smile at the paralysing effect of his return to the initiative – which he had first flaunted to effect in January – it would have passed unnoticed amid the luxuriant whiskers, and remained undetected in the eyes, masked by the peak of the weather-stained campaign cap pulled low on the forehead. His general intention was to make active manoeuvre do the job of numbers, and to fight only on his terms. In other words, to grasp and hold the initiative. Wherever he could reach for a force he reckoned vulnerable, due to isolation, position, numerical strength or feeble handling, he would aim to surprise and crush it, and he was as ever mindful and aware of overall strategic demand, as he was of the developing situation on his immediate front.

Before giving up Winchester, on that night of gloom for the faithful inhabitants, Jackson contemplated a strike after dark, on the hesitant advance. A *"signal victory"* was to be won, he believed, *"by the vigorous use of the bayonet, and the blessing of divine Providence."* A hastily called council of war disagreed, and the regiments were no longer immediately to hand. Looking back at the town as he left, Jackson *"awed"* his medical director, Surgeon Hunter McGuire, as *"he cried out in a tone almost savage: 'That is the last council of war I will ever hold'."*[193] Jackson had experienced the hard way, Napoleon's observation that *"Councils of War … terminate in the adoption of the worst course, which in war, is always the most timid, or, if you will, the most prudent. The only true wisdom in a general is determined courage."*[194]

Ashby, as ever, covered the withdrawal, and catching up with the baggage trains at Kernstown, Jackson moved on to Strasburg – twenty miles back along the Valley Turnpike. When the Federal brigade under General Shields approached just over a week later, Jackson moved further on along the Valley to Woodstock and Mount Jackson; in all a total of twenty-three miles from Strasburg. Here, he had the towering might of the Massanutton at his back. His position could not be turned; but he could watch or move north or south, up or down the Valley, or he could move swiftly east to reinforce Johnston before Richmond, in the best practice

---

193 Henderson.

194 *"The Military Maxims of Napoleon"*, George C. D'Aguilar and David G. Chandler, De Capo Press edition, 1995.

of what was, in one sense, a detached force. If Banks chose to advance along the South Fork of the Shenandoah, he was also well placed to threaten the Federal rearward communications, as soon as they emerged from behind the bulk of the mountain range. At the same time, his scouts had to range west towards the Alleghenies, where a third Federal Army was gathering; somewhat piecemeal and still somewhat distended; but nevertheless, bent on striking at the southern end of the Valley, from where it could go on to threaten Richmond, from the opposite direction to McClellan.

13. FIRST STRIKE

....

*"To the little force in the Shenandoah Valley,
flying southward before Shields, he[195] gave
no thought. It would have been nothing short
of miraculous had he even suspected that
4,500, under a professor of the higher
mathematics, might bring to naught the
operations of his gigantic host."*

Henderson[196]

....

IN his anxiety to prod McClellan into action, Lincoln had resorted to Washington's birthday (twenty second of February) as a quaint, somewhat un-military catalyst. Johnston's giving up his Centreville stronghold was more relevant, and McClellan moved as soon as he did so. However, unlike the President, the General did not want to advance frontally on Richmond in Johnston's wake. This was, in part, due to his believing Johnston's army to be more numerous than it was, and part to the problem of supply, based on a single track railroad. McClellan's numerical misconception was founded on an organisational anomaly on a par with political meddling in tactics. His head of intelligence was not a trained and experienced military officer; but a criminal detective! 'Sherlock' detected a hundred and fifteen thousand, in Johnston's Army of Northern Virginia, which was some sixty-five thousand more than its highest ever total of fifty thousand, which at that time it only ever reached, by

---

195 McClellan (Lincoln also).

196 Lieutenant-Colonel G.F.R. Henderson, CB. *"Stonewall Jackson and the American Civil War"*, Longmans, Green, and Co. 39 Paternoster Row, London, 1904.

adding in the men with Jackson in the Valley. McClellan's plan of choice was to ship the Army of the Potomac to the sea-coast of Virginia and come at Richmond from the East. Thereby approaching in rear of Johnston; maybe even turning his right flank. At no time does he seem to have considered actively pinning Johnston frontally, which would have had the dual advantage of helping to allay Lincoln's obsessional fear for the safety of Washington. Although the President, reluctantly, agreed to the plan, and both General and President were agreed that Banks should secure Winchester, a little over a week after his having done so, Banks was ordered to withdraw, and send two Divisions of five Corps eastwards as lookouts against the unlikely event of Johnston coming back through Manassas to threaten Washington. The third Division of the Corps – that of General Shields, which having reached Strasburg was the most advanced – was ordered to retire back along the Valley Turnpike, to cover Harper's Ferry. The Confederate Valley force had been dismissed from the strategic reckoning as being too few soldiers to even consider, in the overall scheme of things.

Ashby had continued to harry the Banks/Shields advance beyond Strasburg; but on the twenty first of March, he reported that the Federals were turning back. Jackson did not hesitate. It was imperative to prevent Banks's legions from providing indirect support for McClellan's ship-borne move against Richmond, although another four days would elapse before the Confederate High Command realised that McClellan was undertaking a combined sea/land operation. At first light on the twenty-second, the Valley Army marched north in the wake of the withdrawing Federals; the brigade of Colonel Fulkerson from its camp at Woodstock, and those of Garnett and Burke from the nearby area of Mount Jackson. By last light, all had covered the twenty-two miles to Strasburg. That same evening, Ashby attacked Federal pickets just a mile from Winchester, and a brigade group, including cavalry and two artillery batteries, was sent out against him. After a brief flurry Ashby withdrew three miles to the *'tiny village'* of Kernstown. He was not followed.

Ever alert to nuances which would enable him to deduce the 'how, when and where', Jackson demanded more from his cavalry than the formal duties of vedette, picket, frontier patrol, and the basic overall observation that the enemy was either advancing or retreating. He sought the apparently insignificant move, the precise disposition, on which to contrive the swift, unexpected hammer-blows unforeseen by either friends or enemy. Those strikes discussed with no-one; explained to no-one and revealed only on impact. Ashby's rough-riding horse masters were from 'ladhood' ideally fitted for the task of Stonewall intelligence gathering, even if a lack of formal discipline made them sometimes unreliable in the set-piece. For them, as for the fighting freemen of ancient Sparta, night was a cloak and not a barrier to movement. That evening, Ashby's troopers penetrated the Federal lines and reported back that only four regiments of infantry remained in Winchester, and that they were under orders to leave for Harper's Ferry the next morning. In the early hours of Sunday, the twenty-third, Jackson sent four regiments on to reinforce Ashby, and himself hurried forward with the main body. By one p.m. his whole force had covered the fourteen miles between Strasburg and Kernstown. Meanwhile, Shields, his arm fractured by a shell fragment in skirmishing with Ashby the previous evening, had sent Colonel Mason of the Fourth Ohio Volunteers, on a morning reconnaissance of his front. By ten a.m. Mason had reported back, correctly, that only Ashby's troopers were in evidence. Shields conferred with his Army Commander, who was still at Winchester, and both agreed that Jackson with so small and unsupported a force, was unlikely to risk an attack. Apparently comfortable with such a casual rationalisation of convenience, Banks promptly rode away. The current Federal strategic scenario required him to report to Washington.

"Though it was very desirable to prevent the enemy leaving the Valley, I deemed it best not to attack until morning," Jackson wrote afterwards, and on reaching Kernstown, he ordered his leg-weary men to bivouac and rest. Without dismounting, and accompanied by two or three of the staff, he rode forward along the

line of the Valley Pike to see for himself. He was within a grasp of Banks's rear-guard; possibly no more than four regiments of infantry. However, the immediate problem was not the usual one facing a commander, considering whether to delay an attack until the following day or not. That is to say, would the enemy be reinforced overnight, or the general situation be changed to disadvantage; but, specifically, whether Banks would continue to withdraw and so elude the grasp that would land a blow sufficiently threatening to daunt the opposing President. *"But then … should such a blow … any blow … be initiated on the Sabbath?"* Jackson noted Ashby falling back towards and beyond Kernstown; both troopers and gunners firing as they came. Ashby's running-fight had not started on the Sabbath; but had been a continuous process. Although the pounding march of the past forty-eight hours had thinned the ranks, the infantry were keen enough to join-in and bloody the invader. Turning to his left, away from the turnpike, Jackson instinctively took in the details of ridges, forest outcrops, post and rail fences crossing rolling fields, some laid to grass; but many ploughed and heavy-going. He paused, observing the Federal gun position on the prominent hill to his front – Pritchard's Hill – and the long, low, forested ridges stretching east to west across his front, beyond which lay Winchester, *"and what else besides?"* If Ashby gave ground much more, the Federals would reach Kernstown, from where they would be able to see across to the bivouac area. He looked away to the west – to his left. *"On the other hand, their right could be forced to change position and be scattered from the high ground facing the positions they have taken up. High ground including a prominent feature well suited to artillery. Some of Ashby's troopers will need to ride across and cover the open flank, and Ashby will have to stem the advance against him."* Jackson turned to those around him *"Tell Colonel Burke to support Ashby and to hold his brigade in readiness."* The staff galloped off in turn, to set an immediate attack in motion. *"Ascertaining that the Federals had a position from which our forces could be seen"*, Jackson continued in his after-action report, *"I concluded that it would be dangerous to postpone the attack until next day"*[197] – duty before scruple.

Guided by a local man from the Fifth Virginia, the Twenty Third and Thirty-Seventh Virginia Regiments of Colonel Fulkerson's Third Brigade led off from the bivouac area, across the open ground bordering a creek which wound its way northeast in the direction of Winchester. They marched obliquely across the front of the Federal position and, as foreseen, were shelled heavily from the Federal guns on Pritchard's Hill. Two guns of Carpenter's battery, in close support, unlimbered and returned fire. The infantry reached the wooded ridges beyond the creek with few casualties. The Stonewall Brigade, starting from further back, marched due west from the bivouac area, and so avoided a shelling from Pritchard's Hill. Turning north, they moved up through the woods to form the centre of Jackson's attack line-up. A gun-line was speedily defined, and when a further two batteries – each of four guns – together with the remaining two guns of Carpenter's Battery came up, such a concentrated fire was opened on the Federals, in conjunction with the Twenty-Seventh and Twenty-First Virginia skirmishing forward on the Confederate right, as *"compelled the withdrawal of a portion of the* (Federal) *force into a more secure position."*[198] The attack was opening as planned.

However, over to the left of the Valley Turnpike, commanding not only his own brigade against Ashby; but the whole division against Jackson, Colonel Kimball, in the absence of the wounded Shields, read the situation with promptness and understanding. Deducing from the heavy volume of fire suddenly threatening to engulf his right flank positions, that in Ashby he was opposing little more than a distraction, Kimball immediately ordered up General Tyler's brigade, positioned in reserve, directly behind the Federal centre, at a crossroads on the Valley

---

197 Henderson quoting O.R.
198 Report of Major R.M. Copeland, assistant adjutant-general to General Banks (Allan).

Turnpike. Tyler responded briskly, his five regiments moving off to their right in column, before deploying into line to meet the in-coming attack. On Jackson's left, Fulkerson's Twenty-Third and Thirty-Seventh regiments had just reached a low, stout stone wall dividing a patch of open ground, when the colours of Tyler's two right wing regiments emerged into the open, advancing towards them. Holding their fire until the two Yankee regiments were close, the Virginians then *"rose and poured a very heavy volley."* Both regiments broke, one, the Hundred and Tenth Pennsylvania Volunteers could not be rallied again that day. *"The rest of the ... Federal ... line soon rallied and maintained a steady fight."*[199] For the next two hours or so, both sets of resolute men doggedly slugged it out to the continuous crackle and growl of musket and cannon.

Jackson's reaction to the realisation that he was opposed by rather more than the four regiment rump of Banks's withdrawing army was to order the Fifth and Forty-Second Virginia forward into his frontline, and to send for his one remaining, inactive, regiment – the Forty-Eight Virginia of Burke's Brigade – in general reserve at the original assembly area on the Valley Turnpike. For the Federals, Colonel Kimball took the second of two timely and determined decisions which suggest that he should be credited with being the architect of such success, as his side gained from the battle of Kernstown. He sent three regiments of Sullivan's Brigade, tussling with him against Ashby, and from his own brigade, two complete regiments, together with a further ten companies from two other of his regiments, across the Valley Turnpike to reinforce Tyler, and the right flank. But, in those two hours between three-thirty and the approach of sundown, the most fateful decision of all was taken by the commander of the Stonewall Brigade. It is said in parts of Europe that *"All plans are set at naught if an angel pisses in the touchhole of your musket."* For Jackson, the angel was General Richard B. Garnet, who relieved himself by ordering his brigade

---

199 Ibid.

to withdraw from the struggle. It matters little whether he did so because his nerve failed, or because he wished to save some of his men from death or capture. It was a catastrophically bad decision, which could have only one outcome; the surrender of the battle ground. Its immediate effect was to expose the flanks of those fighting on either side of the Stonewall Brigade, forcing them too to pull back. Once the Yankees began coming forward in their greater numbers, they were finally stopped only by the decision of their own commanders, to discontinue the action at the onset of darkness. This was another piece of flawed generalship, based partly on yet another; the incorrect assumption that Jackson would not have chosen to fight unless reinforcements were close at hand. Garnet's was a piece of bad generalship, on the other hand, because a true outcome of fighting in war can only be obtained by the fighting itself. The general who takes it upon himself to pre-judge the outcome of a fight in which he is engaged, simply on the fact that the other side has superior numbers – or even superior weapons – does not understand how battles are won, and makes, as Garnett all too ineptly demonstrated, for a dangerously unreliable leader. It was said that Stonewall Jackson's relations with his most senior commanders were always brittle, and his experience with Garnett explains why. Whilst wanting to press on, during the winter campaign earlier in the year, Jackson came across his old brigade halted and brewing-up. *"What is the meaning of this"*, he asked Garnett, who said *"It was impossible for the men to go further without cooking their food."* Jackson replied tersely, *"I never found anything impossible with this brigade,"* and rode on. Garnett clearly failed to get the point. For Jackson, the senior commanders were those in a position to ruin his plans, and so not to be trusted. He was always considerate of privates and junior officers, with whose staunch fighting qualities he could engineer success. Rather like Wellington, just days before Waterloo, pointing out *'that article'* – an English, red-coated private – as being the key to victory, and, on being asked if any of Bonaparte's marshals had come over to the allied side, replying they would have been *'no use,'* had they done so.

In the event, and disregarding both the approach of night, and the knowledge that Jackson had ordered up reinforcements, Garnett began the tricky manoeuvre of disengaging from a numerically stronger enemy, and in the process, leaving the flank of Fulkerson's brigade un-covered, forcing him to abandon his secure entrenched position lining the stone wall. On meeting the Fifth Virginia moving up, Garnett ordered them back; but, arriving at the scene, Jackson countermanded the order. Henderson has it that, *"seizing a drummer by the shoulder, he dragged him to a rise of ground, in full view of the troops, and bade him in curt, quick tones, to 'Beat the rally!' The drum rolled at his order, and with his hand on the frightened boy's shoulder, amidst a storm of balls, he tried to check the flight of his defeated troops."*! 'Retreating' would be a more accurate term than 'defeated'; but certainly, he ordered the Fifth to establish a line on some nearby trees, and for the retreating troops to form on them. The Forty-Second was coming up. *"many of the brave Virginians lingered in rear of their retreating comrades, loading as they slowly retired, and rallying in squads in every ravine and behind every hill – or hiding singly among the trees."*[200] If many thoughts were on getting clear, Jackson was still bent on victory. *"... covered by a stone wall and thick timber, the two small regiments, encouraged by the presence of their commander, held stoutly to their ground. The attack was pressed with reckless gallantry. In front of the Fifth Virginia the colours of the Fifth Ohio changed hands no less than six times, and one of them was pierced by eight-and-forty bullets. The Eighty-Fourth Pennsylvania was twice repulsed and twice rallied, but on the fall of its colonel retreated in confusion. The left of the Fourteenth Indiana broke ..."*[201] But the Confederate line had been irrevocably fractured, and superior numbers were able to flank the small, two regiment defences. *"Inch by inch"* they were forced to give ground. Halting on their colours, a short distance back, the Fifth reformed once again, and

---

200 Colonel E.H.C. Cavins, Fourteenth Indiana; *"Battles and Leaders of the Civil War"* (quoted by Henderson).
201 Ibid.

the flashes at their musket muzzles glowed ever-more clearly as the evening darkened, and they parried yet another determined assault. Finally, this small rearguard lined-up in a narrow lane behind a stone hedge. Cavalry appeared a short way off to their left rear; but by now it was too dark to charge over the rough ground. Ashby's Major Funston came up with his detachment of troopers, and no shots were exchanged. The Federal infantry halted at the nearby tree-line, and the Fifth was able to follow the rest of the exhausted army back down Stone Lane, and on the mile and a quarter to Bartonsville on the Valley Turnpike.

13/1. Aftermath

....

"I feel justified in saying that, though the battlefield is in possession of the enemy, yet the most essential fruits of the victory are ours."[202]

T.J. Jackson, Major-General

....

BEFORE allowing those fortunate enough to have escaped incapacitating injury to begin moving back to Newtown and the supply train park, Jackson ordered his Medical Director, Surgeon Hunter McGuire, to get wagons for all the wounded and send them back first. He met with Ashby, instructing him to hold a position along Opequon Creek, where it crossed the Valley Pike immediately south of Bartonsville. Thereafter he was to continue

---

202 After battle report – Kernstown (quoted by Henderson)

his customary role of harassment and intelligence gathering, and to *"advise me immediately they start to move."*

Later, after crossing the Creek, Jackson dismounted at a cavalry campfire where some of Ashby's field-hardened horse masters sought sustenance and warmth – and for their horses a break from the saddle – before 'getting their heads down' for an hour or two. Beyond deciding Garnett could no longer be relied upon as commander of the First Division, and that he would replace him, Jackson would have dwelt little on the wretched decision to retreat. 'If only' was not his style, and if, on this occasion, the issue had not been tried by *"the vigorous use of the bayonet,"* the *"blessing of divine Providence"* was ever relevant. In the end, he always thought, *"all things work together for the good of His people."* The facial features were largely masked beneath the weather-stained grey cap, and behind the full, bushy black beard. The silent figure – now cloaked, from throat to spurred cavalry boots – and staring thoughtfully into the spluttering flare of the campfire, was, none the less, easily familiar to the young troopers talking quietly together about the fire. One young man, still in the grip of a youthful excitement, looked across to say brightly, *"The Yankees don't seem willing to quit Winchester, General."* *"Winchester is a very pleasant place to stay in, Sir."* With a grin for his fellow troopers, the young man continued, *"It was reported they were retreating; but I guess they are retreating after us!"* For several moments Jackson did not reply. Just as in the VMI days, the Professor would sit for half an hour silently facing a wall in his living room and, without the aid of either books or notes, meticulously think through his lessons for the next day, so the General would constantly review and update in his mind the ever-changing military situation, and now especially, the implications and possibilities stemming from his recent attack. If this internal assessment could not reveal in every detail, the forthcoming responses of the enemy, his instinctive comprehension of a military situation – both tactical and strategic – would make it virtually impossible for either Banks or Shields to contrive anything approaching a surprise. Their failure to immediately follow-up the battle – *"Night and*

an indisposition of the enemy to press further terminated the battle."[203] –
spoke volumes about Shields and the state of his division. Jackson
instinctively appreciated that the blow had been hard enough to
attract attention, and to paralyse, for the moment at least, the
move by Banks's Fifth Corps to support McClellan. Without
looking up from the fire he said finally, *"I think I may say I am
satisfied, Sir."*[204] A few moments more and he turned away into
the darkness, to where the *'Little Sorrel'*, hitched to a fence post,
cropped grass beneath a wooden rail. As Jackson was mounting,
Dr McGuire found him to report more wounded needing to be
transported than he had wagons, adding that unless this could
be remedied some men would have to be abandoned. He was
told to requisition wagons from the village and nearby farms.
"But," said the surgeon, *"that requires time; can you stay till it has
been done?"* *"Make yourself easy, Sir,"* was the reply, *"this army stays
here until the last man is removed. Before I leave them to the enemy, I
will lose many more men."*[205]

For Jackson, this somewhat unconventional Sunday finally
ended with him breaking his own standing order that field fencing rails should not be broken up for firewood. He said to his
Chief Commissary, Major Wells Hawks, *"We shall have to burn
rails tonight."* The major was the only staff officer still with the
general when they reached Newtown, and amidst an army beginning to litter the countryside around the village, he bustled
round lighting a fire, getting bread and a little meat from a nearby campfire group, and finally laying a rail bed in the corner of
a field, on which the pair slept for the hour or two remaining
before it began to get light.

If the return of the Valley Army to Newtown was a strung-
out affair, by men in shock; thirsty, hungry and exhausted; many
in some degree of pain and discomfort, Stonewall Jackson appears

203 After-battle report – Kernstown (quoted by Henderson).
204 The exact words of this conversational exchange are Henderson's.
205 Ibid.

clearly throughout as being comprehending and quite unflustered. No matter how grim seeming the circumstance to be faced, he was always clear thinking and never at a loss. Secure in his own intellectual ability to thread a way through the unbridled chaos with positive action vigorously undertaken and stemming from right decisions taken at the opportune moment. The instinctive ability to be comfortable with ever-changing and fast-moving battlefield situations, and to fully comprehend their implications, was an important ingredient in the make-up of his genius. This in-bred skill, which Jackson had refined by honing and developing his powers of concentration, had produced in him a remarkable ability to divine exactly what his opponent would do next – and not simply in the immediate aftermath of the battlefield – and is brought into sharper focus, possibly, by its absence in many of those trying to oppose him in the Valley.

Still labouring under the self-induced assumption that Jackson was accessible to reinforcements, and quite failing either to understand Jackson, or to read the situation which had been brought about by the battle his men had just fought, Shields spent a frenzied Sunday night spraying orders in all directions to bring every last Federal fighting man in Virginia to his side. He *"sent an express after Williams's Division, requesting the rear brigade … to march all night and join … him … in the morning."* He *"swept the posts and routes in … his … rear of almost all their guards, hurrying them forward by forced marches to be with … him … at daylight."*[206] In noting his battle casualties six days after Kernstown he wrote, *"The killed and wounded in this engagement cannot even yet be accurately ascertained. Indeed, my command has been so overworked that it has had but little time to ascertain anything."* Douglas writes, *"It was the pride of General James Shields until his death that he was the only Union General who ever whipped Stonewall Jackson."* If true, clearly Shields never did understand the reality of what had taken place at Kernstown. Shields also revised down the estimated strength of his division

---

206 Allan quoting a Shields' report.

engaged at Kernstown, possibly in an attempt to bolster a claim which, deep down, he knew to be more falsely self-glorifying than realistic. Commenting on the revision from the perspective of overall strength returns, McClellan noted drily, *"If Shields's Division, leaving out the cavalry, consisted of only seven thousand, the other Division under Williams, must have contained over twelve thousand men."*[207] (Ostensibly, a division of five Corps was nine thousand strong). If Douglas was right in what he says about Shields, the claim not only sounds rather silly; but even with hindsight is hard to square with the reality. Throughout the Kernstown action, stemming from Jackson's advance and initiated by his left-flanking attack, the Northern regiments were ably directed by a subordinate brigade commander, not Shields. Late in the day, the centre of Jackson's line gave way only because the nerve of a subordinate Confederate General failed. Thereafter, having continued to stem Federal attacks, Jackson's infantry finally withdrew behind Ashby's cavalry screen, to spend the night after the battle, encamped just five miles from the battlefield. The cavalry was no more than two miles distant. There was no immediate pursuit. Subsequently, the Army of the Valley was followed, as it withdrew down the Valley, effectively at its own pace. Shields characterized this follow-up, in a report to Washington, as a *"pursuit … kept up with vigour, energy and activity"*[208]. In reality it was an advance resulting from a change in strategy, and not a pursuit driven by tactical success. To bring about just such a change of thinking was Jackson's purpose in fighting the action. The only vigorous aspect of the Shields/Banks advance was Ashby's constant skirmishing with the vanguard. Jackson achieved his strategic aim of panicking the Federal High Command and bringing about a revision of troop dispositions. Jackson, in his report on the Kernstown action does, indeed, seem *"justified in saying, though the battlefield is in possession of the enemy, yet the most essential*

<hr>

207 Allan.
208 Allan quoting Shields.

fruits of the victory are ours." Shields's attempted self-justification, on the other hand, seems faintly ludicrous.

The Commander of the Federal Fifth Corps had not got beyond Harper's Ferry when news of the action reached him, and he had already counter-marched all but one of the three brigades of Williams's Division – on their way to Manassas – by the time Shields's plea for support arrived. Thus, he began at once, and at the eleventh hour, the process of emasculating the McClellan Plan for a concentrated stroke against Richmond. Banks himself immediately rode back for Winchester, to take command of his shaken advance-guard.

McClellan approved Banks's actions, and accepted that it would no longer be possible for the Fifth Corps to secure the Manassass – Warrenton Junction region. *"In regard to your own movements,"* McClellan wrote, *"the most important thing at present is to throw Jackson well back, and then to assume such a position as to enable you to prevent his return."*[209] By re-instating Banks's brigades against Jackson in the Valley, and finally recognising that *"under the professor of the higher mathematics,"* they were not simply there to observe. McClellan clearly thought that, taken together with his original measures for the defence of Washington – of which his own offensive action was potentially the most effective of all – that he had the situation well in hand. The Yankee President thought otherwise.

Stonewall Jackson's achievement at Kernstown was not that his subtle and full-blooded left flanking attack – probably with little more than two thousand effective 'bayonets' – against, at least three thousand, reinforced by a further three thousand, so nearly carried the field, nor was it that the attack prevented Banks from carrying out the objective of supporting McClellan. The greatest achievement and gain from his acting so promptly and positively at Kernstown was that it caused Lincoln to intervene and

---

209 McClellan from *"Headquarters of the Army of the Potomac, On Board the Commodore, April 1, 1862"* (Allan).

deplete McClellan's means, at the very moment he was moving to implement the agreed plan of attack. First, Lincoln ordered McDowell's First Army Corps – thirty seven thousand men – to remain at Manassas, making it independent of McClellan. To defend the Valley against Jackson, Banks also, was made independent of McClellan. Thirdly, a division under Blenker was ordered to join General Fremont in the Allegheny-West Virginia region, from where they could threaten the southern end of the Valley and co-operate with Banks. For this last disruptive act, a self-indulgent politician relieved himself by informing his principal Army Commander, *"I write … to assure you that I did it with great pain, understanding that you would wish it otherwise."* Overall, civilian meddling left McClellan with just a hundred thousand men for his invasion and the move against Richmond, which, thanks to his poorly performing coppers, left him believing that he no longer had the all-important numerical superiority.

The instigator of the fight at Kernstown was, indeed, reaping *"the essential fruits of the victory,"* although even in the South, this was at first realised only by Jackson himself. However, once the reactions of the enemy became known, and, as a result, it was understood what could be done by an active, ably led, resolute few, against heavy odds, the Valley men received the formal thanks of the Confederate Congress, to which Johnston added; *"his own sense of their admirable conduct, by which they fully earned the high praise bestowed."*[210]

---

210 Henderson.

14. POISED

....

"What I desire is to hold the country
as far as practicable, until we are in a
position to advance; and then with God's
blessing let us make thorough work of it.
But let us start right."
Stonewall Jackson

....

THE ambulances of the wounded led the withdrawal from
Newtown, setting out in the early hours of Monday, with the
last night stars still blanketing the dawn. Unflustered and unhur-
ried, the Army of the Valley tramped in easy stages back along
the Valley Turnpike, their movement masked by the ever-active
Ashby. A few poor souls, for whom McGuire and his medics could
do no more, were left at hospitable homes along the way, prompting the excitable Shields – ever out of touch with reality – to send
"enthusiastic telegrams announcing that the retreat was a flight, and that
the houses along the road were filled with Jackson's dead and dying."[211]
Banks himself did not move from Winchester until the two brigades of Williams's Division had come up. His cavalry achieved
little or nothing, being more or less useless off-road. After seventy-two hours, the Federals had advanced no more than seventeen
miles from Kernstown, when, on the Wednesday evening, they
established pickets along Tom's Brook, a ribbon of water crossed
by the Valley Turnpike. Ashby's men faced them from the other bank. Jackson had positioned Burks' Brigade at Woodstock,
some six miles on from the Brook, and taken the main body on
a further ten miles, to Mount Jackson. A West Point colleague
of Jackson's, commanding the Second Massachusetts Regiment

---

211 Henderson.

in Banks's nineteen thousand-strong force, wrote, on approaching Tom's Brook, *"The superb scenery of the Valley opened before us — the sparkling waters of the Shenandoah, winding between the parallel ranges, the groves of cedar and pine that lined its banks, the rolling surfaces of the Valley, peacefully resting by the mountain side, and occupied by rich fields and quiet farms. A mile beyond I could see the rebel cavalry. Sometimes the enemy amused himself by throwing shells at our pickets, when they were a little too venturesome; but beyond a feeble show of strength and ugliness, nothing transpired to disturb the dullness of the camp."*[212] Banks allowed the men of Fifth Corps nearly seven whole days to enjoy the view. He remained studiously inert, gabbling away to Secretary Stanton, by telegraph, with observations such as *"The enemy is broken, but will rally … At present they will not attack here … His pickets are very strong and vigilant … We shall press them further and quickly … Deficiency in ammunition for Shields' artillery detains us here; expect it hourly, when we shall push Jackson sharply."* Bureaucratic conditions were rarely quite right for Banks. The reality was that he was bereft of constructive ideas on how to make tangible progress, other than by simply marching. He mistook movement for genuine action, and his non-military background probably meant he had little understanding of even the mechanics of an attack. Hence, he talks of *"pushing"* Jackson, without really seeming to appreciate fully what in military terms the word implied. At the end of the week at Tom's Brook, McClellan required his Corps Commander to find out what the enemy had in mind, and to clear him out of the Valley. Banks decided to resume his advance; but another four days passed before he did so. Finally, following a brief exchange with Ashby, his leading units advanced the ten miles to Edenburg, while behind them, the bulk of the force moved up a whole five miles, before halting around Woodstock. A possibly, tongue in cheek McClellan expressed himself, *"much pleased*

---

212 General G.H. Gordon; *"From Brook Farm to Cedar Mountain"* (quoted by Henderson).

with the vigorous pursuit!" – but on the very day of the advance McClellan was removed as commander-in-chief, and Banks reverted directly to his fellow politico, Secretary of War Stanton, expressing the hope *"immediately to strike Jackson an effective blow."*[213]

Although living to an extent off the fertile land around him, Banks believed that he did not have enough wagons to collect sufficient supplies for an advance. The one serviceable railroad, used for bringing up war materials from Washington, via Harper's Ferry, and on to Winchester, became unserviceable, and as they moved back, Jackson had destroyed the bridges on the Strasburg – Woodstock – Mount Jackson stretch of the alternative Manassas Gap railroad. Then the mild spring weather of early April abruptly succumbed to winter. *"... a chill came over us,* Gordon recorded, *"bitter as the hatred of the women of Virginia: the ground covered with snow, the air thick with hail, and the mountains covered in a chilly atmosphere. Our shivering sentinels on the outer lines met at times, the gaze of half-frozen horsemen of the enemy, peering through the mist to see what the Yankees had been doing within the last twenty-four hours."* Precious little, most of the time. Banks demonstrated his idea of 'immediately,' by remaining static for a further thirteen days. During this time, he came to assessing Jackson's army *"as much demoralised by defeat, desertion, and the general depression of spirits resting on the Southern Army. He is not in a condition to attack, neither to make a strong resistance, and I do not believe he will make a determined stand ..."* Poor intelligence gathering, or, as he himself put it; *"good cavalry would help incalculably",* meant that his reporting was more speculative than factual. At least he had detected an increase in Jackson's numbers, which had been stimulated by the Confederate Conscription Act which decreed that all male Whites between the ages of eighteen and thirty-five should sign on for the duration of the War, thus ending the three or twelve months volunteer arrangements, which led to walk-outs at inopportune moments.

---

213 Henderson.

Although Banks saw himself in the dominant position as pursuer, by not acting vigorously and closing with Jackson, he had allowed the character of the 'pursuit' gradually to change. Effectively he had surrendered the initiative. Jackson had progressed from simply withdrawing to manoeuvring. He had written to Johnston at the end of March, saying, *"I will try and draw him on,"* and by mid-April had largely succeeded. Banks was now well down the North Fork of the Shenandoah, and to his left towered the great bulk of the Massanutton, which he would have to go around, if he was to go to Manassas in support of McClellan, for there was only one road-crossing along its fifty mile length; that between New Market – which he had yet to reach – and Luray. Away to his right, the serried ridges of the Alleghenies still inhibited any link up with the substantial, though still widely dispersed, Federal forces under General Fremont, moving in towards the Valley, from west Virginia.

Jackson, at this point, needed to block the continuation of the New Market to Luray road, which would have enabled Banks – at least in theory, – to cross the Blue Ridge through Swift Run Gap and to link up with McDowell, if he came south from Manassas in support of McClellan's advance against Richmond. One of the celebrated forced marches, doubtless grumbled about; but always avoided by Jackson wherever circumstance allowed, was called for. On the eighteenth of April, Jackson marched back the twenty-five miles to Harrisonburg, and on a further six miles to Peale's, at the very southern tip of the Peaked Mountain/Massanutton bulk. Early the next morning he moved on east through McGahersville, crossed the South Fork of the Shenandoah at Conrad's Store, finally coming to a halt in Elk Run Valley – astride the road up to Swift Run Gap – having covered something over fifty miles in three days. *"Banks followed with his customary caution, and when … his cavalry occupied New Market he was congratulated by the Secretary of War on his brilliant and successful operations."*[214] Banks

---

214 Henderson.

did then lead *"a force of cavalry, infantry and artillery"* over Peaked Mountain – the single ridge extension of the Massanutton – to seize and protect the White House and Columbia Bridges over the South Fork of the Shenandoah. In this he succeeded, after a sharp tussle with a detachment of Jackson's, which had been sent to destroy the bridges, they having already demolished the Red Bridge, the next one up-river to the south. During this foray, Banks learnt something of Jackson's movements, which led him to conclude, *"I believe Jackson left this Valley yesterday."* Relieved, if not actually emboldened, by the thought, Banks returned to the main Valley, and marched on down the Valley Turnpike to Harrisonburg, where he established his camp. Remarkably, the situation was now to everyone's satisfaction. Banks believed he had *"thrown Jackson well back,"* as per instructions, and Jackson had *"drawn him on,"* as he intended. But it was a delicate balance, which could not last, and the fruits of the thinking would go to those most able to appreciate, and to get a tangible result from that thinking, by means of imaginative and vigorous action.

In the wider context, Banks, at the end of a lengthy, tenuous supply chain, would look to co-ordinate with Fremont, moving in from the west, and whose advance brigade under General Milroy was already reconnoitring beyond the Great North Shenandoah Mountain, no more than twenty miles distant from Harrisonburg. Fremont was also working towards a plan to concentrate all Federal troops in the region into a single column. This Lincoln approved, with the single exception of ordering the ultimate objective to be Richmond, instead of Knoxville, as was Fremont's original intention. McClellan's landing in the Peninsula country east of Richmond, was proceeding, if not quite to original plan, at least positively. His ferrying system was getting troops ashore in substantial numbers, forcing a somewhat anxious Confederate reaction, which, not surprisingly, given that 'inanimate' Johnston who was commanding on the ground, excluded any attempt to oppose the landings.

Although Jackson's position in the eagle's eyrie of Swift Run Gap was strongly defensible he had chosen it for reasons of offense, as being a most effective position from which to disrupt Banks, as well as keeping him in a position to comply with wider, strategic demands, of which he continued to be mindful. It is just conceivable that an enterprising opponent could have contained Jackson in his Gap position; but given he had a back door, it is more likely that, no matter who opposed him, Jackson would never have allowed a fortress to become a prison. *"My object"*, he wrote on twenty third of April, *"has been to get in his rear ... the Banks rear ... if he gives me the opportunity."*[215] The means with which he intended to do this was still extremely slender, and the increase in his Command to six thousand or so, mostly reflected an increase to Ashby's strength. However, Ashby was a born guerrilla leader, not a trained cavalry commander, and when Jackson tried to instil formal discipline and organisation into a cavalry force now some two thousand strong, Ashby threatened resignation. This, on the strength of his having been the beneficiary of political intervention. So, impressed had Secretary of War Benjamin been with his individual exploits – carried out with a mere handful of loyal followers – that he gave Ashby independent command. Things did not change with the increase in numbers; with the result that the newcomers either swanned about the countryside sponging off the local people or malingered in their own homes. Fully appreciating the value of Ashby's intensive loyalty-based method of making war, Jackson did not press the matter, and his cavalry, for the time being, continued to operate below full capacity.

Almost at the moment that he reached Swift Run Gap, however, Jackson received quite unforeseen news of an extremely rare example of beneficial political intervention. *"In a moment of unwonted wisdom"*, as Henderson has it, *"the Confederate President had charged ... the most clear-sighted soldier in America with the control of all operations in Virginia."* Robert E Lee, the only man Jackson said he would *"follow blindfold"*. At a stroke, the amateur machinations

---

215 Jackson writing on April 23rd (Allan & Henderson).

of Lincoln and Stanton were doomed. Whereas, to some extent, the military ineptitude of Mr Davis was masked by the ability of his generals, those of his Union opposite number were laid bare in the Valley by the appointment of one of whom Henderson, again, wrote *"had a fine career before him until Lincoln 'undertook to make of him what the good Lord hadn't, a great general.'"* It was the misfortune of Banks and his political bosses, to have their combined efforts opposed by the man whom the good Lord very much intended to be the most enterprising, clear-sighted, attacking battlefield commander in America.

As C-in-C, Lee wrote to Jackson in Swift Run Gap on twenty ninth of April, *"General; I have had the honour to receive your letter of yesterday's date. From the reports that reach me, that are entitled to credit, the force of the enemy opposite Fredericksburg is represented as too large to admit of any diminution whatever of our army in that vicinity at present, as it might not only invite an attack on Richmond, but also jeopardizing* (sic) *the safety of the army in the Peninsula. I regret, therefore, that your request to have five thousand men sent from that army to reinforce you cannot be complied with."* Lee suggested a combined effort with General Edward Johnson, currently in the vicinity of Shenandoah Mountain, opposing the Federal force in the Alleghenies. *"A decisive and successful blow at Banks's column would be fraught with the happiest results,"* he continued. Lee had also been concerned for some time about Fredericksburg being used as a stepping-stone to Richmond, and he suggested to Jackson that General Ewell might combine with other Confederate forces east of the Blue Ridge to pre-empt this, adding the proviso *"provided you feel sufficiently strong alone to hold Banks in check. Very truly yours, R.E. Lee."*[216]

Jackson had already been in communication with both Confederate commanders Edward Johnson and Richard Ewell. The former had ridden over from Shenandoah Mountain to confer, during Jackson's brief stop at Peale's, en-route to Elk Run Valley. Jackson had sent an emissary to Ewell while near Mount Jackson.

---

216 Quoted by Allan.

15. A NIGHT RIDE[217]

"A successful and pleasant ride!"
Stonewall Jackson

WHILE the Second Virginia was encamped at Rude's Hill, some two miles from Mount Jackson, Lieutenant Henry Kyd Douglas was sent for by General Jackson. He spent a week or so assisting the Inspector-General, Lieutenant-Colonel Baylor, to organise and allocate new recruits and the returning furlough men, before the Army broke up its camps, and he was sent as liaison to Ashby, who was busy burning three bridges prior to the continuation of the withdrawal. With two bridges securely engulfed in fire, Ashby misjudged firing the third and allowed Federal cavalry to close with him. So much so, that to the watchers on the hill above and beyond the river – including Douglas – the galloping, four abreast files, wreathed in heavy dust, were led *"by an officer on a milk-white horse. It was beautiful,"* Douglas remembered, *"Distance led enchantment to it, as it did on other occasions in my war experience. Look! … said another … see how splendidly that officer on the white horse manages him … By Jove! that's the Colonel … said a watching gunner … see they are firing on him and he on them."* Ashby galloped across the bridge and made to put a match to the brushwood fascines stacked around the wooden framework; but the two leading files of eight, blue-clad horsemen were on to him. A bullet grazed his boot and buried itself in the gleaming white flank of his horse. Ashby sabred the man to the ground and broke free, galloping in a sweeping arc up the slope towards his watching followers. In a rolling gout of smoke and flame a single round crashed out from the supporting artillery piece. As

217 Henry Kyd Douglas, *"I Rode with Stonewall"*.

he reached the summit, *"Ashby's splendid stallion sank to the ground, dappled with the foam of heat and suffering; his wound was mortal ... Thus ...* Douglas wrote *... the most splendid horseman I ever knew lost the most beautiful war-horse I ever saw."* The pursuit recoiled for a time, and Douglas was sent on to Jackson's headquarters with a situation report.

"About the time of setting sun ... General Jackson called for me," Douglas recalled later. *"The sky was covered with heavy clouds, and the rain was falling heavily. The General handed me a paper from under his rubber cape and requested me to take it to General Richard S. Ewell ... on the other side of the Blue Ridge Mountains, somewhere near Culpeper Court House. For a moment I was stampeded, paralyzed. I had never been over a foot of the country and had only a vague idea that Culpeper was somewhere beyond the mountains; but how to get there I could not imagine. Night was upon us; it was raining like the deluge; and I had already ridden to and fro about twenty-five miles that day. But a young man soon rallies, and I pulled myself together quickly. I was being weighed in the balance right there and I determined to throw all my weight on the scales. "General, I will start at once if I can get a horse."*

Lieutenant Kidder Meade, Jackson's Ordnance Officer, lent Douglas his *"spirited dun mare ...* adding the advice *... "strike for Stanardsville first."*

"As I rode away ... in reply to my 'Good night', came the voice of the General — 'A successful and pleasant ride!' It was kindly meant, but it sounded singularly like sarcasm. Forward I went into the night and mud, every minute growing darker and wetter. But all weariness was gone, and I felt as fresh as my mettled horse. In a little while, I was rounding the base of the Massanutton Mountain ... and the towering mass horrified the night. Across the South Fork of the Shenandoah to Conrad's Store. Here, as I approached the Blue Ridge, I felt almost hopeless in the impenetrable stormy night. I stopped to make some enquiries and procured a small bottle of whiskey for emergencies. Then into and up the black mountain.

"Vision was impossible, but fortunately the road was solid and fairly good, and my horse could keep to it. I could reach out my hand and feel her neck and ears, but could not see them ... At times, I heard the water rush under us and across the road and tumble in torrents so far down

below that I knew we were travelling on perilous edges ... At last, we reached the summit of Swift Run Gap. It was from this summit and through this gap that Governor Alexander Spotswood and the knights of the Golden Horseshoe, in 1716, obtained the white man's first view of the Valley of the Shenandoah ... Just here I met a knight of a less romantic order. He was a belated, bedraggled, drowsy courier plodding his way from General Ewell to General Jackson. ... I extracted some useful information as to my route and in return, gave him a pull at my flask. It was vile stuff, but as he seemed to like it, I gave him the bottle and left him on the summit.

"*I soon went plunging into Stanardsville, having done at least thirty seven miles on that blooded mare. Here, I tried to get another horse but failed ... Anxiety for my noble beast added another horror to the night ... Out of Stanardsville, the road forked in the middle of a broad and shallow stream and of course I took the wrong branch. Half a mile beyond, I aroused the inmates of a cabin and learned my mistake. Retracing my steps, I was soon in front of a white farm house. A few well-directed shouts brought an astonished head out of an upper window. I appealed to its owner for a horse ... he declined ... but politely urged me to 'come in out of the wet.'*

"*I then knew that I must play trumps and I said plaintively, 'My dear friend, I am an officer of Stonewall Jackson's staff, carrying an important message, and I must have a fresh horse.' 'The devil!' was the response ... and down went the window ... he soon appeared with Saul, a horse, and a lantern, and helped to exchange the saddle and bridle. As I climbed from the fence to the mare and was about to ride away, he threw the light of the lantern in my face and said in a tender voice, 'Good luck. I have a boy, maybe your age, with Stonewall Jackson.'*

The fresh mount was "*as tall as a dromedary*", but not used to saddle and bridle, and was "*worn out,*" by the time the pair had covered the fifteen miles to Madison Court House, where, at the courier station, "*I exchanged her for a little grey horse ... and having clattered through the streets of that slumbering town, was soon in the open country and on another deep mud road. Suddenly my horse slipped, gave a groan and was down and I rolled off into the mire. I jumped off and asked him to do the same, but he never responded and was apparently dead.*

Standing in the pitch black and pouring rain, with not a light or human habitation in sight, and in what he describes as *"hopeless bewilderment,"* Douglas was suddenly joined by a young negro boy, who jumped *"into the road with a 'Good Lordy, wats dat?' Explanations followed"*. Suitably bribed with a silver dollar, the boy *"disappeared like a rabbit in the dark,"* to procure a re-mount from the nearby tavern. Sitting on a fence waiting, *"covered with mud and soaking … all too conscious of … "the night passing and my spirits … sinking rapidly"*; but the *"little black angel"* soon returned with *"another white horse,"* and duly received his dollar.

"After nine miles more of spurring and splashing, I ran into James City where I changed to a tall gaunt roan that carried me valiantly the eleven miles to Culpeper Court House. As I approached there was a suspicion of light in the direction of dawn and the rain had partially worn itself out. In all directions I heard the drums of an early reveille, and presently encountered a group of men sitting on their horses … It was General Dick Taylor. Learning that he was ordered to march and evidently in the wrong direction, I suggested to him that he should not move until he heard from General Ewell, who, he said, was camped beyond Brandy Station. One of his staff kindly offered me a fresh horse and General Taylor ordered a courier to lead the way and 'ride like the devil.' This the courier did and so did I; but as I had been doing that thing all night it was no novelty to me. We rushed along like a pair of John Gilpins and, as it never seemed to occur to my guide that I might be nearly worn out, I didn't mention it. … We soon made the six miles to Brandy Station. After going several miles beyond, we drew rein at General Ewell's headquarters just as I was beginning to be exhausted beyond endurance.

"The General was just up, and I dismounted and handed him the crumpled and saturated dispatch. … Seeing me totter and about to fall, he caught me, led me to his cot, and laid me there; and then the dear, rough, old soldier made the air blue with orders for brandy and coffee and breakfast – not for himself, but for me. My ride was done, and nature asserted itself by reaction and exhaustion. In less than twenty hours I had ridden about one hundred and five miles … and through rain and mud and impenetrable night, had been under the strain of a cavalry charge for more than eighty miles.

"When I revived and had had something to eat, the General sent me in his ambulance to Culpeper Court House, where I remained in bed in a hotel for twenty four hours. Then I began to retrace my steps ... taking up my horses as I went, and at ten o'clock the second night, I rode up to General Jackson's headquarters near Conrad's Store. It had not ceased to rain for an hour since I left, and except when in bed I had been clad in soaking garments from start to finish.

"I went into the General's room to report. It was empty of furniture and on the hearth were some dying coals of a wood fire. He was lying on the floor upon a thin mattress, wrapped in a blanket and asleep. I awoke him and made my report. He listened politely and then with 'Very good. You did get there in time. Good night.' He turned over to sleep and I left the room. I will not attempt to describe my surprise and indignation at this cool reception. Refusing to be comforted by the Staff, who knew the General better, I threw off my heavy, soggy clothes and retired in grievous disappointment to an uncomfortable bed. A letter that had come through the lines, in a delicate handwriting and with a little gold ring enclosed, did turn my thoughts somewhat in a different direction.

"The next morning the General sent for me. He was alone, sitting on a camp stool gazing into the fire. He arose, holding in his hand a dispatch which he said he had just received from General Ewell, and then remarked, 'Mr Douglas, Major Baylor leaves me today to take command of the Fifth Regiment of the Stonewall Brigade, and I want to assign you to duty as my Assistant Inspector General of my staff.' What I said, I do not clearly remember, but my wounded pride was healed. Thus, I entered the military family of Stonewall Jackson."

16. A 'TERRIBLE MARCH'[218]

*"Now, as it appears to me, is the
golden opportunity to strike a blow."*
Stonewall Jackson

IT may have been Jackson's important recommendation for Ewell to move his Division up to Stanardsville which Douglas carried on his epic night ride – a dispatch including the warning note to be prepared to cross to the western side of the Blue Ridge and occupy Swift Run Gap above Elk Run Valley. The dispatch he had in his hand, when interviewing Douglas, would have been delivered by the courier system established between the two. When Ewell was under his operational command, Jackson was still careful to leave actual moves to Ewell's discretion, although for this move, he did point out *"that there would be no necessity for a forced march; he was to encamp at cross-roads, and ... (very Jackson) ... he was to rest on Sundays."*[219] Lee was equally considerate in the written discussions that took place between him and Jackson, qualifying more detailed views with, *"The blow, wherever struck, must, to be successful, be sudden and heavy ... and ... I cannot pretend at this distance to direct operations, depending on circumstances unknown to me, and requiring the exercise of discretion and judgement as to time and execution ..."*[220]

Jackson's aim throughout, was to clear the enemy from the Valley. Exactly how he would do this depended upon whether or not he could be reinforced. His only caveat was, whether the wider concern of Federal operations against Richmond

---

218 Douglas.
219 Henderson.
220 Lee quoted by Henderson.

should demand his direct involvement. By the twenty ninth of April, he had appreciated that, as things stood then, he was not going to be required east of the Blue Ridge, and that he was not going to be reinforced. *"Now"*, he felt *"was the golden opportunity"*, and he suggested three possible ways of dealing with Banks. One, was to combine with Ewell and attack Banks's rear, should he advance on the important focal point of Staunton, which the Confederates were anxious not to lose. Two, was to unite with General Edward Johnson and throw-back the force approaching from the Alleghenies, leaving Ewell, in his temporary absence, to inhibit Banks. For the Valley Army to hamstring Banks by moving east of the Blue Ridge, before turning back to hit his lines of communication about Winchester – the third possibility – he felt *"with my present force would be rather a dangerous undertaking."* By informing Lee of his intentions amid a screen of alternative possibilities, Jackson was able to maintain his customary high degree of secrecy from which he emerged, having kept his opponents, as well as his colleagues, totally in the dark. So successful was his security, that just three days before he made a move, one of his own staff wrote in a personal letter. *"As sure as you and I live, Jackson is a cracked man, and the sequel will show it."*[221]

Within the short space of a month, this gratuitous opinion must have made its author feel very stupid indeed. On the same day that Jackson wrote to Lee of his plans, Ashby was ordered to make a strong sally against Banks's advance units around Harrisonburg. The following day Federal cavalry pickets were driven in and withdrew to their main lines and camps. That afternoon Jackson marched, and Ewell began moving up from Stanardsville, to take his place in Swift Run Gap, overlooking Elk Run Valley.

For the Virginia Regiments it was back to the campaigning conditions of early January, albeit without the snow and ice. The going was appalling, and it took them two and a half days to cover just sixteen miles. Weeks of near continuous heavy rain had

---

221 Henderson.

turned the road from Conrad's Store to Port Republic into a bottomless bog. With our almost universal ribbons of tarmac laid on firm foundations we have become increasingly unfamiliar with a phenomenon in which wagons bellied-down, and guns sank to their axles – deeper, if heavy enough, or left standing. Men and horses plodded ankle, even knee, deep. By the end of two days, everyone from the general down, was plastered with mud, from carrying wood and stones to provide grip for wheels and hooves, and from pushing and heaving at the heavy equipment. All were soaked to the skin. But then, to the surprise of all, instead of continuing on to cross the Shenandoah beyond Port Republic, the order came to turn east, and begin the climb back up the Blue Ridge towards Brown's Gap. When they made camp on the third day, they were no more than twelve miles from Elk Run Valley, as the crow flies, and largely convinced that they were abandoning the Valley, and marching to the aid of Richmond.

Jackson was criticised at the time, as well as by some commentators later, for taking to the mire of the Conrad's Store – Port Republic road, for what was the first move in his plan to remove the lesser of his two immediate opponents from the immediate reckoning. To suggest that he should, or could, have used either of two alternative routes, is to fail to consider all the factors in play. Something of which Jackson himself was never guilty. His purpose in this instance, was to mask his intentions from the enemy – and, indeed, from friends to achieve surprise – so that Milroy, commanding the advance brigade of the Allegheny force, should in turn be surprised, and Banks kept in a position from which he could not intervene. To have marched up through Swift Run Gap, and so left the Valley directly – although he could then have turned on to the route, he did in fact take to attack Milroy – would have relieved Banks of any pressure and offered him the opportunity to link directly with Milroy, having left a strong force to confront Ewell, when the time came. For Jackson to have headed straight for Staunton and on to Milroy was never a serious possibility, because that way would have fopdoodled no one. When he broke camp; marched up and over Brown's Gap, and down the eastern slopes of the Blue Ridge, to Mechum's River Station, only the weather had changed, and marching now in glorious Spring sunshine, the men still believed they were bound for Richmond. After a night in camp around Mechum's – Jackson had taken the added precaution of closing his lines: no one was allowed through in either direction – the infantry boarded the railway carriages, and with the supply trains, the guns and the wagons continuing by road, all were ordered to proceed, not east, but westwards to Staunton. Morale rose with every step and every mile, and their arrival at Staunton provided a similar boost for the town's people. But to the dismay of the latter, after a day of organisation and rest – the move from Mechum's took place on a Sunday and so needed to be compensated for – the Army of the Valley had no sooner arrived than they were off, taking the turnpike road west to McDowell and Monterey. Edward Johnson's regiments led what became a column some eight to ten miles long on the narrow, dirt roadway. While Jackson was re-grouping, Edward Johnson's regiments had been in camp some eight miles away, at West View.

Whilst Banks's lack of understanding of what was happening to him during these seven days, is amusing in retrospect, it is also a good example of the importance both of swift movement and secrecy – the twin elements of surprise and, for retaining the initiative. On the very day (thirtieth of April), when Jackson was floundering towards Port Republic behind Ashby's cavalry screen, Banks informed Secretary of War Stanton. *"All quiet. Some alarm excited by movement of enemy's cavalry ... they are in pursuit of a Union prisoner who escaped to our camp. The day he left, Jackson was to be reinforced by Johnson ... another report says Jackson is bound for Richmond. This is the fact, I have no doubt. Jackson is on half-rations, his supplies having been cut off by our advance. There is nothing to be done in this Valley this side of Strasburg.* Then a second despatch later the same night *"after full consultation with all leading officers,"* he repeated that *'his troops were no longer required in the Valley'* saying; *"Jackson's army is reduced, demoralised, on half-rations. They are all concentrating for Richmond. I am now satisfied that* (leaving the Valley) *is the most safe and effective disposition for our corps. I pray your favourable consideration. Such order will electrify our force."*[222] As Henderson comments, Banks *"was certainly to be electrified, but the impulse was not to come from Mr Secretary Stanton."* Furthermore, on the third of May, the very day on which Jackson did leave the Valley through Brown's Gap, Banks suddenly got it into his head that he was not headed for Richmond. On the seventh, when Jackson started west from Staunton, Banks's cavalry informed him that Jackson had occupied Harrisonburg – some twenty-five miles in the opposite direction from Staunton, on a line with Elk Run Valley, which Jackson had left a week earlier. Banks immediately withdrew north to New Market. Jackson could hardly have wished for more.

---

222 Quoted by Henderson.

17. M'DOWELL

*"I congratulate you on your recent victory . . .
I request you to unite with me in thanksgiving
to Almighty God . . . and in praying that He will
continue to lead you . . . and make us that people
whose God is the Lord."*
Stonewall Jackson

MILROY had a more effective intelligence network than Banks. On the seventh of May, the day on which Jackson left Staunton and Banks was told he was at Harrisonburg, Milroy was informed that Jackson and Edward Johnson had joined forces and were marching against him. Milroy sent back a request to Fremont for reinforcements. Some eighteen miles out of Staunton, Edward Johnson's brigade, leading Jackson's advance, drove-in a forward picket, and in the early evening, overran a freshly evacuated camp-site, capturing some equipment abandoned for lack of transport. Retiring Union gunners fired a few desultory rounds, and the advance halted for the night. The same evening, Milroy called in his foraging parties, together with their escorting troops, and concentrated his three thousand seven hundred men around M'Dowell. Further west, the Federals too, had been suffering some wintry weather in the western ridges; but before noon the next day, and *"after a march of thirty four miles in twenty three hours"* Schenck's brigade, reduced by detachments to some one thousand three hundred infantry, a battery of guns and two hundred and fifty cavalry, joined Milroy at M'Dowell. Breaking camp early the next morning, Edward Johnson's men encountered no opposition in the first ten miles, which brought the advance to the road pass through Bull-Pasture Mountain – some thirty-three miles from Staunton – and the start of the jumbled array of heavily wooded, conical hills and flat-topped ridges comprising the final three miles to M'Dowell village. Shortly before noon, the point-men drove a Schenck-Milroy picket from the flat summit of Sitlington's Hill and were able to look down and across Bull-Pasture Run to the grid-lines of the Federal artillery, lining a swathe of flat, open ground south west of M'Dowell, and their camp beyond and due west of the village. Jackson and Edward Johnson joined the point-men, having scrambled up the steep rock and tree-strewn ravine in the side of Sitlington's Hill, which was quite insurmountable from the back of a horse. Skirmishers sent up through the trees to probe the Confederate advance were picked-off by Edward Johnson's advance men. The few random rounds, from guns firing at maximum elevation with their trails dropped into pits, buried themselves harmlessly in the hill slopes, or amongst tree-tops, and were ignored.

Jackson decided at once not to deploy artillery on Sitlington's Hill, although from the summit, gunfire could have speedily rendered the Federal artillery park, and the camp beyond, untenable. The task of manhandling guns up the rough ravines and gullies would have been too time-consuming, and their removal, in the event of a withdrawal or a need to move on, too problematical, within a tight time-frame. Furthermore, Jackson did not want to get bogged-down dealing with Milroy, or, more correctly Schenck, who being the senior of the two, was now in charge. Fremont might march hard and concentrate his whole force on Schenck-Milroy, and it was Fremont overall that Jackson needed to knock back, to gain the necessary time and space to deal with Banks. If Fremont was able to concentrate his command, Banks could conceivably find the resolve to join-up with him. In the wider context, Jackson knew that, in Richmond, consideration had been given to putting pressure on Washington by way of the Valley, and that McClellan, largely committed to his Peninsula move, was limited in how he could respond, due to his plan requiring him to operate along exterior lines. Jackson, if he moved swiftly, could exert the necessary relieving pressure, by taking out Banks and dominating the Valley, which would immediately make Federal forces east of the Blue Ridge concentrate their thoughts on the defence of Washington, rather than concentrating their resources on a move on Richmond, in conjunction with McClellan.

The Holy Bible, Napoleon's 'Military Maxims,' an edition of which was published in the Confederate capital that year and a copy given to Jackson by 'Jeb' Stewart, together with a Dictionary, were all three fixtures amongst Jackson's campaign kit. He was said to have referred often to the latter, to maintain his spelling, and to have been a student of the second. It is important to keep the Maxims in perspective, however, for as Bonaparte's somewhat patchy record shows, the Corsican more often than not, talked a better battle than he fought. If and when he did refer to the Maxims, the Virginian would have used them as an aide-memoire only, to check that some aspect or detail had not been overlooked, or to flag-up potential dangers which might exist, when pursuing a particular course of action. Jackson was far too original and fertile a thinker to require creative input from another. Like the so-called 'Principles of War', the 'Maxims' provided a good guide for the pedestrian military mind. The Bible, we know Jackson read daily, whenever possible, in both war and peace. He would have parted company with Bonaparte when he said, *"... many good generals ... see too many things at once ... whereas he – Bonaparte – saw ... only one thing ... the enemy's main body ... which Bonaparte would try to ... crush ... confident that secondary matters would then settle themselves."* Jackson was always comprehensive in his thinking and would certainly not have missed Bonaparte's underlying point about the need to prioritise and concentrate. Like all the truly greats, Jackson would retain the whole military picture in his mind; would comprehend the various implications and possibilities for all the protagonists, and then envisage and constantly update himself – not only as to how the various individual snapshots were changing; but also, how change might be affecting all those concerned; how each in turn, as a consequence, might try to respond. The final strand in this complex and individual skill was the ability to keep the changing kaleidoscope constantly in the mind's eye, whilst unfolding and imposing his own intentions and his own objectives.

During the first three hours after Noon on the Eighth, Jackson was positioning regiments in the case of his being attacked. Four of Edward Johnson's regiments climbed Sitlington's Hill, to go into reverse slope positions behind the crest, which they would do in the order Fifty-Second Virginia on the left, twelfth Georgia on their right – forming the centre of the line – and the Forty-Fourth Virginia on the very right, close to the head of the ravine, which only allowed such torturous access to the summit. The Fifty-Eighth was drawn up close behind the Fifty-Second in immediate reserve. At the same time, staff and engineers were sent away to the left of the advance, to recce any possible route into the rear of Schenck-Milroy, for use either in attack or pursuit. Between Three and three-thirty p.m. it became clear that the process of driving back Schenck-Milroy would begin with a defensive battle phase. Federal regiments began issuing from their camp area and flowing down from the flat ground of their gun line, opposite, to cross Bull-Pasture Run, and begin the clamber over the lower slope of Sitlington's Hill, on up through the trees, finally, to breast the steep open ground before the crest. The attack would also have told Jackson that Schenck-Milroy had failed to appreciate that his overall objective was to manoeuvre them far enough from the Valley, to allow time for the destruction of Banks, and his own re-instatement in the Valley, as a threat to Washington and to Federal action east of the Blue Ridge. Not to have precipitated an action would have been more beneficial for the Federals in the wider context.

As the attacking regiments disappeared amongst the trees below, skirmishers from the Fifty-Second moved down towards the upper treeline, ahead of the Confederate left and centre, and as the flashes of blue started to show amid the darkness of the trees, white spurts of musketry began to fleck the open slope. First out into the open were the Twenty-Fifth and Seventy-Fifth Regiments, *"Western troops"* of whom Jackson had said before Kernstown, *"are familiar with the use of arms. We must calculate on hard fighting ... if attacked only in front, and may meet with obstinate resistance, however the attack may be made."*[223] On the steep slope of Sitlington's Hill, lines rendered ragged by the rough terrain were quickly re-formed, and soon being dappled in turn with grey smoke amid the crack and zing of firing. Men from Ohio came resolutely on, reversing the scatter of skirmishers, frontier men like themselves, who leap-frogged back, alternately turning and firing as they went, darting between whatever inadequate cover the slope provided. A fierce fire-fight developed, wreathing the ridge-line of the summit in swirls of flame-filled smoke. If clambering upward to fire was heavy going, the defending line had to clearly silhouette themselves against the sky to see over the lip, and in firing down, tended to shoot high over the heads of the attack. In their enthusiastic determination to succeed, the Twelfth Georgia suffered most in this way, despite the efforts of their Colonel to re-form their line for a straight shot clear of the edge; but, as one of his brave young men said afterwards, they had *"not come all the way to Virginia to run before Yankees."* The Fifty-Eighth Virginia too, were guilty of a positive disregard of orders. They too caught the enthusiastic anxiety to succeed, and from the reserve position, strode forward on their own initiative, to fight alongside their colleagues in the very forefront of the line, where the firing was fiercest.

With the action against the Confederate left being repulsed and renewed with equal vigour, two further regiments struck at the Forty-Fourth on the very right of Johnson's line, while a third moved up the turnpike at the foot of the slope, with the aim of turning that right flank. (Johnson was fighting the regiments in the battle-line – and would be severely wounded in the foot during the action – while Jackson directed operations overall). Jackson had anticipated some such flanking move and had positioned the Thirty-Third Virginia accordingly, forward of the battle-line, and astride the turnpike. However, all three Federal regiments concentrated on the lone Forty-Fourth at the head of

---

223 Quoted by Henderson.

the ravine, and Jackson swiftly ordered both the Thirty-First and the Twenty-Fifth Virginia up the slope in support of the Forty-Fourth. The firing was *"incessant and at close quarters"* ... Jackson would write later, ... *"the action had now not only become general along the whole line, but so intense that I ordered General Taliaferro to the support of General Johnson. Accordingly, the Twenty-Third and Thirty-Seventh Virginia regiments were advanced to the centre of the line, which was then held by the Twelfth Georgia with heroic gallantry. ... The battle lasted four hours – from half-past four in the afternoon until half-past eight. Every attempt by front or flank movement, to attain the crest of the hill, where our line was formed, was signally and effectually repulsed. Finally, after dark, their force ceased firing, and the enemy retreated."*[224]

During the four hour action, Jackson committed the six regiments of Edward Johnson's command and the three of Taliaferro – his own Second Brigade. All told, they sustained four hundred and sixty-one casualties. (seventy-one killed and three hundred and ninety wounded). The gallant Twelfth Georgia suffered a hundred and fifty six killed and wounded, nineteen of whom were officers. The Third Brigade of the Valley Army, although positioned to secure the right flank, were not attacked, and the Stonewall brigade – like the artillery – remained in rear and out-of-battle throughout. Schenck-Milroy between them had a combined force of some six thousand. Two thousand five hundred were committed to the action, and of these twenty-eight were killed, two hundred and twenty-five wounded and three listed as unaccounted for.

Amid mist, forming as the temperature dropped during the hours before midnight, the Confederates saw to the wounded of both sides, and posted pickets around the battle area, before seeking food and then sleep. Jackson was always meticulous in his care for enemy wounded, and in the Valley, his ambulances were the praise of both sides. The Federals, meanwhile, stoked-up their campfires. Learning shortly before the fighting petered

---

224 Quoted by Allan.

out that a useable track existed which joined the M'Dowell to Monterey road, beyond the Federal camp and west of M'Dowell, Jackson detailed-off a combined force of infantry and artillery to be ready to move the next day. By the time he had finished his rounds, it was near one in the morning. Although he had eaten nothing since shortly after dawn, when Jim, his personal servant, reached him with a plate of food he said, *"I want none; nothing but sleep,"*[225] and, removing only his spurs and boots, fell instantly asleep across his thin, campaign mattress. Awaking later, with the greying dawn, and with the first drumbeats of reveille reverberating around the clefts and defiles of the mountains, he walked out to the *Little Sorrell*, where the staff were gathering. Sending for cavalry to join them, they rode out past the picket line towards the bridge, taking the Staunton road into M'Dowell. To their left, on the flat, open ground beyond Bull-Pasture Run, no guns remained pointing across the darkness of the water. Up ahead, somewhere amid the small cluster of houses, a dog barked. Behind them, the cavalry could be heard coming up at a scrunching trot. No-one stirred. They rode on. Beyond the last house, the Federal tent lines astride the road, gleamed dully in the growing light. A few wisps of smoke and a spurt or two of flame flashed from still glowing embers. Nothing moved, and only the sound of rushing water broke the silence. The camp had been abandoned. The cavalry, as they came up, slowed to a walk, and the General waved them on. *"They will be making for Franklin, Captain Wills. Report as soon as you make contact. Report anyway, no later than ten o'clock. Captain Smith, your Squadron to remain with me. I'll need couriers for Richmond and Staunton during the course of the morning."* Jackson turned to the staff. *"Major Harman, Major Hawks, secure the tents and all other equipment. If it includes breakfast dole it out at once. Major Dabney, Mr Pendleton, get everyone up here. The First and Second Brigades to the camp area. All other regiments on the open ground beside the Run. Get breakfast started right*

---

225 Henderson.

away. We'll move out as soon as we've eaten." The sun, as a fragment of orange disc, showed at the far end of the valley, stretching away to the east, and within minutes, the night sky had vanished. Jackson took a pad from a satchel slung across his saddle, and resting it on the rubber cape and cloak, rolled and strapped across the pommel, wrote in pencil; *"Valley District, ninth of May 1862. To General S. Cooper*[226]*: God blessed our arms with victory at M'Dowell yesterday. T.J. Jackson, Major-General."*

---

226 Confederate Adjutant-General, Richmond (Allan).

18. RETURN TO THE VALLEY

....

*"Why refer to me to learn how
to deal with mutineers?
shoot them where they stand."*
Stonewall Jackson

....

THE trooper riding back to make the ten o'clock, mid-morn-
ing, report reached Jackson several miles out of M'Dowell, on the
Franklin Road. Although Schenck had halted for some hours –
probably on reaching the baggage train he had left some fourteen miles from M'Dowell on his forced march to join Milroy,
he was now on the move again, and had already covered some
twenty-five miles. Beyond thanking the messenger and ordering him back to his squadron, Jackson said nothing. He scribbled a pencil-note for General Winder. *"Press hard. No skirmishing
ahead. T.J.J. ten a.m., ninth."* As Douglas commented, *"To be with
Jackson was to take lessons in brevity."* Brigadier-General Charles S.
Winder was appointed to the Stonewall brigade, in command, on
the first of April, after Garnett was dismissed. Winder would be
killed by artillery fire, at the end of August, early on in Jackson's
very personal victory at the battle of Cedar Run. Apart from
Jackson himself, no commander of the Stonewall brigade lived
long enough to be promoted to Major-General, in the whole
course of the Civil War.

By the evening of Friday, the ninth of May, the Valley men
had narrowed the gap between themselves and the withdrawing
Federals; but were still out of range. Jackson had decided that
Schenck was not going to fight again without being reinforced –
either by Fremont, on whom he was closing, or by Banks from
the Valley. Jackson himself did not want an engagement – he
needed to conserve his numbers for Banks; but he did want to
keep Fremont and his strung-out command clear of the Valley

until he had dealt with Banks, and so, made his presence felt in Washington. His constant, overall, concern was that things might deteriorate around Richmond, due either to McClellan on the Peninsula to the east, or to McDowell in the north, near Fredericksburg. In either instance, probably both he and Ewell would be ordered to leave the Valley. Jackson's acute strategic mind had long appreciated that the way to relieve the pressure from the large numbers around Richmond, was to put pressure on Lincoln and Stanton in Washington. Before turning in for a few hours of sleep on the Friday night, Jackson began preparing to deal with Banks. He sent his Topographical Engineer, Jed Hotchkiss with a cavalry detachment, to block all the roads and passes linking Franklin to Harrisonburg, in the centre of the Shenandoah Valley, and at the southern end of the Massanutton. Chief Quartermaster, John Harman and his Chief Commissary, Wells Hawks, were instructed to concentrate thirty days forage, rations, ammunition and medical supplies, at Staunton.

Both General and infantry were on the road by first light the next morning and were soon amongst the few cavalry pickets keeping in touch with Schenck's rear guard. As they marched on, Federal guns shelled the road from key vantage points, forcing the lead companies to deploy, left and right off the road, and work their way up the tree-girt slopes to move them on. Later in the morning, smoke began to seep back between the trees; horses became fidgety and the point-men heard the crackle of flames. The Federals were torching the trees as they withdrew, and soon the green canopy was overlaid with a pall of grey-black smoke. The head of the advancing column diffused into skirmishing parties, probing cautiously forward for snipers. Progress slowed in the smoky twilight. Jackson, often moving ahead of his men, credited his opponent with *"the most adroit expedient to which a retreating army could resort to embarrass pursuit, ... having ...entailed upon him all the disadvantages of a night attack."*[227] By Sunday evening,

---

227 Allan.

the eleventh, after another day of slow, charred and smoke-impeded progress, Jackson was some two miles from Franklin village, where Schenck had taken up a strong defensive position, to be reinforced by his approaching army commander, and to await an attack, which Jackson had no intention of undertaking.

Monday morning was designated a Sunday with the proclamation, *"Soldiers of the Army of the Valley and North-West: I congratulate you on your recent victory at McDowell. I request you unite with me this morning in thanksgiving to Almighty God, for thus having crowned your arms with success, and in praying that He will continue to lead you on from victory to victory, until our independence shall be established, and make us that people whose God is the Lord. The chaplains will hold Divine Service at ten o'clock a.m. this day, in their respective regiments."*[228] In the afternoon, Jackson turned back for M'Dowell, leaving a small cavalry presence to mask his leaving, under orders to follow after a day or so. The Army passed through M'Dowell two days later, moving on to camp at Lebanon Springs overnight on the Thursday. Here, the road forks for Staunton and Harrisonburg. The following day was spent in camp *"in deference to the proclamation of the Confederate President appointing the sixteenth May as a day of fasting and prayer."* On the Saturday they took the road to Harrisonburg. That night the Army pitched the regimental camps in the fields bordering a five mile stretch of road, in Augusta County, between Mount Solon – more or less equidistant between Staunton and Harrisonburg – and the next hamlet of Bridgewater. While Jackson was establishing his headquarters at Mount Solon, Colonel Grigsby brought the unwelcome news that at least two companies of, original, 'twelve months only' men, in his Twenty-Seventh Virginia Regiment, had reacted against the recent Conscription Act, by laying down their weapons and announcing they would march no further. They would 'soldier no more.' It was mutiny. *"Why,"* Jackson asked the Colonel, *"refer to me to learn how to deal with mutineers …*

228 Ibid.

shoot them where they stand." The Regiment paraded. To the loyal companies, the order was given to load. The mutineers were given the stark choice of instantly collecting their weapons and returning to the ranks, or being shot there and then, by their comrades. In silence, without discussion, all gave in. Jackson's inflexible will was already widely known. The last case of *"organised disobedience in the Valley Army,"*[229] had no sooner been attempted than it was ended.

229 Henderson quoting Major R.L. Dabney, Jackson's Adjutant-General.

19. ANOTHER NIGHT RIDE

....

*"As you are in the Valley District, you
constitute part of my command."*
Stonewall Jackson

....

MAJOR-GENERAL Richard Ewell spent the hours of darkness on that Saturday night/Sunday morning, in the saddle, riding from his camp in Elk Run Valley to confer with Jackson at Mount Solon, over potential confusion caused by the Confederate High Command, which threatened the whole strategy. Since the beginning of April, Jackson had been a clear advocate of destroying Banks's presence in the Valley. Lee concurred, to the extent that he made his, initial, strategy for relieving the pressure upon Richmond, the defeat of Banks; followed by an advance to the Potomac, as a direct threat to Washington. On the very same day that Jackson was moving from Lebanon Springs to Mount Solon, Lee had written *"Whatever movement you make against Banks, do it speedily, and if successful, drive him back towards the Potomac, and create the impression, as far as possible, that you design threatening that line."* The intellectual unanimity between the two, which would yield so many positive successes for the Confederate cause, was about to yield its first fruits. If Jackson could say that, *"Lee was the only man he would follow blindfold,"* Lee was already looking upon Jackson as the man of whom he could say in later years, *"if Jackson had lived, I would not have lost the battle of Gettysburg."* In this second week of May 1862, *"almost the darkest in Confederate annals,"*[230] Lee clearly saw in Jackson the man who could perform the most difficult task of all, the transformation of theoretical strategy into solid success. As practical

---

230 Ibid.

evidence of his confidence, Lee had already ordered the brigades of Generals Branch and Mahone, to move away from Richmond and reinforce the Army of the Valley. By Saturday the sixteenth, Branch had already reached Gordonsville, less than thirty miles from Swift Run Gap, on a straight road.

However, at the very moment that Jackson had manoeuvred, fought and positioned himself to work the oracle – as so often happened on both sides in this War – the fallout from some mal-adroit politician – in this case the Confederate President, whom Henderson characterizes as being even more of a *"marplot"* than his opposite number – threatened to confound the most astute military thinking. Lee had been appointed to the very pinnacle of military power in Richmond; but Davis had appointed Johnston to command all outlying forces around the city, and 'inanimate' Johnston – a general for little movement and even less genuine ac-tion – either knew nothing of what Lee was hatching with Jackson, or, in modern slang parlance, simply did not 'get it.' Learning that Banks was actually constructing earthwork defences at Strasburg, at the northern end of the Massanutton, Johnston *'took council of his fears,'* and ordered Branch back from Gordonsville; Ewell to quit the Valley and move closer to Richmond, and Jackson to do no more than *"observe"* Banks. Jackson had already ordered Ewell forward to Luray, in the eastern valley, between the Massanutton and the Blue Ridge, opposite the New Market Gap in Peaked Mountain; so a good half of the way up the South Fork Valley. Strasburg was situated at the northern end and a little westward of the Massanutton, astride the Valley Turnpike, in the main Shenandoah Valley. The Johnston order prompted Ewell into an immediate discussion with Jackson.

There was a strong touch of the berserker about Major-General Richard Ewell, who was much given at the height of an action, to take part in a charge; to advance with his own skirmish line, or to dash across and assist a nearby gun crew. He was always well mounted and a bold horseman. On the march he would often go 'off-road,' and put his horse at fences and water-jumps. Both mod-est and eccentric, in the way of Blucher, he imagined a serious gut disorder which, although unlike Blucher, did not take the form of his imagining being pregnant with an elephant, did cause him to eat nothing but frumenty, a concoction of hulled wheat boiled in milk. One of his Brigade Commanders described him as having *"Bright, prominent eyes, a bomb-shaped bald head, and a nose like that of Francis of Valois."* Or Wellington, perhaps, but at any rate, a nose which … *gave him a striking resemblance to a woodcock."*[231] Dick Ewell was adored by his officers and men and was admirably suited to operating with Jackson – apart from his *"swearing like a cowboy."* He was *"full of dash and daring, … had seen much service on the Indian frontier … and … was ready to take responsibility, if orders were not forthcoming."* He *"executed instructions to the letter."* Conferring, on Ewell's arriving at Mount Solon soon after first light, Jackson immediately telegraphed Lee *"I am of the opinion that an attempt should be made to defeat Banks, but under instructions from General Johnston, I do not feel at liberty to make an attack. Please answer by telegraph at once."* Ewell proposed he should be given a formal order to move up to New Market, *"on next Wednesday night, unless you receive orders from a superior officer and of a date subsequent to the sixteenth instant."* Jackson agreed and wrote the order, beginning *"As you are in the Valley District, you constitute part of my command."* Given that they were meeting on a Sunday, it is far from unlikely that whilst awaiting Lee's reply, Jackson had the hard-swearing Ewell accompany him to Divine Service. It is no less likely that the pair gestured men to places beside them, in the middle of the congregation, which, out of deference, the dour Presbyterians of the Valley had studiously avoided. What is absolutely certain is that not being exactly over-burdened with sleep, neither general would have heard one word of the firstly, secondly, or thirdly of the Padre's thirty minutes or so of homily. Jackson, at least, had the reputation of sleeping soundly during the sermons of clerics, most of whom would have had no deeper understanding of the Bible and of the Christian religion, than the General himself.

---

231 Henderson quoting General Dick Taylor.

Lee did answer promptly. Ewell returned that afternoon to his command with the already agreed intention of moving up to Luray. The reason for seemingly ordering him to New Market, in the covering instruction of early Sunday morning, was the need to keep Banks at ease and complacent behind the false security of his entrenchments at Strasburg. To make him believe, however unlikely in Jackson's case, that trouble, when it came, would approach him head-on. Jackson, typically, marched early on Monday morning, and made no attempt to enter the eastern valley; but took the Valley turnpike towards New Market. As always, he was planning on the principle that if he could confuse his own side, then he could baffle and surprise the enemy. To further emphasise a march directly on Strasburg, as well as to mask as far as possible that Jackson himself was present, Ewell sent across to Jackson the Louisiana brigade (sixth, seventh, eighth and ninth Louisiana and Major 'Bob' Wheat's Louisiana Tigers. *"An hour or two"* before his death at Cold Harbour, during the relief of Richmond, Wheat *"looking like a mounted Falstaff,"* rode up to Jackson *"with uncovered head, and almost bluntly said; 'General, we are about to get into a hot fight and it is likely many of us may be killed. I want to ask you for myself and my Louisianians not to expose yourself so unnecessarily, as you often do. What will happen to us, down here in these swamps, if anything happens to you, and what will become of the country!' … As he spoke, he looked up frankly into Jackson's face, who was listening attentatively. Then, suddenly taking Wheat's hand and shaking it, Jackson said 'Much obliged to you, Major. I will try not to get into danger unnecessarily. … Each of us has his duty to perform, without regard to consequences; we must perform it and trust in Providence.' … as the General rode away, he said, 'Just like Major Wheat. He thinks of the safety of others, too brave ever to think of himself'."* [232] The Louisiana brigade joined the Army of the Valley, after it had passed through Harrisonburg, and was camped for the night astride the Valley Turnpike beyond Sparta, where the unmade road from Keezletown joined the Pike.

---

232 Douglas.

The Brigade Commander, Major-General Dick Taylor, was the son of the celebrated general of the Mexican War, Zachary Taylor, and another West Point graduate. Henderson describes him as *"a man of high position, of unquestioned ability, an excellent disciplinarian, and a delightful writer,"* which certainly applies to his first meeting Jackson. *"A mounted officer was despatched to report our approach, and select a camp, which proved to be beyond Jackson's forces, then lying in the fields on both sides of the Valley pike."* (Jackson placed the Louisiana brigade at the head of the advance, to help create uncertainty in enemy observers, as to whose force was approaching and thus whether or not he himself was present) *"Over 3,000 strong, neat in fresh clothing of grey with white gaiters, bands, playing at the head of their regiments – not a straggler, but every man in his place, stepping jauntily, as if on parade, though it had marched twenty miles or more – in open column, with the rays of the declining sun flaming on polished bayonets, the brigade moved down the hard smooth pike, and wheeled on to the camping-ground. Jackson's men, by the thousands, had gathered on either side of the road to see us pass.*

"After attending to necessary camp details, I sought Jackson, whom I had never met. The mounted officer who had been sent on in advance pointed out a figure perched on the topmost rail of a fence, overlooking the road and field, and said it was Jackson. Approaching, I saluted and declared my name and rank, then waited for a response. Before this came, I had time to see a pair of cavalry boots covering feet of gigantic size, a mangy cap with visor drawn low, a heavy dark beard and weary eyes, eyes I afterwards saw filled with intense but never brilliant light. A low gentle voice enquired the road and distance marched that day.

"Keezleton road, six-and-twenty miles."

"You seem to have no stragglers."

"Never allow straggling."

"You must teach my people; they straggle badly."

A bow in reply.

Just then my Creoles started their band for a waltz. After a contemplative suck at a lemon.

"Thoughtless fellows for serious work," came forth.

I expressed a hope that the work would not be less well done because of the gaiety. ... Where Jackson got his lemons, "No fellow could find out," but he was rarely without one."[233]

The next morning, as they neared New Market, Jackson surprised everyone by ordering a right turn out of the main Valley, up through the Gap in Peaked Mountain, down into the South Fork Valley, over the river, and on the six miles from White House Bridge to Luray, where forces were joined with Ewell.

---

233 Henderson quoting Taylor's *"Destruction and Reconstruction"*.

20. TURNING THE FLANK

....

"I thought, as I turned towards my camp,
How unconscious all are of the drama
Jackson is preparing for us, and what
'merriment' the morning will reveal!"
Colonel George H. Gordon (United States Army)

....

THE situation threatening his capital, during those second and third weeks of May, failed to produce any constructive or positive thinking in the Confederate President. All too scarce military stores were sent away from the city; Confederate archives were packed for removal, and arrangements were made to evacuate the 'First Family.' The General Assembly, City Council and the populace, however, were in sterner mood. A Confederate States Resolution called upon the President to defend the capital, if need be, *"until not a stone was left upon another."*[234] With ships of the US Navy clearly visible from high ground near the city, as they lay at anchor off Harrison's Landing, the populace turned out en- masse, in the spirit of the Resolution. Soldiers and slave gangs digging and constructing earthworks and ramparts, were assisted by everyone from stallholder to senator. Batteries of heavy guns were dragged into position and registered. When Union gunboats, feeling their way cautiously up rivers and waterways, came within range, they were fired upon, and forced to withdraw. Virginia had proved herself, once more, as the *'Unterrified Commonwealth.'*

One hundred miles north, in Washington, during those May weeks, emotions were running very differently from both the Confederate President and his general public. In the Federal

---

234 Henderson.

capital, the two dominant moods were public gaiety and governmental complacency. Everyone from street-hustler to president was convinced that Union muscle was set to triumph. The books were closed to anyone still wishing to join-up – or, indeed, still left to join-up, for half a million men had come forward to save the Union after Kernstown, so impressed had they been by the Shields version of the event! Entertainers mocked the South and its way of life in public, and in bars and lounges, and in the columns of newssheets, victory and Union skill at arms were the topics of the hour. Personal memos and the knotted handkerchief prompt, made in nervous haste to locate the precise whereabouts of Bull-Pasture Mountain and the hamlet of Franklin, were discarded or untied, as being no longer relevant. Having fragmented their preponderance of manpower into four independent armies – to the detriment, not solely, of McClellan's need for concentration – the Secretary continued to shuffle the deck. Banks was ordered to divest himself of eleven thousand men under Shields, who was ordered eastwards across the Blue Ridge, to cover Washington, in readiness for McDowell leaving the Fredericksburg area to combine with McClellan for the final assault and capture of Richmond. Both President and Secretary planned to be on the saluting dais for a grand review, before McDowell marched on the twenty sixth of May. Confidence was running high. The only person in all Washington, so it seemed, who felt there might be more to Jackson's withdrawal from before Franklin, than a simple retreat in the face of superior numbers, was the President of the Baltimore and Ohio Railroad. *"The aspect of affairs in the Valley of Virginia,"* he wrote to Secretary Stanton, *"is becoming very threatening ... the enterprise and vigour of Jackson are well known ... Under the circumstances will it not be more judicious to order back General Shields, to co-operate with General Banks? Such a movement might be accomplished in time to prevent disaster."*[235] Ashby, who had remained in the Valley

---

235 Henderson.

throughout the M'Dowell sortie, was soon reporting that, following the departure of Shields, Banks had moved still further back up the Valley towards Harper's Ferry, and was digging-in around Strasburg. This in itself, led Lee to conclude that he *"cannot be as strong as has been represented: if so, his course is inexplicable."*

Throughout Thursday, the twenty second of May, the 'architects of disaster' tramped steadily northward up the eastern Valley from Luray. Since leaving their Mount Solon – Bridgewater camps on Monday morning, they had covered some sixty miles, and after halting to eat that evening, and lying mostly in pairs, each wrapped in his own blanket, they were no more than seventy miles from Washington. Jackson's men had covered some two hundred miles in eighteen marching days, since leaving their camps in Elk Run Valley and returning from Franklin. Now they were just ten miles from the hamlet of Front Royal, at the head of the South Fork or Luray Valley, where Banks had positioned Colonel Kenly and his First Maryland Regiment of some one thousand infantry and two rifled guns, both as flank guard for his main position, and to keep watch at the head of this eastern Valley. Two days earlier, Kenly had sent a strong patrol eleven miles along the South Fork of the Shenandoah; and although they had met with no opposition, some locals did say that Confederate infantry was expected. Banks not only did not react in any way to this intelligence; he even withdrew the cavalry from Kenly, leaving him both short-sighted as well as isolated.

As had become customary on marching days, the Army of the Valley broke camp with the dawn of Friday. Within an hour, the strong May sun was lipping the forested heights of the Blue Ridge to their right. It would soon be a hot day for marching. And fighting. The silent, constantly re-assessing; constantly scheming figure on the *'Little Sorrel,'* was riding well-forward amongst Taylor's lead Louisiana companies. Brigade Commander Dick Taylor was moving up through his silent ranks, constantly in touch with both officer and private. The enemy now was too near to allow music. Riding forward at a trot, Taylor rejoined Jackson as they approached Spangler's Cross-roads, just seven miles from Front Royal. A rest halt was agreed. Both had similar views on the benefit of frequent short breaks on long approach marches. Jackson in particular, was insistent that men should lie down for a few moments. *"A man rests all over when lying down,"* he said. This morning he pencilled a brief instruction for the cavalry, handed it to one of the staff for delivery, and within seconds was asleep, slumped in the saddle. Ashby and his guerrilla horsemen, leaving a small detachment on the line of Tom's Brook, had slipped off unseen from before Banks, and in Indian file along twisting forest trails, had come through the Massanutton, crossed Passage Creek and the South Fork River, to join the sleeping army in the small hours. Acting now on the scribbled directive, they moved off to the north on the dirt road towards Buckton, to cut the rail and telegraph links, midway between Front Royal and the Banks HQ at Staunton. Flournoy and the Sixth Virginia Cavalry took the same route and were to come in on Front Royal from the southeast, and prevent any retreat towards Strasburg, that might result from the initial assault. Colonel Munford's Second Virginia cavalry would take care of the telegraph link with Winchester and Washington; destroy the rail bridges approaching Front Royal, and send a strong detachment across the Blue Ridge, to deter and warn against any attempted intervention from the east. The noose was tightening around Kenly. The futility of digging-in around Strasburg was about to be laid bare. By comparison, simply *'observing'* Banks would have contributed nothing to the Confederate dilemma.

One more twist in the plot remained before the attack went in. Jackson was a thorough and continuous studier of the map. It is more than likely, that during the two non-marching days at Mount Solon, he and Hotchkiss had gone over every inch of the ground as far north as Harper's Ferry. Hotchkiss was always given every facility to familiarize himself with the countryside, and would prepare maps and sketches, and scratch diagrams in the earth, to illustrate points under discussion. To the outside observer, Jackson knew every corner of the Valley – as, indeed, he did, by dint of hard study and close reconnaissance but then, probably, no general has or can been truly great without an instinctive feeling for ground.

It had gone noon when they reached Asbury Chapel, little more than four miles from Front Royal, and probably only Hotchkiss was not taken completely by surprise, when Jackson ordered a right turn down a rough track, twisting eastwards through some welcome forest shade. A little over an hour, and one rest halt later, they turned left, and were heading north once again *"on the Gooney Manor road, at Mrs King's."*[236] Still without having bumped an enemy patrol, cavalry vedette, or picket. Jackson had avoided the obvious final approach to Front Royal, and his attack would be better placed to scotch any attempts to retreat eastwards, up across the Blue Ridge, and through the Manassas Gap.

No sooner had the more open ground before the village became visible through the trees, and the First (Confederate) Maryland Regiment of Colonel Bradley Johnson, and Major Roberdeau Wheat's Louisiana Tigers moved swiftly out to right and left into loose skirmish formation, astride the Gooney Road, than the attack broke cover into the hot sunshine, individuals stopping only long enough for well-aimed shots at pickets, placed in the words of Douglas *"within sight of, and negligently near Front Royal."* They were swiftly overrun, and the skirmishers switched their aim to the two infantry companies of the First (Federal) Maryland Regiment, positioned for close support before Front Royal. Behind the skirmishers, bugles screeched, the appearance in the open of the solid assault lines of Taylor's Louisiana men, sending birds fluttering upwards from the forest edge, and chilling the picket residue and support company-men into a dash back into Front Royal. In Kenly's regimental camp, beyond the village and beside the turnpike to Winchester, drums urged the main force of six infantry companies and the crews of two ten-pounder Parrot guns, to arms. While the startled and the curious mingled with the fugitives and uncertain soldiers of a company posted within

236 Allan.

the village, one woman, guessing at once the meaning of the bugles and the firing, slipped out of Front Royal, through the trees and up the slope, towards the advancing men in grey.

Jackson, well forward with Richard Ewell and Dick Taylor, eagerly scanning the scurrying figures, assessing, visualising, pondering – the clearly focusing mind seeing only recognisable patterns and possible opportunities. *"At General Ewell's suggestion,"* he looked back at Douglas. *"You better see what that young woman wants."* Riding towards her Douglas was *"struck ... by ... the tall, supple and graceful figure ... and ... startled momentarily, at hearing her call my name ... but ... not much astonished"* on seeing it was the ardent Virginia patriot and self-appointed Confederate intelligence agent, Belle Boyd, *"whom I had known from earliest girlhood."* Between gulps of air, from the stiff, uphill run, she said, *"I knew it must be Stonewall, when I heard the first gun ... tell him that the Yankee force is very small – one regiment of Maryland infantry, several pieces of artillery and several companies of cavalry."* The Generals may then have ridden across, because, as Taylor recounts the appearance of Belle Boyd, *"... a mounted officer from the rear called Jackson's attention, who rode back with him. A moment later there rushed out of the wood, a young, rather well-looking young woman ... with much volubility. She said ... that the town was filled with Federals, whose camp was on the west side of the river, where they had guns in position to cover the bridge; that they believed Jackson to be west of the Massanutton, near Harrisonburg; that General Banks was at Winchester, where he was concentrating his widely scattered forces to meet Jackson's advance, which was expected some days later. All this she told with the precision of a staff officer making a report, and it was true to the letter. Jackson was possessed of this information before he left New Market, and based his movements on it; but it was news to me."*[237] Banks certainly believed at this time that Jackson was still some fifty miles away at Harrisonburg, while at the same time, Jackson, at least suspected this, as well as being sure that Banks was still at Strasburg – at

---

237 Henderson quoting Taylor.

most ten miles from Front Royal, not yet having moved further north to Winchester.

When Belle Boyd left, to run back down to the village, Douglas recalled, *"I raised my cap,"* and *"she kissed her hand."* Jackson, and those around him, watched as the skirmishers from Maryland and Louisiana swept down the slope, the former suffering the full nastiness of civil war, sniping, not simply at Union sympathisers; but at men from their home state. *"It took very little time to get into Front Royal and clear it out."*[238] Belle Boyd waved *"her white bonnet,"* as she re-entered the village, behind those whom she called *"the darling boys."* *"General Jackson with a semi-smile suggested … to Douglas … that I had better go and see if I could get any more information from that young lady."* When Douglas caught up with her, she was *"standing on the pavement in front of a hotel, talking with some Federal officers (prisoners), and some of her acquaintances in our army. … When I rode up to speak to her, she received me with much surprised cordiality, and as I stooped from my saddle, she pinned a crimson rose to my uniform, bidding me remember that it was 'blood-red' and that it was her 'colours'."*

The pursuit was on; but for Jackson, the straightforward simplicity of a thoroughly planned and skilfully executed surprise attack, had become at once more complex. Close on the far side of Front Royal, the South Fork joins the main (North Fork) Shenandoah River, demanding bridges for rail and 'pike, as well as lesser walkways for lesser streams. Kenly's two, rifled, Parrot guns were formidable weapons, and whilst he frantically worked to get his infantry to hold, he had the guns trained to fire on a bridge ahead of the pursuit. There was an appreciable delay before Jackson's artillery chief, Colonel Crutchfield, could bring up guns to respond. However, the Sixth Louisiana having been ordered into some woods to the left of the line of advance, was working around Kenly's right flank. Belle Boyd had been right to mention cavalry, for two companies of the Fifth New York

---

238 Douglas.

cavalry were just then riding in from Strasburg. However, also closing in from the west was a dust-cloud being thrown-up by Sam Flournoy's Sixth Virginia Cavalry, and they were coming in north of the South Fork, on Kenly's right rear. Sensing the encirclement of his position, Kenly packed what he could into his wagons; fired the rest, and immediately withdrew across both forks of the river, attempting to burn the two turnpike bridges as he went. In this he was only partially successful. Men of the Louisiana regiments ran forward through the smoke from numerous small fires on the abandoned camping ground, to douse the blazing wood of the bridges. However, enough damage was done to the bridges to slow the pursuing infantry. Kenly continued marching clear on the Winchester Turnpike, leaving the two companies of New York Cavalry as a slender rear-guard.

Jackson, riding swiftly through Front Royal, crossed the South Fork and rode on to meet the Sixth. *"Get across and charge 'em, Flournoy! They won't hold."* Troopers quickly began to scour the bank for crossing places both up and down stream, and in a short while the sixth, with the General in their midst, were splashing through the Shenandoah, Company pennons fluttering well to the fore. As they left the water, the troopers were urged swiftly forward *"On you go! On you go! "Don't stop. Charge!"* Sabres flashed in the late afternoon sun. The Virginians spurred into a gallop, dashing piecemeal at the two companies of stationary; but restless, New York horsemen. Pistols cracked on both sides; but at the moment of impact the Northerners turned and rode for their lives. Closing, as they moved forward, 'B' Company charged directly up the turnpike, with 'E' Company moving up through the fields on their left and, 'A' and 'K' on the right of a fast-moving line, made somewhat ragged and jerky by having to cross post and rail fencing.

Just short of Cedarville, some three miles from Front Royal, Kenly decided to make a stand on some rising ground to the right of the 'pike. Possibly, he had not fully appreciated the strength of the force opposing him, or he intended a delaying tactic, to give Banks time to organise. Although he probably did not know it, his telegraphic warning had been intercepted by Ashby at Buckton, when, as ordered, Ashby cut the rail and telegraph link with Strasbourg, and killed or captured the two companies of Philadelphia infantry on guard there. However, a cavalry courier had also been sent to Banks.

"*Charles H. Greenleaf, Company D, Fifth New York Cavalry …* wrote of his experience as the courier, … *Dear Father and Mother, … when we got within two miles of our destination, we heard cannonading. The Major ordered the baggage to stop, and our two companies dashed on, and found several companies of our infantry and two pieces of artillery engaged with several thousand of the enemy. … Colonel Parem, who had command of our force, … ordered me to take one man and the two fastest horses in our company, and ride for dear life to General Banks's headquarters, in Strasburg, for reinforcements. The direct road to Strasburg was occupied by the enemy, so, I was obliged to ride round by another … I rode the seventeen miles in fifty-five minutes. General Banks didn't seem to think it very serious but ordered one regiment of infantry and two pieces of artillery off. I asked General Banks for a fresh horse to re-join my company, and he gave me the best horse that I ever rode, and I started back. … On the Front Royal turnpike, about two miles this side of where I left our men … saw two men … I supposed they were our pickets. … I asked … 'Who are you?'*

'We are part of General Jackson's staff,' they replied. I supposed they were only joking. I rode towards Front Royal till I overtook a soldier and asked him what regiment he belonged to. He said he belonged to the Eighth Louisiana. … I turned back. … When I got out of the enemy's lines I rode as fast as the horse could carry me to General Banks and reported what I had seen and heard. He said I had saved the army."[239] Apart from this oblique, self-condemnation by Banks of his own ability as a general, the letter, which can have done nothing for the peace of mind of Charles's poor mother, was, interestingly, written from far distant Williamsport, on the Potomac, just two days after the battle. Kenly's attempted delaying tactic

---

239 Allan quoting Greenleaf's letter home.

near Cedarville, if such it was, never materialised. While the Marylanders were preparing, the remnant of the Federal cavalry rearguard came belting up the road, crashed through the embryonic defences and disappeared up the turnpike in a cloud of dust. (Given the place and date of Greenleaf's letter, one cannot but wonder where and when they slowed to a walk and drew rein!). A single shot from a Parrot briefly shuddered the advancing 'B' Company; but then the surge of Sam Flournoy's charging horsemen was into the would-be defenders, sabres rising and falling amid the snap of pistols. From right and left, the wings of the charge rode in to envelope the position. Men began dropping their weapons in surrender. In a small orchard towards the back of the mound, Kenly was hacked-down, trying to rally his men around the Regimental Colour. Flournoy's 'I' and 'D' Companies bypassed the fight and rode on up the road in pursuit of the guns and the wagon train. The first gun was taken almost at once, and, continuing to pick-up fleeing horsemen along the way. The two companies went on to capture all Kenly's wagons, and the second Parrot, some four miles from Winchester. The gun was brought in, hitched to a pair of farm horses taken from a nearby field. The final phase of the Front Royal success was complete. Of the one thousand and sixty-three of Kenly's command, fewer than a hundred and thirty escaped. Seven hundred and fifty were captured – mostly by the Sixth Virginia. A hundred and twenty-two were wounded and thirty-two killed. Jackson lost thirty-six men killed and wounded. The attack on Front Royal also yielded quantities of Federal Government stores and equipment, which had been stockpiled *"in the railroad depot and an adjoining store-house."* Just one of Jackson's captures of Federal gear which led General 'Jeb' Stuart to say later that summer, Banks *"has been the best commissary and quartermaster you ever had."*[240]

---

240 Douglas quoting a conversation between Jackson and Stuart *"after Slaughter Mountain"*.

Throughout Friday the twenty third, Banks made no positive response to being attacked at Front Royal, beyond sending the one regiment and two guns towards Buckton, in response to Greenleaf's first report. He later recalled a force without it having either contacted the enemy or gathered any useful intelligence. Throughout this period, he stuck doggedly to his belief that Jackson was still at Harrisonburg, and so opposite him in the main Valley, albeit fifty miles distant. Ergo, the Front Royal attack was either being carried out by Ewell or was a raid. Initial reports of the Confederate numbers involved, which he telegraphed to Stanton, were, he said *"exaggerated."* He would seem to have taken no positive action himself to clarify this crucial point, which clearly, he had to do, if he was ultimately to respond effectively. Then, quite out of the blue, the hard-riding Greenleaf re-appears, and presents him with the one piece of intelligence needed for the mist to clear *"Who are you? We are part of General Jackson's staff."* At a stroke the veil had been drawn aside, and Banks could say *"You have saved the army."*

In response to the somewhat complacent communiques from the Valley, Secretary Stanton sent a telegram, *"Arrangements are making to send you ample reinforcements. Do not give up the ship before succour can arrive."*[241] But in fragmenting, instead of concentrating, the Federal armies earlier, Stanton had played a key role in Banks's decline into the predicament in which he now found himself. On the Friday evening of Front Royal, that fine soldier and erstwhile commander of the Second Massachusetts, Colonel George Gordon, now one of only two brigade commanders in Banks's 'Department of Shenandoah', began to plead at considerable length – to bully almost – his army commander to make a move. Not just any move; but one specific move. The one move that would ensure Jackson retained the initiative. Gordon laboured the point for withdrawal. Not one single aggressive thought in all his forceful pleading. Withdraw, Withdraw, the one move which Jackson wished Banks to attempt above all others.

---

241 Henderson.

21. BITTER SWEET RETURN

....

*"Mr Douglas, what do you think of
the ladies of Winchester? Don't you
think they are a noble set, worth
fighting for? I do. They are the
truest people in the South."*
Stonewall Jackson

....

WHEN darkness fell on that Friday evening at Cedarville, Jackson
was essentially where he needed to be. He had achieved the opening result he intended. The flank of the Strasburg entrenchments
had been turned, and he was poised on the lines of communication from Strasburg, leading back through Harper's Ferry to
Washington. Like Banks, however, Jackson's next move depended upon several uncertainties and uncontrollables. First, he was
not absolutely certain of the numerical strength of the Strasburg
position, yet he needed a swift, clear-cut victory, not an attri-
tional fight, to continue north with the threat to Washington
which could ease the pressure on Richmond. Speed of movement was essential. If Banks decided to tough it out at Strasburg,
inviting Jackson to come after him, time would favour the defender. Jackson's force was not sufficiently large to allow him to
mask Banks with one part, whilst the remainder made an effective gesture towards Washington. Furthermore, Banks needed
to be cleared from the Valley, if only to allow greater freedom
of movement. In theory, overwhelming Federal numbers could
be swiftly concentrated against him. Fremont from the west;
McDowell/ Shields from the east, and numerous units available
to come south from Maryland, through Harper's Ferry. A battle
of attrition was out of the question.

As the day ended with Jackson silently pondering how best to
get Banks out of his entrenchments, and moving in the direction

required, his own infantry finally reached him, having marched some twenty-four miles since five that morning. Ewell's remaining infantry also closed-up, but only after dark, Jackson had sent an order for all those units following the initial attack, to march straight on at Asbury Chapel. However, the despatch courier was one of Ashby's ill-disciplined guerrilla cavalry, and the order was never delivered. As a result, those following Taylor's brigade toiled unnecessarily, tramping the long way around on the twisting, narrow trail to Mrs King's.

To allow for the various options open to Banks, including his deciding to stay put, Jackson's plan was to approach the Valley turnpike on a broad front. *"In the event of Banks leaving Strasburg, he might escape towards the Potomac; or if we moved directly to Winchester, he might move via Front Royal towards Washington city. In order to watch both directions, and at the same time advance upon him if he remained at Strasburg, I determined, with the main body of the army, to strike the Valley turnpike near Middletown, a village five miles north of Strasburg, and thirteen south of Winchester.*[242] On Saturday morning, Ashby, leading a combined cavalry, infantry and artillery group, left Cedarville for the Valley turnpike at Middletown. The main body of infantry followed. The cavalry – the Second and Sixth Virginia under Ewell's cavalry leader General George Steuart, – took the turnpike through Nineveh to Newtown on the main Valley turnpike just eight miles from Winchester, while Ewell himself moved on Winchester with his artillery and one infantry brigade. Shortly before mid-day, as he was nearing Newtown, Steuart's cavalry scouts reported Federal wagons approaching the village on the Valley Pike, away to his left. Steuart struck at once. The crews fled, leaving several wagons in Confederate hands. While the booty of arms and medical stores was being examined, a heavy dust cloud was seen rising amongst the fields and trees to the south. No creak and rumble of laden wagons; but the solid thump of pounding feet. Infantry! Further reconnaissance

---

242 Jackson's report (Allan).

reported infantry and cavalry, and in sufficient strength to force Steuart to withdraw, leaving the road open to Winchester. It seems doubtful if his making no positive attempt to delay, what was possibly, the main body of Banks's force would have commended itself to Jackson.

Ashby, followed by the bulk of the infantry, reached Middletown after Steuart's attack on the Federal wagons. The men were tired. As Douglas put it, *"the army had been marching almost daily for weeks … and had been living for some time on much excitement and very small rations."* In the preceding five days alone, Jackson's command had marched ninety miles or so, and that of Ewell some eighty miles. Jackson had the reputation of marching at dawn, or *'early dawn',* if he did not *'march the night before.'* On this occasion, for whatever reason, he was not in position astride the Valley turnpike before Banks made his move. Henderson almost brings himself to accuse Jackson of the uncharacteristic fault of 'over-caution', but it may have been deliberate, stemming from his not wanting to frighten Banks off from taking the obvious – and for Jackson the best – step of withdrawing along the Valley turnpike. On the other hand, on the morning after Front Royal, the Army of the Valley may simply have made an uncharacteristically late start. Either way, *"When the little village of Middletown came in view … the highway … was canopied with a vast cloud of grey dust, and crowded beneath, so far as the eye could reach, with a column of troops."*[243] Ashby immediately struck at what appeared to be the head of the column, which had already passed through the village in the direction of Winchester. Taylor's Louisiana men raced forward in line and proceeded to volley the flocking crowd of men and animals filling the main street, until *"the road was literally obstructed with the mingled and confused mass of struggling and dying horses and riders. The Federal column was pierced, but what proportion of its strength had passed north towards Winchester I had then no means of knowing.*[244] Jackson

---

243 Allan quoting Jackson's Adjutant-General.
244 Jackson's report (Allan).

rode up the road towards Winchester to direct and reconnoitre. Dick Taylor had provided a hundred Louisiana soldiers to act as an informal bodyguard for Jackson when recceing forward,[245] for he was always un-thinking of his own safety, when on the hunt for details of enemy movements and dispositions. Moments after he had left Middletown, a body of Federal cavalry – approaching from the direction of Strasburg – drew their swords and came on with the intention of cutting their way through the village. Douglas had the bodyguard line a *"stone fence along the road and prevent if possible, the advance of the enemy's cavalry. ... Just as these one hundred men reached the fence, the cavalry came thundering by ... a deadly volley stopped their wild career."* A handful right at the front kept going, but *"behind them, horses and riders went down in a tangled heap. The rear ... plunged on ... upon the bleeding pile, a roaring, shrieking, struggling mass of men and horses, crushed, wounded and dying. It was a sickening sight, the worst I had ever seen then, and for a moment I felt a twinge of regret that I had ordered that little line to that bloody work."* Ashby then rode up, took one look at the small remnant of the cavalry column fleeing in the direction of Strasburg, and put his *"black stallion ... at ... the tottering gate like a hunter, and ... sword in hand, charged into the demoralized rear of that flying squadron."* After a few moments of anxiety for those watching, Ashby was quickly back with a gaggle of prisoners, both on foot and on horseback. Riding back, and watching his return, even Jackson was minded to administer a *"mild scolding ... at such rashness ... but somehow,* says Douglas, *his looks and manner seemed to deprive the reprimand of all force."*

Jackson quickly appreciated that at Middletown, he had captured, destroyed or scattered the Federal wagon-train and cavalry rear-guard, while Banks with his two infantry brigades had already passed through the village, and it was they, leading the withdrawal, who had brushed Steuart aside at Newtown, earlier in the day. The pursuit was on. The Valley Turnpike, winding

---

245 Douglas.

on towards Winchester, was littered with the debris of the hurried and disrupted retreat. *"Wagons broken down, overturned, some with their contents scattered, some sound and untouched, some with good teams, some horseless, sutlers' stores, officers' luggage, knapsacks, Bibles, cards, photographs, songbooks and cooking utensils...*[246] Jackson rode well forward, accompanied by *"a small party of staff and couriers ... in good spirits but ... as ever ... silent and thoughtful.* At one point, having not eaten since breakfast in Cedarville, *"he dismounted and took from an overturned wagon a cracker ...* which, in the view of Douglas ... *was hard and not too clean."* A short while later, *"he suddenly called across the road"* to the youngest member of his staff, *"Mr Douglas, what do you think of the ladies of Winchester?"* The Douglas mind was some way ahead. He had been *"thinking over some social movements ... he ... intended to execute if Banks let us into Winchester."* It was if Jackson had read his mind, and the young man blushed – or rather *"a blush mantled my cheek,"* as he put it, and the General quickly went on *"I mean the ladies generally. Don't you think they are a noble set, worth fighting for? I do. They are the truest people in the South."* With that, he pulled the old campaign cap even lower over his eyes; picked-up the gait of *'Little Sorrel,'* and rode on in silence.

It was dark by the time they plodded into Newtown. At least night had fallen; but ahead the Valley turnpike was ablaze with burning wagons, the aftermath of a gunner's struggle lasting several hours. Whilst the extended conflagration was a signal of hope, telling the locals that Stonewall Jackson was coming, the opportunity for looting had proved irresistible to Ashby's young troopers, many of whom seized wagon horses and rode off with them to their homes, often many miles and more than a day's ride away. *"That the defeat of Banks was not his destruction is due to the failure of the cavalry at the critical moment ...* Douglas noted ... *and General Jackson never ceased to lament and condemn that costly want of discipline."* The following infantry *"were tired and weary and grumbled*

---

246 Douglas.

a bit as usual, but they had faith and ... they too ... plodded on, not cheerfully but resignedly." They would come to be *"proud of Lee"* but they *"loved 'Old Jack.' He was as a father to them, sometimes stern and exacting; they were his children, sometimes sullen but always obedient."* As a captured Federal officer put it *"Stonewall Jackson's men will follow him to the devil and he knows it."* *"They had unbounded confidence in their leader and he in them; that was it."*[247] Taken, together with intellect, single-minded determination and a belief in victory, important ingredients for success since the time of Alexander, a combination against which mere numbers are powerless. While they tramped through the flames and embers of stricken wagons, every man knew that the thought of a brew, a bite and a blissful sleep beneath the stars of early summer, was not a priority for their General. Jackson's sole thought was to nail Banks, and so startle Lincoln and his acolytes that all designs upon Richmond would disperse like mist on a May morning.

They cleared the last burning or burnt-out wreck and plunged into absolute darkness. Jackson – like Alexander at the head of the Companion Cavalry – was the very point of the spear-head. Only a smattering of Ashby's riders, like the Macedonian *acrobolisti*, were between him and the retreating foe. Some of the staff and couriers were still with him, and Ashby himself; others, succumbing to sleep, had fallen away. The hard core that remained crumpled down in the saddle, wrenching against the burden of heavy eyelids, and relying upon the horse to keep pacing behind the relentless stamina of the *'Little Sorrel'* and his rider. Then, without warning, the enveloping blackness; the thick, heavy silence, stirred only by the scuffling clump, clump, of tired feet, shattered by rippling flashes and the crackle of musketry. Seemingly at their elbows. Even the horses showed little energy for more than a twitch of the head, and a token, skittering step. No one cried out; no one was hurt, and investigation soon showed that the ambush-party had fled. The dream-like progress resumed. An hour passed. Two. Once

---

247 Douglas.

more the night-vision was pierced by a nearby, twinkling volley, *"flashing almost in our faces."* A horse squealed; a muttered oath. The staff had earlier pointed out that the General and his Cavalry Chief were not the pairing of choice for springing ambushes; but *"their opinion lacked weight in convincing the General."* Blood having been drawn, however, Jackson ordered forward an infantry spearhead. The next would-be bushwhackers were roughly handled, and a couple killed. Thereafter, the retreat resorted to a few ineffectual skirmishers in a vain hope of deterring the inexorable pursuit. *"An officer, riding hard,"* caught up with the General. Taylor was with him and later wrote, it *"proved to be the chief quartermaster of the army. He reported the wagon trains far behind, impeded by a bad road in the Luray Valley. 'The ammunition wagons?' ...* demanded Jackson *... sternly. All right, sir. They were in advance, and I doubled teams on them and brought them through."* A relieved *"Ah!"* was Jackson's only response, and, to lighten things a little for the tireless John Harman – who was recognised as having the ability to move wagons as Jackson did men – Taylor, laughing, said, *"'Never mind the wagons. There are quantities of stores in Winchester, and the general has invited me to breakfast there to-morrow.' Jackson took this seriously and reached out to touch me on the arm. ... woe to the man who failed to bring up ammunition. In advance, his trains were left behind. In retreat he would fight for a wheelbarrow."*

A silent, shuttered and darkened Kernstown was reached and passed. The deep blackness began to pale and a shaft or two of rose madder gave notice of the approaching sun. Just two miles from Winchester they halted, and where they stopped, they sagged, asleep before the weight had gone from aching feet. Jackson and Ashby hitched their horses to a fence rail and remained, pacing back and forth, to stay awake; each on his own patch; each with his own thoughts. Colonel Fulkerson came up to plead for a rest before a fight. Fulkerson's brigade had led-off at Kernstown and held staunchly to the line. He was a favourite. Douglas says, Jackson's *"eyes filled with tears when he heard of ...* Sam Fulkerson's death *... at Cold Harbour a few months later."* The General listened closely to his Brigade Commander's story of exhaustion winnowing his command at every halt. Men left unconscious in fence corners and around the bottoms of trees. *"Colonel … he finally replied … I do not believe you can feel more for your men than I do. This is very hard on them, but by this night march I hope to save many valuable lives. I want to get possession of the hills of Winchester before daylight … a moment's reflection … Colonel, you may rest your command for two hours. I will go on with my old brigade."*[248]

When full daylight returned, no one moved. A line of battle could be seen to occupy the hills above Winchester. They would have to be fought for. After what to Banks was an eighteen mile withdrawal and to everyone else, given the litter of men and equipment strewing its wake, was a headlong flight, Banks *"determined to test the substance and strength of the enemy by actual collision."*[249] He posted the brigade under Gordon close on the southern approach to Winchester; its left on the Valley Turnpike and the right on the long ridge stretching away to the south west, at the far end of which the Kernstown struggle had been played out. Infantry Regiments were interspersed with cavalry and a total of eight guns. A further eight guns supported Donelly's brigade, which comprised the left of the Federal line, facing south-east; the direction from which Ewell was approaching along the plank road from Front Royal. (A *"plank road" – a supposed improvement in road building … was made of two inch boards securely spiked down to stringers, though this did not prevent their warping. It was quite expensive. For the first few years of use it was a great improvement over the common dirt road, after that, as the boards warped and became loose, it was anything but a pleasure to drive over."*[250]) Ewell, however, had the shorter, more direct route to Winchester, and not having been entangled in any fallout from the retreat, he and his regiments had the luxury of some sleep during the night before the fighting. Their pickets were little over a mile from the enemy. Ewell moved at first-light, four a.m. and within the hour,

---

248 Douglas.
249 Allan.
250 Arnold.

the Twenty-first North Carolina of Colonel Kirkland launched the first attack across an open field. The numerous stone fences intersecting the fields favoured the defence, and they were volleyed both from in front and in flank, by two regiments, and then a third. Having suffered some eighty seven killed and wounded, they recoiled. However, the first Maryland advancing on the left, and the Twenty-First Georgia, with artillery support, on the right, enfiladed the Federal position, which was abandoned for a position nearer the town.

Jackson, meanwhile, seeing enemy pickets on a dominant hill feature close to the Valley Turnpike ordered General Winder with the Stonewall brigade to *"seize the hill as speedily as possible. The Fifth Virginia was accordingly thrown out in advance, as skirmishers, and the Second, Fourth, Twenty-seventh and Thirty-third Virginia being placed in order of battle, the whole line was ordered to advance, which was done in handsome style, and the position on the crest secured, although the enemy made a resolute, but unsuccessful effort to dislodge our troops from so commanding a position,"* Jackson wrote in his report. He then moved up guns to neutralize *"a battery of the enemy, which,* as he put it ... *was playing from the front with great animation and effect upon the hill."* A second brigade was moved up to support the gunners, and Fulkerson's regiments sent round behind, to extend the whole line to the left. Seeing the Federal line being extended to their right by two regiments and a battery, Jackson rode back with Douglas to where Taylor and his Louisiana Regiments were waiting close to the Valley turnpike, behind the right of Winder's position. *"General, can your brigade charge a battery? ..."* Jackson asked Dick Taylor ...

"It can try ..."

"Very good; it must do it then. Move it forward." On his riding across to Taylor, the order was 'no cheering,' and as Jackson passed, men and General simply raised their headgear in an exchange of salutes.

On his way back, *"the troops ... regardless of the proximity of the enemy ... let forth in one of their deafening yells. Old Jack smiled and passed on."* The Federal artillery duly delivered a *"shower of shells"* which

Jackson, as usual, ignored. The scene amused a watching Irishman, either one of Taylor's Louisiana Irishman or from the First (Irish) Regiment of the Stonewall brigade, for Douglas – riding with the General – heard the man say, *"Be jabbers, have your eye on Auld Jack. I'll wager you he thinks them blatherin' bangs are singin' birds ...* and then, laughing *... And look at yon officer behint him, imitatin' the Ginril and tryin to look as bauld as himself."* Shortly after, Taylor rode up at the head of his Louisiana brigade, and turning the five regiments into line, ordered a charge which impressed the watching Douglas. *"I have rarely seen a more beautiful charge. This full brigade, with a line of glistening bayonets bright in that morning sun, its formation straight and compact, its tread quick and easy, as it pushed on through the clover and up the hill ... the battery was not taken, because it did not wait. It departed, and its infantry support was quickly driven after it."*

Over on the right, Ewell, adopting the proposal of his Brigade Commander, had swung wide and General Trimble with his Sixteenth Mississippi and Fifteenth Alabama, together with the Twenty-First Georgia threatened the left flank and rear of the Federal position. The Federal line crumbled. Watching the progress of the battle from high ground, Jackson could see the progress of Ewell's attacks on the right, and then, the men and guns moving back into and through Winchester itself. Abruptly, he turned to Douglas, *"Order forward the whole line, the Battle's won."* As the regiments in reserve on the Valley Turnpike came up, and the whole line gathered momentum, *"the General cried out 'Very good! Now let's holler!' That is the very language the Professor used. He raised his old grey cap, his staff took up the cheer, and soon from the advancing line rose and swelled a deafening roar, which borne on the wind over Winchester told her imprisoned people that deliverance was at hand. A panic seized the enemy and the retreat became a rout. It was Sunday – was Jackson always to fight on a Sunday?"*[251] General and staff galloped down the hill and entered the town with the skirmishers. The people of Winchester were throwing open doors and windows, *"closed for months"* and

---

251 Douglas.

lining the streets to welcome *"their own troops, who soon forgot their fatigue in the joy of their reception. For a moment, but only for a moment, the dead and wounded on the field seemed forgotten. Then a missing face here and there sent relatives scurrying to the battlefield. But the flames from burning buildings, … soon began to shoot up wildly into the sky, and heavy columns of black smoke threw a pall over the town. Terrible as it looked, it only heightened the excitement and enthusiasm of the populace. The reception of General Jackson cannot be described. There were tears and smiles … lips that spoke blessing, and quivering lips that could not speak at all; men, women and children, all joining in the strange welcome. They ignored the suffering they had gone through and their own fortitude, their losses, their anxieties, but they convinced him surely that they were 'worth fighting for'."*[252]

Amongst the dead on the hills above Winchester lay Lieutenant Marshall Barton, a Winchester man who served with the Newtown Artillery. He had been a cadet at the VMI some seven years earlier, and a scrapbook in which he lampooned the faculty of the Lexington Institute, included these lines on *'Hickory'*, as he called Professor Jackson;

"Like some wild beast that ranged the forest wild,
So rude, uncouth, so purely nature's child
Is Hickory; and yet methinks I see
The stamp of genius on his brow, and he
With his wild glance and keen but quiet eye
Fills my heart with love for him who bears
His honours meekly, and who wears
The laurels of a hero."[253]

Despite the reception, Jackson did not linger in Winchester, *"Notwithstanding the fatiguing marches and almost sleepless night to which the mass of our troops had been subjected, they continued to press*

---

252 Ibid.

253 Stanza of a poem by C. Marshall Barton quoted by Douglas.

forward with alacrity … he wrote … The Federal forces, falling back into the town, preserved their organization remarkably well. In passing through its streets they were thrown into confusion, and shortly after debouching upon the plain and turnpike to Martinsburg, and after being fired on by our artillery, they presented the aspect of a mass of disordered fugitives. Never have I seen an opportunity when it was in the power of cavalry to reap a richer harvest of the fruits of victory. Hoping that the cavalry would soon come up, the artillery, followed by infantry, was pressed forward for about two hours for the purpose of preventing by artillery fire, a re-forming of the enemy; but as nothing was heard of the cavalry, and as but little or nothing could be accomplished without it in the exhausted condition of our infantry, between whom and the enemy the distance was continually increasing, I ordered a halt, and issued orders for going into camp and refreshing the men."[254]

Ashby's people, of course were still scattered on the disposal of their loot. The Second and Sixth Virginia had been on the right of Ewell's line at the taking of Winchester, and under the overall command of his then cavalry leader General George H. Steuart. When Jackson's Assistant Adjutant-General, Sandy Pendleton delivered the urgent order to pursue the fleeing enemy, Steuart made the unforgivable response that he could not comply with the order unless it came through his immediate superior. By the time Pendleton had located Ewell and returned, a further two hours had been lost. So, for the second time in forty-eight hours, Jackson was let down by his mounted troops. This second time by a man in charge – a Brigade Commander no less – who should have immediately appreciated that his professional duty was to take up the pursuit, if necessary, on his own initiative, never mind bureaucratic quibbling over the routing of the order. Ashby at least had the excuse that he was not a professional cavalryman; but what Jackson described him as; *"a leader of partisans."* In the event, the Second and Sixth Va did not even overtake Jackson's infantry until it had been halted for an hour and

---

254 Allan quoting Jackson's report.

the enemy *"beyond the reach of successful pursuit."* Jackson did not press charges against Steuart; but contented himself with saying *"There is good reason for believing that, had the cavalry played its part in this pursuit, as well as the four companies under Colonel Flournoy two days before, in the pursuit from Front Royal, only a small portion of Banks's army would have made its escape to the Potomac."* As it was, Banks's remnant covered some thirty-four miles that day, reaching Williamsport as it was getting dark, and crossing the Potomac into Maryland during the night and the next morning. Never before had his command moved quite so far or so fast!

Jackson that morning put the Army of the Valley into camp at Stephenson's, five miles north of Winchester, where they could rest, revive and refit themselves on the glut of captured Federal stores — Trimble reckoned that twenty percent of his brigade were marching on bare feet by the time they took Winchester. Jackson rode back to the town, and establishing his headquarters in the Taylor Hotel, issued the following communique: *"Within four weeks this army has made long and rapid marches; fought six combats and two battles, signally defeating the enemy in each one; captured several stands of colours and pieces of artillery, with numerous prisoners, and vast medical, ordnance, and army stores; and finally driven the boastful host, which was ravaging our beautiful country, into utter rout. The General commanding would warmly express to the officers and men under his command his joy in their achievements, and his thanks for their brilliant gallantry in action, and their patient obedience under the hardships of forced marches, often more painful to the brave soldier than the dangers of battle. The explanation of the severe exertions which the commanding General called the army to carry out, which were endured with such cheerful confidence in him, is now given in the victory of yesterday. He receives this proof of their confidence in the past with pride and gratitude and asks only a similar confidence in the future.*

"But his chief duty to-day, and that of the army, is to recognize devoutly the hand of a protecting Providence in the brilliant successes of the last three days (which have given us the results of a great victory without great losses) and to make the oblation of our thanks to God for His mercies to us and our country, in the heartfelt acts of religious worship. For

this purpose, the troops will remain in camp to-day, suspending as far as possible, all military exercises; and the chaplains of regiments will hold divine service in their several charges at four p.m."

Jackson reported his losses as sixty-eight killed, three hundred and twenty nine wounded, and three missing. Allan reckoned Ashby's losses at twenty or thirty, and Taylor reported ten of his Louisiana men killed at Front Royal; so a total of four hundred and forty for the entire campaign.

22. ON TO HARPER'S FERRY

....

"Quem deus perdere vult, prius dementat."[255]
Lieutenant-Colonel Crutchfield Jackson's Chief of Artillery.

....

*"If Stonewall Jackson ever gets so completely
surrounded that he cannot march or fight
his way out, he will take wings unto
himself and his army and fly out."*
A Federal Army Surgeon

....

JACKSON had established his headquarters at the Taylor Hotel for no more than twenty four hours, when, at around midnight, Sandy Pendleton received from his bed – having *"no idea of getting up for anything short of battle or fire* – a dignified gentleman of *"grey hairs, intelligence and dignity of manner,"* and bearing all the dust and stain of a long, hard ride. He had come from beyond the Blue Ridge especially, with *"information he thought valuable … that the sudden expulsion of General Banks from the Valley had produced the impression in Washington, that General Jackson's Army was large enough to cross the Potomac and sweep over Maryland, if not take the Federal Capital; that General McDowell … near Fredericksburg … had been ordered to march against Jackson; that General Shields with the advance, numbering ten thousand … was already within a day's march of Front Royal."*[256] The gentleman was thanked and given a bed for the night, and next morning he had a talk with the General. Shortly afterwards, Jackson announced his intention of moving forward to Harper's Ferry. The Staff, in the course of

---

255 'Whom a God wishes to destroy He first makes mad.'
256 Douglas.

getting things underway, were flabbergasted. It had been confidently expected that the order would be to withdraw back into the Valley. Jackson, however, had every intention of thoroughly completing the task of shaking up the Federal President and relieving the pressure upon Richmond, which he had begun when he left Elk Run Valley on the thirtieth of April. He was a close student of the map, and if there were those who did not believe him to be a good judge of character, they had to admit that *"his opinion of the generals opposing him … in Douglas's phrase … was always wonderfully correct."* Despite what might look to others much like the jaws of a trap closing behind them, Jackson, the consummate manipulator of time and space, knew that the jaws still had to be closed. He had a clear understanding of those responsible for the closing, and besides, should the jaws of the trap prevent him from returning to the Valley, he had in mind, as always, an alternative plan.

On the twenty-sixth, the same date that the grey haired gent had his talk with Pendleton, 'inanimate' Johnston wrote a letter to Jackson – irrelevant save only to himself and containing the lines: *"If you can threaten Baltimore and Washington, do so. It may produce an important diversion."* The whole tenor of the letter is of a self-justifying man, struggling to stay in the hunt, and ended with the postscript of a man beginning to realise he was out of his depth *"Time will be gained and saved by addressing me always instead of the government. J.E.J."*[257]

Jackson was amongst the most loyal then going; but he was also a realist, with a clear perception of how things were made to happen. The courier with his intentions and crystal clear views on the overall situation, went to Richmond as usual. The twenty-seventh was also a rest day. Early on the morning of the twenty-eighth, General Winder, at the head of the Stonewall brigade and two batteries of artillery, left the camping ground, marching north for Charlestown, seven miles short of Harper's Ferry.

---

257 Quoted in full by Douglas.

Up ahead, the Federals had increased their strength in the area to some seven thousand men with eighteen guns.[258] Learning of this from some of Ashby's men, Winder informed Jackson, who ordered Ewell forward in support. Moving through Charlestown, however, Winder found just two regiments with two pieces of artillery drawn up to oppose him, and deployed one of his four-gun batteries, supported by the Thirty-Third Virginia, and *"in twenty minutes the enemy retired in great disorder, throwing away arms, blankets, haversacks, etc. The pursuit was continued rapidly with artillery and infantry."*[259] These two regiments were an advance party of the Federal force formed at Harper's Ferry under General Saxton, who sent out a third regiment to assist the retreat and drew up the remainder of his seven thousand across the peninsula at the back of the town. Winder, who had covered twenty-one miles since leaving Stephenson's, continued the pursuit as far as Halltown, some three miles from the Ferry, but then pulled back, to go into camp near Charlestown, where he was joined by Ewell.

258 Allan.
259 Ibid.

23. MR LINCOLN RETURNS TO WASHINGTON

....

"Never take counsel of your fears."
Stonewall Jackson

....

IF not quite 'stepping high like roosters' in the 'deep mud' of Southern terminology, when returning from Fredericksburg on the night of Friday, the twenty third of May, Messrs Lincoln and Stanton were certainly up-beat about the way discussions had progressed during their visit to General McDowell's headquarters. As Lincoln told McClellan, Shields, having transferred his Division from Banks to McDowell's command professed himself *"so worn that he cannot move before Monday morning, the twenty sixth … but … McDowell and Shields both say they can and positively will move Monday morning."*[260] McDowell's forty-thousand would increase the fighting strength of the Army of the Potomac by some forty percent. McDowell would move in on the Confederate capital from the north, as the right wing of the Army under the overall command of McClellan. Everyone felt justified in feeling that it was realistic to expect the seizure of the Confederate capital would result.

The President and Secretary, however, had barely finished the first root beer by which they were slaking thirsts after a physically energetic day – and which also served as a modest note of celebration, given the nation was at war – when a despatch was brought in, telling of an engagement at Front Royal, classified as *"only an unimportant raid."* Assured that it was, indeed, the Front Royal just across the Potomac in the Shenandoah Valley, the alarm bells sounded, and the second root beer gave off an altogether more bitter after-taste. McDowell was cabled by the

---

260 Lincoln to McClellan (Allan).

Secretary, *"The President thinks the whole force you designed to move from Fredericksburg should not be taken away, and he therefore directs that one brigade, in addition to what you designed to leave at Fredericksburg, should be left there."*[261]

By Noon next day – the twenty-fourth – any last vestige of euphoria that might have existed in the White House, had vanished like so much snow off a stone wall. Lincoln's morning telegraph to McClellan confirming that McDowell would march on Monday (although already less one brigade) included the classic line *"I wish you to move cautiously and safely."* By four p.m., McClellan was notified that the situation was being viewed more seriously and more drastic measures were being taken. *"In consequence of General Banks's critical position, I have been compelled to suspend General McDowell's movement to join you. The enemy are making a desperate push on Harper's Ferry, and we are trying to throw Fremont's force and part of McDowell's in their rear. A. Lincoln.*[262]

The next day – the Sunday of the battle for Winchester – saw the tension and excitement in Washington rise yet further, and not simply due to Banks's reporting of his ineffectual struggles. General Geary, commanding a force of some one thousand nine hundred, tasked with guarding the Manassas Gap railway, reported the affair at Front Royal and at the same time that he was pulling back to Manassas Junction. *"His troops hearing the most extravagant stories of the fate of the Maryland Regiment, and supposing that they were about to be swallowed up, burnt their tents and destroyed a quantity of arms."* As Allan observed, given that the Maryland Regiment at Front Royal was pretty much *"swallowed up, ... it is hard to see"* how any stories about the fate of the Maryland Regiment might be *"exaggerated."* The panic of Geary's men had a knock-on effect. From further east, General Duryea telegraphed Washington for help, and leaving his Pennsylvania Regiment behind at Catlett's Station, hurried his three New York Regiments

---

261 Stanton to McDowell (Allan).
262 Quoted by Allan.

back to Centreville. He even abandoned quantities of military stores and his *"camp equipage."* The panic lasted for two days at both Manassas Junction and Catlett's Station. *"At night, the camps were kept in constant alarm by the sentinels firing at stumps or bowing bushes, which they mistook for Confederate guerrillas."*[263]

The alarm, if not, indeed, the panic spread through the corridors of power in Washington. *"Secretary Stanton issued orders calling for the militia of the loyal States to defend that city. … This alarm at Washington, and the call for its defence, produced the most indescribable panic in the cities of the Northern States on Sunday, the twenty-fifth, and two or three days afterwards."*[264] Lincoln sent a message to McClellan, by 'US Military Telegraph' from the 'War Department, Washington, DC', telling him that, *"the enemy is moving north in sufficient force to drive Banks before him, in precisely what force we cannot tell. … I think the movement is a general and concerted one, such as could not be if he was acting upon the purpose of a very desperate defence of Richmond. I think the time is near when you must either attack Richmond or give up the job and come to the defence of Washington. Let me hear from you instantly."*[265] Whilst both McClellan and McDowell believed that the President was grossly over-reacting to the detriment of the agreed strategy, the ripples of alarm continued to spread. Governor Andrew issued a proclamation from his headquarters in Boston, at eleven o'clock at night, which began *"Men of Massachusetts! The wily and barbarous horde of traitors to the people, the government, to our country, and to liberty, menace again the national capital. They have attacked and routed Major-General Banks, are advancing on Harper's Ferry, and are marching on Washington. The President calls on Massachusetts to rise once more for its rescue and defence."* The Governor of Ohio began his exhortation *"To the gallant men of Ohio: I have the astounding intelligence that the seat of our beloved government is threatened with*

263 Allan.
264 Allan quoting Tenney's *'Military & Naval History of the Rebellion'*.
265 Allan.

invasion, and am called upon by the Secretary of War for troops to repel and overwhelm the ruthless invaders ..." Governor Curtain of
Pennsylvania proclaimed *"On pressing requisition of the President of
the United States in the present emergency, it is ordered that the several major-generals, brigadier-generals, and colonels of regiments throughout the Commonwealth muster, without delay, all military organizations
within their respective Divisions or under their control, together with all
persons willing to join their commands, and proceed forthwith to the city
of Washington ..."* The Government took *"military possession of all
the railroads in the United States (for the transportation of troops and
munitions of war)."*[266] Within a day of the Government's call for
recruits, some half a million men had responded.

By nightfall on Sunday the twenty fifth, Lincoln had committed all McDowell's regiments to containing what, at one point,
he alluded to as *"insurrectionary combinations"*, less one brigade
to remain at Fredericksburg. McDowell was not in agreement
with how the situation was being handled, and without knowing
Jackson's movements – but at the same time seeming to be more
understanding of what he was about – wrote *"It will take a week
or ten days for the force to get to the Valley by the route which will give
it food and forage, and by that time the enemy will have retired. I shall
gain nothing for you there and shall lose much for you here. ... I have a
heavy heart in the matter ... I feel it throws us all back, ... and we shall
have to repeat what we have just accomplished."* Lincoln excused himself to McClellan by saying, *"If McDowell's force was now beyond
our reach, we should be utterly helpless. Apprehensions of something like
this, and no unwillingness to sustain you, has always been my reason for
withholding McDowell's forces from you. Please understand this and do
the best you can with the forces you have."* Regarding snapping shut
both jaws of the trap in Jackson's rear, McDowell wrote, *"I beg
to say that co-operation between General Fremont and myself, to cut off
Jackson and Ewell, is not to be counted upon, even if it is not a practical impossibility. ..."* Throughout Jackson's operation to destroy

---

266 Allan.

Banks, Fremont had remained immobile at Franklin. It came of something of a surprise when on the twenty-fourth, together with news of Banks's trials and tribulations, came an order from the President to move to Harrisonburg. He moved on the twenty-fifth, but his was a lacklustre performance. He was allowed to choose his own route and began by marching some thirty miles in the opposite direction to where he had been ordered to move. Rain and bad roads delayed his progress. He was fearful lest, if he went to Harrisonburg, Jackson might divert away to Romney or Moorefield, in the area he had just left. From Petersburg, he would have to go a long way around, because *of the different roads leading from Franklin to Harrisonburg. All but one had been obstructed by Jackson in his retreat."* – i.e. Hotchkiss, acting on Jackson's orders on leaving Fremont's front, had made a thorough job of blocking roads running east into the Valley. Finally, and most damning of all the evidence of Fremont's poor showing; he halted for a day in the course of the march *"because of the urgent representations of his surgeon and others that the men needed rest and could not properly go on."* Poor Lincoln, for all his mustering of a military colossus of men and material – admirably suited to squashing the relatively feeble South – he lacked the crucial component; the appropriate intellect for its control and direction. It would take another two years for him to realise that he had not a shred of competence as a military strategist, and he would say to Grant, *"I neither ask nor desire to know anything of your plans. Take the responsibility and act and call on me for assistance."*[267] Meanwhile, the feeble performance of so many of his generals, faced with the military 'dream ticket' of Jackson and Lee, almost demands sympathy, even if not deserving of it.

---

267 Quoted by Henderson.

24. 'IN YOUR OWN TIME'

....

"Old Jack got us into this fix, and with
the blessing of God he will get us out."
A Confederate Soldier

....

JACKSON intended to keep the threat of his advancing into Maryland – with its many Confederate sympathisers – in-play, as a goad to Federal strategic thinking, as long as possible. To deny troops to McClellan, although an on-going requirement, was only a part of the objective. He would not, of course, have viewed the current disposition of his own troops – with the second Virginia glowering down on Harper's Ferry from the Loudoun Heights on the far bank of the Shenandoah – as anything remotely approaching the nature of *'a fix'*. It was simply the stage reached in the working of a thoroughly thought through plan. Jackson knew exactly what he was seeking to achieve; how he would achieve it and had considered every factor that had the potential to prevent him from doing so. He was silently confident in continued progress, with, of course, the blessing of divine Providence. None of the Union generals opposed to him in the field had shown aggressive initiative of any originality. Neither the enemy, nor, for that matter his own side, had divined either his intentions, or the culmination of his moves. All would be revealed only by the action itself. He would consult no-one. *"Mystery,"* he always said, *"mystery is the key to success."*[268] The regiments he was leading may have been comparatively few in number; but they were march and battle hardened. The rank and file did not trouble themselves with thinking about what needed doing, they simply marched – usually at Jackson's favourite start time, *"early*

---

268 Douglas.

dawn" – for as long as required, and in the direction indicated. The move might include a fire-fight; but by no means always. For Jackson, the circuitous manoeuvre would often prove more productive than the un-thinking, head-on clash. For both leader and led, the confidence was mutual and total. He schemed and directed; they marched and fought, with a willingness to kill or to die. The fundamentals for all true soldiers.

Friday, the thirtieth of May dawned wet. It continued to rain all day. Jackson decided he had demonstrated above Harper's Ferry long enough for his purpose and ordered a move back to Winchester. As Douglas put it, *"Having remained before Harper's Ferry as long as he thought prudent – everyone else thought it very imprudent to go there in the first place,"* clearly revealing how little the Staff understood of their Chief's adroit machinations. Jackson planned and manoeuvred dispassionately, on the basis of what he wished to achieve, and not on the distortions of emotional anxiety. It was said that his staff, only *"for the first time realised the true character and magnitude of the Valley campaign"* when, on meeting with Lee near Walnut Grove Church, at the outset of the Seven Days battles at the end of June, they saw *"the eagerness displayed by General Lee's suite to get a glimpse of 'Stonewall."*[269]

In beginning, the march back, south, through the Valley, *"directions were given to General Winder to recall the Second Virginia regiment from the Loudon Heights and as soon as it should return to its brigade, to move with his command, including the cavalry, and re-join the main body of the army."*[270] Jackson and the main body reached Winchester that same Friday night. The General travelled by train, which, as it neared the town, was waved down by an officer riding up to the carriage door. *"What news?"* he asked.

"Colonel Connor has been driven from Front Royal. … Jackson smiled grimly but made no reply. His eyes fixed themselves upon some distant object. Then his preoccupation suddenly disappeared. He read the dispatch

---

269 Henderson.
270 Allan quoting Jackson's report.

which he held in his hand, tore it in pieces, after his accustomed fashion, and, leaning forward, rested his head upon his hands, and apparently fell asleep. He soon roused himself, however, and turning to Mr Boteler, who tells the story,[271] *said: 'I am going to send you to Richmond for re-inforcements.'* As well as being a friend, Colonel Boteler was still a representative for Winchester in the Confederate Congress and was one of three military men serving as volunteers on Jackson's staff, all of whom were colonels. Correct though the *'gentleman with the grey hairs and dignity of manner'* had been, Jackson's intelligence system was more widespread, and did not rely upon the random selflessness of loyal citizens. Ashby's horsemen doubled as scouts, as well as the means of transmitting news, and they were despatched far and wide. Jackson, possibly, agreed with Frederick the Great on the intelligence advantages of fighting in a friendly country, where the very locals provided a network of eyes and ears. He briefed Boteler on the immediate situation. *"Banks ... is being reinforced from Pennsylvania; General Dix* (replaced by General Saxton) *is in my front and being reinforced by the Baltimore and Ohio Railway. ... Front Royal is captured, and Fremont is now advancing towards Wardensville. ...* (twelve miles to the west of Strasburg, with Front Royal a similar distance to the east). At Winchester, Jackson was still some eighteen miles from Strasburg, with the First brigade further away still) *... Thus, you see, I am surrounded by a very large force. 'What is your own, General?'* asked his friend. *'I will tell you, but you must not repeat what I say, except in Richmond. To meet this attack, I have only fifteen thousand effective men.' 'What will you do if they cut you off?' ... 'I will fall back upon Maryland for reinforcements."*

Jackson sent his map-man, Jed Hotchkiss, back to Charlestown, to bring in the Stonewall brigade, telling him *"I will stay in Winchester until you get here, if I can, but if I cannot, and the enemy gets here first, you must ... go ... round through the mountains ... in any case, I will wait for you in Strasburg,"* he added. Before leaving Winchester, Taylor's Louisiana brigade made a sally in the

---

271 Recounted by Henderson.

direction of Front Royal, which froze Shields for twenty four hours. Shields constantly showed himself to be more talker than doer. While still east of the Blue Ridge he had *"condemned the panic that had seized his brother generals, and had told McDowell that he would clear the Valley with his own Division."[272]* On reaching a position from which he could take positive action to interdict Jackson, he dithered about posting pickets on all approaches to the position he had reached, writing letters to McDowell, worrying about the supply situation, exaggerating Jackson's strength, and imagining a Confederate force approaching down the Luray Valley. In short, he did everything, but the task required of him; that is, he did anything apart from taking direct action. Shields had learnt nothing from his bogus boast of a win at Kernstown. Fremont, on the other side of Jackson, was little better. Although he seems to have been less voluble, and he, personally, at least, kept up with his advance guard, he wrote to Lincoln saying he would be in Strasburg on the thirty first. In acknowledging this despatch, the information in it having been passed to McDowell, Lincoln ended on the somewhat forlorn note, *"You must be up to time of your promise if possible."* Fremont halted his approach some six miles short of Strasburg, at Cedar Creek. Jackson entered Strasburg on Saturday the thirty first, unopposed by either of the two generals sent against him. On the same day, Winder reached Winchester, and marched on to camp near Newtown, the second Virginia having covered thirty-five miles, and the rest of the Stonewall brigade some twenty-eight miles, during the day. The trio of tardy generals sent to eliminate the Jackson threat was completed by Saxton, who, having advanced the seven miles from Harper's Ferry to Charlestown found Winder gone, so *"went into camp, and made no further effort to follow ... his men having been 'completely worn out by fatigue and exposure,' consequent upon the skirmishes and movements of the preceding days."[273]*

272 Henderson.
273 Allan.

At Strasburg, Jackson had eliminated the threat from the Federal forces on the Potomac, totalling some fourteen-thousand, by simply marching away from them; but he was now absolutely plumb between the thirty-thousand or so commanded by McDowell – of which Shields with some ten-thousand was the advance – and the fourteen thousand six hundred and seventy-two *"present for duty"* of Fremont. Unlike the pursuing armies on either side of him, Jackson was encumbered with all the gains made in the way of stores and prisoners, during the previous eight days – none of which he was prepared to relinquish – and which, as he recorded, had been considerable. *"The public property captured in this expedition at Front Royal, Winchester, Martinsburg and Charlestown was of great value, and so large in quantity that much of it had to be abandoned for want of necessary means of transportation."* He wrote, *"Major Harman, my chief quartermaster, had but one week within which to remove it; and, although his efforts were characterized by his usual energy, promptitude, and judgement, all the conveyances that within that short period could be hired or impressed were inadequate to handle the work. The medical stores, which filled one of the largest storehouses in Winchester, were fortunately saved. Most of the instruments and some of the medicines, urgently needed at that time by the command, were issued to the surgeons. The residue were sent to Charlottesville and turned over to a medical purveyor. Two large and well-furnished hospitals, capable of accommodating some seven hundred patients, were found in the town, and left undisturbed, with all their stores, for the use of the sick and wounded of the enemy.*

"Commissary supplies, consisting of upwards of one hundred head of cattle, thirty-four thousand pounds of bacon, flour, salt, sugar, coffee, hard bread, and cheese, were turned over to the proper authorities, besides large amounts taken by the troops and not accounted for. Sutlers' stores valued at twenty-five thousand dollars[274] and for want of transportation abandoned to the troops, were captured. Quartermasters' stores to the value of $125,185 were secured (at Winchester) besides an immense

---

274 In terms of the real price of a commodity today: $25,000 = $589,000 & $125,185 = $2,950,000.

amount destroyed. Many horses were taken by the cavalry (Ashby's men had always to supply their own mounts).

"Among the ordnance stores taken and removed in safety were nine thousand three hundred and fifty-four small arms, and two pieces of artillery and their caissons. A large amount of ammunition was also among the ordnance supplies.[275]

Sunday, the first of June dawned bright and clear, following the heavy rain of the previous afternoon, which had continued throughout the night. In the early forenoon, Jackson sent on back two thousand three hundred prisoners, guarded by the Twenty-First Virginia, and the wagon train, bearing such of the captured stores as could be transported. The train of wagons, two abreast upon the road, covered seven miles from front to rear. A further seven hundred and fifty prisoners, both wounded and sick, were *"paroled and left in the hospitals at Winchester and Strasburg. ... The Federal surgeons captured in attendance at their hospitals ... at the suggestion of Medical Director Hunter McGuire, of Jackson's staff, were unconditionally released."*[276] Jackson's losses during the preceding two weeks were: sixty-eight killed, three hundred and eighty-six wounded, three missing and a hundred and fifty-six captured. These last had all been taken on a headlong desertion of Front Royal by Colonel Connor and the twenty-first Georgia, in the face of Shields' approach. Reporting later to Jackson in Winchester, Connor made too carefree an explanation of his failure to take the least offensive action. The General *"asked in his abrupt manner: 'Colonel, how many men had you killed?' 'None, I am glad to say, General.' 'How many wounded?' 'Few or none, Sir.' 'Do you call that fighting, Sir?' ...* Connor stood condemned by his own testimony as another, comparatively, senior officer who could not be relied upon to act effectively when circumstances demanded. ... *Jackson immediately placed him under arrest, from which he was not released for several months."*[277]

---

275 Jackson's report quoted by Allan.

276 Allan.

277 Henderson.

Ashby reported back that Fremont was showing signs of moving against his cavalry outposts, and Ewell was ordered out at the head of a strong deterrent force. Aided by well-sighted artillery, Ewell parried a move forward by Fremont in brigade strength, and then counter-attacked. *"Sheep," says General Taylor, "would have made as much resistance as we met. Men decamped without firing or threw down their arms and surrendered. Our whole skirmish line was advancing briskly. I sought Ewell and reported. We had a fine game before us, and the temptation to play it was great; but Jackson's orders were imperative and wise."*[278] Jackson had not yet reached the position from which he would deal with Fremont. Around noon, Winder and the Stonewall brigade came in – *"the men threw themselves down in the road and went to sleep … It was one of those forced marches which all of General Jackson's army were sometimes called upon to endure, and which won for them the appropriate name of Jackson's 'Foot Cavalry."*[279] In the course of the afternoon Jackson recalled Ewell, and the Army of the Valley left Strasburg, continuing south on the Valley Turnpike. That night, the cavalry rear-guard bivouacked some four miles from Strasburg, while the infantry went on a further six miles to Woodstock. Jackson was effectively clear of the would-be jaws of the trap. On Friday morning, when he had decided to pull-back, his rear-most unit was sixty miles from Strasburg. The 'jaws', in the case of Shields', was no more than twenty miles from Strasburg – reduced to just twelve on Friday mid-day, when he entered Front Royal. Fremont himself was no more than thirty-eight miles away; but with his leading brigade only ten miles from Strasburg. In the three days that followed, Jackson reached and passed Strasburg, before either of the pursuing armies closed with the town or disturbed his progress in any way. Once he had passed by, Fremont, as Allan drily has it *"pressed forward in pursuit with a vigour which might have been more effective if it had been manifested two or three days earlier."* McDowell

278 Henderson quoting Taylor.
279 Douglas.

too seems to have simply failed to appreciate the pace of Jackson's movements. He left the task of interception to Shields, *"with his better knowledge of the roads of that country,"*[280] and Shields dithered, at first, before moving forward briskly when ordered up the Luray Valley, with the Massanutton between him and Jackson, on the Valley turnpike.

Fremont ordered Bayard's cavalry to front his new-found vigour, a brigade of McDowell's command, which had met up with him in Strasburg after the Confederates had departed. Early on, they got inside Ashby's cavalry screen, and, at first, being taken for Ashby's men, caused some confusion; but were soon ejected. Jackson deployed scouts in the direction of Front Royal, including his Staff Engineer Lieutenant Boswell, and the failure of Shields to make any further showing, after having occupied Front Royal, led Jackson to quickly appreciate that a decision had been taken for Shields to move down the Luray Valley, on the far side of the Massanutton. Jackson sent cavalry detachments to burn the only two remaining bridges on the fifty mile stretch of road ahead of Shields, between Front Royal and Conrad's Store. These carried the roads on their approach to the Massanutton crossing above New Market, and their destruction removed any possibility of a link-up with Fremont, or of heading-off Jackson before Harrisonburg, at the southern end of the Massanutton, or, indeed, of Shields being able to take Jackson in flank, in the event of his needing to fend off Fremont outside New Market. On reaching Luray, Shields did indeed hear firing from the direction of New Market, but he was powerless to intervene, even had he been determined to do so which, his record suggests, was unlikely. An hour or two previously, he had written to Secretary Stanton that *'with supplies and forage he could 'stampede the enemy to Richmond.'* Between watching what Shields did, or rather did not do, and reading what he said, even the politician Stanton surely wondered if Shields had the slightest inkling of what he

---

280 Allan quoting McDowell's post-war testimony.

was about. With the bridges gone, Shields was condemned *"to a march of sixty miles over muddy roads, to reach a point not over fifty miles distant now from the Confederates, which they were approaching by a good macadam road."*[281]

---

281 Allan.

25. TO TURN AT BAY

....

"Don't say it's impossible."
Stonewall Jackson

....

AT Woodstock, on the evening of leaving Strasburg, the Staff treated themselves to a slap-up meal of captured provisions, courtesy of Federal sutlers. The menu was nothing if not original, comprising *"cake and pickled lobsters, cheese, canned peaches, piccolomini and candy, coffee, ale and condensed milk. After the dyspeptic supper, we betook ourselves to such rest as it and the constant arrival of couriers would admit of."* But they were soon all back in the saddle. *"The General was up and impatient, and the rumbling of wagons told us that the army was in motion. ... The clouded brow and closed lips of General Jackson were ominous ... Quickly and sharply, he hurried his staff in every direction while, stern and watchful, he rode along the tangled line. ... The trains moved off without unnecessary stoppages, under the controlling influence of Major John Harman, Chief Quartermaster, who seemed to understand the management of teamsters and wagons as well as the General did that of soldiers. ... The General rode up to an officer whose brigade had been divided into two or three parts.*

"Colonel, why do you not get your brigade together, keep it together and move on?"

"It's impossible, General; I can't do it."

"Don't say it's impossible. Turn your command over to the next officer. If he can't do it, I'll find someone who can, even if I have to take him from the ranks." Soon a different state of things showed the effect of the indomitable will of this man.[282]

The *'indomitable will'* had forged the whole two week campaign thus far, driving every phase in accordance with the original aim

---

282 Douglas.

265

and objectives decided upon in Elk Run Valley. While 'maintaining the aim' throughout, he retained secrecy of movement and a firm hold on the initiative, both marked characteristics of his generalship. Whilst clearly appreciating the nominal strength of the enemy opposed to him, it was Jackson who was orchestrating this penultimate manoeuvring phase of the campaign. His was the timetable and the route. The passive posturing of Shields and Fremont were not able to disrupt the orderly withdrawal. Neither of the pair had the strength of character to shift the *'indomitable will'* from its chosen path. Jackson's immediate march objective, after leaving Harper's Ferry and Winchester, was Port Republic, for him, now some thirty-eight miles away, as they left Woodstock behind them. Port Republic was a short distance further on from the head of the Luray Valley, and provided easy access to the Virginia Central Railroad, and so to the east and Richmond. Towering behind and above Port Republic was Brown's Gap, providing, should it become necessary, a strongly defensible position in the Blue Ridge. But, at Port Republic, Jackson would be no longer be between the two columns of pursuers. If Shields exited the Luray Valley, he would be able simply to turn right across the bridge at Conrad's Store, taking a good, macadam road over the South Fork of the Shenandoah, and march towards Fremont, who only had to turn left off the Valley Turnpike, and move to a rendezvous by the same macadam road. In accordance with his precept of concentrating a superior force at the decisive point, and not attacking against heavy odds; but against fractions of the opposition, Jackson's intention was to deal with both generals individually – before they combined. Shields was struggling with a typical, Valley, 'bottomless' road, in a period of frequent heavy storms which had so swollen the rivers below Port Republic, as to make them uncrossable, except by bridges, which were difficult and time-consuming to replace, or construct, under such spate conditions as existed. To slow Shields progress further, therefore; Jackson sent a cavalry detachment to destroy the bridge at Conrad's Store. It so happened that Shields had sent some of his horsemen to report on the condition of this bridge, and to guard it, if in place, against his coming. However, having seen it still intact, Shields's detachment failed to maintain their aim, and "went off on a swan," after some stores which, it was suggested – either truthfully, or as a decoy – were nearby and lightly guarded. The Confederate troopers rode down and burnt the bridge. When in position at Port Republic, Jackson would be in possession of the only remaining crossing point over the South Fork which was still in place. Meanwhile, he sent a cavalry detachment to guard it, prior to his arrival.

As the columns tramped clear of Woodstock on Monday morning, the second of June, the sun was rising; his own herald for a fine day. Ashby, as ever, was covering the rear against Bayard's cavalry, supported by Fremont's leading infantry brigade under General Cluseret. But, as the day ended, just as the Staff were beginning to think of bivouacs, the rain returned in torrents. A courier dashed up to Jackson with the message that Ashby was in danger of losing his artillery. He needed support. Shouting at the staff *"To horse,"* the General splashed at a canter back along the road, cap in hand, to acknowledge the usual enthusiastic cheers at his passing. None had their gum capes, and all were quickly soaked through. No crackle and crump of firing marked their approach to the rearguard, and they soon came across Ashby, plodding forward amongst his troopers, all of whom were well swaddled-up against the rain. The message, he said, had been sent around eight o'clock in the morning, when, indeed for a time, he feared for the guns, and it had occurred to him to wonder why no support had been forthcoming; but in the end he had coped. The staff silently cursed another dilatory courier. Jackson said nothing. Then muttering quietly, *"A water haul,"*[283] he turned his horses head, and rode back through the rain and darkness.

Pendleton was credited by Douglas with knowing *"every good house at which to stop in the Valley,"* and on their returning to the van of the camping army, he soon made a selection approved of

---

283 Douglas.

by the General. *"Fastening our horses to the fence, we entered a small enclosed porch in front of the house and found there an athletic specimen of an infantry soldier. He was seated upon a bench and looked as if he regarded us as intruders. He was nearly bare-footed, his coat was thrown open, and his pantaloons were tattered and torn. Now, the General, after he was completely soaked, had thrown a gum cape over his shoulders, and by it the marks of rank upon his sleeves and collar were concealed.*

"I say Mister, drawled the straggler, what calvary(sic) *do you belong to?"*

"I don't belong to the cavalry," replied the General innocently.

"Don't eh! Must be couriers for some general or other."

"The General smiled and one of the staff stepped forward and presented him. The tramp was speechless, and the General passed into the house. The old soldier pulled his ventilated hat fiercely over his eyes, gave a jerk at his tattered trousers, seized his gun, and moving rapidly away muttered 'Well! If I didn't put my foot into it that time, may I be d-----d'!"

Their uniforms having steamed to a relative dryness by the next morning, General and Staff *"were very early up and off."*[284] The march that day passed relatively quietly, and that evening the headquarters was established in a field close to New Market. Ashby joined them for supper. He had just been promoted to Brigadier-General, and Pendleton expressed the hope that he would now be less inclined to put himself continuously in the forefront of every action. Ashby thought it unlikely. *"He was not afraid of balls that were shot directly at him … he said … for they always missed their mark. He only feared those random shots which always hit someone for whom they were not intended."* A householder arrived to invite the General to spend the night in his spacious home. Jackson *" … declined his invitation and said that he was even now too comfortably fixed with a tent, while his men were bivouacking in the woods without shelter of any kind, except what they could carry on their backs."* He would have had his own views on Napoleon's opinion that *"Tents are unfavourable to health. The soldier is best when he*

---

284 Douglas.

bivouacs, because he sleeps with his feet to the fire, which speedily dries the ground on which he lies. … tents are necessary for the superior officers, who have to write and to consult their maps. Tents should therefore be issued to these, with directions to them never to sleep in a house. Tents are always objects of observation to the enemy's staff. They afford information of your numbers … an army bivouacking is only distinguishable … by the smoke … It is impossible to count the number of fires."[285] Today, it would be more important for soldiers – certainly Western soldiers – to go without tents, to break soft, Twenty-first Century man to the discipline of living close to nature in the field. Satellites, doubtless, can count campfires with ease. That night the rain returned in torrents once more and gathered into a stream which poured through the General's tent pitched, at his direction, in a grassy hollow. *"The next morning the General appeared wet and wearied.* The Staff had been put out by his rejection of the invitation to the nearby house, and as they all made special care *"to administer to the General's comfort and protect his health in every way … were not a little amused and perhaps a little gratified at seeing the general wreck and demoralization in his tent."* There was no action on the following day.

As he retired, Ashby was destroying the bridges, taking the Valley Turnpike over the Shenandoah, and with the continuous heavy rain, water levels were rising fast. It continued to rain, making bridges difficult to construct and repair. A pontoon section, which was part of Fremont's establishment, laboured to fit a floating bridge; but the pace and volume of water was too great, and it was swept away. Despite the weather, it was *"not without some difficulty that the General was prevailed upon to go into New Market and establish his headquarters in a house."*[286]

---

285 *"The Military Maxims of Napoleon"*, translated from the French by Lieutenant-General Sir George C. D'Aguiler, CB, with a new Introduction and Commentary by David G. Chandler, first Da Capo Press edition, 1995.
286 Ibid.

While around New Market, Jackson had a rare encounter with a newspaper reporter. He would not tolerate a correspondent within his command, as being too much of a security liability. Usually, he declined to be interviewed. However, an enemy correspondent who would give the other side a good account of the fighting abilities of his men was a different matter. It was a good propaganda opportunity, and, to the surprise of the Staff, Jackson agreed to be interviewed by the correspondent of a New York paper, who had been captured during Flournoy's decisive cavalry charge at Front Royal, where the man had been covering the Federal First Maryland Regiment. *"He began by expressing his gratification at meeting with Stonewall Jackson, etc.; but being admonished by the General's frown that he cared little for such things, he changed his tactics. ... He said that being well mounted, he could have escaped from Front Royal had he not been suddenly attracted by a conspicuous display of gallantry on the part of some Confederate cavalry. He saw a company or two ... about seventy five or a hundred in number, prepared to charge the Maryland Regiment of Infantry, which had just gotten outside the town. He was amazed at the rashness of the officer leading the charge. On they came, with a resounding yell, and he was so bewildered with wonder and admiration at the magnificence of the charge, that he forgot his own danger. He remained spellbound on the spot; and when he was roused, he was a prisoner.*

"The General was much amused, and to the surprise of the Staff, *"ordered his release as a non-combatant. The incorrigible Yankee at once made an additional request for his horse, and was told that he might take him if he could find him, But having his doubts about the prudence of roaming through Ashby's camp in search of a horse, he took his departure.* Douglas at some stage saw *the next copy of his paper ...* which ... *contained a full account of his capture and adventures and a comical description of the appearance and manners of Stonewall Jackson.* The 'incorrigible Yankee' was, he added *"... the forerunner of the line of war correspondents who became so conspicuous in the Union armies and are now so abundant, enterprising, and dangerous, on the outskirts of all wars: men whose personal courage is often equal to their conceit, but who do not hesitate to attempt to make or mar the reputation of generals and admirals according to their fancy."*

25/1. "An Irreparable Loss"

"Charge, men! For God's sake, charge!"
Turner Ashby

FOR Jackson and his burdened, minority Army, the first five days of June had in the main gone well. His vigilance and forward thinking, combined with the vigour of the Army at every level, had kept them closed-up, and, continuously, one step ahead of Shields, whose units, contrary to McDowell's instruction to keep closed-up, were strung-out along the Luray Valley. Fremont, although aggressively active, like some ponderous Chamois buck at the rut, could think of nothing more original than to keep banging his head against Ashby's screen of horsemen – often dismounting to fight like dragoons.

At one point, as they were approaching Mount Jackson, supported by a handful of straggling infantrymen whom Ashby had lined-up where the road ran through a wood, the troopers demolished with a single crunching volley, an eager charge by a company of Bayard's cavalry. During the hours at New Market on Tuesday and Wednesday – the third and fourth – Jackson sent Hotchkiss and a group of signallers to a high point at the southern tip of the Massanutton, from where they could observe and report on the movements of both Shields and Fremont. Ambulances with the sick and wounded, were sent straight on through Harrisonburg, heading for Staunton by the Valley Turnpike; a ferry-crossing of the North Fork at Mount Crawford having been constructed with difficulty by the pioneers – *"a gang of negroes ... under the superintendence of Captain Mason, a railroad contractor of long experience."*[287]

---

287 Henderson.

Jackson and the main body reached Harrisonburg around mid-day on the Friday. From there they turned off the Valley Pike and took the dirt road through Cross Keys to Port Republic, a distance of some ten miles. Ashby continued to occupy Harrisonburg, until the morning of the sixth, when Fremont approached behind a strong cavalry force of eight hundred or so, led by an English mercenary of, seemingly, no great ability, and whom Douglas, who escorted him – a prisoner – to Jackson, described as *"not an attractive-look-ing warrior … who … looked like what he was, a soldier of fortune."*

Colonel Wyndham had taken paid service in the northern cause and was commanding the first New Jersey cavalry. *"They went through the long main street of the town at a rapid trot,"*[288] and, as ordered, reconnoitred for a short distance beyond. No enemy be-ing sighted, Wyndham decided to exceed his brief and force-on. The seasoned Ashby, who had skirmished with the enemy in de-fence of the Valley of Virginia, on almost every day of this first year of the War, had recently notched-up thirty-eight exchang-es in twenty-eight days. He was commanding both Jackson's reg-ular cavalry, as well as his own 'guerrilla', Seventh Cavalry, and had posted a strong line of horsemen, blocking the road to Cross Keys, at the head of a long low rise. Others he had dismounted, to line the road approaching his blocking force, and having cover from view in a wheat field on the west side of the road. The op-posite side was forested. In hunting parlance, it had already been a brisk and lengthy point for the Northerners; but without so much as a glance, by way of assessing the strength of Ashby's position – let alone a breather for the horses – Colonel Wyndham kept on going, up the slope and straight at Ashby and his men. The ensu-ing volleys from ahead and in flank, reduced the serried, panting files of men and horses to a bloody, shrieking tangle. Wyndham's horse was killed under him, and he was made prisoner by Trooper Holmes Conrad of Winchester – who, Douglas adds, went on to

288 Allan, quoting the account of a participating Federal officer in the *New York Tribune* of *June 7, 1862.*

become Solicitor General of the United States. A further sixty-two of the charging Northerners were also made prisoner. Of the leading companies in the charge, thirty-six were killed and wounded. Ashby had only Major Green, of the sixth Virginia Cavalry, badly wounded. Desultory skirmishing followed; but preparations by the rearmost companies to move up through the wood and turn Ashby's position, were disrupted at the outset, by men and horses from the first ill-advised charge rushing back down the road.

Ashby sensed a stronger attack would be made on his position and called for infantry support. Ewell – whose whole Division was encamped around Cross Keys – sent forward the first Maryland and the fifty-eighth Virginia Regiment. Ashby deployed the First Maryland in the wood beside the road, and the fifty-eighth at the top of the rising ground, astride the road, with himself amongst them. With the sun beginning to set behind them, the anticipated attackers were soon seen deploying into the open fields, and a cloud of skirmishers came forward through the woods on the Federal left. This was no slipshod, ill-conceived and mercenary-led affair. Fremont had ordered forward General Bayard with his first Pennsylvania Cavalry and four companies of Kane's Bucktail Rifles, together with Colonel Cluseret and his sixtieth Ohio and eighth Virginia (Federal) Infantry. Ewell came up, and Ashby pointed out Kane's Rifles and the sixtieth moving in across the fields, and his own dispositions, to meet the attack.

Almost immediately the firing began, the Federals *"reached a heavy fence of timber, whence, under the partial cover, they poured destructive volleys into the ranks of the fifty-eighth Virginia regiment. Ashby, seeing at a glance their disadvantage, galloped to the front and ordered them to charge and drive the Federals from their vantage-ground. At this moment his horse fell, but extricating himself from the dying animal, and leaping to his feet, he saw his men wavering. He shouted 'Charge, men! For God's sake charge!' and waved his sword..."*[289] At

---

289 Allan quoting Jackson's first biographer, and at the time his Adjutant-General (i.e. chief-of-staff).

that moment a bullet smashed into his chest and he fell dying. The fifty-eighth charged as ordered, and from the flank, the Confederate Marylanders rushed forward in support. The attack gave way, and the Confederates, reaching the timber fence *"poured successive volleys into the fleeing mass, until they passed out of musket range."* Skirmishers clashed on the other side of the road, and the Federals advanced as far as a Confederate camping ground, before withdrawing, following the rout of their right wing. Ashby, meanwhile, had died, silent, his body cradled by one of his most ardent followers, Lieutenant Jim Thompson. Besides Ashby, the Confederates lost seventeen killed and fifty wounded. Three went missing. The Pennsylvania Rifles sustained the largest loss on the Federal side, having *"fifty-five killed, wounded and missing out of the hundred and twenty-five carried into the battle."*[290] Their commander, Lieutenant Colonel Thomas Kane, shortly after having been captured, and without realising that Ashby was dead, delivered a memorable first, inadvertent, eulogy to Ashby, in the course of conversation with the captain commanding the Maryland skirmishers, James Herbert, saying: *"I have today saved the life of one of the most gallant soldiers in either army – General Ashby – a man I admire as much as you do. His figure is familiar to me for I have seen him often enough in our front. He was today within fifty yards of my skirmishers, sitting on his horse, unconscious of the danger he was in. I saw three of them raise their guns to fire, but I succeeded in stopping two of them, and struck up the gun of the third as it went off. Ashby is too brave to die in that way."* Kane was true to America in those fratricidal times and, years later, said to someone writing on the war, *"Deal justly with the memory of Ashby. He must have been a noble fellow, a brave soldier, and a gentleman."*[291]

Jackson dismissed Wyndham, whom he was interviewing at the time, when news of Ashby's death was brought to him, and locked the door of the room in the Kemper-house, where his headquarters

---

290 Allan.
291 Douglas.

had been established, a little outside Port Republic. Later, he wrote that, *"An official report is not an appropriate place for more than a passing notice of the distinguished dead; but the close relation which General Ashby bore to my command for most of the previous twelve months will justify me in saying that as a partisan officer, I never knew his superior. His daring was proverbial, his powers of endurance almost incredible, his tone of character heroic, and his sagacity almost intuitive in divining the purposes and movements of the enemy."* His home and lands being, then, behind the Federal lines in Fauquier County, Ashby was buried the next day – Saturday, the seventh – at the Virginia State University in Charlottesville. In glorious June weather, the funeral cortege, including a military escort of Ashby's troopers, passed amid *"the bright green fields and darker woodlands, the rolling hills, intersected everywhere by the valleys of the streams – along the base of the mountains – and – up the valley of the South River, to Waynesboro,"*[292] to journey across the Blue Ridge to Charlottesville. A year after the War ended, Ashby's body was moved to the Stonewall Cemetery in Winchester.

During the two days spanning Ashby's death and burial, Jackson's 'Foot Cavalry' rested and refreshed themselves. In the previous three weeks and three days, they had marched some three hundred miles. Marching, more than fighting, had thinned the ranks, apart from those of the Louisiana brigade, who did not straggle and whose numbers were well up to establishment. Taylor's five Regiments mustered some five hundred each, whereas Winder's four 'Stonewall' Regiments totalled just three-hundred each. Three hundred being the norm too, for all other infantry regiments of the Valley Army. For what he intended should be his final moves against Fremont and Shields, Jackson had just eleven thousand infantry; one thousand or so cavalry, and between five hundred and six hundred gunners,[293] which meant that he had slightly fewer men than Fremont alone, and was slightly superior in numbers to Shields alone.

---

292 Allan.
293 Allan's figures.

The latter, however, had allowed his command to become so strung-out in the Luray Valley, that the chances of his being able either to consolidate in full strength to confront Jackson, or to fully unite with Fremont, were negligible.

Shields himself was still back at Luray, with two of his brigades, apparently due to the Shields's 'intelligence service,' which had a penchant for imagining the approach of non-existent Confederate reinforcements; in this instance, eight thousand coming over the Blue Ridge at Thornton's Gap. Without in anyway proving this, Shields had allowed his advance-guard to reach Conrad's Store, which meant his force was *"stretched out over five-and-twenty miles of road in the valley of the South Fork."*[294] By Saturday the seventh, however, *"a patrol which had managed to communicate with Fremont informed him that Jackson was retreating,"* and Shields sent his advance-guard commander an instruction which Henderson, rather mildly, comments on as being, *"worthy of record,"* but would seem to have reached new heights of bombastic unreality, even for Shields: *"The enemy passed New Market on the fifth, Blenker's Division on the sixth in pursuit. The enemy has flung away everything, and their stragglers fill the mountain. They need only a movement on the flank to panic-strike them and break them into fragments. No man has had such a chance since the war commenced. You are within thirty miles of a broken, retreating enemy, who still hangs together. Ten thousand Germans are on his rear, who hang on like bull-dogs. You have only to throw yourself down on Waynesborough (sic) before him, and your cavalry will capture them by the thousands, seize his train and abundant supplies."*

The next day – Sunday, the eighth of June, whilst still at Luray – Shields wrote to Fremont about *"the demoralised rebels"*... he went on ..." *as my force is not large there* (Port Republic) *yet, I hope you will thunder down on his rear ... I think Jackson is caught this time."* Both Shields and Fremont imagined that they were engaged in a pursuit, whereas the reality was that Jackson was carrying out a military manoeuvre, to position himself to carry

---

294 Henderson.

out the next two stages of the operation which he had planned, overall, and launched, from Elk Run Valley. Despite his numerical inferiority, he continued to retain the initiative he had held throughout, by bold and skilful use of the terrain afforded by the Valley of Virginia; some judicious bridge-burning, and sheer hard marching. Between Elk Run Valley on the eighth of May and Port Republic on the ninth of June, the Army of the Valley had logged some four hundred foot slogging miles.

All attempts by Union forces to unite against them – the fundamental requirement – had failed. Admittedly, initial dispersal had been brought about by political intervention; but, latterly, the inability of Shields and Fremont to combine was due mainly to a lack of resolution, ineffective leadership, and, just possibly, a sprinkling of personal glory-seeking – the sneaking wish, somehow, neither was clear exactly how – to *'bag'*, as they put it, Jackson for themselves. In the case of Shields, these shortcomings were exacerbated by an unprofessional, not to say unhelpful, characteristic which British soldiers a Century later would have unerringly ridiculed as 'flannelling'. The final double-act in Jackson's scenario, however, was not entirely straightforward.

26. THE BRIDGE AT PORT REPUBLIC

....

*"He who does not see the hand of God
in this is blind, Sir, blind!"*
Stonewall Jackson

....

THE General looked towards Mrs Kemper, who inclined her head and smiled, and then turned to his Adjutant-General. *"For what we have received may the Lord make us truly thankful,"* responded the Rev Dr Dabney. As the Kemper family and the four uniformed soldiers stood up, the Kemper's black housekeeper announced, *"An Orderly to see General Jackson, Ma'am."* With no more than a second glance towards their hostess, Jackson left the dining room. Outside on the front porch, he thanked the orderly as he handed over a folded slip of paper. The message, written in pencil, read; *'Shields at Luray still, according to a Federal officers' conversation overheard Harrisonburg by 'snowy-white' who approached my picket. Estimate information four hours old. Fremont not beyond Cross Keys as of this time. R. Ewell, Major-General'* An abrupt, *'No reply'*, and he turned back inside the house. Ewell's note was timed and dated; '5½, Saturday the seventh'. The General did not re-join the group still talking in the dining room; but turned into a small front room he was using as a bedroom. Closing the door behind him, he tore the message into small pieces, and stood looking out on the front pasture, where the horses of the headquarters staff were grazing, and enjoying a much needed respite from the saddle. Recent rain still dappled the window glass before his face. To his left, he looked over Front Royal – the village obscured the Bridge – to the long line of the escarpment-edge running northeast and marking the line of the now swollen South Fork, on its way to Conrad's Store and Luray. Looking further right, the General could see the white patches of his Confederate wagon-train, partially hidden by the village, in their park on the meadowland, stretching back to the forested scarps reaching up to the seemingly endless skyline of the Blue Ridge, above which the eastern sky was brightening. Possibly, he mused, in promise of a fine, summer Sunday *"away from the hum of camp."* The regiments he had already ordered *"to spend the day in camp and the chaplains to hold services."*[295] Those regiments and brigades of his old Division bivouacked in an armed crescent, above the Bridge, the feature of tactical importance to all four, charged with choreographing the blood-stained hours that were to come. Their rifles and rifled guns gleaming in the hands of resolute men possessive of the Bridge. Constantly aware of the steady roar of the river, the General thought for a moment of its tactical value. After passing through Port Republic – and beneath the Bridge – this, the Middle Branch, had been magnified some three miles back – to the south of Port Republic – by the shorter North Branch, and having flowed through the village was joined immediately by the eminently fordable South Branch which, nonetheless, further increased the riverine barrier, for Shields especially, and provided the General with another feature around which to out-think and out-manoeuvre his two less nimble opponents. And to the west of the multi-strand river; across the escarpment, and unseen beyond Winder's Division, the men of Ewell's Division. Albeit, on their own, they are out-numbered nearly three to one by Fremont. Ewell is securely positioned – the General thought – running through once again in his mind's eye, as Ewell himself had outlined it: *"The general features of the ground … a valley and rivulet in my front, woods on both flanks, and a field of some hundreds of acres, where the road …* from Port Republic to Cross Keys runs through the centre of the position, with … *my side of the valley being more defined, and commanding the other."*[296] For the moment, at least, Fremont showing no sign of advancing from Harrisonburg any further than Cross Keys.

---

295 Douglas.
296 Allan quoting Ewell's report.

So far too, he thought, Shields has shown no inclination to cross the tumbling waters of the South Fork of the Shenandoah, flowing north in the shadow of the Massanutton, beyond his abortive attempts to reach the traditional bridges. He has not pushed to combine the – what? – twenty-five thousand? commanded by himself and Fremont, with any degree of urgency. The river still separates them; but as they both near Port Republic, they could come within sight and sound of one another. Their artillery could become mutually supporting, firing across the river, without their having to affect a crossing. A crossing which they may or may not be intending to bring about, by means of the Bridge at Port Republic. A part of Shields' Army, so Ashby's cavalry – or now rather, Colonel Munford's cavalry – report, has advanced beyond Luray; but if the remainder – including their Commander – was still at Luray a little less than twelve hours ago, then it is unlikely that he will be able to concentrate the whole command within striking distance of the Bridge within the next forty-eight hours.

There was a knock at the door and a voice said, *"Lieutenant Douglas, General."*

"Enter": Douglas entered saying: *"Shortly after midnight on the morning of the eighth of June, it was reported that Shields was advancing along the same road that the Army of the Valley had marched in the Spring from Conrad's Store to Port Republic."*[297] Jackson raised his hand, palm outwards, in a frequent and familiar gesture, and motioning Douglas to stay, then turned back to the window, saying nothing for fully five minutes. Conrad's Store: was a little over eleven miles distant, on a dirt, rain-soaked road. Luray: at most twenty-five miles distant; but with at least two, if not three bridges to restore – if the nearest, at Conrad's Store, has not already been fixed.

"Send a cavalry patrol in full squadron strength along the road to Conrad's Store," the General ordered Douglas. *"They are to push-on*

---

297 Douglas.

until they encounter enemy pickets and are to report at once where they first made contact. Stress – at once!" Douglas nodded his understanding of the emphasis. *"Thereafter they will immediately drive in the pickets and advance on the main body, reporting on its strength and position, as soon as it is known. In the face of the enemy's continued advance they are to give way; but remain in contact, reporting frequently on his progress. A sound estimate of their strength would be especially useful; but stress to the officer commanding the detachment the importance of his reporting frequently on any development."*

Alone again, the General turned back to the now darkened window. Nothing, he thought, has been substantially altered by either of the last two pieces of information. Shields to be dealt with first. But at the same time, Fremont will need to be checked. Should Fremont 'march to the sound of the guns', his own extensive artillery batteries could fire across the river into the left flank of any engagement with Shields, even should he be prevented from crossing to give infantry support. If we were to try and dispose of Fremont first, a substantial force would need to be left, to prevent Shields from savaging the wagons and the rear communications, which, in turn, would weaken the force available to engage Fremont.

Jackson moved away from the window. Two steps and he threw himself face down across the iron, single bed. Sword and spurs he had removed before dinner, and they were together on an upright, wooden chair beside the door. Otherwise, he was fully dressed, and asleep, as cheek and beard reached the pillow.

When the General's black campaign servant, Jim, took coffee to the front bedroom, the General was already up, and by seven o'clock was pacing the dirt drive in front of the Kemper House. Sunday morning had dawned fine. Douglas led up his horse, ready saddled, and tied it to the field fence. Having heard nothing from the cavalry squadron sent towards Conrad's Store, he was anticipating an order to 'go and find out', while at the same time, hoping that Mrs Kemper would get in first with a call to breakfast. Suddenly, from the direction of the Bridge, came the clatter of iron hooves rattling loose boards, and a courier galloped into view up the curving track to the house. *"Close enough!"* shouted Pendleton. Reining to a halt some ten yards from them, the courier kicked his left foot free of the stirrup, swung the right over his horse's neck, and slid to the ground, to lean back against the horse's side, clutching reins and a good handful of mane in his right hand. Both were breathing heavily. Jackson walked forward. *"The enemy … cavalry, guns infantry … three miles away … at the Lewis House."*[298] He had no more details and was sent to find out more. Jackson ordered the horses to be readied. Before the courier was out of sight *"a lieutenant of cavalry arrived and said the enemy were in sight of Port Republic. And just then a quick discharge of cannon indicated that the little town was being shelled. … there was hustling for horses … the greatest anxiety was to get the General off … I offered him my horse, running with an orderly to get his, farthest off, of course, in the field. But the General waited and was soon mounted. … If any other crossed the bridge in that John Gilpin race with the General, but Pendleton, I do not remember him. … Few of the staff got off in time. … I was the last to get over."* Douglas galloped down through Port Republic, towards the South Fork, flowing across his front on its way to a junction beyond the village. As he reined left for the Bridge, *"I passed in front of … (enemy) … cavalry as they rode up out of the South Fork ford. I could see into their faces plainly and they greeted me with sundry pistol shots. … I joined the General on a hill overlooking the Bridge."*[299]

The General had already sent Pendleton to bring up the infantry. The Federal cavalry who had fired at Douglas, were milling about at the far end of the Bridge. Jackson *"called to them loudly and sharply not to stop there, but to come over immediately, waving to them at the same time."* Douglas says he told the General they were Yankees, because Jackson may have thought they were his own couriers. Rather more likely, Jackson recognised all along that they were the enemy, and was trying to discourage them from

---

298 Douglas.
299 Ibid.

destroying the Bridge. However, to their *"mutual surprise they wheeled and rode off."* The General ordered over a gun of Captain Poague's Battery, *"posting it in the field overlooking and commanding the Bridge."* While they were setting up, they were *"surprised to see a gun posted at the farther end of the Bridge."* Uncertain as to whose it was, Poague mentioned to Jackson that it might be one of Carrington's Battery, which, apart from several soldiers commanded by Captain Moore, who were recuperating from various wounds and ailments, and had been set to guard the wagons, there were no Confederate forces east of the Bridge and the Middle Branch. Carrington's men, Poague said, had recently been issued with new uniforms. *"The General reflected a moment, and then riding a few paces to the left and front of our piece, called, in a tone loud enough to be heard by them, 'Bring that gun up here;' but getting no reply, he raised himself in his stirrups and in a most authoritative and seemingly angry tone shouted, 'Bring that gun up here, I say!' At this, they began to move the trail of the gun so as to bring it bear on us, ... the General turned to ... Lieutenant Brown ... who had his piece charged and aimed, ... and said in his sharp, quick way, 'Let 'em have it.' Brown sent a shot right among them, so disconcerting them that theirs in reply went far above us."*[300]

Led by Fulkerson's thirty seventh Virginia, Jackson's infantry regiments began closing-in on Port Republic from their nearby camp. The thirty seventh was ordered to take the Bridge and clear the village. They strode down the hill at an angle to the western end of the Bridge, and with Poague's gunners shooting them in, the lead company, sending the wild, 'Rebel Yell,' reverberating through Port Republic, stormed across the Bridge behind their glinting bayonets. A single, random shot in response went wide, and the Yankee gunners limbered-up, turned, and headed for the nearby fords. Fulkerson's men kept coming, and as they spread out through the alleyways, the gun was quickly abandoned to the waters of the ford. Winder's artillery, lining up along the edge

---

300 Allan quoting Captain (later Colonel) Poague CSA.

of the escarpment, began shelling Federal cavalry emerging onto the open meadows and pastures, which there form the northern approach to the South Fork. At the wagon-park, a well delivered volley by the walking wounded had abruptly recoiled Federal cavalry from ravaging the wagon-train and steadied the incipient panic amongst the wagoners. Everywhere, the Federal wave was receding. Eventually all four guns were discarded, as the gunners strove to regain open ground north of the village. Continuing to flee northwards, they edged towards the Blue Ridge, away from Winder's shelling, which kept pace with the retreat from along the escarpment edge; until it moved out of range into the forests at the head of the Luray Valley. Watching from the hill above the Bridge, the General saw evidence of supporting rein-forcements emerging from the tree-line. A column of infantry advanced towards those retreating. At once, the nearest guns on the escarpment switched their aim. *The column showed temporary obstinacy and marched on steadily, but only for a short distance. It was stunned, riddled and scattered, and soon disappeared in the distance or among the adjacent hills.*[301] In the space of about one hour, they had thrown back Shields advance-guard. The advance-guard only, the General decided – despatched to hold the Bridge? Or burn it?

Colonel S. Sprigg Carroll, commanding Shields advance, has been criticised by Douglas and others for not burning the Bridge at Port Republic, as soon as it was in his possession. Certainly, had he done so, it would have made it more difficult, for Jackson to retain the initiative in taking on the Federal advance, whilst the two columns remained separated. Carroll, however, obeyed orders. Shields had instructed him to hold, not burn, the Bridge. However dilatory and incompetently Shields and Fremont may have performed, their theoretical intention remained, to come together, to deal with Jackson. The fact that after a whole week they were no nearer a junction, meant that they too still need-ed the Bridge intact.

---

301 Douglas.

For Carroll, as a relatively junior detachment commander, to take so strategic a decision as to fire the Bridge – on his own initiative and against a specific order from his immediate superior – would have been a court martial offence, even had the outcome been in every way beneficial to the Federal cause.

27. RESOLUTION AT CROSS KEYS

....

*"At present I do not see that I can do
much more than rest my command
and devote its time to drilling."*
Stonewall Jackson

....

THE General rode down the slope and across the Bridge, to position the Thirty-seventh, Twenty-third and the Tenth Virginia – the brigade commanded by Brigadier-General Taliaferro – to hold the fords of the South Fork, and so protect the Bridge, Port Republic itself, and the wagon-park. A lieutenant on Ewell's staff rode up and informed him, verbally, that Fremont was advancing from Harrisonburg; that there had been some skirmishing along the picket line, and that his Division was taking up their pre-arranged positions to receive an attack. *"Thank you. That is all."* The General's expression did not change. No trace of emotion showed beneath the peak of the campaign kepi; but he felt at least, a certain relief in not having to fill in time with drilling, while waiting for the moves of others. As he had speculated somewhat despondently to Lee, Fremont, it seemed, was not going to wait for Shields, and so concentrate their efforts; but instead, intended to attack piecemeal, without thinking.

Jackson rode back across the Bridge and up on to the escarpment, where he ordered Winder's remaining two brigades to be ready to receive an attack from the direction of the Luray Valley, and from where they could swiftly reinforce Ewell, if required. The artillery was drawn-in closer to Port Republic; but the guns remained pointing out over the South Fork, and the meadows and pastures through which Shields would have to approach. Jackson rode back to the road from the Bridge and turned away towards Cross Keys. He smiled for a moment as he thought of a Sunday free: *"from the hum of camp,"* and of *"the wholesome belief of the old soldiers that the side that inaugurated a battle on Sunday, lost it."[302]* He turned his thoughts to Fremont, who had followed the Army of the Valley for fifty miles or so, failing throughout to make an original or resolute attack – or even a genuine attack of any sort – when the Army was encumbered with prisoners and captured stores; but now was about to do so, the prisoners and surplus stores; the sick and the wounded, having all been moved on back, and the Confederate Army left free to manoeuvre. Rippling musketry from heavy skirmish-line firing was becoming continuous not far ahead, indicating that rather more than overnight pickets were becoming involved. *"The Fifteenth Alabama infantry, Colonel Canty, had been thrown out on picket, and, while they were stubbornly resisting Fremont's advance, Ewell carefully disposed his troops along the ridge."[303]* As the General approached the top of one of several undulating ridges, which the road crossed at right angles, he saw first the colours of Ewell's regiments moving, as if self-propelled, across the open ground between the woods on each side of the road. Breasting the ridge, the manpower surrounding them rose rank by rank into view.

The General got no further than the rear-most company of Ewell's Reserve before being recognised, and a great roaring cheer swelled up around him. Instantly, he raised and gave a twirl of the old campaign cap. The yelling-cry rolled forward to a crescendo along the front line, before fading under the consistent crackle of firing. *"The sweetest music … with such men as these,* he thought, *"I have never found anything impossible."* But then, no less important, every Confederate lining up to fight for his country that fine, sunny Sunday morning, drew strength and confidence from the comfort of knowing that Old Jack was with him on the killing ground. On the other hand, that cheering yell may have transmitted a fleeting shudder into Fremont, not the most resolute of leaders or the strongest of characters, especially when compared to the two men he faced that morning.

---

302 Ibid.
303 Allan.

The General moved over into the field beside Ewell's reserve Brigade Commander, Arnold Elzey, whose men were positioned a short way back, behind the summit of the ridge. The last four guns of Ewell's four Artillery Batteries raced-by, to deploy some two hundred yards ahead, on either side of the road to Cross Keys. Ewell himself, coming in from the right of his line, joined Jackson just as the gun batteries began duelling with Federal gunners, on the lower ridge, across the narrow valley. All three looked out to the left of the road for some moments in silence, to where the Maryland line of Confederate Major-General George Steuart's brigade – now including the Forty-fourth, Fifty-second and Fifty-eighth Virginia – were sending skirmishers forward through the trees, to secure the left flank. It would be early afternoon before a Federal brigade felt its way cautiously forward against Steuart's regiments, and although his advanced pickets would pull-back, and Ewell would send the Twelfth Georgia and the Thirty-first Virginia to strengthen his left, no full-blooded attack would develop there. In the centre of the field, the artillery duel would dominate, and Ewell's well-sited batteries, despite taking some casualties, would prevent Milroy – (the opposing Federal General at M'Dowell) – from doing much more than threaten an advance, before Fremont called off the fight, following the mauling given the regiments of his left.

Fremont opened the battle, following the initial skirmishing, with a strong attack by his whole left wing, against Ewell's right. The attack comprised the brigades of General Blenker's Division – the personnel of whose regiments were mainly German migrants. The three New York and one Pennsylvania infantry regiment of Stahl's brigade – to which the Bucktail Rifles had been assigned – fronted this main attack, with support from three artillery batteries. The four Ohio regiments of Schenk's brigade, and the two New York and two Pennsylvania regiments of Bohlen – both supported by artillery – provided the back-up.

Waiting amongst the trees, in a position forward and to the right of Ewell's originally designated position, was the multi-state Confederate brigade of Brigadier-General Isaac R. Trimble.

The Twenty-first Georgia, Twenty-first North Carolina, and Sixteenth Mississippi. His Fifteenth Alabama were already engaged as the command's picket line. Ewell would send them to re-join Trimble during the action. Trimble's ambition in the War, he told Jackson, was to achieve the dignity of a major-general or a corpse. Jackson would promote him, and he would survive, albeit after losing a leg at Gettysburg. Trimble had selected his defensive position as being one less susceptible to being out-flanked. Ewell approved.

Jackson, with his acute ability to read the opposition – both leader and led – had said at the outset of the action, *"Let the Federals get very close before your infantry fire; they won't stand long."*[304] In briefing his regiments before the attack, Trimble did not quite pass on the advice in the form of the immortal rule-of-thumb, 'hold your fire till you can see the whites of their eyes', instead he told them, *"rest quietly in the edge of the open wood …* until, having crossed *the field and hollow,* the attack *should come within fifty steps.* Stahl's men came on seemingly unaware, *"until he was near enough to receive Trimble's fire."*[305] A series of volleys followed in rapid succession. The effect was devastating. Those left on their feet stopped uncertainly for a fleeting moment, then turned about and fled. *"The eighth New York had sixty-five killed in this attack alone."*[306] The back-up regiments, however, did not come forward in support, to sustain the attack, and after a few moments, Trimble counter-attacked, driving the broken ranks *"down the hill, across the meadow, and into the wood from which they had advanced."* Trimble did not pursue amongst the trees; but waited on the crest of the ridge, overlooking the woods in which the enemy was recovering. A Federal Battery, some half a mile away, opened fire on his men halted in the open. The Fifteenth Alabama, having been returned to him, Trimble moved the regiment, under cover of

304 Henderson.
305 Allan.
306 Ibid.

some woods, to within fifty yards of the Federal position, and, *after twenty minutes*, there still being no sign of the Federal attack being renewed, despite their having re-grouped, *"Trimble moved out to his right ... under cover of a ravine and the woods."* Ewell sent across the Thirteenth and Twenty-fifth Virginia, from Elzey's reserve brigade, in a typically Jackson-like tactic, to increase the weight of the manoeuvre. During the flank move, the Thirteenth and Twenty-fifth, led by Colonel Walker, passed into the open near a house and barn, on the extreme right of the attack, and were *"staggered for a moment by a fierce fire of musketry and canister,"* but they kept going. On the left of the attack, the Sixteenth Mississippi were disordered for a moment also, by having their flank pounced on as they passed some woods; but the Twenty-first Georgia immediately charged in support and drove off the attackers. Soon, *"the enemy were driven back in front of our whole line ...* and we then saw *the infantry force in full retreat towards the Keezletown road."*[307] Trimble's sequence of attacks had driven the enemy's left wing back for *"a mile in rear of their first position."*

The hammering, which Trimble had inflicted on the regiments of his left wing Division, so unnerved Fremont that his enthusiasm for attacking Jackson quite oozed away, and he withdrew the tentative advances being made against Ewell's centre and left. The moral courage of the general, not the physical courage of the Northern fighting man, had been undermined. With darkness approaching, Trimble advocated a night counter-attack; but Ewell decided against that, and having driven in the enemy's pickets, he moved forward onto the ground which Fremont had occupied before the battle, in readiness for possibly renewing the action the next morning.

Beyond his physical presence on the battlefield and having masterminded the month-long series of moves leading up to the battle, Jackson had felt little need to play more than a watching brief at Cross Keys. Ewell and Trimble were generals who understood

---

307 Allan quoting a letter from Trimble *dated February 1880.*

the need for swift, clear-thinking and positive risk-taking, if battles were to be won. Both played their parts well in the action of Sunday, the ninth of June. Jackson was well aware that there are 'many ways of skinning a cat' and was alive to the fact that certain subordinates were well able to do the skinning. Watching the pair work towards the decision he required to overawe Fremont at Cross Keys, he had seen no need to interfere. Returning to Port Republic the General, once again, surprised his Staff. If Douglas is to be believed, the Staff expected their General, *"to take advantage of the night and slip out of the trap with his prisoners and stores."* Jackson's was a totally different mindset. He did not look upon the manoeuvrings of his opponents in any sense as 'traps'; one reason why he was never surprised. Mostly, he at least half-expected them to make the moves they did, and when they did, he took them at face value, making related moves of his own by which he, on the other hand, surprised them and achieved the objectives he wanted. That evening, rather than send the wagons away, he ordered them forward so his men could cook and eat their rations. Although *"by the blessing of divine Providence"* Fremont had been dealt a telling blow, the General was no less determined that Shields should be knocked-back by a similar quick, hard action. As he rode, tap-tap-tapping the shoulder of *'Little Sorrel',* he was considering a second strike against Fremont. There would be little resting that night.

He ordered *"a temporary bridge … of planks laid upon the running-gear of wagons … constructed over the South fork,"* so men could cross dry-shod over the ford. Winder was summoned and briefed to march-out at *"early dawn,"* down across the Bridge over the Middle Branch, on over the new, temporary construction across the South Fork, and to instantly strike whatever elements of Shields force had reached the immediate area. In accordance with his habitual practice of personal briefings, Ewell was called in and ordered to follow Winder, having left Trimble and his brigade to distract and delay Fremont. Colonel Patton, commanding the Second brigade in Jackson's old Division, would assist Trimble, and was told, when briefed at around two a.m. on

Monday morning, *"I wish you to throw out all your men, if necessary, as skirmishers, and to make a great show, so as to cause the enemy to think the whole army are behind you. Hold your position as well as you can; then fall back when obliged; take a new position; hold it in the same way; and I will be back to join you in the morning."* Patton asked for how long he would need to delay Fremont. *"By the blessing of Providence, I hope to be back by ten o'clock."*

At the ford, the General joined his staff engineer, seeing to the construction of the wagon and plank bridge. Soon after he turned-in, fully dressed – *"sword, sash and boots all on."* Major Imboden, who had been with him in the final bayonet charge at First Manassas, and was now commanding a Mule Battery, inadvertently entered the bedroom seeking a member of the Staff. *"The low-burnt tallow-candle on the table shed a dim light, yet enough by which to recognise him."* It was an hour before daybreak. *"He checked my apology with, "That is all right. It's time to be up. I am glad to see you. Were the men up as you came through camp? Yes, General, and cooking. That's right; we move at daybreak. Sit down. I want to talk to you."*[308] They chatted at random for a moment, Jackson *"referred very feelingly to Ashby's death, and spoke of it as an irreparable loss."* When Imboden congratulated him on the past four weeks and the *"glorious winding-up yesterday."* Jackson replied, *"Yes, God blessed our army again yesterday, and I hope with His protection and blessing we shall do still better today."* He then discussed with Imboden how the mule battery should be handled and employed among the trees and on the forest trails occupied by Shields leading units. When a little before five a.m. Winder ordered the Stonewall brigade forward across the new construction over the South Fork, the General was riding with the lead Regiment. The Chief Quartermaster had already been sent off with the wagons, and *"looking ... up into the Blue Ridge we saw the long white train, moving on its serpentine way to the top of the mountain."*[309]

---

308 Henderson.
309 Douglas.

28. THE FINAL BLOW

....

*"The only true rule for cavalry is to follow
as long as the enemy retreats."*
Stonewall Jackson

....

THE action fought around the Lewis House – some two miles
from Port Republic – between the South Fork of the Shenandoah
and the thickly forested, lower buttress spurs of the Blue Ridge,
was an altogether more tenacious affair than the tussle before Cross
Keys of the day before. As at Kernstown, Shields, the Federal general who never quite managed to get to the scene of the action,
was again well served by an effective and determined Brigade
Commander. The men of Brigadier-General E.B. Tyler's brigade,
who had combined with Colonel Carroll's composite force the
previous afternoon, were from Ohio (Seventh and Ninth) Virginia
(First Federal) Indiana (Seventh) and Pennsylvania (Hundred and
Tenth). Like the Valley Army, men of frontier stock, tough, determined fighters, who Jackson always rated. Tyler had used his
time well, and created a defensive pattern of strong, interlock-
ing positions. In the grey half-light of the western slopes of the
Blue Ridge, Winder's skirmishers dashed out to right and left
of the Luray road, and quickly cleared the fields on each side of
Federal outposts. As they continued up the road, Jackson registered at once the strength of Tyler's position. The left high on a
chunk of raised ground, from where two batteries of guns, supported by infantry, and with the flank firmly secured amongst
the thick, sloping woodland, covered the whole approach from
Port Republic. With only the twelve hundred or so of Winder's
Division up, at the outset, Jackson was clearly outnumbered by
Tyler's three thousand; but he was in a hurry. He had to be, if
his 'one-two' plan to knock-back Shields, and immediately deliver a heavier blow to Fremont's greater numbers, was to have

any chance of succeeding. But in impetuosity too lay an element of surprise. The Second and Fourth Virginia, supported by two guns, were ordered across and up through the woods to turn the gun-line of Tyler's left flank, which was the heart of his position. Dense thickets beneath the trees made for heavy going and although Tyler, possibly, had failed to realise the speed of Jackson's approach, he already had two regiments supporting the guns and was prompt in moving up two more. With canister and volleys of lead-shot ripping through the undergrowth, the Virginians were forced back. On his left, between the road and the river, Winder tried to establish Poague's Battery and the Fifth and Twenty-Seventh Virginia; but Tyler's guns, both on the right and left of his line, sixteen in all, commanded their front too effectively. Winder called for support. Taylor's Louisiana brigade was closing; but reinforcements were slow in coming. The make-shift bridge had partially given way, and Ewell was struggling across, his troops in single file, intent on using only the one central plank. Surprisingly, perhaps, despite the orders of Jackson's Adjutant-General, Major Dabney, who had been left to superintend the crossing, no efforts were made to wade the *'breast-high'* ford.

The second and fourth having returned, Winder re-formed the Stonewall brigade, and ordered Tyler's right flank positions, between the road and the river, to be taken at bayonet point. *"Jackson was on the road, a little in advance of his line, where the fire was hottest, with the reins on his horse's neck."*[310] As Taylor reached the front, at the head of his brigade, Jackson ordered Hotchkiss to, *"Take General Taylor around, and take that battery,"* pointing to the batteries that had defied the Stonewall Regiments. Taylor and his men turned off to their right to begin the struggle with the undergrowth. Apart from being reinforced by one regiment coming up from the rear, Winder was still isolated on the left, and Tyler's Ohio men were more than holding their own. Tyler

---

310 Henderson quoting Taylor.

himself read the struggle well, and when the Confederates broke amid the vicious exchange of fire, the Fifth Ohio counter-attacked. When Ewell's Thirty-first Virginia reached Winder, he ordered them to cover the guns while he tried to reform his line. One gun switched aim to the counter-attack; but the Ohio charge, *"drove back the half-formed Confederates across a wheat-field and they seized the piece, which they carried off."*[311] Ewell sent the Fifty-second Virginia directly to the aid of Winder, retaining the Forty-fourth and the Fifty-eighth Virginia under his own control.

The General decided that the time had run out for his twin-attack plan. Tyler's defensive had been too stubborn, and he no longer had the time to finish off Shields advance; get back across the river in support of Trimble and Patton, and then to develop a second blow against Fremont. Trimble was ordered to disengage and burn the Bridge at Port Republic. As Fremont continued to feel his tentative way forward towards the escarpment overlooking the South Fork, a column of thick grey smoke rose ever higher into the clear morning sky.

Ewell, watching closely the progress of the rolling attack against Winder, judged the moment, and, as the left flank of the Federal advance drew level, the Forty-fourth and the Fifty-eighth delivered a crippling charge from the cover of the wood. The attack recoiled, and Winder was able to rally his men. Ewell recalled his two regiments and turned back into the woods, in support of General Taylor, who had been having a dogged, see-saw struggle amid the tangled undergrowth. After a stiff fight, the Louisianians eventually succeeded in charging from the trees and taking the two dominant batteries on the Federal left; but as soon as Winder had been repulsed, Tyler sent over reinforcements from his left, and Taylor's men were driven off, abandoning the guns just captured. Despite the horses all having been killed in the course of the tussle, the Federals managed to drag one gun away, before Taylor, now supported by Ewell with the Forty-forth and

---

311 Allan.

the Fifty-eighth stormed back behind a solid volley. Tyler's skilful manoeuvring and his tough fighters were about to be overwhelmed. From between the Luray Road and the Shenandoah, Winder was now able to concentrate the fire of five batteries on the Federal positions. Under fire from in front and in flank, Tyler's men were pushed back all along their line. The remainder of Jackson's command were by now reaching the field, and he ordered Winder, together with Taliaferro's brigade, to pursue. *"They pressed the retreating enemy in a confused mass for several miles, and then handed over the pursuit to the cavalry under Munford, who followed for three miles more."*[312] Nine miles in all. *"About four hundred and fifty prisoners, a few wagons, one piece of abandoned artillery (in addition to the five captured by Taylor in his final charge) and eight hundred muskets were the trophies of the pursuit. Some two hundred and seventy-five of the Federal wounded were paroled in hospitals near the battle-field. About two hundred others were carried off. … Jackson's losses … at Port Republic … were, killed, wounded, and missing, in Taylor's brigade, two hundred and ninety; Winder's, one hundred and ninety-nine; Steuart's, one hundred and ninety-nine; Elzey's, one hundred and twenty-eight; total, eight hundred and sixteen.*[313] Federal reports to the Adjutant-General's office put their losses at *"sixty-six killed, three hundred and eighty-two wounded, three hundred and eighty-two missing, total: eight hundred and thirty."* These figures may not include a somewhat petulant attempt by Fremont to intervene in the aftermath of the action. He drew up some of his rifled guns and shelled Jackson's men as they were tending to the wounded and the dead, at the same time as leaving the field. Jackson's instructions were always that the wounded enemy should be cared for no less than his own men. The *'Medical and Surgical History of the War'* puts Federal losses at: *"sixty-seven killed, three hundred and sixty-one wounded, five hundred and seventy-four missing, total: one*

---

312 Ibid.
313 Allan, and Allan quoting Jackson's report.

thousand and two."[314] Douglas carries the story of a Confederate ambulance in which a Confederate and Union soldier were lying side by side. The latter was killed by a direct hit from Fremont's artillery, and the former survived. *"At the close of the battle, … General Jackson … rode to General Ewell and laying his hand gently on his arm said, 'General, he who does not see the hand of God in this is blind, Sir, blind!'"* His message to Richmond reads, *"Near Port Republic, the ninth of June, Through God's blessing, the enemy near Port Republic was this day routed, with the loss of six pieces of his artillery. T.J. Jackson, Maj. Genl. Comdg." "The next day, as was usual, was one of incessant rain. General Shields sent a note to General Jackson requesting permission to care for his wounded and bury his dead. The General replied that the wounded were being cared for and the dead were being buried; and then called his attention to the unsoldierly conduct of General Fremont's command."*[315]

Jackson has been criticised strongly, for opening the battle of Port Republic before more of his regiments were available for an attack. The reality was, as Jackson appreciated only too well, that he had no option but to attack at the earliest possible moment with the troops that were to hand. He not only had to defeat whatever force from Shields command was 'up'; but he then had to get back across the two bridges and deploy against Fremont. Every second counted. Given the partial failure of the makeshift bridge and the fighting qualities of Tyler and his men, to have delayed the opening attack even until Ewell was on the scene, would have removed at the outset, whatever chance there was of making the second strike.

---

314 Ibid.

315 Douglas.

28/1. Deception

....

*"If I can deceive my own
friends I can make certain
of deceiving the enemy."*
Stonewall Jackson

....

IN the immediate aftermath of the battle, Jackson could not be certain exactly how Fremont and Shields would react to their twin defeat. He therefore withdrew from Port Republic into the lower slopes of the Blue Ridge, along the road to the defensible fastness of Brown's Gap, and on, if necessary, to the Virginia Central Railroad and to Richmond. In the event, neither of the defeated decided to try conclusions further. Fremont left the area the next day, to bivouac overnight at Mount Crawford, before continuing on to Harrisonburg – where he left *"two hundred wounded in the hospitals, some medicine and other stores, and about two hundred muskets"* – when he moved on, as he put it, due to, *"Significant demonstrations of the enemy."*[316] Never, in fact, more than Munford's cavalry; but which none the less, caused him to continue north up the Valley to Mount Jackson, then Strasbourg, and finally to Middletown, where he joined Banks and Sigel (the latter now commanding the Harper's Ferry force) on the twenty fourth of June, sixteen days after his defeat at Cross Keys. Neither of these generals had thought fit to support their colleagues in their attempts to *'bag Jackson'*; but, then, perhaps their brief was the security of Washington!

Shields had got little further than Conrad's Store when the fugitives from Port Republic reached him, in a state of bemused defeat. He decided on immediate withdrawal, citing as an excuse

---

316 Allan.

for his lack of enterprise, an order from McDowell instructing him to return. McDowell was the one Federal commander – not excluding the President – who seems to have realised what Jackson was up to and was not panicked by him. McDowell was consistently ignored or overruled. His chief-of-staff had in fact written to Shields, *"If you are about to fall on the enemy and can do so with reasonable chance of success ... the General is not disposed to recall you."* McDowell himself wrote later *"Both the condition of General Shields's Division, and that of the roads and rivers by him, indicated anything other than the success he anticipated."*[317] When the reports from Munford's cavalry made it clear that he was not going to be disturbed by either Fremont or Shields. *"Jackson moved out from his confined bivouac at the foot of Brown's Gap, and crossing the South River near Weyer's Cave, camped in the noble, park-like forest between the latter place and Mount Meridian. Here, for five days of that splendid June he rested and refreshed his army. ...* Jackson himself wrote ... *"For the purpose of rendering thanks to God for having crowned our arms with success, and to implore His continued favour, divine service was held in the army on the fourteenth."*[318]

The fighting phase of the Valley Campaign was complete. Douglas, having served on the Staff throughout, sums up the campaign as having *"... driven the Federal Administration in Washington to the verge of nervous prostration. In thirty days, his army had marched nearly four hundred miles, skirmishing almost daily, fought five battles, defeated four armies, two of which were completely routed, captured about twenty pieces of artillery, some four thousand prisoners, and immense quantities of stores of all kinds, and had done all this with a loss of less than one thousand killed, wounded and missing."* While, *"the troops were encamped in a range of woodland groves between the two rivers, surrounded with the verdure of early summer and the luxuriant wheat-fields whitening to the harvest ... and ... in this smiling paradise ... solaced themselves five days for their fatigues ... by ... reposing under the shade*

317 Ibid.
318 Allan, and Allan quoting Jackson.

or bathing in the sparkling waters of the Shenandoah, and the horses feeding in the abundant pastures,"[319] for the General, the period of sustained, intellectual concentration needed to be continued, in order to contrive one final extended marching manoeuvre by the Army of the Valley, for the final bafflement of Yankee generals and their political bosses.

Ever since leaving Elk Run Valley, Jackson had kept in his reckoning the possibility of being required to march to support an attack on McClellan, to take the pressure off Richmond. The moment had now arrived. The inanimate General Johnston had finally launched an attack on McClellan's positions – at their closest now no more than five miles from the Confederate capital – and, in the process of organising badly, the initial build-up, had contrived to get himself wounded. Doubly fortunate for the Confederacy, his successor fell ill, and Lee was ordered to command the army in the field. Lee wrote to Jackson three times during the first half of June. In the first he said, *"I congratulate you on defeating and then avoiding your enemy. Your march to Winchester has been of great advantage and has been conducted with your accustomed skill and boldness. ... Should there be nothing requiring your attention in the Valley so as to prevent your leaving it in a few days, and you can make arrangements to deceive the enemy and impress him with the idea of your presence, please let me know, that you may unite at the decisive moment with the army near Richmond. ...* Lee added, ... *should an opportunity occur for striking the enemy a successful blow do not let it escape you."*[320] Jackson received the letter immediately after the back-to-back victories of Cross Keys and Port Republic and set about the deception of the enemy with his *"accustomed skill"*, promptness and thoroughness. Before withdrawing from Harrisonburg, Fremont sent officers to Colonel Munford, asking for his wounded to be returned under a flag of truce. In a despatch, Jackson told Munford, *"Please impress the bearers of the flag of truce as much*

---

319 Allan quoting Jackson's Adjutant-General.
320 Allan quoting Lee.

as possible with an idea of a heavy advance on our part and let them return under such impression."[321] Munford arranged for the Federal officers to overhear a fictitious report from a courier, telling of numerous reinforcements coming up from Staunton. The 'news' was leaked for the excitement of the town, and the Federal officers sent back, their request having been turned down. In general, the Federals were admiring of Jackson's arrangement for the care of those wounded in the Valley fighting. It was another aspect of war to which he applied himself, especially after his experience in the Mexican War, where *"I have since my entry into this land … he told sister Laura … seen sights that would melt the heart of the most inhuman of beings: my friends dying around me, and my brave soldiers breathing their last on the bloody fields of battle, deprived of every human comfort, and even now, I can hardly open my eyes after entering a hospital, the atmosphere of which is generally so vitiated as to make the healthy sick. I would not live in one a week, under the circumstances in which I have seen them, for the whole of Mexico. To die on the battlefield is relief, when compared to the death in a contaminated hospital."*[322]

Jackson's subsequent order to Munford for the cavalry, who would maintain the false front in the Valley after the infantry had departed, were typically thorough. *"Do all you can to cut off communication across the lines between us and the enemy; also let there be as little communication as practicable between your command and that of the infantry. Let your couriers be men whom you can trust, and caution them against carrying news forward, as it may reach the enemy. …* on arranging to meet Munford, Jackson wrote … *I will be at Mount Sidney to-night about ten o'clock. Can you meet me there? I will be on my horse at the north end of town, so you need not enquire after me. … Say to those who come on this side (the lines) that for a few days, they will have to remain on this side, as no one is permitted to pass the lines to the enemy's side."*[323]

---

321 Allan.

322 Letter to Laura from *City of Mexico, October 26, 1847* (Arnold).

323 Allan quoting Jackson.

Over the next week, Jackson did not spare himself – without saying a word to anyone, in his efforts to bamboozle the enemy. Lee entered fully into the deception campaign, writing in his second June letter, on the eleventh: *"Your recent successes have been the cause of the liveliest joy in this army as well as in the country. The admiration excited by your skill and boldness has been constantly mingled with solicitude for your situation. The practicability of reinforcing you has been the subject of earnest consideration. It has been determined to do so at the expense of weakening this army. Brigadier-General Lawton, with six regiments from Georgia, is on the way to you, and Brigadier-General Whiting, with eight veteran regiments, leaves here today."*[324] On arrival, Whiting rode some twenty miles to see Jackson, getting back to his own headquarters *"after midnight,"* and in a *"towering passion,"* declaring *"that Jackson had treated him outrageously … he didn't say one word about his plans. I finally asked him for orders … he simply told me to go back to Staunton, and he would send me orders tomorrow. I haven't the slightest idea what they will be. I believe he has no more sense than my horse."*[325] In their Shenandoah rest camp, the rank and file were oblivious to their General's instigation of a watertight deception plan. When the march to Richmond was underway, however, they were forbidden either to speak to the locals, or to ask what village they happened to be passing through. One of the Texans in General Hood's brigade of Whiting's Division was spotted by Jackson *"climbing a fence to go to a cherry-tree near at hand. … 'Where are you going?' asked the General … 'I don't know' … 'To what command do you belong?' … 'I don't know' … 'Well, what State are you from?' … 'I don't know' … 'What is the meaning of all this?' …* Jackson asked another soldier nearby *… 'Well,' was the reply 'Old Stonewall' and General Hood gave orders yesterday that we were not to know anything until after the next fight.' Jackson laughed and rode on."*[326]

---

324 Allan, Henderson quoting Lee.
325 Henderson quoting Imboden.
326 Henderson.

The Staff fared no better than Whiting. During the five days the troops were resting, they had little idea of their General's whereabouts from one day or night to the next. He had instructed Richmond to use no more than *"Somewhere"* as his address on all written correspondence. The Staff, however, contrived some personal advantage from the security clamp-down. *"Left very much alone, …* Douglas writes, *… Jackson's young staff – they were nearly all young men – did not go through the green fields and valleys of Albemarle and Louisa without seeing many of their lighted parlours, in which they were always welcomed by bright and pretty girls and merry music. … all enjoyed that little holiday and made the most of it, seeking new Desdemonas at the close of each day."* At one point he says, *"some of us reported to General Ewell for duty. He said with grim humour that he was only a general commanding a Division, marching under orders, but he didn't know where, and that at that time he had more staff than he had any use for."* The day after reporting to Ewell, the Staff *"detected'* the General getting off a train at Mechum's River Station. *"He had no instructions to give and did not trouble himself to ask the whereabouts of anybody. He had his trunk put on the train, remained about fifteen minutes, and shaking hands all round and saying goodbye as earnestly as if he was off to Europe, he departed and gave no sign."* When they next came upon the General *"It was afternoon and he was in bed. … His wet and muddy uniform was being dried by the fire and the appearance of his ponderous boots indicated that he might have been wading all night through mud and mire. No one seemed to know where he had been or what doing."* Lee had ended his second June letter *"…if practicable precede your troops, that we may confer and arrange for simultaneous attack."* In response to this suggestion, Jackson had been to Richmond. His travel pass he had had signed by Whiting, authorising *'one officer'* to go to Richmond, and, throughout, his one companion was instructed to address him as *'Colonel'*. He had conferred with Lee. It was the first face-to-face meeting between the two since the outbreak of the War. From Jackson's reports, Lee's assessment of the situation in the Valley, agreed exactly with Jackson's, and the third June letter, sent by Lee on the sixteenth, said, *"… the sooner you unite with this* *army the better …in moving your troops you could let it be understood that it was to pursue the enemy in your front … dispose those to hold the Valley so as to deceive the enemy."[327]* Douglas writes that Lee ended the letter with, *"if you agree with me, the sooner you make arrangements to do so the better."* Apart from providing a clear indication of just how much store Lee set by Jackson's skill and judgement, Jackson had, of course, for the past few days, been assiduously paving the way for the march in exactly the way expressed by Lee. For the General, the rest camp days had been anything but a rest.

For the Army, the period of 'R & R' ended when they broke camp, on the delivery of Lee's third letter, early on the morning of the seventeenth, and the columns of Jackson's outstandingly enduring 'Foot Cavalry,' once more began tramping, now, eastwards towards Ashland Station and the left flank of Lee's Army, one hundred and twenty miles away. The objective was to assist in the prizing of McClellan from his threatening but uneasy posture astride the Chicahominy River, east of Richmond.

"It will always seem to the average soldier", Douglas would write, that all the secrecy *"was carrying mystery to extreme lengths."* Absolutely, and the secrecy is a good illustration of a slightly different point. Jackson was very far from being the *"average soldier"*. To achieve an unblemished record on the battlefield, such as that of Stonewall Jackson, requires military genius, intellectual focus and the unrelenting determination and vigour of an Alexander, a Cromwell, or a Marlborough; a very far from average genius. In attempting a completely secure operation, the *"average soldier"* – or general – would have done less and achieved less. As it was, McClellan and Lincoln suspected something was brewing, although they could not fathom what. McClellan's view of things is best summed-up by his comment, *"I don't like Jackson's movements, he will suddenly appear when least expected."* Banks, with his crucial numbers stolidly entrenched at the head of the Valley, just north of the Massanutton, never got further than thinking that Jackson was

---

327 Allan quoting Lee.

not *"within thirty miles"* of him. Two days after Jackson's men had marched from their rest camp in the area of Mount Meridian, *"… on the nineteenth … Banks telegraphed to Washington … No doubt another immediate movement down the Valley is intended with a force of thirty thousand or more. He opposed the withdrawal of Shields strongly in the same telegram. On the twenty second, he is still on the alert for Jackson's and Ewell's movements, and on the twenty eighth, when Jackson was fighting at Richmond, … and three days after the Valley men reached Ashland Station … Banks telegraphs that he believes Jackson meditates an attack in the Valley!"*[328]

The arrival at Ashland Station marked the end of the marching element of Jackson's Valley Campaign, in its widest definition. Henderson computes the dates and distances of the Campaign as beginning on the twenty second of March with the forty mile march from Mount Jackson to reach Kernstown early the following afternoon, and as ending with the one hundred and twenty miles to Ashland, which was reached on the twenty fifth of June. These parameters give a total marching distance of six hundred and seventy-six miles in forty-eight marching days, for an average of fourteen miles per day. This remarkable feat of endurance was achieved by what was in reality a volunteer army. Although technically conscripts, the Confederate Act conscripting them did not make them trained regulars. In March the previous year, all but a fraction of both officers and men were enjoying the civilian existence which, up until the outbreak of the Civil War, had been their life since birth. In addition, not being thoroughly broken to military discipline, they straggled badly, as Jackson admitted; apart from the Louisiana brigade of Ewell's Division, that is, whose men had been assiduously taught march discipline and field hygiene by their General, Dick Taylor. These bare marching statistics too, leave out of the reckoning the fighting and the winning achievements of those resolute men. Men fighting for their country and their homes and, more and more,

---

328 Allan quoting Federal official telegrams.

as the days went by and the successes mounted up, for a leader even more unyielding than themselves, in whom they came to have implicit faith and trust. The spirit of the Valley Army was the spirit of its leader and provides as fine an example as may be found in any era, of the value of inspirational leadership. Of what can be achieved in war, with very limited means, by a truly great leader. The physical achievements of his men are an indisputable panegyric to the intellectual accomplishments and abilities of Jackson the General. Nor does the bald statistical statement 'fourteen miles per day' give the least clue to the stark conditions surrounding the achievement; incessant rain, mud and bottomless roads, random rations – often absent and having to be cadged from farmers or captured from the enemy – worn out or non-existent footwear, and for sleeping, no more than a blanket and rubberized cape. At the outset, the men of the Valley were no different from many others who signed-up, for both South and North, and, as the fighting showed, the battles were often close, and fiercely contested. The men of the Valley gained an edge because they had 'Old Jack'.

29. "THE HOODED FALCON"

*"To move swiftly, strike vigorously,
and secure all the fruits of victory
is the secret of successful war."*
Stonewall Jackson

BY persuading the Federals to believe that the strength of the Valley Army had been increased to thirty thousand and denying them the understanding that he had actually withdrawn his eighteen and a half thousand, Jackson had kept the Yankee President so fearful for his capital that he in turn, denied McClellan any support from the numbers of Fremont, Banks and McDowell. In March, Lincoln was working to reinforce the Federal Army of the Potomac to around two hundred thousand. When, in late June, Lee moved to prize McClellan from his earthworks just five miles from Richmond, the invading numbers remained no more than the one hundred and five thousand or so, that had come ashore originally at Harrison's Landing. In addition, McClellan had continued his absurd practise of relying on police detectives for his intelligence, and they persisted in grossly over-estimating Confederate numbers. McClellan got it into his head that he was facing some two hundred thousand whereas, even with Jackson's men from the Valley, Lee could deploy eighty five thousand at most.

The brief campaign against McClellan began on the twenty sixth of June, and ended on the second of July, after seven days of more or less continuous fighting. Jackson was the only General on either side – not excluding the two Commanders-in-Chief – who had a proven record of sustained battlefield success. However, he was reverted to being just one of seven Divisional Commanders in Lee's Army – excluding the cavalry commander J.E.B. (Jeb) Stewart. The Campaign bears not a trace of his genius; but, not surprisingly, bears all the hallmarks of the principal contenders, Lee and McClellan. Lee showed himself to be vigorous, attack-minded and daring; but also, unimaginative, predictable, and unable either to take control or to react quickly to change of circumstance. McClellan throughout, was bereft of the slightest spark of aggressive intent, and simply edged ever backwards to the comfort zone of his gunboats and his support ships. He was tentative, also unimaginative, well stocked and fitted-out; but ill-informed.

To go on to the offensive was a daring move, shot through with risk; but Lee had no option but to take the initiative. To continue to remain static, and simply maintain an already uneven and precarious balance was to play the invader's game. For him, unlike McClellan, time had not the potential to yield significantly more resources in either men or material, so the imbalance in favour of the Federals could only increase. The options and risks for a Confederate offensive were brutally clear. They would have to take on superior numbers with inferior equipment, and not only in small arms. *"The smooth-bore pieces, with which at least half the artillery was equipped, possessed neither the range nor the accuracy of the rifled ordnance of the Federals."*[329] Anticipating reinforcements, McClellan had reached out towards their coming, by moving his Fifth Corps northwards across the invious swamps and sluggish waters of the Chickahominy. With few, irregularly placed bridges, albeit in Federal hands, the river effectively split the Army of the Potomac. A reconnaissance cum raid by 'Jeb' Stuart and one thousand two hundred troopers, scouted right around the besieging Federal army, covering some one hundred and ten miles in less than three days, and disrupting, capturing and destroying supplies and equipment, and bringing in one hundred and sixty-five prisoners and some two hundred and sixty horses and mules. The exploit told Lee that McClellan's right flank was 'in the air', secured neither by natural obstacle nor entrenchment. At the same time, the ride shook Northern faith in their Field

---

329 Henderson.

Commander and devalued their massive Army in the eyes of the South. Lee made his opening move against the unsupported Fifth Corps, in an ungainly, complex plan, which he was lax about controlling effectively. First, he had to withdraw thirty-five thousand men from in front of McClellan's main position, in order to join them with Jackson's eighteen and a half thousand, already on the north side of the Chickahominy. By doing so, he would gain a two to one superiority over Fitz John Porter, commander of the Fifth Corps. To leave no more than twenty-eight thousand facing McClellan's seventy-five thousand was, seemingly, to invite a strike for Richmond; but Lee, like Jackson, was a shrewd reader of an opponent. Lee knew McClellan from the old US Army, and it was his understanding of the man that made his acceptance of an unavoidable risk viable – and ultimately successful – at least to a degree. Lee counted on McClellan remaining entrenched on the defensive until forced out, when his instinct would then be to retreat rather than to advance. Lee surmised, in addition, that McClellan would neither be alert for an offensive opportunity, nor sufficiently bold to take advantage of one, should it present itself. In the series of engagements undertaken for the purpose of relieving the immediate pressure upon Richmond, this psychological appreciation of the Federal Commander proved correct.

29/1. Mechanicsville

LEE's opening gambit required three Divisions, each starting from a different position and moving by different routes, to unite in the face of the enemy. *"According to Moltke,"* Henderson observed, *"to unite two forces on the battle-field, starting at some distance apart, at the right moment, is the most brilliant feat of generalship. Haste,* he adds, *is even more to be dreaded."*

Jackson departed Ashland Station on the twenty-fourth with the intention of joining-up with the Divisions of Longstreet, Hill (A.P.) and Hill (D.H.), at Beaver Dame Creek – some twenty-eight miles distant – on the twenty-sixth. This he duly achieved, although not without some difficulty. At a planning meeting on the twenty-third, Lee had put the onus on Jackson – the Divisional Commander with the least familiarity with the area; but having the farthest to march – to set the timetable. Fully appreciating the vulnerability of the army divided, Jackson opted for the earliest seemingly feasible date; but hardened to prolonged fighting marches as they were, the Valley men had a tough approach *"over an un-mapped country, unknown either to Jackson or his staff, which had lately been in occupation of the Federals. Bridges had been destroyed and roads obstructed."*[330] Over the last sixteen miles, skirmishing in the thickly wooded country was continuous. *"Federal outposts contested every favourable position."* At one point, a burnt bridge was rebuilt and made serviceable in just one hour, by a black labour force, *"which had already done useful service in the Valley,* under Captain Mason *"a railroad contractor of long experience."*[331] The heavy going, and the obstructive efforts of the enemy kept Jackson behind his own suggested timescale on both the twenty fifth and the twenty sixth, and for this he has been criticised. Nonetheless, by the evening of the twenty sixth, Jackson, at least, was where he needed to be, at Hunley's Corner on Beaver Dam Creek. However, without knowledge of either Jackson's or anyone else's whereabouts, late that afternoon, A.P. Hill took it upon himself to launch an immediate infantry attack. In the brief, brisk affair that followed, he was repulsed with some slaughter, sustaining two thousand killed and wounded, to the three hundred and sixty of the defenders. Jackson was just three miles away; but separated from Hill by thick woods laced with Federal sharpshooters. He has been criticised for not 'marching to the sound of the guns',

---

330 Henderson.

331 Ibid.

in support of Hill's ill-advised and unauthorised evening attack. Given the ground surrounding the position he had reached, and the time of day, it was simply not possible for him to have supported Hill's unexpected attack. In addition, his men had been stood-down to cook and rest, and he had no expectation of an attack by Hill; was not in communication with him and had no up-to-the-minute knowledge of his whereabouts. Lee's plan for the first attack on Porter, called for *"the four Divisions of the army to move forward <u>in communication with each other</u> …* (Henderson's italics) *… and drive the enemy from his position."* But ONLY, when all four Divisions had crossed the river. The further criticism that Jackson getting behind the clock was somehow due to *"indifferent tactics"* makes no sense either. Faced with a string of Federal strongpoints, one cannot see what else he could have done, other than halt the column, attack, overcome, and then move on; halt, attack, overcome, move on, which is surely what he did.

At least some of this criticism would have emanated from Generals in the aftermath of the War, honing their own reputations for posterity; but, in reality, to criticise the Divisional commanders during this build-up phase is to wrongly apportion blame. The sole culprit for Confederate difficulties in the days leading up to the evening of the twenty sixth is Lee. He failed to take charge of the implementation of his plan from the very outset. That is to say at the planning stage. In the first instance, the commanding general should not have put the onus on a Divisional commander to set the deadline for the initial concentration. Once having done so, and presumably having agreed to the deadline, he should, at least, have given himself the capability of being able to control and co-ordinate actual progress between all four of his Divisions, in real time. This Lee could have done by the simple expedient of using Stuart's troopers – many of whom were familiar with the region – both to keep himself informed, and to deliver his orders. The troopers could also have been used to advantage, as guides for Jackson's march. Munford's cavalry had not yet come in from the Valley; but even had they done so, by no means all would have been familiar with the new area of operations, and to leave

Jackson and his small Staff to find their own way in unfamiliar territory seems less than sensible. As it was, Lee seems largely to have let the whole phase unfold according to the premeditated, written plan, rather than imposing firm control as things developed in the conditions pertaining. Surely fatal under constantly changing circumstances and untried conditions. Hill's lone, late evening attack was certainly a mistake; but it was probably an honest mistake. Having no idea how things had progressed around him, he did what he thought was best. If blame for this as a failure is to be made, then the blame for this also should be laid at Lee's door. A message he was said to have sent by Captain Sydnor of the Fourth Virginia Cavalry *"ordering ... Hill ... to postpone all further movement, arrived too late."*[332] Clearly Lee failed to anticipate such an eventuality until it was too late. In war there are no marks for intent, only for the minimum of mistakes (that pass un-punished) and for actions successfully carried out.

29/2. Action Near Gaines Mill and Cold Harbour

"ON the morning of the twenty seventh we moved forward, cautiously and slowly, pushing the enemy gradually. A junction was formed with A.P. Hill and pleasant greetings exchanged. General D.H. Hill reported with his Division, and was thenceforth under the command of General Jackson, his brother-in-law. The troops marched and assembled for the battle of Cold Harbour. Longstreet and A.P. Hill had been fighting for some time vigorously, but it was late in the afternoon when Jackson's command got actively to work, and the general battle became fast and furious."[333]

---

332 Henderson.
333 Douglas.

Jackson's approach route was once again blocked by trees felled into the road and covered by the sniping fire of Federal sharpshooters. To avoid them and keep moving, he moved off the direct road to Cold Harbour and swung wide to his left towards Bethesda Church. Once again, his command had the farthest to march to come up on the left of Lee's line; but the detour did not affect the start of the action, which Lee began at two-thirty p.m., with an assault by A.P. Hill. Jackson for a time stayed put, out of the action. Porter had chosen a strong position on rising ground, encircled to front and flank by streams, and a jumbled confusion of swamp, trees and tangled undergrowth. McClellan had reinforced him during the day, with a Division of nine thousand under General Slocum. Some thirty four thousand Federals – including a Division of regulars of the old US Army under General Sykes – were well positioned to receive Lee's bludgeoning, unimaginative frontal assaults, by no more than fifty six thousand, all ranks.

It was on this morning, when Jackson met with Lee near Walnut Grove Church *"that the staff officers of the Valley Army, noting the eagerness displayed by General Lee's suite to get a glimpse of 'Stonewall', then for the first time realised the true character and magnitude of the Valley Campaign."*[334] The pair considered in which direction Porter might retreat on being driven from his Gaines Mill – Cold Harbour defensive. Uncertainty stemmed from their believing McClellan was still using a supply line running east of south to White House on the Pamunkey River, as well as his main line south to Harrison's Landing. This doubt, possibly, explains Jackson's delay in joining in the general attack. Porter's position covered at least four bridges by which he could cross to the south side of the Chickahominy, and so link up with McClellan and the main Army of the Potomac, but if he extended his line in the opposite direction – to his right – to secure a possible line of retreat to the Pamunkey, then Jackson was ideally placed to

334 Henderson.

take him in flank. However, Porter accepted Jackson was now nearer to White House than he and made no attempt to do so. Late in the afternoon, therefore, on deciding that Porter would not withdraw in his direction, Jackson sent his engineer staff officer to Lee with the message that he had *"closed upon the flank of the enemy and will open the attack at once."*[335] For this delay Jackson has been criticised. *"It is said,"* Douglas writes *"officers and men in other parts of the army had begun to doubt whether Stonewall Jackson had really come from the Shenandoah Valley."* Ever since the 'Stone Wall' dubbing by Bee at First Manassas, and even more so now, after what he had achieved in the Valley he had become widely known and appreciated, Stonewall Jackson had become an iconic, talismanic figure to the South – both civilians and military alike. *"In the crowded steeples of Richmond where men and women had gathered to watch the distant signs of a struggle fraught with such vital consequences to them, the welcome sound was heard from a new direction and not understood. When someone said 'Those are Stonewall Jackson's guns,' all hearts and eyes grew full, and no more fervent prayers were ever spoken from the chancels beneath them than those unspoken ones that went to Heaven that day."*[336] When word spread that Jackson was in action at Cold Harbour *"A staff officer dashed along Longstreet's wearied lines, crying out, 'Stonewall's at them!' and was answered with yell after yell of joy, which added a strange sound to the din of battle."*[337] In the final assaults at the close of that bloody, dying day at Old Cold Harbour *"the shout was carried down the line, 'The Valley men are here!' and with the cry of 'Stonewall Jackson!' for their slogan, the Southern Army dashed across the deep ravine."*[338] Along the length of the entire front, it was a savage bludgeoning affair of shot, shell and bayonet. Of A.P. Hill's opening assault against the three tier lines of infantry and eighty rifled field guns, Porter wrote later

---

335 Douglas.
336 Ibid.
337 Ibid.
338 Henderson.

314

"brigade after brigade seemed almost to melt away before the concentrated fire of our artillery and infantry, yet others pressed on, followed by supports daring and brave as their predecessors, despite their losses and the disheartening effect of having to clamber over many of their disabled and dead, and to meet their surviving comrades rushing back in great disorder." As the evening drew on, and the fire fight continued with no slackening by either side, even *"Jackson grew anxious … and for the first time and the last, his staff beheld their leader riding restlessly to and fro, and heard his orders given in a tone which betrayed the storm within."[339]* Jackson was riding *"a large and useful chestnut given to him by Major Harman … his 'Gaunt Sorrel,' and as he moved more to the front … someone handed him a lemon. … Immediately a small piece was bitten out of it and slowly and unsparingly, he began to extract its flavour and its juice. From that moment until darkness ended the battle, that lemon scarcely left his lips except to be used as a baton to emphasise an order. He listened to Yankee shout or Rebel yell, to the sound of musketry advancing or receding, to all the signs of promise or apprehension, but he never for an instant lost his interest in that lemon and even spoke of its excellence. His face, nevertheless, was calm and granite-like. His blue eye was restful and cold, except when now and then it gave, for a moment, an ominous flash. His right hand lay open and flat on his thigh, but now and then was raised into the air as was his habit – a gesture which the troops learned to believe was as significant as the extended arm of Aaron. But the lemon was not abandoned."[340]*

Jackson's brigades were opposed by Sykes's regulars of the old US Army, who stuck with unyielding, grim professionalism to the frenzied task of grinding down the successive attacks surging up at them. As the grey ranks emerged from the trees, to wade through swamp and stream, and scramble up over clumps of abattis, formation, inevitably, was lost, as well as being further disrupted by incessant musket and cannon fire. The regulars exploited the ragged gaps by coolly changing alignment, and counter-charging

339 Henderson.
340 Douglas.

with the bayonet, to take the struggling attackers in flank. As their position was exposed by those yielding stubbornly around them, Sykes's men withdrew in good order, steadily fighting back up the slope as they went. The first Confederate colours to reach the summit, and break Porter's savagely defended line, were those of the Fourth Texas of General John Hood, in a charge *"in which upwards of one thousand men fell killed and wounded before the fire of the enemy, and in which fourteen pieces of artillery and nearly a whole regiment were captured."*[341] Shortly before, at Hood's request, Douglas had delivered an order from Jackson to silence a Federal Battery blocking the advance of the Texans. Then Douglas saw Jackson stand in his stirrups and say fiercely to Pendleton, *"Ride to General Ewell and direct him, if the enemy do not retire before dusk, he must sweep them from the hill with the bayonet!"* ... *"That's the order!" shouted Jeb Stuart, waving his plumed hat in the air. ... Night was settling on the bloody scene ... there was a momentary lull ... then ...the battle grew louder ... 'at once there rose so wild a yell' ... 'There goes Old Dick!' broke from us all ... it was Ewell's last grand charge at Cold Harbour. ... that battery had been silenced; the enemy swept from the hill ... the noise of battle was hushed and soldiers wandering in the darkness over the field in search of fallen comrades, told each other that Richmond was saved."* Going forward, amid the confusion and the gloom of those final moments, Jackson rode into a Federal picket. Their surprise submitted to his brisk determination, and he spurred amongst them demanding surrender. On being escorted to the rear, the twenty or so men of the picket *"amused the troops they met on the march by loudly proclaiming that they had the honour of being captured by Stonewall Jackson."*[342] As other incidents would show, on other battlefields later that year, while already a lucky talisman to his own people, Stonewall Jackson was on the way to being claimed with something like pride by the North. The great 'Rebel Patriot' was claimed as a great 'American,' while the guns of discord were still firing.

---

341 Henderson.
342 Ibid.

When Douglas last saw the lemon *"it was torn open and exhausted and thrown away, ...* but only when *the day was over, and the battle won."* The Confederates lost an estimated eight thousand killed and wounded at Cold Harbour, of which at least half were Jackson's men. The Federal defenders lost half that number, plus a further two thousand eight hundred and thirty either captured or reported missing, several of whom would have been amongst the dead. Lee had been more fortunate than his unimaginative tactics deserved. His original reading of McClellan, however, had been spot-on. Apart from Slocom's nine thousand and the brigades of Meacher and French who crossed the Chickahominy at around six thirty p.m. to cover the retreat, McClellan did absolutely nothing to support his gallant and resolute Fifth Corps. Apart from one fleeting glance from the opposite bank of the river, he showed no interest in supporting Porter. Nor did he make the slightest attempt to turn Porter's defensive battle – ably fought against superior numbers – into a Federal victory. Instead, he kept some sixty six thousand cosily entrenched, doing little more than brushing aside the feint demonstrations of twenty-eight thousand Confederates when, probably, no more than ten thousand fresh troops would have been sufficient for Porter to have held his position, and gone on to demolish Lee's now thoroughly disorganised and, in parts, demoralised, Army. McClellan even whinged to Lincoln, *"I have lost this battle because my force is too small."* Such inertia, and a total misreading of the situation – or, perhaps, simply a complete failure to read the situation at all. With Porter's withdrawal over the two bridges being covered by the two fresh brigades and the sturdy regulars, the Confederate impetus for victory drained down into their own confusion. Lee failed to make effective use of Stuart's cavalry to instil an element of panic. Instead, when Porter's lines were giving way, Stuart *"had dashed down a lane which led to the river, about three miles distant ...* but *... finding no trace of the enemy, he had returned to Old Cold Harbour."*[343]

---

343 Henderson.

29/3. Affair at Frayser's Farm

ALTHOUGH the threat to Richmond had been eased, Lee still had to get McClellan to go, and although he remained convinced that he would go, Lee was uncertain as to the direction he would take. Having convinced himself that aggressive action was not feasible, McClellan did, indeed, intend to withdraw; but he faced the difficult task of manoeuvring in all, some ninety-five thousand men, five thousand ammunition and supply wagons, his siege train, and fifty field batteries, across the slough of the White Oak Swamp, which meandered glutinously between him and the protection of his gunboats, some ten or eleven miles distant – a short but fraught traverse, to be made in the face of a mauled yet determined enemy which, possibly, he still could not bring himself to believe was inferior in numbers. Lee – now the one with the divided army – faced a similar problem with the marshy going. His tactical problem was equally clear. He had to deliver a sufficiently hard blow to eject McClellan – to prevent him from simply being reinforced and returning in greater strength – with an army split into four parts. The three of the original attacks north of the Chickahominy and the fourth, of twenty-eight, to the south of the river. A co-ordination and concentration conundrum, which he had shown himself far from adept at controlling during the opening phase of the campaign.

From the outset, the Confederate cavalry were allowed, or given, an irrelevant role, Stuart going off at a tangent after a Federal detachment and stores stockpiled on McClellan's now discontinued supply line to the Pamunkey. If it had not become clear from Porter's actions at Cold Harbour that the Pamunkey line was discontinued, and Lee really did not appreciate that McClellan would not want to add an opposed river crossing – back across the Chickahominy – to his withdrawal complications, then; on the day after Cold Harbour, all was made clear to the Confederates by their finding the railroad to White House on the Pamunkey unguarded, and a railroad bridge destroyed. Lee had not learnt anything from Jackson's brilliant use of his horsemen in the Valley – despite the limitations imposed on him by their lack of professionalism – a fundamental which was not lacking with Stuart and his squadrons.

Lee's next move was an attack on McClellan's rear guard at Savage's Station, north of White Oak Swamp, which was harshly repulsed by two Federal Army Corps. Jackson's approach on Lee's left was held-up by his having to re-build the Grapevine Bridge, destroyed by the Federals in their withdrawal. McClellan, meanwhile, was negotiating the Swamp, albeit at the expense of abandoning some two and a half thousand of his wounded and having either to leave behind or burn great quantities of stores. McClellan then established a defensive arc south of White Oak Swamp, centred on Frayser's Farm and astride the Quaker Road, his withdrawal axis to Harrison's Landing. Longstreet, from Lee's centre, attacked the latest Federal defensive position, while A.P. Hill, alongside him, was held back. Longstreet was successful in forcing McCall's Division from its position; but when McCall was strongly reinforced, Longstreet was forced on to the back foot *"by superior numbers, and when Hill was at length put in, it was with difficulty that the fierce counter-blows of the Federals were beaten off."[344]* Both Longstreet and Hill (AP) moaned that surrounded by some fifty-five thousand colleagues they fought unsupported. One must wonder, though, what Lee really had in mind. With neither of these first two attacks does he seem to have been attempting a concentrated, co-ordinated effort. The Divisions of his right tacked about somewhat aimlessly, and failed to engage, and Jackson on the opposite wing, having reached White Oak Bridge around noon, was not able to fight his way across the Swamp by nightfall. *"Here … at the Bridge … the enemy made a determined effort to retard our advance … Jackson wrote … we found the bridge destroyed, the ordinary place of crossing commanded by their batteries on either side, and all approach to it barred by detachments of*

344 Henderson.

sharpshooters concealed in a dense wood close by … A heavy cannonading in front announced the engagement of General Longstreet at Frayser's Farm and made me eager to press forward; but the marshy character of the soil, the destruction of the bridge over the marsh and creek, and the strong position of the enemy for defending the passage, prevented my advancing until the following morning."[345]

Here again, there is no overall impression of a firm, directing hand. Lee seems not to have 'taken charge'; but to have simply let things take their course, without attempting to consider, and to adjust for the realities with which local commanders were struggling to deal with. To blithely dismiss the blame with *"The staff proved incapable of keeping the Divisions in hand"* – as Henderson does – seems not only unfair; but quite wrong. The directing hand is everything, as Jackson clearly demonstrated throughout the Valley Campaign, and would demonstrate yet again, with a very personal victory at Cedar Run, just one month later. In this Frayser's Farm phase of his hounding of McClellan, Lee required Jackson's Command to guard the left flank of the continuing push against any possible incoming attack from across the lower Chickahominy. This was to be done by moving down the road to White Oak Swamp, crossing the Swamp, and continuing a mile and a half or so along the road to Long Bridge. Jackson was to advance no further *"until he received further orders."* He received no further orders and carried out the original brief with typical determination and vigour, not to say precision. *"General Jackson demanded of his subordinates implicit, blind obedience, …* said his Staff Medical Director. *He gave orders in his own peculiar, terse, rapid way, and he did not permit them to be questioned. He obeyed his superiors in the same fashion."*[346] The comments that have been made about Jackson's struggle to get across White Oak Swamp, in the face of McClellan's rear-guard, are numerous and varied. Their very variety indicates clearly that the problems stemmed, not from Jackson's

---

345 Ibid.
346 Henderson quoting Dr McGuire.

undertaking of his assignment; but from the plan itself, and with Lee's handling of it. It was said that Jackson's troops were *"worn out by long and exhausting marches and reduced in numbers by numerous sanguinary battles."*[347] Given what they had achieved in the first half of the year, they were certainly battle-hardened, which implies a certain amount of wear and tear. On the startling imputation of his 'inactivity', he himself was said to have been *"utterly exhausted."* Given how he had consistently performed during the previous three months, he was surely down on sleep; but he had not, noticeably let-up since leaving the Valley. In the last three days alone, he had had a midnight meeting with Stuart and a ride to Magruder, on the far right flank, at three-thirty in the morning. Nor was he curtailed by the weather. He mentions in a letter to his wife that *"in consequence of heavy rain he rose 'about midnight' on the thirtieth"*[348] – the night when the troops were shaken at two-thirty a.m. In the effort to cross White Oak Swamp, the General was ahead of his men, as Colonel Munford attested, in experiencing the purest of Stonewall Jackson moments. Munford and the Second Virginia Cavalry had recently re-joined from their decoy and deception duties in the Valley. *"When I left the General on the preceding evening …* Munford wrote later … *he ordered me to be at the cross-roads (five miles from White Oak Bridge) at sunrise the next morning, ready to move in advance of his troops. The worst thunderstorm I ever was in came up about night, and in that thickly wooded country, one could not see his horse's ears. My command scattered in the storm, and I do not suppose that any officer had a rougher time in any one night than I had to endure. When the first grey dawn appeared, I started off my adjutant and officers to bring up the scattered regiment; but at sunrise I had not more than fifty men, and I was half a mile from the cross-roads. When I arrived, to my horror, there sat Jackson waiting for me. He was in a bad humour, and said, 'Colonel, my orders to you were to be here at sunrise.' I explained my situation, telling him that we*

---

347 General D.H. Hill quoted by Henderson.

348 Henderson.

had no provisions, and that the storm and the dark night had conspired against me. When I got through, he replied. 'Yes, Sir. But, Colonel, I ordered you to be here at sunrise. Move on with your regiment. If you meet the enemy drive in his pickets, and if you want artillery, Colonel Crutchfield will furnish you." Munford rode on with the few men he had, and as his bedraggled command began gathering after their scattering by the storm, Jackson sent him two couriers to inform him his "men were straggling badly'. In the hope of getting a more sympathetic hearing, Munford rode back and repeated his woes to the chief, only to be told "Yes, Sir. But I ordered you to be here at sunrise, and I had been waiting for you for a quarter of an hour." Munford then "determined to give him no cause for complaint," and rode on with the few he had to hand, sending his Adjutant to re-form the remainder. When, with Jackson, he reached the creek, the Colonel "did not think we could cross. ... the General ... "looked at me, waved his hand, and replied, 'Yes, Colonel, try it. In we went and floundered over." Dr McGuire recalled that the cavalry was followed by "Jackson himself, accompanied by three or four members of his staff, of whom I was one." The cavalry was then out-gunned by the artillery and infantry on the far bank and were forced to move "down the Swamp about a quarter of a mile ... to re-cross ... with great difficulty by a cow-path." Following further recce, Jackson had an approach path cut to one side, and parallel with the road. When "this was done, thirty-one guns, moving forward simultaneously ready-shotted, opened fire" on the position's opposite; but although the initial surprise was total, fresh rifled-gun batteries were brought up by the Federals, and the day faded away in an artillery duel in which the observation and fields of fire of both sides were obscured by thick woods. A mile upstream was a further crossing place at Brackett's Ford; but in trying to find a way of turning the enemy's position "every road and track ... was obstructed by felled trees and abattis." Jackson, by now, had ascertained that he was opposed to the enemy in some strength; but would not have known precisely that some twenty-two thousand – two Divisions and three Batteries – were in place, to prevent his crossing the Swamp. It was not until the following day, when he was joined by a brigade from the right flank – from the Division of Magruder, his old battery commander in Mexico – that Jackson was stronger in men, if not in effectiveness of equipment.

Despite the natural obstacles and the substantial strength of the enemy faced at White Oak Swamp, Jackson has been criticised for not marching to the aid of Longstreet. That General himself even went so far as to propose an alternative plan and route which Jackson might have taken and arrived *"in season for the engagement at Frayser's Farm* – i.e. in time to support him. One cannot but wonder what would have been the Commander-in-Chief's reaction to Jackson's blithely marching quite counter to his brief; but here again, to suggest an alternative plan is as much an indictment of the overall plan and its implementation, as of Jackson's handling of the situation he faced, in working the plan he been ordered to follow. When, some ten days later, Crutchfield, Pendleton and the Doctor were discussing whether Jackson should have ordered a move to assist Longstreet at Frayser's Farm, the General came in and, overhearing them *"curtly said: 'If General Lee had wanted me, he could have sent for me.' … If Lee had wanted Jackson to give direct support to Longstreet, he could have had him there in under three hours."*[349] Clearly Lee was either, once again lax in having his plan carried through, or he did not wish Jackson to move in support of Longstreet.

Long after Jackson was dead and the Civil War over, even the opposition got in on the act of critical comment. General Franklin, commanding in the area of White Oak Swamp, began with the unlikely observation – heightened by his, presumably, not having been in Lee's confidence – that *"Jackson seems to have been ignorant of what General Lee expected of him."* That Franklin was ignorant of what Jackson had been doing, is clear, for he added Jackson was *"badly informed about Brackett's Ford."* Jackson's Brigade Commander reported the impassable nature of the approaches to Brackett's Ford, and *"…Franklin himself admits that directly Wright's … (Jackson's Brigade Commander) … scouts were seen near the ford, two brigades of*

---

349 Henderson.

Sedgwick's Division were sent to oppose their passage."[350] Franklin seems
not to have been able to appreciate his own situation, never mind
that of the opposition. He continues with a truly asinine observation: *"In fact, it is likely that we should have been defeated that day had
General Jackson done what his great reputation seems to make it imperative he should have done."* Jackson's past achievements, of course,
are irrelevant, and have no bearing, regarding specific comment
about his actions during the Seven Days. In the Valley, he was operating according to the dictates of his own intellectual genius and
understanding of war. To clearly thought out moves, both of his
own devising, as well of his own directing. He was not trying to
make the second-rate devising of another succeed. In this case, a
plan of Lee's of which even Henderson is tentatively critical, saying, *"Lee's design was by no means perfect. It had two serious defects. In
the first instance, it depended for success on the co-operation of several con-
verging columns, moving over intricate country, of which the Confederates
had neither accurate maps nor reliable information. … In the second place,
concentration at the decisive point was not provided for."* And again, *"…
in justice to the reputation of his lieutenants, it is only fair to say that Lee's
solution was not a masterpiece."*

Had Lee wished to apply a firm, co-ordinating hand, having
considered the conditions under foot, he could rather more easily
have concentrated the Divisions from his right flank, in support of
the attacks from his centre, than those of Jackson on his left. It is
probably true to say that it was the prominent position Jackson had
achieved in the perception of others, which continuously makes
his actions the subject of comment. In the event, however, Lee got
his result. McClellan's dwindling, increasingly demoralised army
withdrew from the Frayser's Farm position overnight, to an even
stronger one on the slopes of Malvern Hill, already partly prepared
by the Federal Fifth and Sixth Corps. Five Corps Commander,
General Fitzjohn Porter, who had already proved himself so extremely able a defensive general, would be in overall charge

---

350 Ibid.

29/4. Losers at Malvern Hill

....

JACKSON's brother-in law, General D.H. Hill, wrote that, *"Jackson's genius never shone when he was under the command of another. It seemed to be shrouded or paralysed. … Jackson his own master, (was not more different) from Jackson in a subordinate position … The hooded falcon cannot strike the quarry."*[351] In one sense Hill is making a point so obvious as to be of little value. With someone else calling the shots, the intellectual part of Jackson's genius for War would, of course, always be curtailed. However, he seems to be making the point in the physical sense, and Henderson seems to have interpreted the comment in the context of physical action, when he writes, *"The reader who has the heart to follow this chronicle to the end will assuredly find reason to doubt the acumen, however he may admire the eloquence, of Jackson's brother-in-law.* There is nothing in Jackson's make-up or character, to suggest that in every aspect and action of his life he did other than give one hundred per cent to everything he undertook; including the parts, he had to play in the projects of others. If Hill is applying his lovely metaphor to intellectual Jackson, then there is no reason on earth to 'doubt the acumen'. It is perfectly apt. As Napoleon commented upon the situation in which Jackson found himself *"… nothing cramps so much the efforts of genius as compelling the head of an army to be governed by any will but his own."*[352]

Probably it is arid and meaningless to speculate on how Stonewall Jackson might have tackled and solved the problem of ejecting McClellan from in front of Richmond; that is, the problem facing

---

351 Henderson quoting D.H. Hill.

352 *"The Military Maxims of Napoleon"* translated by Lieutenant-General Sir George D'Aguilar, Da Capo Press edition 1995, with introduction & commentary by David G. Chandler. (Quoted by William E. Cairnes in the 1901 edition).

Lee before the outset of the Seven Days Campaign. And yet, had Jackson been in control, one cannot help but believe that the solution would have been very different and the outcome dramatically so. Just as had he been the commanding Confederate General after First Manassas, it is reasonable to say that Washington would have fallen. So, in the end, in the June and first three days of July operations, south and southeast of Richmond, it is hard not to envisage Jackson, his Valley men augmented by no more than a further ten thousand – so giving him a total of around thirty thousand and leaving, in round numbers, some fifty thousand to pin McClellan in front – while, with Stuart under command, Jackson swept round McClellan's right flank, with devastating attacks against the Federal rear and rearward communications. Swift, selected, hard-hitting attacks, enforcing situations where there would have been no question of McClellan withdrawing his army in measured steps, but rather of it being destroyed corps by corps, until the whole was either dead, wounded, straggling, or captured, and with the remnant capitulating long before it reached Harrison's Landing. Fanciful, possibly, but we know from Malvern Hill how profoundly – even before the outset – Jackson disagreed with aspects of that awful, unimaginative, blood-stained action. If, of his own volition, any General was less likely to resort to the horrors of the mindless, frontal assault on a strongly prepared defensive position it was Stonewall Jackson.

Jackson and the Stonewall brigade led Lee's Army in the march of nearly four miles from White Oak Swamp to the stooked and standing corn surrounding the sides and base of the one hundred and fifty foot high plateau of Malvern Hill. They marched through a litter of discarded weapons, personal kit and equipment, abandoned wounded, wagons and hospital carts, and a continuous stream of stragglers. Clear evidence of a widespread demoralisation. Reconnaissance by Lee, Jackson and then Longstreet, revealed sharpshooter/skirmishers covering the forward slopes of the hill, a solid, encircling line of guns – including the massive thirty-two pound smashers of the siege train – and, finally, the massed regiments of infantry in defensive positions prepared earlier by the Fifth and Sixth Corps, to whom the remainder of the Federal Army had fallen back. McClellan, seemingly as demoralised as anyone in his army, left the fighting to the able General Fitzjohn Porter, thereby denying himself from the outset, the possibility of taking advantage of any opportunities to counter-attack.

Jackson recommended turning the right flank of the position. James Longstreet, the oldest of Lee's Divisional commanders *"thought it probable that Porter's batteries, under the cross-fire of Confederate guns posted on his left and front could be thrown into disorder, and thus make way for the combined assaults of the infantry."*[353] O, but *"thou shouldst not have been old, till thou hadst been wise.'*[354] Poor, plodding Longstreet! In the coming months he was destined to play the all-important anvil to Jackson's forensic hammer; but he never understood what was going on, beyond the march he had been ordered to carry-out – and even then, he could only get thirty miles out of his men in the time Jackson's covered fifty.

On detached command he could not integrate what he was looking at, into the strictures of the wider strategy, and he would even procrastinate a direct order from Lee, in a situation where time was critical, while he tried to grope his way to an understanding of what was happening immediately in front of him. At Malvern Hill – and showing a lack of thought and imagination – Lee opted, not for the turning movement proposed by Jackson, but for the catastrophic, frontal option proposed by Longstreet. From then on, nothing went right for the Confederate attackers. The moment the artillery, struggling amongst *"the swamps and thickets … at last emerged from the cover and unlimbered for action … the … concentrated fire of the Federal guns overpowered them."* General Hunt, McClellan's Chief of Artillery, having deployed all his guns and sited them well, was able to concentrate between fifty and sixty pieces on each floundering Confederate battery in

---

353 Henderson quoting from Longstreet in *"From Manassas to Appomattox".*
354 Shakespeare's 'King Lear'.

turn. Scant if any consideration had been given even as to how the inferior Confederate field pieces were to be brought to a position where the Federal artillery could be *"thrown into disorder."* Infantry deployment suffered no better. Hunt's gunners pounded all approach roads and bombarded woods which provided cover from view but not from fire. Lee's original attack plan, however, described by Henderson as *"an extraordinary production"*, actually contained the statement: *"Batteries have been established to rake the enemy's line."* When this piece of wishful thinking could not be made reality, Lee, according to Longstreet, ordered his Division, together with that of A.P. Hill, who were in the rear, to move round to the left in a move to turn the Federal right flank. The original order, however, was not cancelled, and when sometime before six p.m. D.H. Hill took the sound of skirmishing fire for the signal for him to attack, as originally ordered, his *"ten and a half thousand men, absolutely unaided, advanced against the whole Federal army. ... There was no attempt at concentration ... The Divisions that should have supported him had not yet crossed the swamp in rear ... The blunder met with terrible retribution ... death reaped a fearful harvest. ... 'It was the onset of battle,' said a Federal officer present, 'with the good order of a review.' But the iron hail of grape and canister, laying the ripe wheat low as if it had been cut with a sickle, and tossing the shocks in the air, rent the lines from end to end. Hundreds fell, hundreds swarmed back to the woods, but still the brigades pressed on ... the Federal infantry had yet to be encountered. Lying behind their shelter they had not yet fired a shot; but as the Confederates reached close range, regiment after regiment springing to their feet, poured a devastating fire into the charging ranks. The rush was checked. Here and there small bodies of desperate men, following the colours, still pressed onward, but the majority lay down. ... there was no further support at hand. ... Federal gunners held fast to their position, and on every part of the line Porter's reserves were coming up. As one regiment emptied its cartridge-boxes it was relieved by another. The volume of fire never for a moment slackened.*[355]

---

355 Henderson.

Jackson made no attempt to move brigades forward to support Hill (D.H.). The original attack order applied to Hill only. One cannot help but suspect that Jackson, the ever-thinking General and conserver of his men's lives, realising from the outset the futility of what was being attempted, had decided to act solely in accordance with his orders. Magruder and Huger on Lee's right attacked next. Their brigades were not mutually supporting. Fatally, they attacked piecemeal, and the lethal Federal artillery exacted an even heavier toll than they had with Hill. No progress, meanwhile, had been made with a left flanking manoeuvre by Longstreet and Hill (A.P.) and there, with the approach of darkness, the encounter ended.

Some thirty thousand – nearly half – of Lee's infantry had been severely mauled. His army was in a state of confusion and disorder. Men divorced from their regiments, lost and straggling, many wounded, roads blocked by guns, waggons and ambulances. Such was the state of the disorder and demoralisation, which McClellan had denied himself any opportunity to capitalise upon, in the wake of Porter's largely artillery-won victory. Porter, probably, had been ordered to do no more than block Confederate attacks that day. The Federal Commander-in-Chief had not even witnessed the battle. After watching the first salvoes of early evening he had ridden back to Harrison's Landing.

During the first hours of darkness, Jackson's Divisional commanders reported to him on the state of their units and were given their night orders. *"… after many details of losses and disasters, they concurred in declaring that McClellan would probably take the aggressive initiative in the morning, and that the Confederate army was in no condition to resist him. Jackson had listened silently, save when he interposed a few brief questions, to all their statements; but now he replied: 'No; he will clear out in the morning'."*[356] At the first glimmer of dawn, Jackson rode forward in pouring rain, and saw, as he forecast, that Malvern Hill had been abandoned by all but a few

---

356 Henderson quoting the Reverend. Dr Dabney.

Federal cavalry patrols. Below the summit, *"the slopes … were … covered with hundreds of dead and dying men, the surgeons were quietly at work."* He rode back to his headquarters and *"ordered his chief of staff to get the troops under arms, to form the infantry in three lines of battle, and then to allow the men to build fires, cook their rations, and dry their clothes."* He then rode back up the Quaker Road, to the house Lee was using as his HQ, which was where Dr Dabney found him later in the morning, to report that *"his orders had been fulfilled. … ammunition had been replenished and his four Divisions formed up."* *"Here I stayed much of the day, …* Dabney recalled … *and witnessed some strange things."*

Longstreet arrived, wet and muddy from having ridden round the battle-field. *"His report was not particularly cheerful. Jackson was very quiet, never volunteering any counsel or suggestion, but answering when questioned in a brief, deferential tone. His countenance was very serious, and soon became very troubled."* For Stonewall Jackson those wasted, irretrievable hours in the Poindexter Mansion headquarters must have been exasperating in the extreme.

Outside, his weather-beaten and battle-proven 'foot cavalry' were once more ready for whatever, and for wherever he should lead them. A few miles down the road, as he appreciated full well, was a demoralised and disorganised enemy. In the past six days of fighting and marching, McClellan's generalship-by-proxy, had cost his side no more than sixteen thousand battle casualties; but his fighting strength had been reduced by nearly fifty percent, to no more than fifty thousand due to desertion, straggling, sickness; lost and missing, and the debilitating effect of demoralisation. Lee's unimaginative, uncoordinated battering had cost the Confederates twenty thousand killed and wounded. For Jackson, the time to strike was now, this very moment; but with every passing minute the opportunity was fading, and he was forced to sit idle, and to witness an interminable quite profitless debate. Was McClellan beaten or manoeuvring? The direction of his retreat was not clear! Was he bent on getting away, or on embarking, simply to come back at Richmond from a different direction? Irrelevant, irrelevant, all irrelevant. When a clatter of hooves heralded the arrival of a sodden President Davis and his nephew, 'Old Jack's' heart surely must have sunk still further. It would be the fatal inertia of post–First Manassas all over again. *"Davis and Lee drew to the table and entered into an animated military discussion."* Jackson's worst fears were realised. No movement without further information. *"Jackson … sat silent in his corner. I watched his face. The expression changing from surprise to dissent, and lastly to intense mortification, clearly showed the tenor of his thoughts. He knew that McClellan was defeated, that he was retreating and not manoeuvring. He knew that his troops were disorganised, that sleeplessness, fasting, bad weather, and disaster must have weakened morale. He heard it said by General Lee that the scouts reported the roads so deep in mud that the artillery could not move, that our men were wet and wearied. But Jackson's mind reasoned that where the Federals could march the Confederates could follow, and that a decisive victory was well worth a great effort.*[357]

Finally, that unnecessary, enervating discussion between President and Commander-in-Chief decreed, *"The enemy was not to be pursued until Stuart's cavalry … should obtain reliable information."* As allowed to perform by Lee, in admittedly not ideal cavalry country, Stuart's misplaced, and largely irrelevant cavalry were proving themselves – quite literally – a 'loose cannon'. Riding on down past Malvern Hill, they occupied the Evelington Heights – the ground of tactical importance which dominated Harrison's Landing. In their dispirited trudge back to the area of the Landing, the Federals had failed to occupy these Heights. Stuart un-limbered the single howitzer he had with him and lobbed a shell or two amongst the mass of tents, stacked muskets, parked guns, wagons and mounds of stores, spread out below. It is unlikely that McClellan or Porter waved a plumed hat in thanks for the tip-off; but following Stuart's revealing and futile gesture, the Federals secured the Heights.

---

357 Henderson quoting a letter he received from the Reverend. Dr Dabney, adding; Dr McGuire writes to the same effect.

When at last Lee ordered an advance, led by Longstreet's Division, they found the River Road had been blocked. Lee ordered a change of route, and the army counter-marched to the Charles City cross-roads. Incompetent guides led to further delay, and by evening, Lee had failed even to contact a Federal outpost. Behind Longstreet in the order of march, the Valley men progressed just three miles in the day. Even Jackson's patience and iron self-control snapped, and he rounded on the useless guide; *"in fierce anger and ordered him from his presence with threats of the severest punishment. ... he said to the Staff, 'Now, gentlemen, Jim will have breakfast for you punctually at dawn. I expect you to be up, to eat immediately, and be in the saddle without delay. We must burn no more daylight."* The General's anger flared again the next morning, when only Major, the Reverend Dr Dabney met him for breakfast at the ordered time, the rest of the Staff being still asleep. He *"turned in a rage to the servant; 'Put that food into the chest, have that chest in the wagon, and that wagon moving in two minutes."* The Major *"suggested very humbly, that he had better at least take some food for himself. But he was too angry to eat, and repeating his orders, flung himself into the saddle, and galloped off. Jim gave a low whistle, saying: 'My stars, but de general is just mad dis time; most like lightnin' strike him!"*[358]

When the pickets finally closed and engaged, and the troops deployed for action, Lee and Jackson went forward on foot to recce McClellan's remnant. They found the Evelington Heights strongly fortified, and gunboats positioned to provide covering fire for both flanks, of what was, in effect, a great semi-circular redoubt. They had no option but to declare McClellan's position at Harrison's Landing impregnable. Lee had failed to get a genuine result from Malvern Hill, and on two counts. First, he was defeated at every stage in the tactical battle of the first of July. Second, by not instigating an instant and vigorous pursuit the morning after – as Jackson expected and immediately prepared

---

358 Henderson quoting Dr Dabney.

for – he allowed not only hope and confidence to seep back into McClellan and his troops; but gave a boost to the whole Northern people, helping to instil in them a more positive feeling towards their own fighting men. For the South, Lee's Campaign was a success only to the extent that it eased the immediate threat to Richmond. No positive advances were made. The relief was purely temporary. Although Jackson was involved as a subordinate Divisional commander, in all actions, the Campaign bears none of the hallmarks of his genius. Surprise and speed of movement; unexpected and unforeseen initiatives; swift and relentless follow-ups, all were lacking. Lee had failed to take McClellan out of the reckoning, and he remained for the time being, crouched in his corner of the Peninsula, a brooding threat, writing to Lincoln of his urge for aggressive action which was most notably lacking when he had ample opportunity to act positively. If McClellan had not actually 'snatched defeat from the jaws of victory', he had certainly made sure defeat was safe from those jaws.

30. 'MAN OF MYSTERY'

*"A defensive campaign can only
be made successful by taking the
aggressive at the proper time."*
Stonewall Jackson

TEN days after Malvern Hill, Jackson was back near Richmond with his command encamped astride the road to Mechanicsville, some two to two and a half miles from the Confederate capital. Not wishing to disturb local householders unduly, the General established his headquarters under canvas in *"a yard in front of a gentleman's house."* He spent his days shaking-off a fever which had plagued him since the action at White Oak Swamp, and in equipping and refreshing the organisation of the Valley Army, after some three months of fairly continuous marching and fighting. *"He received many visitors of all ranks and condition and treated them cordially by giving them as much time as he could. ... He was at that time the favourite of the army and the people, but his style and manners were unchanged, and his Headquarters was maintained in all its Valley simplicity ... He might have been lionized in Richmond as no one else ever had been, but that did not accord with his tastes, and the simplicity of his character made him shrink from it."*[359]

It was a hardened core of fit and resolute men Jackson had around him on the Mechanicsville Road, Albeit that their original, naïve camaraderie had been blown away, and their numbers brutally attenuated since the turn of the year. Now, the prospect of serried ranks of steel-tipped blue, and a vista of dust-laden miles, stretching beyond the distant peaks of the Blue Ridge, had

---

359 Douglas.

coalesced into a way of life, that with the assurance of his leadership, they could even thrive on in these times of kill or be killed. He, who now saw tirelessly and patiently to ration strengths, the fit of cloth and shoe leather; slow-healing wounds, the maintenance and the loading of ammunition wagons, the shining and sharpening of weapons, and the application of cold water to weather-scourged skin.

Their unshakeable confidence, and the selfless application to everyday tasks came from a belief born of mutual sacrifice. He was not simply the Old Jack who emerged bleary-eyed from a tent washed through by rain; but the embodiment of the master-artist of the cruelly complex art in which they were immersed, and which dominated their every waking moment. In action, faith alone had become sufficient to make death alone synonymous with defeat. 'Old Jack' was both *"a rallying cry and a term of endearment."*[360] For many everyday needs, the enemy, that looming, ever-present evil to soldier and civilian Virginian alike, had been a prolific, if inadvertent, supplier during those Spring days in the Valley, and McClellan's recent undeviating determination to go backwards had also proved a ready source of bits of kit and equipment; wagons, rifled-guns, and newer, more up-to-date rifles complete with ammunition. The cavalry, for example, no longer carried their original double-barrelled shotguns; but carbines courtesy of the Union.[361] They never did get hold of the Winchester repeater in any numbers, which, in the closing stages of the War, made Union cavalry formidable. In camp at Mechanicsville meals were regular, if not overly plentiful. By and large, fellow Virginians were generous and grateful, given their own increasingly constrained means. The 'Foot Cavalry' remained severely lean, as well as

---

360 Captain Charles M. Blackford, *"Letters from Lee's Army"* compiled by Susan Leigh Blackford, Charles Scribner's Sons, New York and London, 1947.

361 Ibid.

hardened. In death, their spare frames would resist decay longer than those of a well-glutted foe.[362]

Accompanied by three of the staff, the General went once into town to attend a Presbyterian morning service in the comforting surroundings of wooden pews, church bells and consecrated stone. The unassuming horseman, in dull, weather-stained grey, whose name was never far from every tongue, and no discussion on the War could long exclude, rode slowly and unnoticed through the Sabbath streets. The service was drawing to its ultimate blessing when the congregation quickened into the sudden, excited realisation that the figure at prayer in the side-pew was Stonewall himself. The living embodiment of the unyielding sobriquet, which was their most treasured balm for the frustration of resentment in the face of oppression. Young and old swarmed around him for a few precious moments of relief. The Staff had to help their chief get clear. Outside, a lady, whom Douglas took for an old friend, hurried him down the street. They waited by the horses; but he was soon back, and apologising quietly for having kept them waiting, mounted, and led the group of uniformed figures away to their soldier's camp without the walls. He, at least, to be recognised amongst them once more only, through a pall of grief that would shroud his passing.

---

362 Douglas mentions that after Second Manassas: *"It was noticeable in how much better condition were the Confederate dead, who had been lying on the field for several days, than those of the Union army. … The Federal troops were well cared for, well fed, fat, and in good physical condition; upon them decay and decomposition made quick work. The Confederates had little flesh upon them, no fat, nothing to decay."* Visiting the same area some four months after the first battle, Captain Charles Blackford remarks how *"The earth having been washed off, many of the bodies were exposed entirely to view. Strange to say, they seemed to have just dried up without decay. It was the same way with the horses, none of which have either decayed or been devoured by buzzards."*

30/1. "A Glow-worm with the Moon"

....

IMMEDIATELY following the Seven Days battles, Jackson had once more proposed an immediate invasion of the North. Although he had been ignored on the way to proceed at Malvern Hill, Lee was clearly approving of Jackson's methods and achievements, although the Confederate C-in-C himself may not have been much of a student of Napoleon, amongst whose many tips for generals was the admonition *"Never attack a position in front which you can get by turning."* Barely more than a month passed, after the McClellan redoubt at Harrison's Landing had been declared impregnable, however; before Lee wrote to Jackson, *"there should be no more Malvern Hills. You are right in not attacking them in their strong and chosen positions. They aught always to be turned, as you propose, and thus force them on to more favourable ground."*[363] Turning movements with Jackson generally had something more far-reaching in mind than simply *'forcing on to more favourable ground.'* To the invasion proposal though, Lee said *"nothing",* and Davis was said to have *"considered"* but *"disregarded."* Jackson seems to have been alone in understanding the importance of timing; that *"a defensive campaign can only be made successful by taking the aggressive at the proper time."* Davis certainly seems to have failed to understand either the importance of the initiative, or the war they were fighting.

Lincoln, on the other hand, like Jackson, understood full well the unyielding nature of the fight he had brought about, and was determined to remain on the front foot – against what he termed *"insurrectionary combinations"* – no matter how little he understood what it took to make such a stance successful. With McClellan knocked-back on the Peninsula, a further Union Army, was mustered south of the Potomac in Virginia, under a fresh commander, appointed from the Western Theatre.

---

363 Henderson quoting Lee.

Major-General John Pope believed in making war on un-armed civilians. He would hold local people responsible for guerrilla sabotage to railways, telegraphs and roads, and have his units subsist off the inhabitants of the country. He ordered his subordinate generals to administer an oath of allegiance to the Union, to the men and women of Virginia within their military jurisdiction, and to expel from their homes any who resisted. One of his German brigadiers went a stage further in depravity and ordered the arrest of five prominent citizens who were then to be held in readiness for judicial murder, on a quid pro quo basis, in retaliation for any soldier bushwhacked. The Confederate Government reacted as far as it could, *"by declaring that Pope and his officers were not entitled to be considered as soldiers ... and ... if captured were to be imprisoned so long as their orders remained un-repealed; and, in the event of any unarmed Confederate citizens being tried and shot, an equal number of Federal prisoners were to be hanged."*

"It was said to Jackson "This new general claims your attention." "And please God, he shall have it" was the quiet reply."[364]

The opportunities were not long in coming, for Lee wanted Pope's activities curtailed, and the vital rail link for supplies coming south from Gordonsville, protected. The task was allotted to Jackson, amongst whose initial preparations was the order for a cavalry Company to be attached to his headquarters, whose men were intimately acquainted with the countryside around Fredericksburg. Having spent much of his boyhood roaming the area, and knowing many of the families thereabouts, Captain Charles M. Blackford was the ideal person, and 'B' Company, Second Virginia Cavalry, duly reported to Jackson on the Mechanicsville Road. Jackson had a last meeting with Lee and the President, and Sandy Pendleton invited Captain Blackford to join the staff on this second trip into Richmond. Blackford was dismissed for one hour, whilst various Generals met with the President, and he *"rode around to Cousin Mary G.*

---

364 Henderson.

Watkins' and got a very nice lunch, which she kindly prepared for me in an hour ... any kind of hospitality is a strain now ... Blackford wrote to wife Susan – when bacon is seventy-five and fresh meat fifty cents a pound, potatoes sixteen dollars a bushel, and other things in proportion."

Lee and Jackson were the last to leave the President's house, "and stood talking on the steps. Lee was elegantly dressed in full uniform, sword and sash, spotless boots, beautiful spurs ... the highest type of the Cavalier class, to which by blood and rearing, he belongs. Jackson, on the other hand, is a typical Roundhead. He was poorly dressed, that is, he looked so, though his clothes were made of good material. His cap was very indifferent and pulled down over one eye, much stained by the weather and without insignia. His coat was closely buttoned up to his chin and had upon the collar the stars and wreath of a General. His shoulders were stooped, and one shoulder was lower than the other, and his coat showed signs of much exposure to the weather."

"He had a plain sword belt without sash, and a sword in no respect different from that of other infantry officers that I could see. His face in repose is not handsome or agreeable and he would be passed by anyone without a second look, though anyone could see determination and will in his face by the most casual glance – much I would say to fear but not to love. I, of course, speak only from a casual observation ... that might be likened to that of a glow-worm with the moon."

He got on his old sorrel horse, which his courier was holding for him, and without saying a word to anyone, in a deep brown and abstracted study, started in a gallop towards the Mechanicsville Pike, which we soon reached." Movement on the Pike was much impeded by wagon trains moving in both directions. Jackson was in a hurry to get back, and be gone, and he ... "first dodged in and out among the wagons, but his progress was ... much slower than his needs demanded. ... He told his Adjutant to have the cavalcade fall into single file, and thereupon dashed into an extensive field of oats, over ripe for harvest". His "orders, published to his Corps, very strictly enjoined the preservation of the crops ... and forbade all officers and men from riding out into the fields on each side of the road." Unfortunately, the move was observed by "a round and fat little gentlemen ... sitting smoking his pipe, with bald head and red face, in his shirtsleeves with an eye on his morning

'Examiner' and the other on his field of oats." He rushed to confront the column, and *"standing like a lion on the pathway ... puffing and blowing, wiping the perspiration off his forehead and so bursting with rage that all power of articulation seemed for a moment suspended. ... The General saw him, and for the first time in his career seemed inclined to retreat, but our irate friend had regained his speech and made his attack as Jackson drew rein before him.*

"What the hell are you riding over my oats for? The little man shouted ... dammit, don't you know it's against orders? ... What's your name, anyhow?"

"My name is Jackson", said the General, half as if, for the occasion, he wished it were something else."

"Jackson! Jackson! In a voice of great contempt. ... I'll report you to Stonewall Jackson myself, that's what I'll do!"

"They call me that sometimes," said the General in the same subdued, half-alarmed tone. "What name?" "Stonewall" "You don't mean to say you are Stonewall Jackson, do you?" "Yes, sir, I am." Waving a *"big bandana around his head,"* and with a loud cheer for Stonewall Jackson, the 'stout party' duly collapsed with a *"By God, General, please do me the honour to ride all over my damned old oats! ... and with an admiring look that was adoring ... tears stood in his eyes ... he pressed the General to take every variety of strong drink, but buttermilk was all he would accept. So great was our friend's admiration for old Stonewall, that even his refusing to take something stronger did not lower him in his estimation, as I think it might have done, had the refusal come from a lesser light."*

Captain Blackford told his wife. *"I shall watch Jackson closely ... and put down what I see and what I think of him ... he is, of course, a military genius ... the army is full of stories about him ... whenever he is recognized by the soldiers, he is cheered ... he tries to go about unrecognized ... he seems to have no social life ... he divides his time between military duties, prayer, sleep and solitary thought. He holds converse with few."*

Ordering the Valley Army to follow, Jackson's headquarters took to the road, north in the direction of Gordonsville, at 'early dawn' the next morning. Soon after, on accepting an invitation to breakfast, General and Staff were entertained by a young lady playing the piano. To her surprise, Jackson asked her to play "Dixie". *"I heard it a few days ago and it was, I thought, very beautiful."* *"Why, General … she replied … I just sang it a few moments ago – it is about our oldest war song."* *"Ah, indeed, I did not know it."* Douglas, recalling the incident, claims *"the General had the least knowledge of music … and had so little of it in his soul that he was necessarily "fit for treason, strategy and spoils."* …and goes on to suggest Jackson *"thought he would startle the young lady with his knowledge of music."*

Rather more likely, he had been so engrossed in considering the minutiae of the operational situation facing him that he had not fully registered the rendition, and with the instinctive courtesy and sensitivity of feeling of a true countryman at ease with the honest, unsentimental harshness of nature, was simply asking to hear a tune which pleased him. As a boy *"Thomas displayed some interest in music. The old melodies of the slaves were known to him and he could sing them through in their dialect. … he became expert in making 'corn stalk fiddles' … and when …he came into possession of a regular violin, badly in need of repairs … Conrad Kester, the gunsmith at Weston, with whom he was on most friendly terms … soon had the instrument in serviceable condition. After hours of practise, Jackson gained proficiency on it."*[365] He would have been aged about sixteen at the time.

Having ridden for the rest of the morning that followed, under a hot, mid-July, sun, Jackson led the few members of Staff and Blackford's 'B' Company cavalry escort up to the gate of a house set back from the road and covered in a profusion of flowers and climbing roses, where *"a very plainly but neatly dressed matron of forty, with a pleasant face and neat looking children, was sitting on the steps watching the soldiers go by."*

He asked for a drink of water, and the woman immediately went indoors and came out with a blue pitcher which she handed

---

365 Cook.

to Jackson. There was nothing about the group to suggest other than *"Damned quartermasters and commissaries"* but the woman, noticing the respect shown to Jackson, asked Captain Blackford who he was. *"On being told, her eyes riveted on him with a look of combined curiosity and devotion."* When the General returned the pitcher, she poured the remainder of the water on to the ground and, to the dismay of the rest of the party, turned back into the house. However, she was soon out once again with a *"large white pitcher and dipper"* from which she amply slaked the remaining thirsts. Blackford *"asked her why she carried the other pitcher into the house, and she replied she never intended anyone else should drink out of it and would hand it down to her children as a memento of Jackson's visit."*

When they rode on, *"General Jackson made me ride up beside him and directed me to go with my Company to the neighbourhood of Fredericksburg, which is occupied by the Federal General Augur, to send into the town and find out all I could about their force, movements, etc., and report to him by couriers; … then … we rode on like a couple of dummies,"* wrote Captain Blackford who, from time to time tried, vainly, to make conversation. When they reached the turning for Fredericksburg, *"I told him so, touched my hat and left him, but I have my doubts as to whether he knew of my presence or absence."* The General had much to consider, and many possibilities to anticipate and allow for. To pick his way through the complex skein of what might or might not occur required every iota of his formidable powers of unremitting concentration.

30/2. Paving the Way

....

*"You, a man, and belonging to Jackson's
Army, and talk of him being defeated!
you ought to be ashamed of yourself."*
Miss Crittenden to Dr Dabney

....

APART from terrorising local non-combatants, Pope was using his five thousand cavalry effectively to gather intelligence.
Patrols and pickets ranged up to twenty miles ahead of his infantry Divisions; but they were operating in an increasingly hostile
environment. The women of Virginia were incensed, and keener than ever to support their own.

When Dr Dabney proposed precautions in case of Jackson
being defeated, he was taken sharply to task by the ladies of the
Crittenden Family, whose home was close between the two sides.
*"You, a man, and belonging to Jackson's Army, and talk of him being
defeated! You aught(sic) to be ashamed of yourself."* Captain Blackford
wondered *"How much is it possible for the men of a country to be sub-
jugated when the women show so much spirit? ... All, of every degree
and every age, with praying heart and tearful eye, with one consent are
engaged everywhere in unceasing labour, plying the busy needle, handling the constant shuttle, twirling the ceaseless wheel, nursing the sick,
watching the dying or binding the wounded limb."* He quoted to his
wife the ancient story of Greece, unconquerable, and how *"its
maidens twined their soft tresses into golden bowstrings that their lovers
might send winged death hissing to the Persian heart ... adding ... neither history nor romance shows a parallel to the devotion our women are
displaying in every hamlet of our land. This is the age of heroines and I
glory in the fact that my wife and mother are among them."*

In his unceasing quest for intelligence of the immediate enemy, Jackson quickly appreciated that Pope's forty-two thousand
infantry were widely dispersed, in Division-sized groups, which

suggested possibilities according to his second tenet for commanding Generals *'never fight against heavy odds, if by any possible manoeuvring, you can hurl your own force on only a part, and that the weakest part, of your enemy and crush it. Such tactics will win every time …* he said … *and a small army may thus destroy a large one in detail, and repeated victory will make it invincible.*"[366] His opening move was to begin the application of his overall *modus operandi "to mystify, mislead, and surprise."*[367] His own men were at first held back to encourage Pope to come forward. At the same time, he requested reinforcements. Odds of four to one against were plenty long enough, even for one who was never in the least overawed by mere numerical strength. Lee sent up the Light Division of A.P. Hill plus the Second brigade of Louisiana Volunteers. At two to one against, this made the achieving of superiority at decisive points potentially achievable for Jackson's customary swift, attacking style, especially now that he would be wielding a force of some twenty-three thousand. For all his braggadocio, Pope may well have had a legitimate degree of uncertainty, at first, about how great a threat Jackson represented numerically, because McClellan, with his extraordinary capacity for over-estimating the opposition – largely thanks to his Pinkerton Agency detectives – had reported Stonewall Jackson as heading for the Valley with a force of sixty to eighty thousand.

Jackson identified Culpeper Court House as the key strategic focal point, where four roads converged. He reckoned on Pope using three of the roads to concentrate his units from Fredericksburg in the east, and from Waterloo Bridge and Sperryville in the north. If he could reach Culpeper, ahead of Pope's concentration, using the fourth road from Orange Court House, he would be well placed to attempt the destruction of Pope's Army piecemeal. The 'if', however, like so many of the ifs of war failed to congeal fully.

---

366 Henderson quoting Imboden.
367 Ibid.

In the interests of intelligence gathering, 'B' Company, Second Virginia became immediately and effectively active within the Federal cavalry screen around Fredericksburg. The Company Commander patrolling and reconnoitring with one half of the Company and his Lieutenant scouting with the other, Blackford set up some brisk and profitable huckstering – profitable both militarily and financially – within Fredericksburg itself. *"I have one of my men in town … with his horse hitched to a two-wheeled wagon selling eggs, chickens and tobacco, and picking up all the information possible. … He looked as if he had been raising peanuts and potatoes all his life in Caroline* (County). To reduce the likelihood of his troopers, in numbers, being detected by Pope's numerous and active cavalry, Blackford took to going behind Federal lines with only a single companion, who, like himself knew the country intimately. *"I fear you shared the anxiety of my army friends that I had been captured near Fredericksburg …* he wrote to Susan from; *Dr Pendleton's on the twenty second of July … I was in danger of it, but owing to my perfect acquaintance with the neighbourhood, I was able to elude pursuit, although the enemy in large force, had thrown their line far in my rear. The people everywhere kept me posted, regarding their movements."* Jackson was pleased with Blackford's close observation of Federal camps and sent for him on his return to headquarters. *"I found the General in a tent with nothing but a roll of blankets strapped up, two camp-stools and a table. He was seated on one stool and motioned me to the other, asking at once for me to tell what I had seen. After I had been talking a few minutes I perceived he was fast asleep. I stopped and waited several minutes. He woke up and said "Proceed". I did so for a few minutes when I noted he was asleep again, so I stopped. … when he awoke, he said without any explanation, apology or further questioning; "You may proceed to your quarters." I did so although I felt somewhat put out that my narrative had proved such a good soporific."*

Some days later, Blackford's servant, John Scott told him the Army was about to move. Asked how he knew, Scott replied that General Jackson had sent for his washing. Although, when asked, the Adjutant-General did not know of any proposed move; but duly sent for his washing, as did Blackford, who also ordered 'B' Company to get their impedimenta sorted and to prepare for the road. Within an hour, Blackford was scribbling a note. *"The whole army is moving somewhere … I can see a train of wagons five miles long … yet nobody but General Jackson knows where we are going. It seems strange to see a large body of men moving in one direction, and only one man in all the thousands knowing where they are going. I am at headquarters and know nothing, nor does the adjutant-general. They will go until ordered to stop.*

Jackson was moving forward and was close to moving up to Culpeper Court House, and to *"hurling"* his reinforced Army on Pope's isolated leading Division, commanded by his old opponent from the Valley, General Banks. Jackson himself was incessantly active, both physically and mentally. Scouting and reconnoitring was continuous. One afternoon, Blackford was riding with Jackson, *"investigating some roads I expect he intends to use … when the General suddenly stopped, dismounted at the foot of a tree, unbuckled his sword and stood it by the tree, then laid down with his head on the root … and was asleep in a second … He laid with his eyes shut for about five or six minutes, got up, buckled on his sword, mounted and rode on, without any explanation or comment. He is a curious, wonderful man … He has no social graces but infinite earnestness. He is a zealot and has stern ideas of duty.* The silence of a masterful concentration was absolutely focused on a complex intellectual task, with every aspect and nuance held entirely within the compass of a single mind. Nothing in the planning and preparation stage committed to paper; no other opinions either required or necessary. A virtuoso intellectual performance, demanding profound moral fortitude and assurance.

Blackford was witnessing not Tom Jackson the Man; but Stonewall Jackson the General. Blackford was experiencing the art of pure generalship by a consummate exponent. An individual genius which was both inherent and self-developed in and by the man. If it can be said that the artist and the man are two separate entities within a single being – and the greater the artist, the greater the separation between the two[368] – then it is as true of the artist with war, as it is of the artist with the word, or with the brush. In none of the select handful of truly great battlefield leaders is this gulf between the fabric and the torment of the man, and the intellectual activity of the artist, greater than it was in Thomas 'Stonewall' Jackson.

30/3. One Man's Will

....

"Where's my Stonewall brigade?"
Stonewall Jackson

....

POPE began his forward concentration on the very same day that Jackson began his advance, and for once, Jackson's command hung-fire. They were painfully slow getting from Gordonsville to Orange Court House, from where Culpeper was still twenty miles away. Ewell made no more than eight miles in a day, and the Light brigade of A.P. Hill just two miles. Federal cavalry held river crossings, and staff work was sketchy. A march route for Ewell was changed, with the result that Hill was held up when the designated paths crossed. The weather too, did not help. At the end of the first week of August it was stiflingly hot, and the march claimed lives. Because of this poor initial progress, Jackson

---

368 From T. S. Elliot's contention; the greater the exponent the greater the separation between the human experience and the intellectual creativity.

"feared … the expedition … would be productive of little good."[369] He was facing a delicate situation. Pope knew he was on the move, and Jackson could not get intelligence precise enough to be able to tell exactly how Pope's dispositions were changing, although he, in turn, knew Pope was also on the move. Despite the uncertainty of being in close proximity to so superior a force, Jackson unhesitatingly forced on. The favoured early dawn start was made on the second morning, and good progress achieved during the forenoon. All the while the advance skirmished on and off with Pope's cavalry. They approached the southern end of Slaughter's Mountain, a long, low ridge, to the right of the line of march, and running at right angles towards the Cedar Run, whose several twisting and turning branches, were crossed by the road to Culpeper, now just seven miles distant. Word came back around Noon that the Federal cavalry had massed in a position of some strength about two miles ahead of the advance. On his leading brigade coming under artillery fire from a ridge ahead, Jackson rode forward. At least one of Pope's Divisions was clearly in the offing. He immediately secured the tactically important forward slopes of Slaughter's Mountain with two batteries of eight guns. From there, they could enfilade any attack coming in from the direction of Culpeper Court House. From that initial move by Jackson, the struggle on the Cedar Run, in the shadow of Slaughter's Mountain, evolved according to his understanding and his will. He deployed a brigade to left and right of his axis of advance and ordered all the artillery forward; but the eleven thousand infantry of Hill's Light Division would take some two hours to arrive and deploy fully. Colonel Henderson reckoned that Jackson's twenty three thousand strong force occupied some seven miles of track-way when advancing in column.

"Jackson got impatient, especially for the ordinance wagons."[370] He rode back, accompanied only by Captain Blackford, to where his

---

369 Henderson quoting Jackson.
370 Blackford.

Chief Quartermaster, Major John Harman, was personally supervising the crossing of the Crooked Run. Wagons were getting stuck in the heavy mud as they exited the water. *"It is said that (Harmon) can swear at a mule team and make it jerk a wagon out of a mudhole as nothing else will. … he was using his utmost endeavours at the ford that day … and the air was blue with his oaths. As Jackson came up, he rather increased his energy. Jackson stood a moment and said very mildly: "Major, don't you think you would accomplish just as much without swearing so hard?"*

"Harmon turned with a smile that was almost contemptuous and said: "If you think anybody can make a set of damned mules pull without swearing at them you just try it, General! Just try it! I'll stand by and see how damned quick you get tired of it!" … he commenced impatiently to walk backwards and forwards while Jackson watched the ford."

"The first wagon was light and had a good team and pulled out. Jackson turned with some triumph to Harmon and said, "You see, Major, how easy it is?"

"Just wait," Harmon said, "till one of those damned ordinance wagons come along! You haven't had anything but a bunch of damned empties yet; don't holler till you're out of the wood, General!"

"As he said it a monster came to the exit of the ford and stalled. The driver jerked the reins and whipped and did everything but swear, having recognized the General on the bank, and after some moments got it out, while Harmon stood by obviously enjoying Jackson's impatience."

"Better let me damn 'em, General, nothing else will do!" Jackson made no reply and another ordinance wagon came along. It was obviously heavily loaded and stuck at the edge of the ford, despite every effort of the driver, some suggestions on the part of the General, and some pushing by other drivers. Harmon was delighted and laughed a most triumphant laugh. "What do you say now, General? Try swearing at them yourself, General, since nothing else will suit a mule!"

"The General stood impatiently a moment longer, then gathered up the reins of his horse and moved off, saying in a crestfallen tone: "Well, Major, I suppose you will have to have your way!" Before he had moved fifty yards all the pent up energy of Harmon's nature found vent in a fluent damnation which so startled the mules and their negro driver that

the wagon was jerked out of the stream and was alongside the retreating General in half a minute."

Jackson had ordered forward most of his artillery, some twenty-six guns in all, and they were already in noisy, vigorous action, as he returned to the front. Ordering Blackford to remain at the edge of the woods – just in rear of the gun-line – and to direct Hill to support the attack, as his brigades marched up, Jackson continued on forward through the trees. Jackson attacked *"impetuously",* according to Douglas. An unfortunate word, indicative of a failure to appreciate the time factor. Few at the time seem to have understood how Jackson used time – or had his competence in its use; least of all his staff and fellow Generals. As is so often the everyday norm in any War, here on the banks of the Cedar Run, Jackson could not afford a moment's delay. In two hours, Pope might have double the number on hand. Orders were swiftly delivered, and as swiftly obeyed; but in those two hours from *"about four and a half"* on that hot, summer afternoon (what in the South was termed 'evening') – the whole opposing brigade, of the familiar opponent Banks – some nine thousand in total; was committed to the assault. The attack was checked by Ewell, on the right of the Confederate line, where the flank was secured by the artillery on Slaughter's Mountain. But on the left, where Jackson had at once pointed out the weakness, the flank was open, against a dense wood, impenetrable to cavalry, but not to determined infantry. He had ordered it to be reinforced; but before the order could be complied with, Winder, the Stonewall Brigade Commander, was mortally wounded by a cannon shot, and soon after, a line of one and a half thousand determined Northerners – in part shrugging their way through heavy sniping fire from Confederate riflemen – swept forward across some three hundred yards of open wheat field, and part, on the right, working their way through the unguarded woods. The advancing line curled around the open left flank and scattered the First Virginia. The now exposed Twenty-first were forced to give ground, and the Federal infantry bore on towards the twenty-six strong gun-line, and the centre of Jackson's still deploying infantry.

At the point of deployment *"where troops were thrown into the line of battle,"* Captain Blackford was at the epicentre of the action. *"… the smoke was so dense I could see very little … I was in the rear of two batteries firing in different directions and drawing upon themselves a very heavy fire from the enemy. The two lines of fire converged so as to cross about where I was standing.* Two things surprised Blackford, as he waited to direct the oncoming battalions. *"I could see them in column down the road run out of the ranks and hide something under the leaves in a hedge corner. I found out later they were playing cards, being superstitious about taking them into battle. Here, too, I saw what I had never seen before: men pinning strips of paper with their names, company and regiment to their coats, so they could be identified if killed. After what seemed to me a long time the firing on my front and to the left of the road, became very sharp and was nearing me rapidly … I could not see because there were some low bushes in my front, but in an instant, a regiment or two burst through into the spot where I was standing, all out of order and mixed up with a great number of Yankees. … I could not tell whether our men had captured the Yankees, or the Yankees had broken through our line."*

The General, on the other hand, despite the smoke and the trees, saw exactly what had happened and knew instantly what remedial action was required. *"In an instant … I was put at rest, for Jackson … came dashing across the road from our right in great haste and excitement. As he got amongst the disordered troops, he drew his sword, then reached over and took his battle flag from my man, Bob Isbell … and dropping his reins, waved it over his head and at the same time cried out in a loud voice, "Rally, men! Remember Winder! Where's my Stonewall brigade? Forward, men! Forward!"*

"He dashed to the front, and our men followed with a yell and drove everything before them. It was a wonderful scene – one which men do not often see. Jackson usually is an indifferent and slouchy looking man but then, with the 'Light of Battle' shedding its radiance over him, his whole person changed. His action was as graceful as Lee's and his face was lit with the inspiration of heroism. The men would have followed him into the jaws of death itself; nothing could have stopped them, and nothing did. Even the old sorrel horse seemed endowed with the style and form of an Arabian."

Watching, mid the smoke and the shout of conflict; the crash of gunfire and splintering wood, Blackford felt a hand on his leg, and looked down on the curly blond head of a very young Union lieutenant, clutching a broken sword, who shouted up at him *"What officer is that, Captain?" … when I told him, fully appreciating the magnetism of the occasion … and …with a touch of nature that makes the whole world kin, he waved his broken sword around his head and shouted, "Hurrah for General Jackson! Follow your General, Boys!" I leaned over, almost with tears in my eyes and said, "You are too good a fellow for me to make prisoner; take that path to the left and you can escape." He saluted me with his broken sword and disappeared in an instant. I hope he escaped."* Next up was General Hill, and Blackford, to his considerable relief, was able to deliver Jackson's order, and Hill to direct his two leading brigades to advance to the left in support of Jackson's charge.

Brigadier-General Taliaferro worked his way forward and up beside Jackson, to say that the head of the frontline was no place for the Army Commander. Watching, it was thought Jackson *"looked surprised."*[371] It was an unexpected intrusion into his concentration, and, unlike his subordinate, Jackson knew that crisis moments such as the Confederate ranks had just experienced, demanded nothing less than the intervention of the true leader, if disaster was to be averted. Victory would go to the strongest will. Jackson reined-in, and the Stonewall brigade surged on, killing or driving back the attackers. Troops were rallying to colour officers. Lines began reforming and to move forward. The General had done enough. Sheathing his sword – the one time he drew it 'in anger' during the War – Jackson turned away, muttering his familiar expression *"good, good,"* and rode back to direct newly arriving regiments into the counter-charge, on either side of the Culpeper axis road, and on the road itself. He had already initiated this counter-stroke <u>before</u> leading the charge which drove back the Federal break through; a striking example of his ability to read and control a situation, amid

---

371 Henderson.

the chaos of fighting. When the Federals staunchly tried to stem the strengthening surge coming at them, they were volleyed from all along the Confederate line, and forced to give ground. Cavalry squadrons charging the Confederate centre were shot down. The advance of a fresh Federal brigade was shot to a stuttering halt. Those no worse than wounded turned away. Jackson ordered two of Hill's brigades to move out wide through the woods on the left, and to turn the Federal right. He now had superiority all along his two mile line, and was cheered loudly by his men, as he rode back to the front.

All around, the shambles of dead, dying and wounded men, abandoned weapons and equipment, and men giving themselves up, bore evidence to a hotly contested two hours. Wearied men threw themselves down to sleep, wherever the advance had taken them. From the dissolving chaos a Union Staff Officer galloped up to Jackson *"and said, "General, General Banks says."* Then the ghastly truth dawned, and he whirled to ride away ignoring the shouts to surrender. An infantry office downed him with a single shot and brought horse and despatches to Jackson. But, was it only the broken remnant of Banks's staunch, but now demoralised, regiments that spattered the woods and trails over the final seven miles to Culpeper Court House? Jackson still could not be sure. He continued to press forward. Two fresh, hitherto uncommitted, brigades were moved up through the re-grouping ranks, and, shaking out into line, led a cautious advance. The moon soon rose after the onset of darkness. Scouts came in reporting a defensive line no more than a mile ahead. The rattle and flash of musketry followed. An artillery battery was galloped to the front; unlimbered and opened fire, prompting strong counter-battery fire. From the right of his line, Jackson's horsemen reported having taken prisoners from a Federal Army Corps commanded, not by the defeated Banks, but by General Sigel. *"Believing it imprudent to continue to move forward during the darkness, I ordered a halt for the night."*[372] The next morning, cavalry patrols confirmed

---

372 Henderson quoting Jackson's Report.

that in addition to Sigel, half of McDowell's Corps had already reached Culpeper, and the second ten thousand of McDowell's troops was no more than twenty miles distant. Altogether, a total of thirty-two thousand excluding the five thousand unscathed after the recent battle, were now on Jackson's immediate front. He withdrew back across the Cedar Run, to wait in a strong defensive stance for two whole days, before heading back for his original starting point of Gordonsville, *"with the hope that General Pope would be induced to follow me until I should be reinforced."*[373] Pope made not the slightest twitch of aggression. Left to his own devices he may well have fallen for Jackson's wishful lure; had he not been restrained by written order from Lincoln's recently appointed military Chief of Staff in Washington, the more perceptive General Halleck, who warned *"Beware of a snare."*

With Jackson having drawn back from his immediate front, however, Pope promptly and loudly proclaimed Slaughter's Mountain a Federal victory, which must, at the very least, have been something of a surprise to General Banks and his Command, which Pope was still claiming *"unfit for service"* two weeks later. It would also have surprised two friends of Cavalry General Stuart's, both of whom were Federal Generals, and with whom he had met and had a friendly chat after the battle. They disagreed that the action would, as usual, be claimed a Union victory. Stuart bet them a hat that it would, The Northern Media picked-up on Pope's claim, and the hat was duly delivered, under the same flag of truce through which Pope was allowed to bury Banks's dead. It took a whole day for the Federal medical and burial parties to clear up. Blackford estimated the ratio of killed and wounded as three to one in favour of the Confederates.

In the aftermath of the fighting and having had *"a very poor breakfast of hardtack and stone-cold fried middling"* Blackford took some twenty of his 'B' Company troopers and went on *"a scout ... towards the Orange and Alexandria Railroad."* He and his men captured

373 Ibid.

a Federal picket, under an *"intelligent Sergeant"* who was *"communicative"* and whom he took to the General's tent, *"thinking he might give some valuable information."* The Staff were gathered outside the tent, one of them holding the *"Little Sorrel."* and all waiting for Jackson to emerge. *"My prisoner took his stand ... at the rear of the horse, and ... at once commenced, I supposed in nervous agitation, to stroke the sorrel's rump with his right hand and to pass his left hand through the tail, pulling out each time a number of hairs. This he did so often that his hand was quite full of them and one of the staff, with some asperity, just as the General came up to the horse's head, ordered him to stop, which he did, cramming the hairs into his pocket. General Jackson saw what he was doing and, to my infinite relief, said in a mild voice, "My friend, why are you tearing hairs out of my horse's tail?" The prisoner took off his hat most respectfully and with a bright smile said, "Ah, General, each one of these hairs is worth a dollar in New York." The General was both amused and pleased."*[374]

30/4. All for Nothing

....

"Groan!"
Stonewall Jackson

....

IN John Pope there was much of James Shields. Pope too was prone to bombastic, swaggering proclamations – whistling in the dark even – which, in his case, the Northern Media ridiculed as 'Pope's *'Ercles vein'*. He was also extremely lacking, to the point

---

374 Susan Blackford, *"Letters from Lee's Army"*.

of reluctance, when it came to genuine constructive action. Like Shields, and most Generals who opposed Jackson on the battle-field, Pope showed himself quite unable to 'read' Jackson in any meaningful way. Having lost the opening round, Pope then assumed that because Jackson marched away from him, that he was retreating. Big mistake. True, Pope had been ordered not to move forward before being reinforced; but when halted, even preparing for an initiative seemed beyond him. For Jackson, on the other hand, manoeuvre itself meant positive action.

On the morning, he turned from the banks of Cedar Run, the General had his map-man ride beside him. He wanted maps of the whole area between Gordonsville – where they were headed, and which was some twenty miles from Cedar Run in the lee of South West Mountain – and Washington. *"He required several copies – I think five …* Hotchkiss wrote in a letter to Henderson … and … *it was important to have it done at once."* (Even although it was a Sunday).

Far from retreating, Jackson was already beginning his next offensive move. He would rest the Army for two days at Gordonsville, and then move away east, into the cover of Clark's Mountain, to await reinforcements, poised, just a few miles off Pope's left flank. The whole move was masked by a thin screen of cavalry, and the resulting secrecy caused widespread speculation. Not least amongst a largely admiring Northern Media. Where would the now invisible *"Man of Mystery"* strike next? *"Where would the next blow fall?"* *"I don't like Jackson's movements"* … *wrote McClellan to Halleck* … *"he will suddenly appear when least expected."*[375] McClellan was in the process of removing himself, by water, from the Peninsula. His men were to reinforce Pope. Lee did nothing more than observe their going – a less than vigorous piece of generalship – which ignored an opportunity to reduce the number of Federals who would live to fight another day. Secondly, his inactivity led to the assumption that the Confederates were gearing-up to deal with

---

375 Henderson.

Pope, and so allowed the spotlight to focus on Jackson, when it was especially unwelcome. In the event, Jackson positioned himself behind Clark's Mountain without detection.

Once there, Blackford was *"ordered, a little after sundown, to report with twenty men to the General for scout duty.* Together *"with Colonel Pendleton … we started off, the General leading the cavalcade. He wandered about all night in by-paths and unused roads in places where neither friend nor foe would ever pass; as far as we could see, without aim or purpose and that it was one of those freaks which sometimes seized him and which make many people think he is deranged."*[376] Such comments say as much about the amateur cavalry officer (Blackford had no military training or experience prior to the outbreak of the Civil War) as they do of the professional General.

Jackson was insatiable in his quest for information about the enemy and was, clearly, reconnoitring, and seeking ways to surprise and get at Pope. What is surprising about Blackford's reaction to his night's experience, though, is that even with so little military experience, after more than a year of pretty full-on active service, he was not more aware of the value and need for reconnaissance. Jackson was equally as relentless and thorough when it came to secrecy, and certainly, Blackford – a mere company commander – and one whose duties made him more than commonly liable to capture outside of a battle, would certainly not be privy to the General's intentions. Jackson, of course, was equally and unquestionably correct in his stance on secrecy. It will be remembered that in the Valley – immediately after the battle of Front Royal – two of his Staff, no less, told an unknown horseman they were on *"General Jackson's staff,"* and within the hour, that horseman had galloped back to put General Banks out of his ignorance, and be told *"you have saved the Army".* Three unthinking words to a stranger had, if not totally set at naught, at least devalued the end result of all those painstaking hours of planning, and sleepless days and nights of marching.

---

376 *"Letters from Lee's Army".*

"About daylight" ... Blackford continued, we ... *rode straight to the top of Clark's Mountain ... and then had a magnificent view, including the whole Federal Army stretched out before us..."* As a result of seeing for himself, Jackson established a signal station on Clark's Mountain. Blackford sets the start of this scouting incident as the *"evening of the nineteenth"* (August), by which time Pope was in the final stages of withdrawing behind the Rappahannock, having been made aware of his predicament on the eighteenth. Blackford's experience would have taken place on the night of the sixteenth or seventeenth at the latest. Blackford says in the same letter, dated as covering the period *"August the nineteenth to the twenty sixth"* that *"I am suffering much from dysentery"* and *"I was very sick ... suffering so much from dysentery, that I could not keep my sword belt buckled without great pain."* None the less, he goes on to make an elaborate comparison between Jackson and Lee. Of the latter; *"I felt myself in the presence of a great man, for surely there never was a man upon whom greatness is more stamped. He is the handsomest person I ever saw; every motion is instinct with natural grace, and yet there is a dignity which, while awe-inspiring, makes one feel a sense of confidence and trust that is delightful ... Lee ... does not hesitate to avail himself of some of the aids of martial pomp ... wears well-fitted undress grey uniform, with the handsomest trimmings, a handsome sword and cavalry boots, making him the grandest figure on any field. The men, in addition to the confidence they have in the genius of Jackson, have for Lee a proud admiration and personal devotion "passing the love of woman."* Of Stonewall Jackson, Captain Blackford says at this time; *"There is a magnetism in Jackson, but it is not personal. All admire his genius and great deeds; no one could love the man for himself. He seems to be cut off from his fellow men and to commune with his own spirit only, or with spirits of which we know not. Yet the men are almost as enthusiastic about him as over Lee, and whenever he moves about on his old sorrel, with faded uniform ... most men shout with enthusiasm. ... It is a saying in the army if a shout is heard, "There goes Old Jack or a rabbit."* Having commented that Lee and his *"favourite horse ... a handsome grey called 'Traveller,' ... looks like a picture whenever he is seen. ...* Blackford says *"The old sorrel is not more martial in*

appearance than his master … but when once roused there is no stopping either of them until the enemy has retreated." Blackford makes much of Jackson as the archetypal Roundhead, and Lee as the typical Cavalier. All his opinions of both men, of course, are based on a comparatively short acquaintance, and that 'in the field' only. It is conspicuous that only with Jackson does he link greatness to deed. To Lee, greatness is manifest in appearance and manner only. Blackford, possibly, sets too much store by shiny boots, and was, perhaps, one of those men who *"discovers in a sense of tidiness a moral superiority,"[377]* for surely, he was of a tiny minority for whom Jackson's appeal was not personal. For many, both friend and even foe, the magnetism was very personal indeed, as numerous anecdotes show.

Douglas writes, if the soldiery *admired and were proud of Lee; they loved Old Jack.* Blackford too seems to strain the Roundhead analogy when he goes on about Jackson *"communing with spirits of which we know not."* Surely, his being *"cut off from his fellow men"* was, in the main, his being in the grip of an intense focus and concentration, absorbed and engrossed, on the relentless and hugely complex and ever-changing demands of Victory in War. Just as it was the Roundhead, and not the Cavalier, who was able to create the greatest and most successful army of that era in Europe, so it is the abilities of Jackson which raise him, and not Lee, into the exclusive handful of the very greatest captains.

Lee reinforced Jackson, behind Clark's Mountain, with the Army of Northern Virginia, less two brigades left behind to cover Richmond in the Peninsula. Unfortunately for the Confederates to be effective, the Falcon's plans required the Falcon to apply the talons. On joining Jackson, Lee took command and botched the end-game. He approved the intention to crush Pope from his left flank; but failed to appreciate the time factor. An error Jackson was never guilty of. Stuart would lead the advance; but then a day was wasted waiting for a cavalry brigade to reach Stuart. During

---

377 Buchan, *"John Macnab"*.

the day of delay, Stuart contrived to get his despatch-box captured by a Federal patrol, not to mention his plumed hat, and very nearly himself. In the box was a letter from Lee telling of Jackson having been reinforced.

Very much against the least delay, Jackson pointed out that the signal station he had established on Clark's Mountain reported Pope's Army basking in August sunshine and in comfortable ignorance, and that he had enough cavalry to protect the advance. Further cavalry was not needed, to provide intelligence. Lee surely heard what he said; but seemingly did not understand. Jackson was not heeded. Other objections to an immediate attack were brought up, such as horses and men needed resting after the march from the Peninsula, which had been rapid, and had left wagons and supplies far in rear. Jackson pointed out that not only was there a large Federal supply depot at nearby Brandy Station; but *"the intervening district promised an abundance of ripening corn and green apples."*[378] He was disregarded. How wrongly was such fare considered unsuitable for the task! Presumably, experience during the Valley Campaign had either never been appreciated or had been already forgotten.

Jackson was said to have groaned so loudly at the postponement decision that Longstreet accused him of being disrespectful to the C-in-C. Poor Longstreet! He too failed to appreciate the importance of valuing time. Vital though his role would be, as an all-important anvil for Jackson's fire and hammer, the feeling is inescapable that Jackson's combinations were beyond his understanding. As subsequent marches demonstrated, an army led by Jackson marched twice as far in a day as one led by Longstreet.

The period of dithering lasted essentially for the forty eight hours between the seventeenth and the eighteenth of August. As an objective comment on Jackson's unwavering 'just do it' view, his West Point contemporary and Federal General, George Gordon, then serving under Pope, wrote afterwards *"it was fortunate that*

---

378 Ibid.

Jackson was not in command of the Confederates on the night of August the seventeenth; for the superior force of the enemy must have overwhelmed us if we could not have escaped, and escape on that night was impossible."[379] On the eighteenth a Federal spy awoke Pope to the Confederate presence behind Clark's Mountain. He made haste to be gone. Eventually, on the morning of the nineteenth Lee himself took post on the Mountain *"but the weather was unfavourable for observation"* due to thick haze. It was only late in the afternoon, that as he watched, the remaining Federal tents *"fifteen miles away to the north-west"* disappeared from sight, and the awful realisation dawned that the golden opportunity created by Jackson was no longer an option. Pursuit was promptly instigated; but the reality was clear. All that the Falcon had so skilfully schemed and manoeuvred for had been spurned at the point of consummation. Pope, unscathed, was now closing with McClellan, and Lee faced a very different ball-game.

The hasty departure and prompt follow-up led to the two sides confronting each other across the Rappahannock, a substantial river flowing roughly north west to south-east. Pope, on the north side, effectively shielded Washington and had the Orange and Alexandria Railroad, as a substantial though obvious umbilical cord, passing through Manassas Junction. Due east, and distant no more than twenty-eight miles from the Federal left flank, McClellan's Federal Army of the Potomac was coming ashore in Acquia Creek. From Acquia Landing, a railroad track ran south through Fredericksburg, direct to Richmond, which meant that McClellan's men, once ashore, were closer to the Confederate Capital than was Lee's Army of Northern Virginia. However, it would have needed the Stonewall Jackson the North lacked, to exploit such a situation.

After a week or so of skirmishing at crossing places, some seriously heavy rain, and an incursion by the cavalry, in which Stuart got his own back by capturing *"One of Pope's staff officers,*

---

379 Henderson quoting Gordon's *"The Army of Virginia".*

together with the uniform and horses of the Federal commander, his treasure chest, and his personal effects." Lee "removed his headquarters to Jefferson, where Jackson was already encamped, and on the same evening, with Pope's captured correspondence before them ... (amongst Stuart's haul was Pope's dispatch book) "containing most detailed information as to his strength, dispositions and designs ... a plan of operations was determined upon."[380]

If the detail that produced the plan of operations has led to continuous subsequent discussion on who proposed the plan, the implementation by Jackson was unequivocal, and devastatingly successful. It is hardly possible to believe, however, that such a plan can have stemmed from any other intellect than his. Lee did not select Jackson's headquarters for the planning meeting by accident.

The plan called for Jackson to withdraw, unseen, from before the right of Pope's line, and to march away to the west – (Jackson's left) – to pass through the forested ridges of high ground north of Warrenton, before turning back east, in order to pass down through Thoroughfare Gap, and across the Manassas Plain, from where he could fall swiftly and unexpectedly upon the massive Federal supply depot, established at Manassas Junction, directly in rear of Pope's Army, fifty-five thousand in number, even before being reinforced by McClellan's men returning from the Peninsula. The manoeuvre would force Pope to trend away from McClellan's returning units, to counter the threat in his rear. Lee would then bring up the units of Longstreet – whose role was to distract Pope while Jackson was marching – together with those of Confederate General Anderson, and so re-unite the Confederate Army. Henderson accords "the higher merit" to the risk inherent in this decision of Lee to divide the Confederate Army, which he calls "the supreme exhibition of the soldier's fortitude ... it is easy to conceive ... he says ... it is less easy to execute."

---

380 Henderson.

How wrong that was! As Lee himself said *"the disparity of force between the contending forces rendered the risks unavoidable,"*[381] One needs to look no further than the record of Lee himself, to see the flaw in such thinking. After Jackson's death it was observed that Lee never executed another great turning movement. After Jackson's death it may be said, he no longer had access to a brain capable of conceiving such brilliant manoeuvres. Henderson pleads that in executing a plan, the soldier/General risks *"cause and country, name and reputation on a single throw."*

The reality is that a commanding General is risking all this during every moment of every day in which he holds office. It is his duty and his honour. The plan – the *"single throw"* – which yields success, is what justifies him in honourably holding that office. To do nothing, and thereby, for a time at least, to risk neither defeat nor victory, is fraudulent generalship; craven and dishonourable.

As Jackson simply and succinctly put it *"War means fighting. The business of the soldier is to fight."* As the undistinguished records of so many Generals throughout the history of warfare show, it is extremely difficult to *"conceive"* for success, and certainly it is far from easy to *"execute."* But these two stages of a process are sides of the same coin. The true brilliance lies in the ability to combine and control conception and execution right through to the desired outcome. That there are no more than six or eight men in all recorded history, who have been able to work the oracle consistently and unfailingly, when faced with widely differing conditions of complexity, is a measure both of their brilliance, as well as of the difficulty.

---

381 Henderson quoting Allan, *"The Army of Northern Virginia".*

31. POPE'S END

....

"It is always as well to be wide awake, and not to allow ourselves to be taken by surprise."
Tom Jackson to sister Laura

....

WE catch fleeting glimpses of Jackson during the intellectually and physically demanding period – the twenty fifth to the thirtieth of August 1862 – the six days following the missed opportunity at Clark's Mountain, in which was wrought the final confusion of Pope as a General, and the crumbling and demoralization of the General and his more numerous Federal array.

Dr Dabney wrote in a letter to Colonel Henderson. *"The day before we started to march around Pope's Army, I saw Lee and Jackson conferring together. Jackson – for him – was very excited, drawing a map in the sand with the toe of his boot, and gesticulating in a much more earnest way than he was in the habit of doing. General Lee was simply listening, and after Jackson had got through to him, he nodded his head, as if acceding to some proposal. I believe from what occurred afterwards, that Jackson suggested the movement as it was made, but have no further proof than the incident I have just mentioned. … (Jackson was so reticent that it was only by accident that we ever found out what he proposed to do)."*

In truth, the whole concept and its unfolding is pure Stonewall Jackson. No other commander on the battlefields of Virginia demonstrated that they may have had either the mental or physical capacity for such an accomplishment. Today, we can see how the flank march up to and including the battles of Groveton and Second Manassas are Jackson inspired; whilst we are less able to feel and comprehend the extent and depth of the physical sacrifice wrenched from the twenty thousand ill-clad and under-nourished men with whom it was achieved. Those who, given his direction, inflexible determination and unflagging moral courage, turned theory into practical reality; those who carried the weight and worry about their loved-ones, who too lived amid the daily uncertainties and strictures of a poor country at war. Those Virginians, above all – who followed out of a fierce, personal and spiritual belief in their home-State, and an equally unshakeable confidence in a leader, whom all admired, and many, but not all – if Blackford is to be believed – actually loved. That God-fearing, uncommunicative, man, who may be likened – more specifically than Blackford's Roundhead analogy – to Oliver Cromwell, to the disapproval of some and the approval of others. If Thomas Jackson, second-generation Virginian-American, of Irish-Scotch stock, differed from the great Englishman, it was in the main due to the vastly differing importance of religion in the respective wars in which they both fought. Religion had no relevance beyond the personal, in Old Jack's war, whilst for Old Ironsides, religion was at the very centre of the political stage. Both men had a similar depth to their spirituality and looked to the Almighty alone, as the font of all success. The man who said, *"I would rather that Muhammadanism was allowed amongst us than one Christian should be persecuted for his faith"*, was no less tolerant than the Presbyterian Confederate who believed, like Frederick the Great of Prussia, that *"everyone must find their own way to heaven,"* and, indeed, with Jackson, were encouraged to do so, in their own way. With both Jackson and Cromwell, to have touched a man's life was to influence it ever after. If Macaulay could recount the belief that, following the demobilisation of the soldiers of the New Model, a thorough job was honestly done in England, then it was more than likely that the artisan or trader had been *"one of Oliver's soldiers,"* then it was no less true, in the Southern States, of those who once numbered themselves amongst Jackson's 'Foot Cavalry.'

"No one, when he had gone, ever left behind him among the ranks greater reverence or a more tender memory," wrote the youngest member

of Jackson's staff[382]. Although he had first-hand experience of serving with Stonewall Jackson, surely Blackford got it wrong, if not for himself, at least for the great majority – both soldier and civilian – when he wrote that the appeal was *"not personal."*

31/1. Flank March: Day One

....

"Who could not win battles
with such men as, these?"
Stonewall Jackson

....

THOSE who slept that last time at the foot of the Richmond statue, after the War was over and Jackson long dead, would not have been amongst the leading files that had marched some twenty miles by early evening on the twenty fifth of August 1862. Two Corps had left their assembly area around Jackson's Headquarters at Jefferson, before first light. For the Stonewall brigade – now commanded by William Booth Taliaferro, pronounced 'Taliver' by him, a Virginian, whose antecedents hailed from Venice, by way of London – was marching around the middle of the column. As evening drew on, and the sun lowered, Jackson rode through the cloaking dust – which both masked and revealed and was roused by every bare-foot step and iron-shod hoof – to halt ahead of the staunchly striding Army, and a short distance behind, the small cavalry escort surrounding Captain Boswell. His engineer staffer, familiar with the locality

---

382 Henry Kyd Douglas, *"I Rode with Stonewall"*, The University of North Carolina Press, Twelfth Printing 1940.

since childhood, was defining the route, and using cavalrymen to mark turning points in danger of being missed. The General commended the leading group of mounted officers on the march discipline; the brisk pace being maintained, and the few stragglers. As the leading files of the point infantry company approached, the General nudged his horse to the side of the unmade track and motioned with his right for silence. *"No shouting, lads, the Yankees might hear,"* was relayed back along the line. File after file, in column of fours, they tramped by; in silence, but for the shuffling thump of feet. The guns duelling across the Rappahannock may have faded; but the enemy might still hear if a band struck up, although no Federal outpost or picket had been seen all day. Every man looked across at the mounted, grey-clad figure, as weather-stained and tattered of uniform as themselves. The brown film of dust shrouding both horse and rider, sheened red-gold in the setting sun. In passing, all lifted a wave; a fist; a hand at the forehead, and the old familiar campaign cap was as unfailingly doffed in response. A momentary settling of dust on the evening breeze, a lull in the passing files. Then a fresh surge at the shadow line, and from out of the green-gloom of oak and pine, and from their own gold-tinged dirt-cloud, emerged the men of Virginia. The Old Dominion which begat the Union, and to which primitive inhabitant and encroaching incomer alike, owed their original cohesion and their entity as a nation state. On they came, tattered, ragged, skeletal figures. Only the eyes and weapons shining back the sun's glint. *"No shouting ..."* the injunction got no further. As the leading files came abreast their General, a great, swelling yell rolled back along the ranks, to mingle with cheers, enthusiastic laughter and, amid the trees, the clatter of startled birds. The *'Little Sorrel'* jerked up his head and skittered a pace or two. An eager smile creased the dusty features, and the General stiffened bolt upright in the saddle, hoisting the familiar cap to full reach. He half-turned in the saddle, looking back at one of the nearby staff, saying, *"It is of no use, you see, I can't stop them."*[383] And,

---

383 Henderson's wording.

turning back, half to himself, *"Who could not win battles with such men as these?"* The unanswered truth being, of course, none but he. He alone had brought them to this pitch of their own self-realisation. They alone had enabled him to achieve, with his own unconquerable intellect, resolution and understanding – *"What I Can I Will."*

After dark, they covered a further six miles, to litter the road in sleep just wherever they happened to be around midnight, when the order to halt reached them. Within four hours they were roused, to resume their tramping; but the General was long gone. When dawn came, he had already climbed the gorge on Bull Run Mountain, to the east of where the Army had stopped so briefly during the night, and which took the railway up and through Thoroughfare Gap.

31/2. Flank March: Day Two

....

"Reports are never entirely to be relied upon, they are seldom full, they are often false, and they are generally exaggerated."
Lieutenant-Colonel G.F.R. Henderson CB

....

WITH the sun sculpting the tops of pines from the clinging darkness of the crags and corries at the head of the Pass, the 'Falcon' rode forward to look down on the Plain of Manassas. To a Union spyglass, his lone figure would have seemed no more ominous than a cavalry scout, and if the young troopers of the Black Horse Cavalry, providing an escort and couriers, were in view behind him, then they were simply vedettes of the picket. But lone – isolated would be more fitting – the 'Falcon' most certainly was.

Far more so, than any casual observer could have envisaged. The strain of the Valley Campaign was more prolonged than this march into the rear of Pope's Army; but the implications and the concentrated intensity were less. Throughout those early days of August, the continued existence of the entire Army of Northern Virginia – the northern bulwark of the Confederacy – hung in the balance. Yet for all that, the Army could not have been more secure, amid the insecurity of Generals, than in the cool, resolute, bold and vigorous mental and physical grip of her most imaginative and most consistently successful General. From another perspective, the fate of both Lee's Army and that of Pope – some one hundred and thirty five thousand men, if taken altogether – would be choreographed by the intellectual skill; the genius of Jackson alone. The enormous strain and loneliness inherent in the task, being disarmed by the seemingly impregnable and inexhaustible font of moral courage – the vital ingredient – in the make-up of the man.

To his satisfaction, Jackson could see no clouds of dust rising from the feet of regiments and brigades, turning back from the Rappahannock to oppose his coming. Boswell rode by with his escort and his guides, his buoyant *"top of the morning, General,"* eliciting the merest flicker of an approving half-smile by way of acknowledgement. The telescope showed-up the intense, steam-revealed activity of supply trains plying in both directions along the Orange and Alexandria Railway, and isolated bodies of men marching and riding on the few tracks where they appeared in the open between the secretive forest, and the farming symmetry of tilled fields. Directly below lay Gainesville where the railroad, directly below where the General had halted, crossed the road from Warrenton to Fairfax Court House. There, he decided, he would rendezvous with Stuart, whose troopers in the hours before dawn, had been spreading out to cloak his right flank from prying eyes. A courier cantered away to confirm the rendezvous with the Army's cavalry chief. The cavalry tentacles searching out and observing, ahead of the striding columns – the regiments of Thomas Munford – would move on and seize all such Federal scouts and pickets, as were lounging, unaware, on the line of approach. Sending a second Black Horse trooper back to ensure that the Army was up and doing – and pressing hard in the wake of the *"Little Sorrel,"* – the General nudged the little horse forward and followed Boswell down the slope from Thoroughfare Gap.

By evening, the Division had covered some fifty-six miles in the forty-eight hours since dawn the previous day. *"After dark, a regiment of cavalry passed our plodding infantry … at the invitation of the officer in command* (Colonel Munford) *… I joined him …* Douglas wrote later … *"A charge was made upon the place, the Federal guard of cavalry put to flight with a few prisoners, and I got a horse and a pair of pistols. Instantly a train of cars, loaded with stores, came dashing past. The dismounted cavalry poured an ineffective volley into it, but it rushed on its way and bore the alarm to Manassas Junction.*

In a few minutes more, the advance of the infantry, their weariness forgotten in the excitement, came up at double time, and were more successful in their attempt to stop two trains … they had no stores of any value and were subsequently burned. … It was after nine o'clock at night when we got entire possession of Bristoe Station; yet, before midnight General Jackson sent General Stuart with some cavalry and General Trimble with his brigade, to take possession of Manassas Junction, the great depot of supplies. The work was quickly and well done; before daylight Trimble took the works at Manassas with little loss."

31/3. Behind Union Lines: Day Three

*"What sort of man is your Stonewall Jackson
anyway; are his soldiers made of gutta-percha,
or do they run on wheels?"*

Union Prisoner at Bristoe Station

*"On the morning of the twenty-seventh, leaving Ewell at Bristoe Station,
General Jackson moved with the rest of his command* (the Divisions of
Taliaferro and A.P. Hill) *to Manassas Junction."*[384] The cavalry spread
out to picket all approaches. For the under-nourished and ill-clad
infantry, the haul secured by Trimble's Twenty-first Georgia and
Twenty-first North Carolina Regiments beggared belief. *"The
valuable stores captured were far in excess of what any Confederate ever
conceived to be in existence. … Famished soldiers appeasing the hunger
that had tormented them, declared that … as a Commissary, Pope was
even superior to Banks."*[385] *"Streets of warehouses … a line of freight
cars two miles in length … thousands of barrels, containing flour, pork,
and biscuit, covered the neighbouring fields … brand-new ambulances …
packed in regular rows …field ovens; all the paraphernalia of a large bak-
ery and great pyramids of shot and shell."*[386]

The wagon train was back with Lee beyond the Rappahannock,
so when turned loose on the cornucopia, Jackson's men could do
no more than satisfy their immediate appetites, replace their tattered clothing with Union blue, top-up with ammunition, and
select such as they considered choice items, and could be carried by themselves during the marching and fighting to come.
In the main, liquor was secured early on; but *'cegars'*, tobacco and

---

384 Douglas.
385 Ibid.
386 Henderson.

coffee were popular. Basic medical necessities, so lacking in the Confederacy, were of special value, and for those accustomed to green corn and apples, the luxuries of *"lobster salad, sardines, potted game and sweetmeats"[387]* were irresistible.

Although valuable for sustaining his men, and as a disruptive to Pope and his Army on the Rappahannock, for Jackson, the capture of the Federal's strategic supply dump was a secondary consideration. The main aim was to lure Pope from the river line; to get him moving, uncertain and vulnerable; to keep him in play, while Lee re-united the two wings of the Army of Northern Virginia, and – although numerically inferior – to administer a crushing defeat. Early that morning, a Federal attack in brigade strength, from the direction of Union Mills, less than three miles north of Manassas Junction, was brushed aside with little effort, and a pursuit taken to within ten miles of Alexandria. It told Jackson that, in Washington at least, they were still imagining him to be a cavalry raid. By mid-afternoon, Ewell at Bristoe, however, was skirmishing with an altogether heavier probing attack from the south. five and a half thousand men under General Hooker, of McClellan's Army, were sent by Pope, to find out the strength of the Confederate force which had appeared without so much as a 'by your leave', some twelve miles in rear of his headquarters. Ordered not to become involved with superior force, Ewell withdrew after an hour or so, and re-joined the main body at the Junction. Stuart's patrols were now reporting that, everywhere, Pope was decamping northwards. Then a trooper of his Black Horse escort – *"disguised as a countryman,"[388]* reached Jackson with the news from Lee's headquarters that Longstreet was on his way, and would be following in his footsteps, to approach through Thoroughfare Gap. Jackson had now to take into reckoning how long Longstreet would take to reach him – always provided Pope did not intervene. He doubtless was well

387 Gordon.
388 Henderson.

aware that Longstreet did not have his Alexander-like ability to induce an army to move swiftly across country.

Pope obviously realised by this time that Lee had divided his Army. Indeed, he had ridden forward, to ascertain for himself what he was facing, in time to witness the spectacular pyrotechnic display when Jackson, having tallied the original content, burnt the Manassas Depot, just as it was getting dark. Although Pope imagined Ewell's withdrawal to be a defeat inflicted on Jackson's Corps, he had rid himself of all thoughts of a cavalry sortie. Pope set himself to accomplish a task which, hitherto, had proved quite beyond the capacity of Union Generals, and to which he was not to prove, in any way, a shining exception to the catalogue of failure. He, Major-General John Pope would surround and *"bag"* Jackson. He was doomed to disappointment almost from the moment of conception, for his first units did not move forward until midnight, and the remainder, as he ordered it, not until *"the very earliest blush of dawn."*[389] Jackson, on the other hand, was already into his next move, while Pope was watching the fireworks, and Stuart's troopers were still feeding the flames like so many Hell's Stokers. As ever with Stonewall Jackson, it was not only the speed with which he and his men covered the ground; but the speed with which he implemented the move he intended making. As with Alexander, so with Old Jack; *'to think was to act.'*

---

389 Ibid.

31/4. Back on their Flank: Day Four

....

*"Move your Division and
attack the enemy."*
Stonewall Jackson

....

DURING the hours of darkness Jackson feinted north towards Centreville, in three roughly parallel columns, before his centre and right – Hill and Ewell respectively – marched six miles to the west, over the old battle ground of last summer, to join Taliaferro in the cover of the heavily wooded area about Groveton. The Light Division covered fourteen miles overnight; Ewell some fifteen, and Taliaferro – with such ammunition wagons as they had either brought with them or appropriated – between eight and ten miles. One cannot help wondering if they barbequed the long-distance cattle in the fiery holocaust of Manassas, before setting off, or, as is more likely, they simply made do with pickled lobster and jugged game. Pope, on his northerly advance, had trended to the east with his right wing, which, on reaching the area about the Junction found he had surrounded no more than the odd man who had over indulged, and was sleeping off the effects in the surrounding woods. His clutch at thin air being observed with some interest, if not in every detail, by Stuart's troopers, ranging from vantage point to vantage point on the distant high ground. However, Pope's left flank, under McDowell, took a more northerly route than Pope, moving up the road from Warrenton (town) to Fairfax Court House, which took a west – east line some six miles to the north of the railway line from Warrenton Junction to Manassas Junction. Having only a rough idea what Pope was about, Jackson's aim was to keep his attention, whilst remaining as accessible as possible for Lee to bring about the concentration. Apart from concealment, and having strong defensive potential, Jackson had selected the Groveton woods area because it enabled him to keep open a wider range of options. He was now just twelve miles from Thoroughfare Gap; but, if Longstreet was either blocked by Pope or otherwise delayed, or even if Jackson alone, became too hard-pressed, he had an escape route north to the Aldie Gap, a pass at the far, northern end of the Bull Run Mountain ridge. Above all, the position enabled him to remain poised for an attack on Pope's left flank. As the forenoon of that 'Glorious twenty eighth' drew on, Bradley Johnson, the Colonel commanding the right hand brigade of Taliaferro's Division, was warned by the cavalry that the enemy was moving up the road from Warrenton and Gainesville in strength. After some skirmishing, Johnson, finding himself so heavily outnumbered, drew off into the woods north of the road. McDowell's leading brigades under Generals Sigel and Reno, still marching on the original order to surround Jackson at Manassas Junction, plodded on. During the afternoon, the cavalry brought in a captured Federal courier, carrying McDowell's orders for dealing with Jackson at Manassas Junction. The captured despatch was sent immediately to the General.

"Johnson's messenger found Confederate headquarters established on the shady side of an old-fashioned worm-fence, in the corner of which General Jackson and his Division commanders were profoundly sleeping after the fatigues of the previous night, notwithstanding the intense heat of the August day. There was not so much as an ambulance at headquarters. The headquarters' train was back beyond the Rappahannock … with remounts, camp equipage, and all the arrangements for cooking and serving food. All the property of the general, the staff, and the headquarters' bureau was strapped to the pommels and cantles of the saddles, and these formed the pillows of their weary owners.

"The captured despatch roused Jackson like an electric shock. He was essentially a man of action. He rarely, if ever, hesitated. He never asked advice. He called no council to discuss the situation disclosed by this communication, although his ranking officers were almost at his side. He asked no conference of opinion. He made no suggestion, but simply, without a word, except to repeat the language of the message, turned to me and said: 'Move your Division and attack the enemy;' and to Ewell: 'Support the

attack.' *The slumbering soldiers sprang from the earth at the first mur-mur. They were sleeping almost in ranks; and by the time the horses of their officers were saddled, the long lines of infantry were moving to the anticipated battlefield."[390]*

When the two brigades reached a position overlooking the Groveton Turnpike – halting on some higher ground at the edge of the woods – not an enemy of any sort was in sight. However, from his headquarters north of Gainesville (on Jackson's right as he faced Pope) in the country towards Bull Run Mountain, Stuart had been skirmishing with Federal cavalry for much of the day, and his couriers had informed Jackson that Longstreet's advanced-guard had engaged elements of McDowell's command on the far side of Thoroughfare Gap. Soon another Federal Division came into Confederate view on the Groveton Road – *"a regimental band having just struck up a merry quick-step."* Although Jackson could not be certain what part of Pope's Army was approaching (in fact this Division of Wisconsin and Ohio regiments, with no cavalry support, was counter-marching under McDowell's orders to go in support of the action against Longstreet) two Confederate horse-artillery batteries *"trotting forward from the wood, deployed upon the ridge. The range was soon found, and the effect was instantaneous. But the confusion in the Northern ranks was soon checked ."[391]* Trees and uneven ground gave cover to both sides, and the comparatively brief action which followed was bitterly contested. *"In many places the lines approached within a hundred yards, the men standing in the open and blazing fiercely in each other's faces. Here and there, as fresh regiments came up on either side, the grey or the blue gave way for a few short paces; but the gaps were quickly filled, and the wave once more surged forward over the piles of dead. Men fell like autumn leaves. Ewell was struck down ...* losing a leg which kept him out of action for a year; but *"he was never old ironsides again"[392]* ...

---

390 Henderson quoting Brigadier-General Taliaferro.
391 Henderson.
392 Douglas.

and Taliaferro, and many of their field officers"[393] also. Night brought an end to a fight in which the Federals, probably had some one thousand one hundred killed and wounded, and Jackson lost around one thousand two hundred.

However, the Groveton action alerted Pope to Jackson's location, of which up to that point he had become entirely ignorant. It did not, on the other hand, make him any more understanding of what Jackson was about. Thinking Jackson was making for Thoroughfare Gap, Pope's order that night, for an attack the next morning, including the lines, *"McDowell has intercepted the retreat of the enemy ... I see no possibility of his escape.[394]*

31/5. Fronting the Enemy: Day Five

....

*"General, your men have done nobly;
if you are attacked again, you will
beat the enemy back."*
Stonewall Jackson

....

DESPITE having misread the situation that had evolved, Pope was preparing to do exactly what Jackson intended he should do. That is, to focus the main Federal effort against his, by then, probably no more than eighteen thousand strong Corps. Although Pope had contrived to get his array scattered, at his disposal, barring the dispersion, were some fifty thousand all ranks, a figure

---

393 Henderson.
394 Ibid.

which was being rapidly increased to sixty-five thousand by men from McClellan's Army, and also by Federal forces from the far west of Virginia. Fully appreciating the disparity, and fully real-ising that Longstreet was not capable of moving troops as rapidly over the ground as himself – in this instance, Longstreet covered no more than thirty miles in two days, as opposed to Jackson's recent fifty-six in two days – the pressure upon Jackson was re-lentlessly building. During the hours of darkness, following the Groveton action, Jackson pulled back to the nearby area of his Light Division (A.P. Hill) – which he had left in rear to cover the earlier possibility of his having to withdraw to Aldie Gap – and took up a compact defensive position in depth. The flanks of the position were secured by Stuart's cavalry, together with the Bull Run on his left. The right of the chosen position, hav-ing a frontage of a little over a mile and a half, Jackson secured with an artillery concentration of forty guns. The 'Stone Wall' was once more being set in place and, on much the same ground as in what, after the fighting of the coming two days, would be re-designated the First Battle of Manassas.

Jackson had already ridden round his lines, when the first Federal attack came in, shortly after five a.m. on the morning following the evening action on the Groveton Road. His sim-ple order would demand almost superhuman effort. *"Hold the line of the railway embankment."* In all five attacks, a total of some thirty thousand Northerners, would attempt to overwhelm the Confederate position. All would bite deep into the grim defence, before being fought to a standstill, and then hurled back, most-ly at bayonet point. Pope himself did not reach the scene until shortly after Noon. Longstreet's brigades began insinuating them-selves amongst the woods on Jackson's right, during the forenoon. When told of Longstreet's arrival, Jackson permitted himself no more than a brief release of breath. Their arrival did nothing to deflect the Federal attacks from his front. *"The heaviest fighting was in the afternoon. … Douglas would write … Time and again, the heavy lines of the enemy rolled against us, like roaring waves of the sea, but they were broken and thrown back. Each attack was weaker, each repulse more difficult … It was a fearfully long day. … For the first time in my life,* Douglas continued … *I understood what was meant by 'Joshua's sun standing still on Gideon,' for it would not go down. No one knows how long sixty seconds are, nor how much time can be crowded into an hour, nor what is meant by 'leaden wings' unless he has been under fire of a desperate battle, holding on, as it were by his teeth, hour after hour, minute after minute, waiting for a turning or praying that the great red sun, blazing and motionless overhead, would go down."* One can scarcely even begin to imagine what the pressures must have been for the one man – in terms of numbers of soldiers the numerical underdog – alone bearing the entire moral responsibility for success or failure. The calm, collected and apparently ice-cold figure, was constantly seen amongst them. After nine hours of fighting, and with some four thousand dead already piled before the lines of the Light Division, Douglas brought Jackson a message from A.P. Hill saying, *"if he was attacked again, he would do the best he could, but he could hardly hope for success. … I … delivered the message. …* Douglas wrote … *It seemed to deepen the shadow on his face, and the silence of the group about him was oppressive; but he answered promptly and sharply, 'Tell him if they attack him again, he must beat them."* Jackson rode after Douglas and they soon met up with Hill who *"repeated his fears. The General said calmly, 'General, your men have done nobly; if you are attacked again you will beat the enemy back."* As he spoke, they heard firing on Hill's front, and Hill galloped off shouting, *"Here it comes … and … Jackson calling after him, 'I'll expect you to beat them.' The attack was fierce and soon over. The Rebel yell seemed to follow and bury itself among the enemy in the wood … A staff officer rode up, 'General Hill presents his compliments, and says the attack of the enemy was repulsed. … 'Tell him I knew he would do it,' answered Jackson with a smile."*

The late afternoon attack upon Hill turned out to be Pope's last attacking effort of the day. The Valley Army and their Leader could claim another hard earned success. However, there would have been a Confederate counter-attack that evening, if Lee had had his way. Longstreet demurred. *"Three times Lee urged him forward. The first time he* (Longstreet) *rode to the front to reconnoitre, and found that the position, in his own words, was not inviting."*[395] Three times, Longstreet disobeyed his superior, and on the third occasion responded with the classic reasoning of the second-rate General *"I suggested ...* Longstreet wrote later *... that the day being far spent, it might be as well to advance before night, on a forced reconnaissance* (whatever that may be); *get our troops into the most favourable positions, and have all things ready for a battle the next morning."* A laughable proposal from a probationary second lieutenant; but pathetic coming from a lieutenant-general in command of an Army Corps. Lee's *"reluctantly given consent"* may or may not be the classic decision of a feeble C-in-C; but it can be said with some certainty, that had Longstreet been working for Stonewall Jackson in that instance, he would have been relieved of his command and facing a court martial before he could get off his horse, and having decided upon the counter-stroke, Jackson would have been well to the fore, and urging it on himself.

31/6. The Pope Recul: Day Six

....

"The effect was not unlike flushing a covey of quails."
Union Officer

....

LONGSTREET's failure to obey Lee's late afternoon orders to attack, meant that when daylight came, before he could decide his immediate next move, Lee had no option but to thoroughly

---

395 Henderson.

assess a situation which could well have changed significantly overnight. Essentially, he was going to have to start from the beginning with an enemy that had been allowed to catch his breath. Apart from one or two minor readjustments to the position of brigades, and tending to matters of routine, such as ammunition re-supply, feeding and caring for the wounded, both wings of the Confederate Army remained largely concealed, and in their original positions. No attacking moves were made by either side during the forenoon.

Pope, on the other hand, never did seem to get a realistic grasp of the situation he was facing. As has been said, he had not reached the battlefield until after Noon on the first day. He planned based on what others told him, rather than making any attempt to see the situation for himself. He acted in accordance with how he wished things to be, rather than on how they were. After the failure of all five of his bloody, mindless, frontal assaults, solely against Jackson's line, he reported to Halleck, *"We fought a terrific battle here yesterday with the <u>combined</u> forces of the enemy, which lasted with continuous fury from daylight until dark, by which time the enemy was driven from the field, which we now occupy. … The news has just reached me from the front that the enemy is retreating towards the mountains."* The 'news' came in the form of *"a Union prisoner, recaptured from Jackson …* who could quite conceivably have been a plant, and who … *declared that he had heard 'the rebel officers say that their army was retiring to unite with Longstreet."*[396] Porter, whose men recovered the man, sent him back to Army HQ with the cover note: *"In duty bound I send him, but I regard him either as a fool or designedly released … No faith should be put in what he says."* *"General Pope believes that soldier …* Porter was told in reply … *and directs you to attack."*[397] Pope wanted to believe that the Confederates were retreating, and with no more corroboration than this meagre 'intelligence' – which was against

---

396 Henderson.
397 Ibid.

every instinct of most of his subordinate commanders and not only Porter – Pope attacked. For once, according to Douglas, Jackson, although prepared, predicted wrongly, and was not expecting another attack. His battle lines were concealed in the woods, and Pope could see only a few skirmishers on the open ground before the long line of the railway embankment that marked the front of Jackson's defensive position. By now Pope could call upon some sixty-five thousand men, together with twenty-eight artillery batteries, and not long after Noon, in Henderson's words, *"to the dismay of his best officers ... Pope ... issued orders for his troops to be 'immediately thrown forward in pursuit of the enemy'."* Shortly after two thirty, Jackson *"was sitting on the ground with his back against an old straw stack writing a note to General Lee ... containing words to the effect ... notwithstanding the threatening movements of the enemy, I am still of the opinion expressed this morning that he does not intend to attack us.* A single starting gun from a slope opposite brought Jackson instantly to his feet, with the words *"That's the signal for a general attack."*[398]

Wanting to believe that his advancing twenty thousand were about to snatch the batteries of guns, he could see seemingly isolated, on the opposite slopes; but which, in reality, were securing Jackson's right flank, the Federal Commander watched the clouds of skirmishers deployed by his assaulting Generals, to confirm or allay their anxieties, as they pushed forward against Jackson's sparse pickets, which to Pope covered no more than a sparse rearguard. Suddenly, a strident clang of bugles amid the booming of the guns, and a torrent of Confederate bayonets – over a mile wide – poured forward from the woods. *"The effect, said a (Union) officer who witnessed this unexpected apparition, was not unlike flushing a covey of quails."*[399] Another commented later *"We were sent forward to pursue the enemy, who was said to be retreating; we found the enemy, but did not see them retreat."*

---

398 Douglas.
399 Henderson.

Despite the underlying misconceptions and concerns, the Union brigades hurled themselves at Jackson's thin Grey Line with the greatest bravery and determination. Those guns coveted by Pope were precisely sited to enfilade an assault and opened a relentless bombardment as the initial waves of the attack moved forward over open ground; then, in places passed through a strip of woodland, before more open grassland fronting the linear stockade of the railway embankment. Prominent ahead of the long lines of Blue, and alone upon a bright chestnut horse, a single Union officer survived all the cannonading and the initial, close-quarter, volleys of musketry, to put the chestnut at the very slope of the embankment itself. The gallant pair, to the admiration of many of the defenders, reached the summit of the parapet, he with unsheathed sword still raised, before both man and horse were dissolved into a gory heap, to many shouts of *"Don't kill him!"*[400] from the admiring regiments of the Stonewall Division. Elsewhere, with all ammunition expended, stones from the unfinished track were pressed into supporting cold steel. When the numbed survivors of the final convulsion had stumbled away across the grass and through the trees, one regimental colour lay close against the embankment. Around the tattered silk lay the drained bodies of one hundred Union soldiers, who had given their lives, selflessly but in vain, to keep it defiantly aloft.

It took a little over one hour for one third of Pope's Army to shatter itself, in three consecutive, rolling attacks, against Jackson's attenuated but durable lines. Pope made no attempt to increase the weight of his assault, and shortly after four o'clock Lee counter-attacked. Unlike Pope, Lee punched his weight. The entire Confederate Army pressed forward from the positions in the woods which they had held for the previous thirty six hours. Jackson's controlled advance met steady resistance from regular US Army regiments, which gave ground in good order. He reformed lines, disrupted by the fighting advance, on at least two

---

400 Ibid.

occasions. Initially, to take a combined artillery and infantry position on high ground to his left. The Light Division captured six guns at bayonet point, in the face of musketry and canister. *"They came on ...* reported a Northern Correspondent ... *like demons emerging from the earth."*[401] Reforming again, the Valley men forged on, to take the Matthew's House Hill, overlooking Bull Run and the Stone Bridge, which they occupied when darkness put an end to the fighting. Across to their right on the Henry House Hill – the ground on which Jackson had been immortalised as 'Stonewall' in the battle of the previous year – the Regulars of General Sykes, the Pennsylvania Regiments of General Reynolds, together with elements of Porter's doughty Fifth Army Corps held firm until nightfall against Longstreet's men. This standalone prevented the complete disintegration of the Army, which Pope had so boastfully and bombastically assumed command of, some eight weeks previously. The Confederates awoke, after a night of pouring rain, to find that the Federals had withdrawn *"leaving thousands of wounded on the field."*[402] The cavalry reported that defensive positions had been taken up utilising old Confederate earthworks on the high ground around Centreville, some four miles to the east. *"Pope, with an audacity which disaster was powerless to tame,* commented Henderson, *reported to Halleck* (from Centreville) *that, on the whole, the results of the battle were favourable to the Federal Army. 'The enemy, largely reinforced, assailed our position early to-day. We held our ground firmly until six p.m. when the enemy, massing very heavy forces on our left, forced that wing back about half a mile. ... with horses and men having been two days without food, and the enemy greatly outnumbering us, I thought it best to move back to this place at dark. The enemy is badly whipped, and we shall do well enough. Do not be uneasy. We will hold our own here."* If Halleck was reliant on his Field Commander for the true state of affairs, he was misled. As Douglas noted, *"Pope certainly had*

---

401 Ibid.
402 Henderson.

the courage of his mendacity." More surprisingly, McDowell – the General who had seemed more aware of Jackson's intentions in the Valley than any other Union Commander – informing his wife of the battle, ended with *"The victory is undoubtedly ours."*[103] Possibly McDowell's purpose was to say nothing to dint the morale of the Home Front in the North.

On the day after the battle, Jackson included Federal field hospitals in his visits to the wounded. *"There was great curiosity to see him … Douglas observed … wounded soldiers climbed over each other to get a glimpse of him."* Passing near the railway embankment of his defensive position, he rode over to a wounded Confederate soldier and asked *"to what regiment he belonged. '… the Fourth Virginia, your old brigade, General. I have been wounded four times, but never before as bad as this. I hope I will soon be able to follow you again."* The man was suffering from a deep wound in the thigh, and Jackson *"placed a hand upon his burning head and in a low husky voice said, "You are worthy of the Old brigade, and I hope with God's blessing, you will soon be well enough to return to it."* He ordered the Staff to carry the man to a more comfortable place, and asked Dr McGuire to tend to him whilst a courier went for an ambulance. *"The grateful soldier tried to speak but could not; sobs choked him, and tears ran from his eyes over his ashen cheeks: words would not come, and he submitted to everything in silence. But the General understood."*[104]

Lee had no intention of allowing Pope to sit tight around Centreville. Stuart was soon in rear of the Federal position, shooting up supply trains and harrying outposts. Inevitably Jackson's Corps led the ten mile slog through mud and wet, moving around Pope's right flank, to threaten his rearward communications. Pope had *"ordered all wagons to be unloaded at Centreville, and to return to Fairfax*

---

403 J.B. McMaster, *"Our House Divided"* (Originally entitled *"A History of the People of the United States During Lincoln's Administration"* – a work seemingly skewed in sympathy towards the North).

404 Douglas.

Station for forage and rations.'[405] He had informed Halleck that, *"he would hold on"* in the Centreville position; but no sooner did he get wind of Jackson's approach than he immediately retreated the eight miles along the road to Fairfax Court House, no more than fourteen miles from Alexandria on the Potomac, opposite Washington. The clash came amid the heavy and incessant rain of a violent thunderstorm. During the action, in which the Federals had one thousand or so killed and wounded, and the Confederates half that number, Jackson received a plaintive message from a Brigade Commander doubting if he could hold his position because of sodden ammunition. He was told in no uncertain terms to 'hold his ground, for if his guns would not fire, then neither would those of the enemy'. During the action, Confederate General Philip Kearney – who had served with Jackson in the Mexican War and had a great reputation for bravery – presumably disorientated by the extreme weather, rode into the Confederate lines and was shot trying to ride clear. Jackson had the body and all Kearney's accoutrements returned by special ambulance under a flag of truce. The streak of chivalry was broad in the unrelenting nature of Stonewall Jackson. As ever, the Union Rank and File fought staunchly and honourably; but their General was a broken man. He passed the buck. *"There was an undoubted purpose, on the part of the enemy, ...* Pope reported to Washington ... *to keep on slowly turning his position so as to come in on the right, and that the forces under his command were unable to prevent him doing so in the open field. Halleck must decide what was to be done."*[406] Pope was told to get his Army behind the Washington fortifications *"as best he could."* In his subsequent report Lee wrote *"It was found that the enemy had conducted his retreat so rapidly that the attempt to interfere with him was abandoned."*[407] Once the Army was secure, Pope was allowed to resign – *"before being relegated to an obscure command against the Indians of the North-west."*

---

405 Henderson.

406 Henderson.

407 Henderson quoting Lee's dispatch.

32. "NOW ADMIT THE LADIES"

....

(Stonewall Jackson)

....

HAVING rid Virginia of both Pope and McClellan's Army of the Potomac – apart from the fortified zones in the area of Arlington – Lee decided on invasion. He was not confident about the condition of the Army of Northern Virginia and told Davis. *"The army is not properly equipped for an invasion of the enemy's territory. It lacks much of the material of war, is feeble in transportation, the animals being much reduced, and the men are poorly provided with clothes, and in thousands of instances, are destitute of shoes.*[408] Probably the only realistic chance the South ever had of coercing the North into halting the Civil War was during the three days following the victory of First Manassas. Thereafter, the Northern juggernaut became daily more powerful. Lee's only hope was to strike for a victory over the Northern Field Army on their own soil, and impose upon Northerners in their own back yards, until they so disliked the disruption, that they would decide the game was not worth the candle.

Having been granted a day for rest and personal administration, for once, the Valley-men were not in the van when the Army of Northern Virginia crossed the Potomac behind Stuart's ubiquitous, ever-active, cavalry. The Division of Jackson's brother-in-law, General D.H. Hill, provided the advance guard. They were, however, back in front the next day, when Jackson's Corps occupied Frederick. The invasion of Maryland was not an especially fortunate time, either for the Confederacy or for Stonewall Jackson personally. The *'dirty darlings',* as the ladies dubbed the men in shoddy grey, were very unprepossessing compared to the

---

408 Henderson quoting Lee's letter.

trim-blue of the well-stocked Yankees. In western Maryland, at least, there was little sympathy for the Southerners. Food and clothing, however, were freely given; but the gift of a horse to the celebrated Corps Commander had an unfortunate outcome, Jackson being dumped when, having mounted, a band struck-up; the horse reared, and the girth broke. A bruised General retired to his headquarters tent to catch-up on the paperwork. Douglas, on the other hand, remembers the unhorsing of the General as having taken place when they were moving on, and with Jackson having to spend the day flat on his back in an ambulance, with control for the day having been devolved on to D.H. Hill. It was about Frederick too that the poet Whittier concocted his ficti-tious slur against the memory of Stonewall Jackson. As Douglas recounts, *"There was such an old woman in Fredericksburg ... as Barbary Frietchie ... in her ninety-sixth year and bedridden ... we did not pass her house."* Douglas was with the General all day and says, *"she never saw Stonewall Jackson and he never saw her."* Shortly af-terwards, in Middletown, *"two very pretty girls with ribbons of red, white and blue in their hair and small Union flags in their hands ...* appeared from a house as Jackson, Douglas and the Staff passed by, and ... *"laughingly waved their colours in the face of the General. He bowed and lifted his cap, and with a quiet smile said to the Staff 'We evidently have no friends in this town.' The young girls abashed turned away. ... That ...* says Douglas ... *is about the way he would have treated Barbara Frietchie!"* Sadly, the versified lie sticks in the mind's eye, and is recalled even today.

Once across the Potomac, Lee was concerned for his com-munications with Virginia. Through Manassas Junction, they were susceptible to interdiction by Federal cavalry. Leading back further north, through the Shenandoah Valley, they would be a prime target for raiding parties sent out by Federal garrisons still remaining in Winchester, Martinsburg and at Harper's Ferry. The combined garrisons totalled some fourteen thousand. Lee gave immediate priority to removing this threat to his supply lines in Virginia, rather than taking offensive action against any Army sent out from Washington. Because of his comparatively small numbers, Lee once more had to divide his forces. Disagreeing with the Commander-in-Chief's priorities, James Longstreet declined the task of reducing the three Federal garrisons. Within five days Jackson had the job done. Cloaking his initial move with a display of interest in the area immediately north of Frederick, and calling for maps of Pennsylvania, he marched swiftly south, to re-cross the Potomac at Williamsburg, the regimental bands playing *"Carry me back to Ole Virginny, to the old Virginny shore."*

That afternoon, Jim, the General's servant, overtook Douglas and rode with him for a while. *"The faithful fellow has become historical by reason of his association with General Jackson, to whom his devotion was a kind of superstition. ...* Douglas wrote *... he never denied an anecdote told of him, however incredible, if the General was in it. He was a handsome mulatto, in the prime of life, well-made and with excellent manners, but perhaps altogether true only to the General. He was a great admirer of the General's temperance views, although they did not apply to himself, for he was fond of liquor ... he could always tell the condition of the military atmosphere by the General's devotions ... when he got up in the night to pray, 'Then I begin to cook rations and pack up, for there will be hell to pay the next morning.' ... He would politely answer all questions regarding the General's habits and peculiarities of life, but not so much with strict regard to truth, as to make his master a very mysterious personage. ... Once ... he was asked to drink General Jackson's health so frequently, that the 'hospitality of the people was too many for Jeems (sic)' ... he galloped* (back) *into camp ... his face suffused with the red cast of liquor ... but the General never heard of it, for the Staff always screened him. When the General died Jim's, honest grief was almost inconsolable. ...* He looked after Sandy Pendleton for a bit; but when he was killed, went home on leave, saying *... he would come back and join someone of the 'old staff;' Jackson's own. But he was taken ill and died in Lexington ...* and, like the General, Jim too *... lies buried in that historic town."*

With his customary rapid marching, Jackson induced the outlying Federal garrisons to herd together at Harper's Ferry, which he surrounded and isolated. On his taking over Martinsburg, after the Federal departure, unlike Middletown, the friends and admirers of Stonewall Jackson almost overwhelmed him. When crowds gathered around the Everett House, the General *"took refuge in the parlour and had the door locked and the windows on the street closed. ... Soon voices were calling him at the windows and rattling the shutters."*[409] He needed to get a dispatch away to Lee and, ignoring the blandishments, wrote on. Outside, people were gathering around his charger and *"about to despoil the unsuspecting beast of mane and tail. They were soon stopped by a sentinel, but not before they had obtained little licks of hair for bracelets and the like. ...* the horse was not the 'Little Sorrel', that was absent for a few days, having been stolen; but one *"that had been lent to him by that gruff soldier and woman-hater, General William E. Jones."*[410] *But the horse did not satisfy them. Some boys, urged on by the ladies, managed to open the shutters of one of the windows ... they called out 'Dear, dear General', and managing to force up the window a little way they threw red and white roses all about him. Soon a smile broke over his face, for there is a point beyond which to resist the pleadings of a woman is not a virtue. At any rate his dispatch was finished and, giving it me* (Douglas) *with very definite instructions for a courier, he said, 'Now admit the ladies'."*

"*They came and swarmed about him. They all tried to get his hands at once ... they all talked at once with the disjointed eloquence of a devotion that scorned all coherent language. Blushing, bowing, almost speechless, he stood in the midst of this remarkable scene, saying 'Thank you, thank you, you're very kind.' ... There were daughters and mothers and sweethearts of his soldiers, and he was too tender at heart to resist them. And when a rosy-cheeked little girl reached both her chubby hands up to his coat and begged him for a button for a breastpin, he cut one off and gave it to her. It was a fatal let-down: in a twinkling half the buttons on his coat were gone, and boys, taking advantage of the pressure, robbed his coat tails of their buttons. Another young lady wanted his autograph in her album ... and he wrote it. Of course, they all wanted autographs ... On sheets of foolscap paper, he wrote that modest "T.J. Jackson" and*

---

409 Douglas.
410 Ibid.

distributed it amongst them. He seemed to have given way entirely. But when one woman, more adventurous, hinted for a lock of hair – of which he had no super-abundant supply, he drew the line and put an end to the interview. He declined innumerable invitations to dinner and a little after noon disappeared. … it was said he went to dine with a plain old man and his wife … whose son was a private in the General's Old brigade."[411]
In the afternoon he moved on, and the next day – Saturday the thirteenth – he was within two miles of the Bolivar Heights, which overlook Harper's Ferry from the south. With General McLaws approaching the Loudon Heights, on the east side of the Shenandoah where it flows into the Potomac, and General Walker closing on the Maryland Heights, overlooking Harper's Ferry from the north bank of the Potomac, the ring was in place and simply had to be tightened.

411 Ibid.

33. "HE'S NOT MUCH FOR LOOKS"

....

"He's not much for looks, boys;
but if we'd had him, we wouldn't
have been caught in this trap."
Union Soldier at Harper's Ferry

....

ON Sunday the fourteenth, Jackson tightened the noose, ordering
the shelling of Harper's Ferry from both banks of the Potomac, in
preparation for an assault *"along the left bank of the Shenandoah …*
in order to … turn the enemy's left flank and enter Harper's Ferry.[412]
At first light on Monday morning, Jackson's 'old Division' – now
commanded by General D.R. Jones – opened proceedings with
diversionary fire on *"the steep bluffs of Bolivar … and … filled the*
air with a din of war that echoed along the Potomac and reverberated in
multiplied repetitions against the rocks of Maryland Heights."[413] Fire
was immediately opened from north and east of the Ferry, and
Hill's Division moved forward to the assault. As Douglas rode
back from having delivered Jackson's order to General Jones, *"a*
white flag went up on Bolivar Heights and all firing ceased." Douglas
was soon escorting a group of Federal officers along the Halltown
turnpike, to discuss formal surrender terms. It was to be uncondi-
tional, Jackson told General Julius White, the senior Federal officer, before turning him over to A.P. Hill to finalise the details.
"I took occasion to note the appearance of General White … Douglas
wrote … *There was nothing strikingly military about his looks, but he*
was mounted on a handsome black horse, was handsomely uniformed,
with an untarnished sabre, immaculate gloves and boots, and had a staff

---

412 Henderson quoting the order issued by Jackson from *'Headquarters,*
     Valley District, September 14, 1862.
413 Douglas.

fittingly equipped. He must have been somewhat astonished to find in General Jackson the worst dressed, worse mounted, most faded and dingy-looking general he had ever seen anyone surrender to, with a staff, not much for looks or equipment." Beware giving too much credence to shiny boots!

Jackson's haul at Harper's Ferry was thirteen thousand small arms, seventy-three pieces of artillery, and a large quantity of military stores of various kinds. The collective garrisons yielded twelve thousand five hundred and twenty prisoners. When Jackson rode down into Harper's Ferry, the road *"was lined with Union soldiers curious to see Stonewall Jackson. Many of them saluted as he passed, and he invariably returned the salute. ... Douglas ... heard one of them say: 'Boys, he's not much for looks, but if we'd had him, we wouldn't have been caught in this trap. ... there was an echo of endorsement around the candid soldier.*"

34. "BOYS, IT'S ALRIGHT!"

....

(Confederate Soldier before Sharpsburg)

....

LEAVING A.P. Hill to take care of the surrender details at Harper's Ferry, Jackson marched, with customary celerity, to re-join Lee around Sharpsburg, some ten miles north across the Potomac in Maryland. The C-in-C was experiencing a tricky forty-eight hours. McClellan was approaching from the east, with an Army of between eighty-seven and ninety thousand with which to confront Lee's thirty-five to forty-five thousand all ranks. The Federal advanced-guard had been able to force both the Gaps in South Mountain – a long ridge of high ground shielding the eastern approach to Sharpsburg. Although Lee had ordered the reinforcement of D.H. Hill's detachments picketing the Gaps, Longstreet's command did not move until the day following the order, and then took thirteen hours to march ten miles. As Henderson commented *"not all the Confederate Generals appear to have possessed the same 'driving power' as Jackson."* How often does Longstreet's attitude to war seem way too complacent, and his views at odds with Lee's. In their twin defeats at Crampton and Turner's Gap the Confederates lost a total of three thousand four hundred men, of whom nearly two thousand were taken prisoner. A number which Lee could ill-afford to lose, given his initial numerical inferiority, and a wholesale and continuous straggling problem which bordered on desertion.

In the immediate prelude to the battle of Antietam Creek, Douglas experienced two revealing aspects to Jackson the man and the general, and the regard in which he was held by the rank and file. Jackson was conferring with Lee and Longstreet *"on what is now Cemetery Ridge ...* Douglas recorded, and *... "as I approached some soldiers who were loafing near, I overheard an animated and amusing conversation as to whether Stonewall Jackson had* *arrived or not. One insisted he had arrived while another repeated a re-port that he was 'over in Virginny, somewhere, up to something lively, I'll be bound.' One of them expressed his determination to ask me about it and, approaching me, did so.*

"I told him Jackson had arrived and said, 'That's he, talking to your General, 'Old Pete' — the man with the big boots.' 'Is it? Well, bless my eyes! Thankee, Captain.' And returning to his squad, flourishing his tattered tile, he exclaimed, 'Boys, it's all right'!"

This ability to allay anxiety at the prospect of battle; to reassure and instil trust and confidence, is given to few, and is a certain indicator of true greatness in the General. An example in relation to Oliver Cromwell has already been mentioned; *"Old Ironsides has come to lead us."* A little over fifty years after Cromwell, Captain Robert Parker of the Royal Regiment of Foot of Ireland, under orders to assault entrenchments at the siege of Bouchain, wrote *"I must confess I did not like the aspect of the thing. ... But while I was musing, the Duke of Marlborough (ever watchful, ever right) rode up quite unattended and alone, and posted himself a little on the right of my company of grenadiers, from whence he had a fair view of the greater part of the enemy's works. It is quite impossible for me to express the joy, which the sight of this man gave me at this very critical moment. ... I was now well satisfied, that he would not push the thing, unless he saw a strong possibility of success; nor was this my notion alone; it was the sense of the whole army, both officer and soldier, British and foreigner. ... He stayed only three or four minutes, and then rode back. ... He had not been longer from us, than he stayed, when orders came for us to retire."*[414] A Century or so after Marlborough, soldiers of another 'astonishing infantry' looked in vain for Wellington before the battle of Albuera, *"Whore's oor Arthur? ...* asked a Geordie private in the Seventh Fusiliers of ... *"his mate George Spencer Cooper ... I don't know, I don't see him, replied Cooper. Aw wish he wor here, said*

---

414 *"Military Memoirs of Marlborough's Campaigns 1702–1712"* by Captain Robert Parker, Edited by David Chandler, Greenhill Books, London, 1998.

the man. And so, mused Cooper, did I."[415] It is a fair bet too, that the hardened fighters of Alexander's Phalanx would have joked to no other General but their young King, that victory against the vast number they would face on the morrow, was assured by the hircine smell of which they all reeked.

415 Richard Holmes in, *"Wellington – The Iron Duke",* quoting Cooper, *"Rough Notes from Seven Campaigns."*

35. "MY GRATEFUL APPRECIATION"

*"Well, as she has sent me my breakfast
to the field I will call her Miss Fairfield."*
Stonewall Jackson

THE morning before battle, Jackson was invited to breakfast with the Grove family in Sharpsburg, with whom Stuart and Longstreet were billeted. He was too busy with his preparations to accept, and *"a daughter of the house, sent a delightful breakfast to him by one of General Longstreet's servants. … he … asked what young lady had sent it. 'I dunno, General, but it was the fair one.' 'Well,* replied Jackson, *as she has sent me my breakfast to the field, I will call her Miss Fairfield.' … he took a pencil and wrote the following note: Sharpsburg September sixteenth 1862. Miss Fairfield, I have received the nice breakfast, for which I am indebted to your kindness. Please accept my grateful appreciation of your hospitality. Very Sincerely Yours, T. J. Jackson. … This note has become well known. I have seen it spread upon satin and nicely framed, doing duty at bazaars and fairs for 'Confederate Homes', since the war. During the war, … Douglas wrote … it was lithographed in Baltimore, and $500 was realized from the sale of those lithographs for the use of Confederate hospitals."*

During the afternoon, skirmishers and sharpshooters began the overture to battle, as McClellan's Army poured down from the South Mountain ridge–line, to deploy along the line of Antietam Creek. The Confederates continued siting their sparse and shabby brigades amidst the knolls and hillocks; the woods and cornfields between the Creek, and the nearby village of Sharpsburg, which lay behind rising ground immediately to their rear. From within the village, a turnpike ran north to Hagerstown, and a second, from Boonsboro to the east, continued on to Shepherdstown on the nearby Potomac. Jackson held the left of the Confederate line; Longstreet the right. The Division of Jackson's brother-in-law, D. H. Hill, linked the two. *"Lee was not on the left at all; as usual he trusted General Jackson to fight his own battle."*[416]

_____

416 Douglas.

36. "GOD HAS BEEN VERY"

....

"God has been very kind to us this day."
Stonewall Jackson

....

SHORTLY before the battle, the Federals picked up in Frederick a copy of Lee's Operation Order, including the entire Order of Battle for the Army of Northern Virginia. The order was found wrapped around three cigars.[417] Longstreet wrote after the War *"that the lost order was sent by General Jackson to General D.H. Hill but was not delivered."* He, seemingly, produced no evidence for his claim, and as to his motives for it, who can say? Jackson no longer being around to refute the statement. Possibly it was an attempt to divert attention from a lapse in which either Longstreet himself, or his Staff, were implicated. D.H. Hill wrote after the War: *"I have now before me (1888) the order received from Jackson. My adjutant-general swore affidavit, twenty years ago, that no order was received at our office from General Lee. Jackson was so careful that no one should learn the contents of the order that the copy he furnished to Hill was written in his own hand. The copy found by the Federals … was signed by Lee's adjutant-general."*[418]

His inherent caution at least quietened by the intelligence windfall – as well, presumably, by even his detectives being unable to exaggerate Confederate numbers – McLellan opened the battle promptly the next morning with an attack by his First Corps alone – fourteen thousand eight hundred and fifty-six all ranks, with forty guns[419], commanded by General 'Fighting Joe' Hooker. Skirmishers began moving against the Confederate Left at around

---

417 Henderson.
418 Henderson quoting both Hill and Longstreet.
419 Henderson's numbers.

five a.m.; but were held-off by gunfire. An hour-long artillery duel followed, before the densely packed columns of Hooker's infantry swarmed to the assault. This opening, and main, phase of the battle was bloody in the extreme; a see-saw affair, lasting some five hours, during which McClellan was forced also to commit his Twelfth Corps – ten thousand one hundred and twenty-six all ranks, with thirty guns, commanded by General Mansfield – to shore-up the attack. To no avail. Although giving ground, supported by Hood's Texans and Lawton's brigade from the Confederate Centre, and with Stuart's gunners enfilading the attacks from out beyond the left flank, the thin line of Valley soldiers held firm. 'Old Stonewall' had been mostly towards the right of his line during the morning, allowing the Commanders of Brigades and Divisions to act for themselves, whilst he maintained his customary calm overview. As he watched, McClellan was preparing to follow-up the failed attacks with another eighteen thousand eight hundred and thirteen men and forty-two guns – the Second Corps of General Sumner. The Confederate Left had comprised some nineteen thousand four hundred at the start of the action, and after fending-off attacks by around twenty-five thousand was hardly in a position to resist an assault from a fresh Corps, whose numbers almost certainly now exceeded their own. *"But ... as Henderson has it ... Jackson's hand still held the reins of battle."* The Confederate Right had not yet been attacked, and despite the battering to his line, for Jackson, the moment to counter-attack had arrived. *"He had already demanded reinforcements from General Lee"* and at their approach, Jackson ordered General McLaws to detach a brigade to sustain Stuart on the left, and *"to drive the enemy back and turn his right."* Some six thousand Federals advancing through the West Wood immediately to the front, were taken in flank. *"Nearly two thousand men were disabled in a moment."*[420] A brigade was sent to their assistance; but McLaws reformed his attack-line and drove on. *"The*

---

420 Federal General Palfrey, present at the battle, quoted by Henderson.

Southern yell, pealing from ten thousand throats rang with a wild note of anticipated triumph, and Jackson, riding with McLaws, followed … the progress of his counterstroke … 'God', he said to his companion, as the shells fell around them … has been very kind to us this day'." But, inevitably, the attack had become ragged. The attackers had no back-up. The defence was too numerous. The Confederates fell-back, and the firing died away. Jackson re-established his position at the West Wood.

37. "DR MCGUIRE THEY HAVE . . ."

....

"Dr McGuire, they have done their worst."
Stonewall Jackson

....

CONCERNED, from the sheer number of wounded struggling back to his medical station and ambulances, that the battle was going unfavourably, Dr McGuire gathered-up some peaches and sought out the General. He suggested the wounded be evacuated to relative safety across the Potomac. Jackson was sitting on the 'Little Sorrel,' immediately behind his sparse, front line. Pointing to the lowering masses of the enemy – beyond the heaps of dead and wounded, the cries for water, the litter of weapons, and the scattering of stragglers – he pointed, saying quietly *"Dr McGuire, they have done their worst."* The General was grateful and turned his attention to the peaches.

If being handed complete details of the opposing army, almost literally 'on a plate', went a long way to curbing McLellan's over-weaning caution, it did nothing for his methodology. The old folly of committing formations piecemeal, if not as blatant as at First Manassas, was still evident at Sharpsburg, and if McLellan had been told of the brilliant, all-embracing counterstroke that rounded-off the Confederate victory of Second Manassas, the implications had passed him by. Having failed to dislodge Jackson on the left, McLellan launched elements of his Second and Fifth Corps – Generals Sumner and Franklin – against the Confederate Centre. More bloody, close quarter fighting ensued. A sunken lane, running in front of D.H. Hill's Division, was packed with bodies, and became ever after 'Bloody Lane'. Longstreet was forced to give a little; but, once more the sparse Grey line held. Having checked the assault, Longstreet ordered an advance. Fortunately for the Confederates, he rescinded the order on being told that Lee had already ordered a turning attack, against

McLellan's Right, which Jackson was preparing. Longstreet, up to now at least, does not seem to have understood the destructive power of artillery fire against troops in the open, nor, despite all subsequent examples, the futility of isolated, stand-alone, frontal assaults on a strongly defensive position. The Federals had some two hundred rifled guns at Sharpsburg – including a number of heavy calibre. In the event, the turning manoeuvre could not be carried out, because the Federal Right was too well secured by artillery, and the close proximity of the Potomac.

McLellan launched the third, and final, of his major assaults, in mid-afternoon, against the, as yet untried, extreme right of Lee's line. The Ninth Army Corps of General Ambrose Burnside – thirteen thousand eight hundred and nineteen men, with thirty-five pieces of ordnance – pressed up towards the ridge overlooking Sharpsburg, to threaten the rear of the Confederate position. Guns, Lee had posted centrally, tore gaps in the attacking ranks, and infantry support from the left was on the way; but to McClellan it surely looked as though he was, at last, poised to turn the defence, and roll-up the Confederate line from right to left. He had some twenty-five thousand men who, up until now had not fired a shot. If ever a moment in battle cried-out for an all-or-nothing, decisive hammer blow, then it was this moment, late in the afternoon beside the Antietam Creek. The blow duly came; but it was delivered not by McLellan's many; but by Lee's few.

At that supreme moment, on to the reeking, smoke-stained battle field rode the Commander of the Confederate Light Division. General A.P. Hill, having been left to tidy up Jackson's capture of Harper's Ferry, had received an urgent order, around six thirty that morning, to join the main body. Within the hour the Light Division was on the march, to cover the intervening seventeen miles in eight hours. In the warm sun of late summer, Hill had removed his general's jacket, and was riding ahead of his advanced-guard resplendent in blood-red battle shirt. He grasped the situation in an instant, and without a moment's hesitation, swung his three brigades forward from column into line.

Once again, it was *'the flash of the kingfisher across the surface of the lake.'* With barely a breaking step, two and a half thousand[421] veteran fighters of the advanced-guard crashed against the head of Burnside's attacking column. *"The blue line paused, stopped, hesitated, and hesitating was lost. … Jones rallied on Hill and they drove Burnside back to the Antietam, and the protection of his heavy guns, so rapidly that Hill's other brigades could not catch up and get a share in the fighting. … For the day, McClellan's grand army was beaten."*[422] And there the blood-stained encounter ended. Reading extensively on that ferocious encounter from the perspective of today, Douglas certainly would seem to be right in his judgement that McClellan *"made a grave error when … he listened to General Sumner and refused to let Franklin renew the assault with his troops … either by making an assault on Jackson's frazzled front, or by moving simultaneously with Burnside … directly on Sharpsburg. I cannot see how such a movement, with fair fighting, could have failed. … if Lee had been in McClellan's place, with Jackson and Longstreet and the Hills, the Army of Northern Virginia would have ceased to exist that day."* For Douglas himself, *"fighting at my own front door … it was a fearful day."* He had been ill the night before, and *"the day was hot … the suspense racking … the anxiety intense."* By Noon he had exhausted two horses and was riding a third *"trying to dismount, I fainted on the field … but … soon recovered … with the aid of food and brandy."*

Lee held his position overnight, against the views of his immediate subordinates – including Stonewall Jackson, so it has been said. *"… strengthen your lines … Lee said, …collect your stragglers … If McLellan wants a fight in the morning, I will give him battle."*[423] Douglas never did believe that Jackson was amongst the advocates of withdrawal. *"If so … he wrote … it was the first time in their joint career that Lee ever wished to make an aggressive movement that Jackson did not concur with. He never consented to a retreat unless he*

---

421 Douglas.
422 Ibid.
423 Henderson quoting Lee.

could give a stunning back-hand blow to the enemy," and for Douglas, the next morning, Jackson *"seemed ready for fight at the drop of a hat."* From sometime soon after the fighting petered-out, Lee considered a flanking attack to turn McClellan's right. Douglas may not have known of the incident the following morning, when the Commander-in Chief ordered an Artillery Colonel – Stephen Lee – to report to Jackson, saying *"he will tell you what he wants."* The pair rode alone to the left of the Confederate line and climbed a hill. *"be careful not to expose yourself, for the Federal sharpshooters are not far off,"* Jackson said, before ordering a careful examination of the Federal position opposite. The Colonel's considered view was that it was *"a very strong position, and there is a large force there."* The General then asked him if he could crush the force – the Federal Right – with fifty guns. After further examination, the Colonel said *"General, I can try. I can do it if anyone can."* Jackson was relentless. *"That is not what I asked you, Sir. If I give you fifty guns, can you crush the Federal right? … I want your positive opinion, yes or no."* Eventually; reluctantly, Colonel Lee said *"General, it cannot be done with fifty guns and the men you have here."* Immediately, Jackson ordered Lee to report back to the C–in–C, and to tell him all that had taken place, including his being forced to give his opinion on the viability of an attack with fifty guns. Having done so *"I saw a shade come over General Lee's face, and he said, 'Colonel, go and join your command'."*[424]

As Henderson noted, it is conceivable that Jackson had already recced the Federal Right during the evening following the battle, and having decided a flank attack would not succeed, was an advocate of withdrawal. With typical rectitude and consideration, Jackson used a chosen and trusted emissary of Lee, to convey the same, negative, view on the up-to-date situation the next morning. No attack was made on the Federal Right, and no attacking move was made by either side throughout the

---

424 Henderson quoting a letter written to him by (then) General Stephen Lee, after the War.

day. Having learnt that McClellan was being reinforced – the Confederates withdrew after dark, across the Potomac, back into Virginia. A few severely wounded men and the odd straggler were all that was left behind. *"wagons and guns, useless wagons, disabled guns, everything … was removed … if a scavenger had gone over the field the next day, he would have found nothing worth carrying off. … General Jackson on horseback, spent much of his time in the middle of the river urging everything and everybody to push on. But the genius of this retreat was Major John Harmon, Jackson's Quartermaster, big-bodied, big-voiced, untiring, fearless of man or devil, who would have ordered Jackson himself out of the way, if necessary, to obey Jackson's orders."* It was daylight before Jackson finally crossed, just ahead of the last cavalry scouts. Although he was not fired on, later that evening, McClellan sent infantry across the river under a heavy artillery barrage from the Maryland side. The two-brigade Confederate rear guard was surprised and had four guns captured. *"The affair disgusted General Jackson beyond words. He took the matter in his own hands and his staff were little out of the saddle that night."* When Lee's courier reached him the next morning, with an instruction to deal with the matter, he found Jackson alone upon the Shepherdstown road observing the approach of more Federal infantry. However, the Divisions of A.P. Hill and General Jubal Early (now commanding Ewell's brigades) soon appeared, and their being ordered to attack at once, the Federals were driven back to Maryland. *"The dash across the river was daring and admirable: the result a failure."*[425]

In accordance with what was becoming something of a habit with Northern Generals, McClellan duly proclaimed Sharpsburg a brilliant Federal victory. In this, he was probably more justified in the claim than were either Shields or Pope, given that however unimpressive and irresolute his tactical handling of the battle may have been, he had put an end to Lee's invasion of the North without anything of value having been achieved.

---

425 Douglas.

McClellan made no further incursions into Virginia. The Army of the Potomac was sorely in need of a thorough overhaul. It too had serious deficiencies in kit, equipment and horses, and it had suffered heavy losses, under both Pope and McClellan. In the wake of an estimate by General Banks – now in a command at Washington – that the Confederate field strength was some ninety-seven thousand, McClellan, once more, began reporting *"Lee's overwhelming strength."*[26]

President Lincoln had an amusing take on what he seemingly realised was the extraordinary capacity of his Generals to over-estimate Confederate military strength. Questioned by a delegate visiting the White House as to how many men under arms he reckoned the South had, Mr Lincoln replied *"Sir, I have the best possible reason for knowing the number to be one million of men, for whenever one of our generals engages a rebel army, he reports that he has encountered a force twice his strength. Now I know we have half a million soldiers, so I am bound to believe that the rebels have twice that number."*[27] Certainly, the presence of Stonewall Jackson on the battlefield was worth twice as many bayonets, so perhaps estimates by Lincoln's Generals were not so far out!

426 Henderson.
427 Quoted by Henderson.

38. "LET US TAKE A DRINK"

....

"Come, gentleman, let us take a drink."
Stonewall Jackson

....

IN the three months following the return from Maryland, Jackson established his headquarters once more in the Valley of Virginia. Initially, where he could *"could keep an eye on either ford of the Potomac."* Later, he moved nearer Winchester. The Army was reorganised; its numbers built up by recruitment and stragglers brought back to the Colours. Jackson and Longstreet were promoted Lieutenant General – *to take preference according to previous rank* – and to command the Second and First Corps of the Army of Northern Virginia, respectively. The Confederate authorities never fully realised just how great a General they possessed in Stonewall Jackson. Whether or not it was a comment on his promotion, or his practice of not writing to Anna of official military matters, in a letter home, soon after being promoted, Jackson told her that there was *"no position in the world equal to that of a minister of the Gospel."*[428]

In the course of a headquarters move soon after the return to Virginia, a supper invitation was accepted from a kindly house-holder, whose offer of quarters the General had *"politely declined"*, Jackson startled the Staff by accepting a glass of whiskey. *"It was a cold, damp evening, unpleasantly suggestive of Autumn; …* Douglas remembered *… we were chilly, and our wagons had not arrived, the hospitable host appeared with a decanter of whiskey and glasses … and deferentially suggested … an appetizer either straight or with water.* "Have you any white sugar?" *smilingly broke in the General. … It was instantly forthcoming.* "Come, gentlemen, let's take a drink!" *was the General's startling announcement. … he … walked to the table, under the guidance*

---

428 Henderson.

of his Medical Director, who of course doubled the prescription, and with a skill and ease which seemed in shocking contrast to his reputation, mixed a stiff toddy and drank it off." Jackson complimented the host *"upon its flavour and purity, although not old."* Douglas declined to drink for various reasons, and ended by saying *"Besides, General, I do not like the taste of spirituous liquors."* Jackson turned to him and said *"quietly, but with a distinct seriousness, 'In that I differ with you … I like the taste of all spirituous liquors. I can sip whiskey or brandy with a spoon with the same pleasure the most delicious coffee or cordial would give you. I am the fondest man of liquor in this Army and if I had indulged my appetite, I would have been a drunkard. But liquors are not good for me. I question whether they are much good for anyone. At any rate I rarely touch them.' This was the only time I ever saw him take a glass of spirits.* (except by mistake on one occasion, on the march to Bath, during the Winter Campaign early in the year) … *Some gentlemen of Frederick presented his Headquarters with several baskets of claret; it was on the table daily, bur he rarely tasted it."*

Yet another side to his character and intellect was revealed when General Bradley Johnson escorting Colonel Garnet Wolseley (later Field Marshal, and Commander-in-Chief of the British Army) – the Hon. Francis Lawley (Special Correspondent to 'The Times' newspaper) – and Mr Henry Vizetelly (Special Correspondent to the 'Illustrated London News') *"By order of General Lee"*, introduced them to Lieutenant-General Jackson. *"We were all seated in front of General Jackson's tent, and he took up the conversation. …* when in England, *he had been very impressed by Durham Cathedral and with the history of the bishopric. … he cross-examined the Englishmen in detail about the cathedral and the close, and the rights of the bishops. … he kept them busy answering questions, for he knew more about Durham than they did. … As we rode away, I* (General Johnson) *said; 'Gentleman, you have disclosed Jackson in a new character to me, and I have been carefully observing him for a year and a half. You have made him exhibit 'finesse', for he did all the talking to keep you from asking too curious or embarrassing questions. I never saw anything like it in him before.' We all agreed that the general had been too much for the interviewers."*[429]

---

429 Henderson quoting from the *'Memoirs'* of General Bradley T. Johnson.

When the Second Army Corps was encamped around Bunker Hill, a widespread interest in religion was stimulated by the Reverend Dr Stiles, a seventy year old cleric and native of Virginia, who was chaplain in Ewell's old Division, now commanded by Jubal Early. Douglas remembered him as *"a most eloquent preacher. ... Meetings were held in one of the camps nearly every night. Jackson often attended ... offering a fervent prayer –* 'in former pauperis' *– to God, in the midst of the camps. ... General Jackson's step at any time could hardly be called a walk; with his heavy army boots on he simply plodded ... talking about sundry things ... he never 'talked shop.'* The word would spread of his approach, and Douglas noticed that in many of the tents, the soldiers would be *"absorbed in games of cards, sitting in squads of four, around a candle in an inverted bayonet stuck in the ground as a candlestick. As the General approached the light would go out, the cards would be put down in place just as they were held, the players would crawl out and fall in behind; and when he had reached the place of prayer, lo, the camp was there. Bowed heads, bent knees, hats off, silence! Stonewall Jackson was kneeling to the Lord of Hosts, in prayer for his people! Not a sound disturbed his voice as it ascended to Heaven on their behalf and, in their faith, the very stars seemed to move softly and make no noise. When we left, a line of soldiers followed him in escort to the edge of the camp, and then, doubtless, returned to their cards."* Douglas remembered on one occasion, at least, *"that as the hour for tattoo came, and the rolling drums scattered it through the camps ... suddenly out upon the beautiful night there broke forth that wild and joyous yell for which the Stonewall brigade was famous. Other brigades and Divisions took it up, and it sprang from camp to camp with increasing vigour, until the bright arch of Heaven seemed to resound with the thundering acclaim. The mingled roar was grand, peculiar, impressive in the extreme. When it was at its height, I saw the General come out, bareheaded, from his tent, walk to the fence and lean his elbow on the topmost rail. Resting his chin upon his hand he waited in silence for the climax, fall, and the conclusion of this strange serenade. The shouts decreased, the noise became fainter and fainter, and when it had almost ceased to be audible, he lifted his head to catch the last note and its last echo. When it was all over, he returned slowly to his tent, and said in soliloquy as he entered, 'That was the sweetest music I ever heard."*

39. "WE WILL WHIP THE ENEMY"

"I am opposed to fighting on the Rappahannock. We will whip the enemy but gain no fruits of victory."

Stonewall Jackson

THE weeks of rest and resuscitation for the Army of Northern Virginia ended in early November. Wishing to make another strike against Lee before Winter set in, McClellan was preparing to invade Eastern Virginia. Unfortunately, both for him and the Union cause, his preparations were deemed too slow. Political considerations intruded on this occasion, slowness was prompted not by McClellan's innate caution; but by the very proper need to refurbish the Army of the Potomac, and to repair shattered morale after the defeats of the previous months, which were all too apparent to the rank and file, whatever their Generals may have claimed. McClellan was the only Union General who had the confidence of the Northern soldier, and who could complete the vital rejuvenation process; but just at that moment, Lincoln opted to change the whole character of the War, by *"violating"* the Constitution. He needed to sustain support for the War, and his keen political insight sensed that the United States had reached a point where, for many, probity had superseded the once-sacred text of the Constitution. *"For the clause which forbade all interference with the domestic institutions of the several States, …* he substituted … *a declaration that slavery should no longer exist within the boundaries of the Republic."*[430] From here on, the Northern soldier was to fight for the freedom of the negro. Like William

---

430 Henderson.

Wickham, Colonel of the Fourth Virginia Cavalry and Member of the Confederate Congress, many in the South, especially from Virginia, would continue to say, *"Remember, if I am killed tomorrow it will be for Virginia, the land of my fathers, and not for the damned secession movement."*[431] Having made so controversial a political move, the last thing Lincoln wanted was inaction, which would allow time for reflection, especially on the part of an influential General who, unlike the President, was a Democrat, yet who, nonetheless, was in the perfect position to blur the controversy by fighting. McClellan was fired, and Burnside, the outstanding failure of Sharpsburg – worthy and plodding, but having little or no initiative – was appointed Federal Field Commander. Burnside shared the President's political perspective. Shortly before the dismissal, Lee had added to McClellan's woes by sending Stuart on one of his predatory sweeps, which encircled the entire Army of the Potomac, and kept him *"for fifty six hours inside the enemy's lines,* during which time he, and his six hundred, covered one hundred twenty-six miles – the last eighty miles without halting – and returned having appropriated some five hundred horses, as well as disrupting Federal communications, and gaining the required intelligence. In the process, Stuart had gained the added bonus of knocking-up practically the entire Federal cavalry force, which had been sent in every direction in an effort to apprehend him, but which had achieved nothing more than the capture of the odd skirmisher. One Federal cavalry General covered seventy-eight miles in twenty-four hours, and another two hundred miles in four days. Neither so much as glimpsed Stuart. The Northern people were acutely aware that this was the second occasion on which the Confederate Cavalry Leader had been able to play fast and loose with their Army and its Commander-in-Chief, but *"until his cavalry should have recovered … McClellan believed … it was impossible to invade Virginia."*[432]

---

431 Blackford in his account of the battle of Fredericksburg.
432 Henderson.

Throughout October and early November, Lee kept his two Corps separated. The strategy agreed with Jackson was to oppose by manoeuvre, and not, either by entrenching or head-on confrontation with an enemy greatly superior in number. The Second Army Corps, therefore, remained in the Valley, with their supply lines secured by running back along the North fork of the Shenandoah – in the lee of the Massanutton – to Staunton, and from where Jackson was nicely poised for a swoop on the communications of any invader moving against Richmond. He had, in fact, already proposed a pre-emptive strike against the rear echelons of the Army of the Potomac. As usual his ever-constructive vigour was not adopted.

Burnside had at his disposal a field force of one hundred and twenty-five thousand men, and some three hundred and twenty guns. Behind this frontline were a further eighty thousand protecting Washington; ten thousand at Harper's Ferry, and another twelve thousand spread along the Baltimore and Ohio Railroad, four thousand of whom were at Sharpsburg. A total of two hundred and twenty five thousand. To oppose them Lee had some seventy-one thousand eight hundred and nine officers and men, in two Army Corps, including a Cavalry Division of seven thousand one hundred and seventy-six, a Reserve Artillery of nine hundred men; the whole backed up by a total of two hundred and seventy-five guns.[433]

Jackson, easing back to the area of Winchester, caused considerable perturbation to Northern businessmen and bankers, never mind politicians and public opinion, and ultimately, of course, a freshly appointed, and far from self-assured, Federal Army Commander. Appreciating that Burnside was being driven ultimately by political, and not military, imperatives, Lee had anticipated that this might have the effect of causing Burnside to trend away to his left, without abandoning the intention of moving on Richmond, despite the onset of the first snows of Winter.

---

433 Henderson's figures.

Longstreet's First Corps was close to Fredericksburg, barring the direct line South to Richmond. Lee ordered the Second Corps across from the Valley to take up positions, east of First Corps, on the lower reaches of the Rappahannock, in the direction of Port Royal.

Did Jackson sense he would be leaving the Valley for the last time? Before departing, he rode into Winchester *"to make some calls. This was the only day during the war he ever spent on social duties. … He dined at the house of his Medical Director's father, Dr Hugh McGuire, and, … at the request of Miss McGuire, went to Lupton's gallery to have his photograph taken for her. This is the best likeness that was ever taken of him during the war and may be called his official photograph."*[434] According to Henderson *"he spent his last evening with his old friends, … the Rector, Dr Graham, and his wife. …* *"He was in fine health and fine spirits, …* Mrs Graham wrote to tell Anna … *The children begged to be permitted to sit up to see 'General Jackson,' and he really seemed overjoyed to see them …he … talked a great deal about the hope of getting back to spend this winter with us, in the old room, which I told him I was keeping for you and him. He certainly has had adulation enough to spoil him, but it seems not to affect or harm him at all. He is the same humble, dependent Christian, desiring to give God all the glory, looking to him alone for a blessing, and not thinking of himself."*

Second Corps left the Valley on the familiar old Valley Turnpike, marching at the usual, swift Valley Army 'Foot Cavalry' pace. Down the 'Pike to New Market, a sharp left turn up over the Massanutton, and down the far slope, to cross the Shenandoah and the Luray Valley, before climbing once more up through the deep forests of the Blue Ridge, to cross through Fisher's Gap. The Corps covered one hundred and twenty miles in six marching days, plus two rest days en-route, and with scarcely a straggler. Rigorous steps had been taken to stamp out the ill-discipline and weakening effect of straggling.

---

434 Henderson.

Whilst the General was engaged in relocating Second Corps below Fredericksburg on the lower Rappahannock, Anna Jackson was delivered of a baby girl. The General received the news that both mother and child were well, by sealed letter, typically, having requested that news of the birth should not be allowed to leak out by way of a more public telegram. He gave vent to his longing to see his daughter in letters to his wife and to relations; but otherwise told no one he had become a father. *"My mother was mindful of me when I was a helpless, fatherless child, …*he wrote *… and I wish to commemorate her now."*[35] The baby was baptised Julia, and also Laura, after his much-loved sister, the only other living member of his childhood family.

Appointed for the purpose of taking the war to the South, and goaded by the Northern media, Burnside moved briskly up to the Rappahannock, aiming to cross at Fredericksburg where the river was still navigable for ship transport; which would provide a secure line of supply for an onward advance. However, despite arriving at the river over three weeks before an engagement actually took place, and while the opposite bank was still weakly defended, Burnside missed an important opening trick by denying his advance-guard the opportunity to cross and establish a bridge-head. Lee opted to block Burnside on the Rappahannock. The river presented disadvantages for both Generals, which either they failed to appreciate or chose to ignore, with the result that, apart from stopping the Federal advance into Virginia by a few miles, achieved nothing apart from the killing of men on both sides.

An irregular escarpment fronted the river on the south (Confederate) bank, and the intervening plain, intersected by narrow Runs (streams) a few tracks, and crossed in two directions by the railroad, varied in width from a half to two miles. In the possession of the Confederate infantry, despite inferior numbers and inferior quality guns, the heavily wooded slopes would prove

---

435 Ibid.

impervious to Federal unimaginative, but ever-heroic, frontal assaults. The battle would, once again, prove Jackson's dictum *"My men may sometimes fail to take a position; but to hold one, never!"* His quick eye for ground, however, immediately saw that the south bank presented no more than a strong blocking position, which, in reality, might have been turned from further up-river, although probably only he of the Generals involved would have thought to undertake such an evolution. Certainly, Burnside did not have the essential skill and imagination, as Lee fully appreciated. For the Confederates, however, the unsurmountable downside to the position was, that once the Federal attacking nerve was exhausted, it was an impossible position from which to counter-attack and to instigate an annihilating pursuit. *"I am opposed to fighting on the Rappahannock. …* Jackson said to his brother-in-law, more than two weeks before the battle … *We will whip the enemy but gain no fruits of victory. I have advised the line of the North Anna but have been overruled."*[436] The North Anna was a further thirty-six miles on from Fredericksburg. For Jackson that meant thirty-six miles of exposed communications, and almost limitless opportunities for destructive 'flanking and rearing', and the very real possibility of being able to demolish Burnside's entire command. It was fortunate for the Federals that wintery December, that the one man who would never willingly surrender the initiative, and wait in passive defence, was not in command of the Army of Northern Virginia.

The battle of Fredericksburg was eventually fought on the thirteenth of December, and unfolded as Jackson had envisaged. At the end of Lee's last minute briefing, around nine a.m. on the morning of the battle, with the clammy winter fog lifted, Burnside's vast army, sprawling across the open terrain over a frontage of some four miles, was starkly visible from the escarpment. Longstreet apparently said to Jackson (of all people) *"General, do not all those multitudes of Federals frighten you?"* It was

---

436 Henderson quoting Dabney.

probably the only moment during the entire day when Jackson was confronted by a moment to which he could not instinctively relate, and one would give much to know what his thoughts on the question – and, indeed – the questioner, were. He had long ago reduced fear to an abstract notion, on which he wasted nothing of his concentration. It would simply not have occurred to him to be afraid of mere numbers, and for want of anything better, he said dismissively *"We shall very soon see whether I shall not frighten them"*, and rode across to the thirty thousand men of his Second Corps, and to the business of repulsing the initial attacks of Burnside's Left Wing – some fifty-five thousand men and one hundred and sixteen field guns[437] – commanded by General Franklin. Once more the Falcon was being condemned to fight hooded.

The left of the Confederate line was held by Longstreet's veteran First Corps *"against which ... in Henderson's words ... forty thousand Northerners were madly hurled by the General of Mr Lincoln's choice. By those hapless and stout-hearted soldiers, sacrificed to incompetency, a heroism was displayed which won the pity and the praise of their opponents. The attack was insufficiently prepared, and feebly supported by the artillery. The troops were formed on a narrow front, ... the strongest portion of the position, where the Confederate infantry found shelter behind a stout stone wall, and numerous batteries occupied the commanding ground in rear, was selected for assault. Neither feint nor demonstration, the ordinary expedients by which the attacker seeks to distract the attention and confuse the efforts of the defence, was made use of; and yet Division after Division, with no abatement of courage, marched in good order over the naked plain, dashed forward with ever-thinning ranks, and then, receding sullenly before the storm of fire, left, within a hundred yards of the stone wall, a long line of writhing forms to mark the limit of their advance."* Lee justly relied upon Longstreet to deal with whatever came against him in a defensive situation; but none the less, remained mainly in his half of the field during the battle. As was

---

437 Henderson's figures.

seen at Malvern Hill and Sharpsburg, imaginative and realistic match-winning combinations were not Longstreet's forte.

Similar bludgeoning, unthinking heroics were displayed against Jackson's Corps, on the right of Lee's line, where Jackson steered the action with customary unflappable calm. Early on, in his unceasing quest to know for himself the evolving action at any given moment, he appeared on foot, forward of the frontline, accompanied by a single aide. Without warning a Federal sharpshooter sprang from the grass some two hundred yards away and snapped off a round which swished between the pair without hitting either. Smiling, the General said cheerily *"Mr Smith, had you not better go to the rear? They may shoot you!"*[438] As it happened, he himself was looking especially tempting to snipers that morning, being dressed, not in the old, familiar weather-beaten cap; but one sporting a broad ribbon of gold braid – a present from the people of Richmond – together with a brand spanking new uniform coat, with the insignia of a Lieutenant-General, which Jeb Stuart had made, and which one of whose aides had presented to Jackson some weeks previously. In early afternoon, a smoke and mud be-grimed young gunner caught his *"first glimpse of Stonewall Jackson … when … a general officer, mounted on a superb bay horse and followed by a single courier, rode up through our guns."* Although the dense cover on the position prevented the immediate siting of no more than forty-seven of two Corps total complement of one hundred and twenty-three guns, Jackson's 'favourite arm' had, unaided, shelled the initial Federal attack to a halt. Jackson's customary skilled use of cover had led Burnside to under-estimate the strength of the Confederate Right Wing, and wrongly assuming that Jackson was not yet present in full strength – the final Divisions of Early and Taliaferro having only closed-up around dawn that morning – had ordered a Divisional attack solely against Lee's Right. Some thirty-eight thousand men of the Grand Division of General Franklin, reinforced by some

---

438 Henderson.

twelve thousand of Hooker's command, stood idly by, as nearly five thousand of their fellows were halted and cut about for nearly thirty minutes by a single two-gun horse artillery battery, ordered forward by Jackson. Despite constant changes of position to unsettle the ranging of Federal Artillery, one gun of the pair was disabled, before all ready-use ammunition was expended, and Stuart ordered the Battery Commander to withdraw. The dense yet leafless trees protected Jackson's ranks from the heavy shelling which followed. The attack was then resumed *"bayonets glistening in the bright sunlight ... the Pennsylvania infantry came on ... waving their hundreds of regimental flags which relieved with warm bits of colouring the dull blue of the columns and the russet tinge of the wintery landscape."[439]* With the range down to eight hundred yards, Jackson sent forward all the guns he had been able to deploy, and with the Federal Artillery still firing, they blasted the approaching lines to a shuddering, corpse-strewn halt. A pause, and then the attackers – in the new buzz-word of 1862 – 'skedaddled'. Taking a breather after the intense activity of barrage firing, the young gunner watched the General *"gazing intently on the enemy's line of battle. ... the cap, coat, top-boots,[440] horse and furniture, were all of the new order of things. But there was something about the man that did not look so new after all. He appeared to be an old-time friend of all the turmoil around him. ... Although a somewhat bashful and weak-kneed youngster, I plucked up courage enough to venture to remark that those big guns over the river had been knocking us about pretty considerably during the day. He quickly turned his head, and I knew in an instant who it was before me. The clear-cut, chiselled features; the thin, compressed and determined lips; the calm, steadfast eye; the countenance to command respect, and in time of war to give the soldier that confidence he so much craves from a superior officer, were all there. He turned his head quickly, and looking me all over, rode up the line and*

---

439 Henderson quoting an *"eye-witness."*

440 *"The boots, stout, useful, able-bodied, were a present from Staunton. ... the trousers had been given to him in the Valley"* (Douglas).

away as quickly and silently as he came.'[441] Jackson's locked-in concentration upon the unfolding battle was in no way interrupt-
ed or disturbed by simply a look in the young man's direction.

As that bleak, winter afternoon ground on, fighting intensi-
fied along the entire battle front. Out of the *"smouldering ruins"* of
Fredericksburg, the sombre blue masses of Sumner's Grand Division
strode forward, to shoot and strive in vain before the shallow,
icy weapon scrapes of Longstreet's seasoned fighters. Franklin,
commanding Burnside's Left, re-grouped, reinforced and butted
again at Jackson. In the lead still, the men of Pennsylvania, made
for an area of trees, swamp and tangled scrub that protruded forward from the defended embankment, and broke the symmetry
of Jackson's frontline. Defenders in a later war would have extensively mined and wired the whole enclave. In this Civil War,
the trees could well have been felled; but the area had been left
untouched and undefended, on the grounds it was impenetrable – although Jackson pointed out beforehand that it would be
a point of bitter contention. That no terrain is impassable to the
killer ape in military guise, is a lesson soldiers of each new gen-
eration have been slow to appreciate, and may be even slower
today, given the insidious, enfeebling process of civilisation. At
Fredericksburg, the men from Pennsylvania tore their way through
nature's scrub and swamp obstacle, and in ever-decreasing but
ever-heroic numbers, strove for the very entrails of Jackson's position. Three quarters of his Second Corps brigades were back,
concealed amongst the trees, carefully sited in reserve, where he
could swiftly and penetratingly deploy them, as he deemed fit,
and the fierce, ever-changing kaleidoscope of battle demanded.
On being brought the message *"'the enemy have broken through …
and General Gregg says he must have help or he and General Archer will
both lose their position.'… Jackson turned … and without the least trace of
excitement in either voice or manner, sent orders to Early and Taliaferro,*

---

441 Henderson quoting *"A Confederate artillery-man."*

in the third line, to advance with the bayonet and clear the front."[442] He turned back to continue his observation of the enemy's build-up through *"field-glasses"*, having already noted that the breakthrough was unsupported, and that the Regiments following up had been checked by artillery and rifle fire. Early and Taliaferro, whose advancing ranks included the Stonewall brigade, swiftly restored the situation; but then, despite Jackson's clear and specific orders to the contrary, the counter-charge was allowed to over-reach itself. Having swept the attackers back down the slope, the Confederates were blasted in turn by Union guns firing canister and grape-shot, and forced to withdrew back up the slope, with some loss, in men killed, captured and taken prisoner. However, the repulse and counter-stroke had exacted a considerable price. The Federal Left had been further demoralised beyond their in-itial lack of faith in their commanding general. Some five thou-sand had been either killed or wounded in the abortive attacks on Second Corps, and although Jackson's men, having had less time to prepare, and only the benefit of metaphorical stone walls in defence of the position, had suffered more casualties than the regiments on the left of the Confederate line, he and his men had imposed themselves no less emphatically upon the resolve of the opposing commanders. Whilst the regiments of Second Corps were restoring the integrity of their position – and the attacking Northerners were realising all too clearly that the failure to sup-port the breakthrough was another failure in the competence of command – Burnside was experiencing a fourth repulse at the hands of Longstreet's First Corps. He called on Franklin, his left flank commander, for aggressive, distracting support on his front; but Franklin had had enough. *"He had lost all confidence both in his superior and his men, and he took upon himself to disobey."*[443] With the short winter afternoon drawing in, Jackson was carefully watch-ing what appeared to be preparations for another attack against his

---

442 Henderson.

443 Henderson.

position. *"I waited sometime to receive it ...* he wrote afterwards ... *but* (Franklin) *making no forward movement, I determined, if prudent, to do so myself."* However, as Jackson foresaw, *"the artillery of the enemy was so judiciously posted as to make an advance of our troops across the plain very hazardous; yet it was so promising of good results, if successfully executed, as to induce me to prepare for the attempt. In order to guard against disaster, the infantry were to be preceded by the artillery, and the movement postponed until late in the afternoon, so that if compelled to retire, it would be under cover of night."*[444] Stuart's troopers had been keeping their customary close watch upon the enemy and had reported the plummeting morale in Franklin's ranks. Stuart himself was an enthusiastic supporter of a counter-stroke, and after conferring with Jackson, set off on the right flanking attack which, it was agreed, should co-ordinate with the main, infantry assault. However, although at first, Stuart was able to sustain his advance with sporadic rounds from the pair of guns of his leading horse artillery battery, he met swiftly increasing resistance. Jackson too led with his artillery; but had only advanced a short distance before the *"great array of* (Federal) *artillery ... reopened with vigour,* and to use Jackson's words, *'so completely swept our front as to satisfy me that the proposed movement should be abandoned."* Franklin's Division alone had some one hundred and sixteen field guns, and these were backed-up by the heavier calibre gun-line established on the Stafford Heights to the rear, of which some thirty were ranged against the Second Corps. On Jackson's courier reaching him, Stuart withdrew into the gathering darkness without loss.

However, Jackson's determination to achieve something positive from an otherwise futile tussle, was not yet exhausted. He immediately set about preparations for a night attack. Corps Medical Director, Dr McGuire, was not at all pleased on being asked *"how many yards of bandaging"* he had, when he learnt the General wanted *"a yard ... to put on the arm of every soldier in this*

---

444 Henderson quoting *"Jackson's Reports."*

night's attack, so that the men may know each other from the enemy." He replied, seemingly somewhat huffily, that he *"had not enough cotton cloth for any such purpose* ... adding that the General ... *would have to take a piece of the shirt tail of each soldier"* to supply the need. The problem with that being that half the men had no shirts! Jackson *"showed his annoyance"* that his head quack did not know exactly how much bandage cloth he had(!) but in the event, *"the expedient was never tried. General Lee decided that the attack would be too hazardous."*[445]

With a night attack no longer an option, much preparation, reorganisation and resupply was still needed, if the Second Corps was to be ready to repel assaults the next day, and, having successfully done so, to force a counter-stroke with immediate pursuit, against a further weakened enemy. Jackson allowed himself no more than three hours sleep that night, and by four o'clock the next morning had returned to the demanding task of writing and issuing instructions, and despatching couriers. On being told that General Maxcy Gregg was close to succumbing to wounds received in the breakthrough attack of the previous afternoon, Jackson ruffled McGuire further, by interrupting his tending the wounded, and sending the busy doctor to see if the dying General could be helped in any way. Jackson himself soon followed, to give what comfort he could to a fine and gallant soldier whom the command could ill-afford to lose; but with whom he had recently had one of his, frequent, 'senior officer spats'. Old Jack, typically, wanted to ease Gregg's last moments as far as he possibly could.

Returning daylight gradually revealed the Federal Army drawn out in full battle array, the turgid, dull-December water of the Rappahannock flowing at their backs, and looking, but for the littered, grizzled ground before them, as if the costly, bloody disorders of the previous day had never taken place. *"The skirmishers of the two armies were not much more than a hundred*

---

445 Dr McGuire in a letter to Henderson.

yards apart, concealed from each other's view by the high grass in which they were lying, and above which, from time to time, rose a small cloud of blue smoke, telling that a shot had been fired.'[446] The Confederates looked forward with some keenness to attacks on their position being resumed; but although both artillery and rifle fire was exchanged with varying degrees of intensity throughout the day, no Federal attacks materialised. The next morning – the second after the battle – Burnside finally signalled his intention to make no further attacks and admitted defeat by sending across a flag of truce, with the request he be allowed to bury the dead, amongst whom were a number of wounded who had been lying, untended, between the lines for nearly forty-eight hours. That night, their movements masked by a heavy and prolonged storm, the entire Federal Army withdrew, skilfully and un-challenged, back across the Rappahannock, taking with them all their guns and wagons. Only the fallout from the first day's fighting, was left behind on the battlefield, together with a few very seriously wounded in the blasted ruins of desolated and otherwise abandoned Fredericksburg.

If perceived wisdom harps upon the dangers of giving battle with a river immediately in rear, Burnside's experience highlights, yet again, that all general verbalising on the conduct of war can never be anything more than an *aide memoire,* covering points worth considering, in the actual conditions prevailing. No matter by whom they are uttered, they can never be a handbook to success. For Burnside, the several road bridges across the Rappahannock provided more avenues for a swift, clean disengagement, than would probably have been the case had he been in more open country, and dependent upon a single road together, possibly, with a railway line. The river speeded his exit, and, once across, provided an effective bulwark for the defence of an orderly withdrawal, and at the same time a serious obstacle to hot pursuit. Yet again, the hard-fighting, long-suffering

---

446 Henderson quoting Stuart's Chief-of-Staff.

soldiers of the Confederacy had shot and bayoneted their way to a battlefield success which yielded no, off-site, strategic gain. For Jackson it was surely doubly frustrating to have to fight the action, for which, weeks previously, he had predicted so accurately, a barren outcome.

After Fredericksburg, the armies effectively went into Winter Quarters, although between Christmas and New Year (1863) Stuart made another of his morale boosting; but as a direct contribution to war-winning, irrelevant; sweeps through Union territory.

He contrived to confuse those sent after him by breaking into Federal telegraph traffic with bogus messages purporting to indicate his position and movements. On this occasion he took more casualties than on previous jaunts, losing twenty-eight officers and men – out of an original one thousand eight hundred – in the course of covering some one hundred and fifty miles in four days. He signed-off in typically cavalier Stuart fashion, with a telegraph signal to General Meigs, Lincoln's Chief Quartermaster in Washington, requesting a better class of mule be supplied to the Army of the Potomac, as he was quite embarrassed by having to use the current crop to pull captured wagons into Confederate lines.

During the second half of January, Burnside *"made a futile attempt to march his army round Lee's flank"*; but the winter weather was so severe, and the Virginia roads at their bottomless worst, such that he soon gave up what came to be dubbed his *"Mud Campaign."* Intensive lobbying finally induced President Lincoln to disregard his own watchword *"never swap horses when crossing a stream,"* and on the twenty sixth of January, he replaced Burnside with General Hooker, the 'Fighting Joe' of Sharpsburg.

40. WINTER QUARTERS

....

*"Whilst it would be a great comfort
to see you and our darling little
daughter, duty appears to require
me to remain with my command.
It is important that those at
headquarters set an example
by staying at the post of duty."*

Tom in a letter to Anna

....

WRITING as the Victorian Century was drawing to a close, yet
while a number of those who had campaigned with Jackson were
still living and could answer queries and respond with first hand experiences, brought Henderson to the belief that *"the early spring of
1863 was undoubtedly one of the happiest seasons of a singularly happy life."*
Writing when all – including the great biographer – are long gone,
it is not possible to accept quite so sanguine a view of the emotional
Stonewall Jackson, either for his life overall, or during the final four
months. True, his natural instinct was to be up-beat, despite having been taken from a mother whom he adored; orphaned, when
she died two years later – his father having died when he was only
four – and being one of only two siblings out of four to advance
through adulthood. True too, that he would quite often say – especially in the pre–Civil War years *"Ah, now that is not the way to be happy."* Furthermore, although the sudden death of his first wife caused
him the greatest grief, he had two happy marriages. This, his second
marriage had just been blessed with a daughter, whom he would
see briefly, for the first time, during that final, first quarter of 1863,
when wife and daughter – *"Little Miss Stonewall"*[447] – visited him

---

447 Douglas.

in the field, and whom he would only see again in the final week before his death. Jackson set great store by marriage, and the very happiness of his own, surely contributed to his describing enforced separation on war service as a *"continual sacrifice."* In a letter to sister Laura, from the Mexican War, he wrote *"If any happiness is to be had in this world, it lies in the married state."*[448] In a letter to his sister-in-law, at the end of campaigning in 1862, he wrote *"I trust God will answer the prayers offered for peace. Not much comfort is to be expected until this cruel war terminates. I haven't seen my wife since last March, and never having seen my child, you can imagine with what interest I look to North Carolina."*[449] Professor Jackson did not share the Virginia passion for field sports; but, at the Virginia Military Institute, preferred driving out from Lexington into the glorious countryside of the Great Valley; walking, working on his small farm, or sightseeing in the country and cities of the Northern States, always in the company of his wife. Without question, to be joined by his wife and daughter, whilst *'remaining with his command'* would bring him great happiness, and he had far too great a control over his own mind and thoughts not to be able to take great pleasure from their visit. Without doubt too, Jackson had a great, even singular, capacity to garner happiness from life, However, he had far too clear an understanding of the War itself, and of the situation which the Confederacy faced after some twenty months of war, for an everyday happiness not to be shrouded by an internal, unexpressed anxiety.

The Second Army Corps went into Winter Quarters along the South Bank of the Rappahannock, with Corps Headquarters some eleven miles south-east of Fredericksburg, at Moss Neck. The General chose the Corbin mansion for his command post. Not wishing to disrupt the family, he settled on an outbuilding, the hunting lodge – or gun-room – of the estate, for his quarters. Having reached an understanding with the lady of the house, a Mrs Corbin, Jackson walked out to his horse, being held at the

---

448 Arnold.
449 Henderson quoting Jackson.

gate by a single, mounted, courier, his sole companion. *"Do you approve of your accommodation, General? The Trooper asked. "Yes, Sir, I have decided to make my quarters here." "I am Mr Corbin, Sir ...* replied the soldier ... *and I am very pleased."* The gun-room was adorned with sporting memorabilia. Hunting, shooting and fishing trophies, and engravings. The slot or head of a deer, the mask or pad of a fox or wolf, and the likenesses of an especially audacious hunt terrier, or bold, front-running hound. All of which Jeb Stuart, when he visited, was quick to play-on, suggesting with gay good humour that the collection reflected Jackson's own sporting tastes – *"indicating a great decline in his moral character, which would be a grief and disappointment to the pious old ladies of the South."*[450] Whilst Stuart's devil-may-care good humour was enjoyed by Jackson as much as anyone, he openly admitted – when the laughter had subsided – that he had probably had more to do with racing horses than his boisterous younger friend realised. As an orphan teenager, Nephew Tom had been Cummings Jackson's jockey of choice, and the Uncle's pairings had led to some memorable wins on the racetrack close by the family homestead. On days of ordinary, headquarters routine, on the other hand, with Stuart absent, *"His gravity of demeanour seldom wholly disappeared, his intense earnestness was in itself oppressive, and he was often absent and preoccupied. 'Life at headquarters ...* Henderson wrote, quoting a letter from Dr McGuire ... *was decidedly dull. Our meals were often very dreary. The General had no time for light or trivial conversation, and he sometimes felt it his duty to rebuke our thoughtless and perhaps foolish remarks. Nor was it always quite safe to approach him. Sometimes he had a tired look in his eyes, and although he never breathed a word to one or another, we knew that he was dissatisfied with what was being done with the army.'"* Emotionally, Moss Neck was a far cry from the relatively carefree, child-infused romping of the previous Winter, which he had so enjoyed as home life with Mrs Jackson. Absent also was the stimulus of discursive, intellectual

---

450 Henderson.

ponderings, enjoyed amid the learned volumes in the library of the Graham Manse in Winchester.

Jackson's own relationship with the War – and, probably, his perception of where the Confederacy stood with regard to an outcome – would have changed radically in the twelve months intervening between those first two winters of the War; not simply because of his promotion to Lieutenant-General and resulting position within the Army of Northern Virginia. In the first winter there was an exciting optimism, a confidence and positive anticipation. A degree of novelty, from which any thought of failure was absent. By the second winter, Jackson's own record as a battle-field commander had so escalated, as to stand higher than that of any other General – South or North – and was widely recognised and acclaimed as such, by both soldier and civilian, on both sides of the Divide. On riding out from Moss Neck, on his rounds of the positions picketing the Rappahannock, on one occasion, for example; the usual yells and cheers greeted his arrival, and the Union pickets on the far bank would shout across asking what it was all about. On being told who was visiting, a cry of *"Hurrah for Stonewall Jackson"* rang out from the ranks of the enemy. It is a more than a fair bet that no other General – Grey or Blue – could have elicited such a response from the opposition. It is just this unparalleled achievement and reputation, which his genius had crafted, which throws more than simply doubt upon any but momentary, passing flashes, of personal happiness. His very reputation, placed alongside the overall conduct of the War, would have been enough to provide grounds for concern, despite his seemingly impervious self-control.

Stonewall Jackson had achieved an unbroken run of success against every Northern General who had opposed him and, consistently, the numerical odds had always been against him. His tactical imagination and aptitude had got the measure of every situation and had been matched by no other commander fighting in Virginia. And yet! And yet! For all the pounding manoeuvres, the vigorous marches, incisive attacks, and deft, finely-held defensives, the cause of securing States Rights, for which the

Confederacy of Secession was originally constituted, had not been advanced one iota since the outbreak of war. Despite the bruising, the numerical might of the North was as strong as ever, and despite inept Generals playing commissariat to Jackson's lightning strikes, and Stuart's all-embracing sweeps, the Northern soldier still received an un-interrupted torrent of ammunition, guns and equipment. Hostile armies still squatted on Virginian soil, and an alien uniform still oppressed her citizens.

Not a single proposal for *"taking the aggressive"*, put forward by the South's one consistent winner, had been taken up, since the failure to follow-up battle-field victory at First Manassas seventeen months earlier. The complacent do-nothing weeks of the culpable and fatally inanimate Johnston, of the previous summer and autumn, to the barren convulsions of the Seven Days Battles south of Richmond, and the recent, wholly unproductive achievements of Second Manassas, and the Sharpsburg and Fredericksburg battles, to Jackson above all, his instincts and profound intellectual assessments largely being ignored, can only have proved frustratingly correct. Such local successes as Confederate arms had achieved in the past eighteen months, had been achieved by his intellect and his unrelenting, vigorous application. That as late as January 1863, the Confederate political establishment could still believe that the War could be resolved in its favour by nothing more than a passive defence and the wishful notion of outside intervention, was surely a source of acute anxiety to Jackson, with his closely observed understanding of the War in all its aspects, and in every theatre. Whilst the outside world beat a path to the enforced, requisitioned door of his encampment, in recognition of his unique ability, the 'hooded falcon' would have felt very much the 'prophet crying in the wilderness', despite his clear and often-stated loyalty and support for Lee. A most unhappy condition, and one, probably, only made tenable by his unshakeable belief in the Almighty, and, at best, only fleetingly alleviated by the visit of a much-loved wife and new-born daughter.

The War attracted soldiers of fortune from overseas to fight on both sides, and the reputations of fame attracted the curious, simply to visit. One English Captain, who had fought in the Crimea, brought with him a *"box of goods (a present from England) for General Stonewall Jackson,"* and having reached Richmond was invited to Moss Neck. Around ten o'clock one morning, he reached the nearest rail station, and then walked the *"eight or nine miles"* to Corps headquarters. *"Wet to the skin, I stumbled through mud (Virginia mud is quite as villainous as that of Balaclava) – a heavy fall of snow had covered the country for some time before, to the depth of a foot ... but ... my journey was made in a drenching shower. I waded through creeks, I passed through pine-woods, and at last got into camp at about two o'clock."* An orderly took the Captain's name and he was immediately ushered in. *"The General rose and greeted me warmly. I ... was most agreeably surprised and pleased with his appearance. He is tall and handsome, and powerfully built, but thin. He has brown hair and a brown beard. His mouth expresses great determination. The lips are thin and compressed firmly together; his eyes are blue and dark, with a keen and searching expression. I was told his age was thirty eight. He looks forty. The General, who is indescribably simple and unaffected in all his ways, took off my wet overcoat with his own hands, made up the fire, brought wood for me to put my feet on, to keep them warm while my boots were drying. ... At the dinner hour we went out and joined members of his staff. At this meal the General said grace in a fervent, quiet manner, which struck me very much.* After dinner, Jackson chatted with his guest, and when Jim came in and laid out his mattress and his blankets, he offered to share them with the Captain. *"I thanked him very much for his courtesy but said 'Good-night' and slept in a tent, sharing the blankets of one of his aides-de camp. ... at breakfast time I noticed the General said grace ... with the same fervour I had remarked before."* For his return to the station, the Captain had borrowed a horse, and on his going to say farewell, found his greatcoat being dried in front of the fire in the General's room. He came in, saying *"Captain, I have been trying to dry your greatcoat, but I am afraid I have not succeeded very well."* For the guest, the act was typical of his host. *"With the care and responsibilities of a vast army on his shoulders, he finds time to do little acts of kindness and thoughtfulness."*

"Of military history", said another English soldier-visitor, *"he knew more than any other man I met in America; and he was so far from displaying the somewhat grim characteristics that have been associated with his name, that one would have thought his tastes lay in the direction of art and literature."* For 'The Times' Correspondent – the Hon. Francis Lawley – *"who knew him well, ... His chief delight was in the cathedrals of England, notably in York Minster and Westminster Abbey. He was never tired of talking about them or listening to details about the chapels and cloisters of Oxford."*[451] On being visited by a future Chief of the Imperial General Staff, he *"certainly had very little to say about military operations ...* Lord Wolseley wrote ... *although he was intensely proud of his soldiers ... it was impossible to make him talk of his own achievements. ... His manner ... was most attractive. He put you at your ease at once, listening with marked courtesy and attention to whatever you might say; and when the subject was congenial, he was a most interesting companion. I quite endorse the statement as to his love for beautiful things. He told me that in all his travels he had seen nothing so beautiful as the lancet window in York Minster."*

In the winter months at Moss Neck, Jackson showed himself clearly as both man of God and unflinching soldier. *"The Stonewall brigade set the example ... the men of their own volition built a log church where both officers and men, without distinction of rank, were accustomed to assemble during the winter evenings."* Both Lee and Stuart were frequently of the congregation. Jackson led the drive to appoint padres at both Regiment and Brigade level, throughout the Army, as well as the inviting of ministers *"from all parts of the country,"* to visit and to preach. Earlier in the year, on the Rappahannock, Captain Blackford had witnessed Jackson in the role of, what he termed, 'warrior-saint'. At a temporary halt, the young wife of a railway worker, fetched from a nearby cottage, her baby boy *"of about eighteen months and handing it up to the General asked him to bless* (the child) *for her. ...* Without showing any surprise ... *he*

---

451 Francis Lawley in 'The Times', June 11, 1863 – and other visitor comments – quoted by Henderson.

turned to her in great earnestness, and with a pleasant expression on his face, took the child in his arms, held it to his breast, closed his eyes and seemed to be, and I no doubt was, occupied for a minute or two in prayer, during which we took off our hats, and the young mother leaned her head over the horses shoulder, as if uniting in the prayer. ... Around-about the soldiers in their worn and patched clothing, in a circle at a respectful distance, ... Jackson, the warrior-saint of another era, with the child in his arms, head bowed until his greying (sic) *beard touched the fresh young hair of the child, pressed close to the shabby coat ... so well acquainted with death. For the first time, it brought to me that this stern, enigmatic man ... had another side to him ... that of a tender man of family. He handed the child back to its mother without a word, who thanked him with streaming eyes, while he rode off back down the road."[52]* The man too, who amid all the pressure and uncertainty of the night following the battle of Fredericksburg, made time to comfort the last moments of the dying Confederate General Maxcy Gregg, in a scene which *"made a deeper impression on those who witnessed it than the accumulated horrors of the battle field,"* so Dr McGuire told Henderson. The man who, having ridden back to his battle headquarters, the Doctor then *"put the question as to the best means of coping with the overwhelming number of the enemy ... gave the uncompromising reply ... Kill them, Sir! Kill every (single) one."* The same leader who was meticulous in caring for the wounded enemy. Jackson too, could listen with tears welling in his eyes to a plea of leniency in the face of a court martial death verdict – and would even suggest further reasons for clemency – but would nonetheless confirm the sentence with his signature, on the grounds it was for the good of the Army and the Cause, and it was, therefore, his duty to uphold the findings of the Court. In the final reckoning, the man for whom duty was absolute, and could be undertaken in no other way, but to the very limit of his considerable ability.

With the coming of April, and the approach of Spring, Jackson moved his headquarters nearer to the river, and put himself under

---

452 Blackford.

canvas. *"It is rather a relief ...* he wrote *... to get where there will be less comfort than in a room, as I hope thereby persons will be prevented from encroaching so much upon my time."*[453] On the arrival of Anna and Julia, he moved back into a house, on *"Mr Yerby's plantation, near Hamilton's Crossing. ... but ... he did not permit the presence of his family ...* Mrs Jackson recalled *... to interfere in any way with his military duties. The greater part of each day he spent at his headquarters but returned as early as he could get off from his labours and devoted all his leisure time to his visitors – little Julia having his chief attention and his care."*[454]

It was still dark, when early on the morning of the twenty ninth of April, messages began coming in that the enemy was stirring. Heavy and sustained gunfire soon followed. Jackson, at once, arranged for Anna and Julia to leave immediately for Richmond, and himself rode off to the outposts. With his unmatched understanding of the importance of time in war he, typically, did not wait for breakfast.

---

453 Jackson quoted by Henderson.
454 Anna Jackson quoted by Henderson.

41. AGAINST THE ODDS

....

*"I do not profess any romantic sentiments
as to the vanity of life. Certainly, no man
has more that should make life dear to him
than I have, in the affection of my home;
but I do not desire to survive
the independence of my country."*
Stonewall Jackson

....

AS he rode to where, amongst the cheerful vagrants of his front-line, he could read for himself the emerging turmoil of the enemy, the General concentrated on earlier, equally solitary, meditations on the options open to the would-be controlling mind opposite. On General Hooker. *"A strict disciplinarian with a talent for organisation."*[455] Jackson was well versed on how the North had made good use of the months of Winter Quarters. From bitter experience, Lincoln and his Secretary of War had learnt to support and not to meddle, and *"unity of purpose and concentration"* of effort had resulted. Their current C-in-C, General 'Fighting Joe' Hooker, had worked hard over the winter, to repair the morale of the Army of the Potomac, as it lay mired and depressed in the glutinous Virginia mud, following defeat at Fredericksburg. Hooker's take-over muster found *"two thousand nine hundred and twenty-two commissioned officers and eighty-one thousand nine hundred and sixty-four non-commissioned officers and privates absent … the majority from causes unknown."* An absentee problem bigger than Lee's entire army. Hooker reorganised both cavalry and infantry; replaced ineffective generals; recruited new regiments; recovered absentees and instigated intensive

---

455 Henderson.

field training. It was a rejuvenated Army of the Potomac opening the campaign one hundred and thirty thousand strong, with four hundred and twenty-eight artillery pieces, and some faith in their new commander.

Apart from the training and refitting of regiments by officers in the field, the South, by contrast, had largely frittered away the cold months of inactivity. Davis and his new Secretary of War, Seddon, had reverted to the old evil of political meddling.

Lee had been induced to detach two Divisions to secure Richmond from what the politicians imagined was a threat from the Atlantic coast. Given the threat posed by the Army of the Potomac, it was an unfortunate irrelevance, made doubly so, by the appointment of Longstreet to the command. He seems to have had little understanding of the overall strategic situation; of the responsibility of a detached commander, or of the vital importance of time in all military undertakings.

Once again, Longstreet went against Lee's better judgement, which was *"so to dispose his troops that they could return to the Rappahannock at the first alarm."*[456] Instead, at Seddon's instigation, he undertook the irrelevant siege of the town of Suffolk, some one hundred miles distant from the Rappahannock, at the mouth of the James River. When Hooker opened the 1863 campaigning season, Lee had to face the main threat with an army of just sixty-two thousand all ranks and all arms, equipped with one hundred and seventy guns. In addition, *"sufficient supplies for a forward movement ... which Lee was determined to make ... had not yet been accumulated ... and ... two brigades of cavalry ... sent to South Carolina and the Valley, had not re-joined."*

Jackson's ultimate intention too was to attack the enemy. Knowing the strength of the Federal build-up, a member of staff had suggested that in the face of such numbers, there would be no other option than to retreat. Jackson responded *"sharply ...*

---

456 Henderson.

No, Sir, we shall not fall back, we shall attack them."[457] Two Divisions on Hooker's Left Wing, bridged the Rappahannock below Fredericksburg, under cover of early morning fog. As it lifted, Jackson watched them crossing, and entrenching the ground on which their attacks had been driven back last December. The thirty-seven thousand men of Second Corps he had moving-up into positions along the wooded ridge from where they had triumphed last December. The relatively small number busy below indicated that Hooker was, probably, on the move elsewhere, and, if so, had divided his Army. Over the winter the Confederates had fortified some twenty miles of the river's south bank. A frontal attack was, therefore, unlikely – especially in the light of Fredericksburg – but given Federal numbers, the fortified lines could be overlapped with some ease. Having considered the ground in front of him, Jackson and Lee agreed, that he could not exploit the opportunity presented by the small number before him. The Rappahannock both secured the flanks of the position and would bar any attempt at a turning manoeuvre. Hooker would have to be turned elsewhere. Where exactly, would depend on how he had chosen to come forward.

In the close, heavily wooded country, enemy movements were not easily detectable. To Jackson's left, the great Wilderness of Spotsylvania, stretching some twenty miles to the westward, and fifteen miles north-south, was crossed by only two roads and an unfinished railway line, and had few tracks and clearings amongst *"the groves of pines … immersed in a sea of scrub-oak and luxuriant undergrowth."*[458] In that direction, Hooker had goaded the right flank of the refurbished Army of the Potomac into un-typical vigour and activity. *"In three days, they had marched forty-six miles over bad roads, had forded breast-high two difficult rivers, established several*

---

457 Henderson quoting Jackson.
458 Ibid.

bridges[459], *and captured over one hundred prisoners.*" Hooker had insinuated seventy thousand men – their rations, equipment and ammunition either carried or on pack-mules – into Lee's rear, and "*saw victory within his grasp.*" The Federal Commander-in-Chief crowed in a General Order "*It is with heartfelt satisfaction that the Commanding General announces to his army that the operations of the last three days have determined that our enemy must either ingloriously fly or come out from behind his defences, and give us battle on our own ground, where certain destruction awaits him.*" Henderson described Hooker as "*skinning the lion while the beast still lived.*" Jackson's hard-swearing Chief Quartermaster would doubtless have advised "*Don't holler till you're out of the wood, General!*" For all his commendable vigour and aggressive activity, Hooker had failed to realise the supremely important element of surprise. Stuart's brilliant handling of his cavalry had enabled him to observe all and to report on all, and on this basic information – with the agreement of Lee – the 'ardent genius' of Stonewall Jackson went unhesitatingly into over-drive.

---

459 Henderson notes: "*The total weight carried by each man, including sixty rounds of ammunition, was forty-five lbs. The reserve ammunition was carried principally by pack mules, and only a small number of wagons crossed the Rappahannock. Four pontoon bridges were laid by the engineers. One bridge took three quarters of an hour to lay; the other three, one and a half hours to lay, and an hour to take up. Each bridge was from one hundred to one hundred and forty yards long.*"

41/1. Final Triumph

....

*"I feel that His hand led me –
Let us give Him the glory."*
Stonewall Jackson

....

LEAVING General Jubal Early with ten thousand men to watch and contain the thirty-five thousand of the two Federal left wing Divisions, Jackson led the twenty-seven thousand bulk of the Second Corps westwards on the plank road, through the darkness of the night and the forests of the Wilderness. By the early morning of the first of May, Second Corps had reached the extreme left of Lee's line, held by the eight thousand men of General Anderson's Division, approximately half of what was left of First Corps, after Longstreet had spirited the other half, far beyond recall, for his irrelevant besieging of Suffolk Town. The Division of General McLaws had also joined-up, having moved parallel to Jackson, on the Wilderness turnpike. *"With the help of Lee's engineers, Anderson had strongly entrenched the whole front,"* facing west, the direction from which Hooker would approach. Jackson was not of a mind to surrender any initiative and wait on the defensive. He stopped work on the fortifications, and by eleven o'clock the whole Confederate Army was moving westwards, through the heart of the Wilderness, in three columns, with Stuart's cavalry well forward.

Hooker, having got his main body on to Lee's left flank, had drawn up his three great Corps in the form of a gnarled hockey stick; its handle resting on the Rappahannock; the knobbly shaft running south for some three miles, before the arc of the foot curved back and up to the west, to take-in Chancellorsville, situated at a junction of the plank and pike roads. The fatal flaw in Hooker's plan was, that the colossus – for all military purposes – was effectively blind and, unlike Cyclops, the blinding was self-inflicted. Hooker's manoeuvrings would seem to have been undertaken with the intention of positioning the Army of the Potomac closer to Richmond, rather than focusing on the destruction of the Army of Northern Virginia. To this end, he sent his newly constituted Cavalry Corps, some ten thousand horsemen wide out ahead of his advance, to threaten Lee's supply lines, on the misguided assumption that Lee would protect them with an immediate retreat towards Richmond. (Apart from failing to appreciate the attacking styles of both Lee and Jackson, it does not seem to have occurred to Hooker that the Confederates might have looked on the Army of the Potomac as a more generous source of supply than the straightened resources of the Confederacy!) Only a single Cavalry brigade accompanied the Federal advance, and this, Stuart easily dominated, concentrating his horsemen at the place of vital importance – between the armies – from where he was able both to accumulate intelligence and deny it to the enemy. Hooker believed that so massive a cavalry presence *"would draw off the whole of the Confederate horse;"* but Stuart was not so easily to be taken out of the reckoning. Detaching just two of his mounted regiments, under General W.H.F. Lee, to monitor the cavalry incursion, he wheeled away to the west, before coming in along the length of the advancing Federal right flank, to take prisoners from the Fifth, Eleventh and Twelfth Corps, which enabled him to define the strength of Hooker's main body. *"… having obtained the information he required, Stuart, moved across the front, and routing one of Pleasonton's regiments …* part of the solitary Cavalry brigade Hooker had retained with the Army … *in a night attack near Spotsylvania Court House, regained touch with his own Army."*

Hooker was taking several quite admirable expedients intended to cope with how the situation might unfold; but, at this point, none were based on the actual situation, and how it was unfolding in reality. To all intents and purposes, he might have been issuing orders in a vacuum, as if no thinking, active enemy existed. But the three-column Army Jackson was advancing through the Wilderness was strenuously driving forward;

constantly on the alert, and ever-scheming. Even at this stage, Jackson would have had in mind one of his trade-mark turning manoeuvres which, in the expression of a mercenary officer on Stuart's Staff, made him *"the supremest flanker and rearer,"[460]* but, for the moment, he did not have all the pieces of the pattern he needed, to make it happen. Hooker pointed the unseeing juggernaut east, towards his two left flank Divisions, crouched and contained by Jubal Early's ten thousand, despite the injunction: *"to observe the enemy's movements with the utmost vigilance; should he expose a weak point, to attack him in full force and destroy him; should he show any symptom of falling back, to pursue him with the utmost vigour."[461]* In the Wilderness, a clash soon followed, and the Confederate right-hand column speedily deployed. *"the fight was spirited but short."* Jackson, riding with the centre column, *"informed of the encounter, had ordered troops on the* (central) *plank road to move briskly forward, and the Federals, finding their right in danger of being enveloped, retired."* Soon afterwards, cavalry and skirmishers of the Confederate central column, engaged the enemy coming towards them on the plank road. Again, Jackson ordered forward a brigade, from the left-hand column this time, out to his left, moving on the unfinished railway line. Again, a threatening enveloping movement caused the Federals to fall back.

It was by now around two thirty in the afternoon, and Jackson sent a written message to General McLaws, in command of the right-hand column, from *"Headquarters, Second Corps, Army of Northern Virginia, first of May 1863, two thirty p.m. 'General – The Lieutenant-General commanding directs me to say that he is pressing up the plank road; also, that you will press on up the turnpike towards Chancellorsville, as the enemy is falling back. Keep your skirmishers and flanking parties well out, to guard against ambuscade. Very respectfully*

460 Major Heros von Borcke quoted by Douglas.

461 Henderson.

etc., etc.[462] Still the situation cannot have been exactly clear to Jackson. Out beyond the right-hand column, the Third Virginia Cavalry reported a brief encounter with a Federal force of cavalry, infantry and artillery. After a short fight, the Federals, again withdrew. One attempt at reconnaissance nearly ended in disaster, when Jackson, accompanied by Stuart, various of their staff members, and a battery of horse gunners, rode forward along a narrow woodland bridle-path, heading for a small patch of high ground. *"Scarcely had the smoke of our first shot cleared away, when a couple of masked batteries suddenly opened up on us at close range and enveloped us in a storm of shell and canister, ... did fearful execution among our party, men and horses falling right and left. ... that Jackson and Stuart with their staff officers escaped was nothing short of miraculous."*[463] But, as the evening drew on, and Federal resistance stiffened, further reconnaissance revealed Hooker *"... had assumed a position of great natural strength, surrounded on all sides by dense forest, filled with a tangled undergrowth, in the midst of which breastworks of logs had been constructed, with trees felled in front, so as to form an almost impenetrable abattis."*[464] At much the same time as Jackson and Lee came to realise that Hooker had gone over to the defensive, Hooker recognised that, far from *"ingloriously flying"*, the Confederates were coming at him with unrelenting vigour. His aggressive initiative, so forcefully and actively begun, seeped away. Given his superiority in numbers, it is a change of heart difficult to understand, unless 'Fighting Joe' simply lost his nerve in the face of unexpected aggression. Or, he was inhibited by what he himself was surely coming to realise was an ill-founded misuse of his newly refurbished cavalry arm. Given all that the Army of Northern Virginia had accomplished with inferior numbers, since July of the previous year, it seems hardly

462 Henderson quoting instruction sent by the hand of J.G. Morrison, Acting Assistant Adjutant-General.
463 Henderson quoting Heros von Borcke.
464 Henderson quoting Lee.

possible that Hooker could have imagined his immediate opponents capable of self-destruction in another Longstreet-instigated, Malvern Hill-style attack.

That night, General Hooker indulged in what leaders of the stature of Stonewall Jackson, in every era, have dismissed as a recipe for enervating ineffectiveness. He held a Council of War, the result of which was typical of such a craven measure. Some said attack; some said wait to be attacked. On the right, Hooker's subordinates *"were confident of the strength of their entrenchments. … Hooker himself wished to contract his lines so as to strengthen them. … it was at length determined that the army should await attack in its present position."* In other words, avoid a positive decision, and do nothing.

That same night, no more than three miles distant on *"the plank road, under a grove of oak and pine, Lee and Jackson, while their wearied soldiers slept around them, planned for the fourth and last time the overthrow of the great army with which Lincoln still hoped to capture Richmond."* Their deliberations were of a very different character from those of their opponents.

Jackson was firmly of the view that Hooker should be attacked the next day – in the event he had not retreated. Given his defensive move, Jackson felt Hooker was already becoming demoralised. Earlier, before dark, Lee himself had reconnoitred the Federal left, stretching back to the Rappahannock, and *"two of Jackson's staff had reconnoitred the front."* No weaknesses were detected along the length of the Federal line; but then *"Stuart rode in with the reports of his cavalry officers, and the weak point of the position was at once revealed."*[465] The right of the Federal line was a bare, open end, secured neither by natural obstacle nor engineering work.

Before daybreak the next morning, Jackson had roused Jed Hotchkiss, and sent him to the nearby house of a Colonel Welford, to see if local knowledge might reveal a practical road round to the rear of the Federal position, that was not shown on the engineer's

465 Henderson.

maps. Back in little more than an hour, Hotchkiss found the two Generals conferring once more, sitting facing one another on recently abandoned Federal *"cracker boxes."* Hotchkiss spread out his freshly marked map on a third. Colonel Welford had recently constructed a road *"for the purpose of hauling cord-wood and iron to his furnace."*[466] It led away from the Federal position – the required direction; and linked with the Brock Road, which ran at right angles, and wound its way to the Plank Road, which it reached a mile and half or so beyond the right of Hooker's line. Less than a mile further on was the Wilderness Turnpike, more or less parallel, as it led out from Chancellorsville, and the very heart of the Federal defences.

Hotchkiss having indicated the Welford Road, *"General Lee then said, 'General Jackson, what do you propose to do?" He replied, 'Go around here,' moving his finger over the road I had located upon the map. General Lee then asked, 'What do you propose to make this movement with?' 'With my whole Corps,' was the answer. General Lee then asked, 'What will you leave me?' 'The Divisions of Anderson and McLaws,' said Jackson. General Lee, after a moment's reflection, remarked, 'Well go on,' and then, pencil in hand, gave his last instructions. Jackson, with an eager smile upon his face, from time to time nodded assent, and when the Commander-in-Chief ended with the words, 'General Stuart will cover your movement with his cavalry,' he rose and saluted, saying, 'My troops will move at once, Sir.' The necessary orders were forthwith dispatched."*[467]

Discipline on the flank march was tight. Henderson even writes *"all stragglers were to be bayoneted."* Such a measure is very much at variance with the rest of Jackson's conduct throughout the War. Not at all typical. Due process was always a pre-requisite, and such a measure is too obviously open to abuse. Just possibly, like his reaction to Colonel Grigsby's mutineers during the Valley Campaign, the threat might be seen as a bluff; but bluffing was

---

466 Henderson quoting a letter received from Major Hotchkiss.
467 Ibid.

about the last characteristic to associate with Stonewall Jackson. In his recently issued, general marching instruction to the Second Army Corps, Jackson makes no such threat, so possibly, it was a stipulation inserted by Lee, specifically for this operation. In which case, it would have had Jackson's tacit approval when, as Jed Hotchkiss recounted, he witnessed Lee pencilling the final operation order. Such a measure is not typical of either General.

Lee stood watching as the column moved out, preceded by the Fifth Virginia Cavalry, with squadrons of the Second, Third and Fifth providing an active, fluid screen in 'no-man's land' to the right of the line of march. Riding close behind his leading infantry, Jackson *"drew rein,"* and a military pairing of the stature of Marlborough and Eugene conversed briefly for the last time. A Federal General observed the column moving away from him and shelled the turning point on the Welford Road. Then, noticing that the wagon trains were following the front line troops, Hooker *"jumped to the conclusion"* that Lee was retreating. The situation was developed, and infantry became involved in a brief but vigorous skirmish, from which the Federals were driven back. Jackson, with the bulk of the Second Corps, was well on, and he ignored the intervention. Lee had overall control of the diversionary 'sniping' being actively carried-out on Hooker's Front, by the Divisions of Anderson and McLaws. Reaching the Plank Road, the first of the two roads leading out from Chancellorsville, Stuart's leading cavalry commander, General Fitzhugh Lee, requested Jackson to accompany him to some high ground, where he could see down upon the Federal position.

"Bring only one courier … as you will be in view. … The situation was still as Fitzhugh Lee had first observed. (*"Two cannons … upon the high road, the horses grazing close at hand. The* (Federal) *soldiers were scattered in small groups, laughing, cooking, smoking, sleeping, playing cards, while others were butchering cattle and drawing rations."*) *I watched him closely …* General Fitzhugh Lee recalled … *His expression was one of intense interest. His eyes burnt with a brilliant glow, and his face was lightly flushed, radiant at the success of his flank movement. To the remarks made to him while the unconscious line of blue was*

pointed out, he made no reply. And yet during the five minutes he was on the hill his lips were moving. 'Tell General Rodes,' he said, suddenly turning his horse towards his courier, 'to move across the plank road, and halt when he gets to the old turnpike. I will join him there.' One more look at the Federal lines, and he rode rapidly down the hill.[468]

With the Stonewall brigade and squadrons of Stuart's cavalry securing the Plank Road, Rodes moved his Division as ordered, and by four p.m. on the afternoon of the second of May, Stonewall Jackson had poised twenty-five thousand men on Hooker's open and oblivious right flank. The Federal Commander-in-Chief, and his subordinate Generals were, all of them, none the wiser. Almost at this very moment, Hooker sent a message across to his Left Wing, still immobile beyond Fredericksburg, under the steady gaze of Jubal Early, which contained the line *"We know that the enemy is fleeing, trying to save his trains."* During the day, the Federal C-in-C had imbued his Generals with his own belief that they were unlikely to be subjected to a flank attack. Once again, in opposing Stonewall Jackson, a Federal General was making the fatal mistake of interpreting a situation according to his own wishes, rather than defining and interpreting the possibilities inherent in the reality. An hour earlier Jackson had sent a final note to Lee *"Near three p.m. May the second, 1863. General – The enemy has made a stand at Chancellor's, which is about two miles from Chancellorsville. I hope as soon as practicable to attack. I trust that an ever-kind Providence will bless us with success. Respectfully, T.J. Jackson, Lieutenant-General.* Adding the postscript *"The leading Division is up, and the next two appear well closed. T.J.J.* He spent two hours meticulously preparing and aligning the Second Corps for the imminent attack. He *"was determined that the troops should move forward in good order, and that every officer and man should know what was expected from him. ... The whole force was to push resolutely forward through the forest ...* Having taken the first, crucial, objective, *an open hill – about a thousand yards eastwards,* which overlooked a

468 Henderson quoting General Fitzhugh Lee.

ridge-line running back, northwards, into the heart of Hooker's position, where, *if the Federals … then … showed a determined front, Rodes was to halt under cover until the artillery could come up and dislodge them. Under no circumstances was there to be any pause in the advance.*"[469] Jackson had a Field Hospital set up, in rear of the start line, at the Old Wilderness Tavern.

By around six p.m. the brigades of General Rodes – forming the first line of attack – had moved up, spreading out into the forest on either side of the Turnpike. Bayonets were fixed and with Regimental Colours streaming free, even those who had already marched some fifteen miles that day, were champing to be let loose against the complacent invader, slack and unaware beyond the immediate thickets. On the Turnpike, in the centre of his attack formation, *"Jackson, watch in hand, sat silent on 'Little Sorrel,' – the peak … of his reassuringly familiar old campaign cap … drawn low over his eyes, and with his lips tightly compressed."* There were little more than two hours of good shooting light left in the day. Jackson's unwavering resolve to attack marked him – yet again; but for the last time – as the truly great battlefield commander. The common run of everyday Generals would likely have delayed, in an attempt to shore-up a fainter heart with the pretext of more daylight at the beginning of a day; thereby missing the ever-fleeting opportunity. Longstreet's defiance of Lee's order to go forward at the end of the day at Second Manassas – and Lee's own second-rate acceptance of his subordinate's crass 'await the morrow' reasoning, is a case in point. With Jackson, one thinks of Nelson at the Nile, swooping, without a moment's pause, on the inert enemy fleet, at the tail-end of a Mediterranean summer day. Jackson could hear the rumble and screech of the gun, and gun limber wheels, as the artillery closed-up, and the steady, resolute thump of A.P. Hill's Light Division shaking-out behind the vanguard. Possibly, with a final searching gaze to left and right and a last glance at the watch, he looked across at Rodes.

---

469 Henderson.

"You can go forward, Sir." A curt jerk of the head towards his skirmish-line commander, Major Blackford, before a gesture for the single bugle call that Rodes set ringing through the forest – to be immediately matched and embraced by a dozen others – and the surprise attack was set in motion.

Thrusting strands of skirmishers threaded forward amongst the bushes, before the surging battle lines turned the, initial, seeping trickle into a raging torrent, and the bugle's call was displaced by the resounding 'Rebel Yell', flaring birds and beasts into honest flight, and, beyond the advance, freezing guilty men to momentary inactivity. Inside half an hour, Old Jack was riding by Talley's Farm, the signs of surprised confusion strewing the ground in every direction. Dead and wounded men; dead and dying horses; broken and abandoned wagons; camps and camp fires deserted by all but bodies, and *"knapsacks piled in regular order"* still; prisoners being rounded-up and marched to the rear, through the *'smoke and dust'*, Distant Federal guns added to the confusion, lobbing shells about the *'open hill'*. The ground sloped away from Tally's into a shallow open valley, now with a smothering of men and horses running and hobbling through the spurts of dust and smoke. Beyond, the ground rose gradually into a low ridge, ablaze from end to end with gun and rifle fire from the last, manned, entrenchments of Hooker's Right Flank Corps. Running forward, to pause and take aim, to fire, reload and run on; disordered by the speed and strength of the successes amidst thick undergrowth, and with more space being shot in the wavering attack-line, the momentum for a moment began to sag. Officers ran out ahead, swords drawn, and with a wild, supporting yell, the Second Line of the Light Division swept in behind the thinned; but still leading, files. Beneath their mingled Colours, the boosted mass swirled up the slope in one solid, unstoppable torrent. The hitherto gallant defenders leapt from behind their abattis, scrapes and parapets, and ran for their lives. In no more than sixty minutes, Jackson's lean, ill-nourished, veterans had dispersed and demolished a discipline Corps ten thousand strong.

Darkness was seeping in; but Old Jack had in his sights Hooker's line of escape, a road, not more than half a mile distant, leading back to the fords of the Rappahannock. On and around the Turnpike, close amongst his front line troops, he had one urgent, stark and simple, unavoidable message; *"On! On! On! Press them!"* Something less than a mile and a half away, the demeanour and temper of the opposing Command-in-Chief had been somewhat different. As seven o'clock approached, Hooker, accompanied by two Aides, was sitting back on the verandah of the house in Chancellorsville serving his Headquarters. Spurred boot-heels rested on the light wood rail. He had strengthened his front line; such cavalry as was with the Army had been sent forward, and the firing from the front had slackened, and was fading. What was, in reality, the diversionary skirmishing being carried out by McLaws and Anderson – under Lee's overall charge – was, for Hooker, the Confederate retreat. All was going well and fitted his personal scenario. Pleased and at ease, he continued chatting with his two Aides. Still talking, the three glanced around, casually, towards the east. Firing. From a fresh direction. After a few moments, a Staff Officer walked past, and out into the roadway, to scan with field glasses, the steadily increasing racket. After several minutes careful scanning, he abruptly lowered the glasses, and swung round towards the verandah, bellowing at his Chief as he did so *"My God! Here they come!"* Even given 'Fighting Joe's' active career, it must have been something of a defining – not to say paralysing – moment, made all the more acute, when having sprinted for his horse and galloped towards the action, he learned from amid the fleeing chaos of men and animals, that a Confederate Army had rounded and disintegrated his whole right flank and, was already well in behind his fortified line, and bearing down on the heart of the whole defensive, about which he had earlier, a trifle smugly, commented *"How strong! How strong!"* Still more enervating, he learnt that the Confederates were led by the General whom Federal Generals least wished to be confronted by; Stonewall Jackson. For Hooker, the realisation that his considerable fighting qualities were insufficient to ensure success, that, in war, extreme mental and physical vigour, of a high order, are paramount, must have been sobering in the extreme. As Marshall Saxe has it *"The legs ... directed by the intellect ... – not the arms – are the key to the battlefield."* Or, as was said in the Century before Saxe took the field, and Jackson understood so completely, *"Wars are won by industry and cunning, rather than the actual clash of arms."*[470] But, for his all too languid periods, the Federal General was to get off rather more lightly than he deserved. He was to be let off the hook, as it were, with nothing worse than a retreat; a retreat without even the complication of a pursuit.

41/2. Controlling Mind Withdrawn

....

" . . . and all my wounds are from my own men".
Old Jack

....

IN the increasingly heavy darkness of the Wilderness, the Confederate attack and follow through strained to a halt, with some mixed company remnants occupying emplacements less than a mile from Chancellorsville, and the Federal centre of control. All the leading Regiments had become more or less disorganised in the course of the rapid fighting through the rough going, in increasingly poor light, and were active in correcting the confusion. *"... tell the troops from me to get into line and preserve their order,"* Jackson ordered Colonel Cobb of the Forty-forth Virginia,

---

470 Fuller quoting Paolo Vitelli and Prospero Colonna.

before riding *"through the ranks of the Eighteenth North Carolina."* The General was now technically ahead of his front line, engaged in his usual relentless quest for precise information on which to force the ongoing situation. A short distance ahead, Federal orders could be clearly heard, amid the plink of axes, as the enemy strove to shore-up his much frayed position. *"General, you should not expose yourself so much,"* one of the few officers with Jackson admonished him. *"There is no danger, Sir, the enemy is routed. Go back and tell General Hill to press on."*

Totally focused on the all-important priority of maintaining the pressure, and keeping the thoroughly discomforted opposition off balance, Jackson had already begun implementing his intention of maintaining the attack during the hours of darkness, at least until he was astride Hooker's line of retreat, just half a mile further on, the White House Road to the United States Ford of the Rappahannock. The Light Division had been ordered to take over the lead, and Hill, pleading unfamiliarity with the country, provided with a guide. None understood better than Stonewall Jackson that success is inherent in swift, positive action against the half-stunned opponent, as well as, in this specific instance, the inestimable strategic gains to be reaped from a comprehensive destruction of the Amy of the Potomac. With each second that ticked-by without progress, the major triumph was becoming that much less attainable; the floundering enemy gaining time to rise. Not seeing the approach of Hill's point sub-unit, in the lurid-yellow light of a rising moon filtering feebly through heavy tree shadow, Jackson turned back towards his own lines.

To the Eighteenth North Carolina, horsemen coming at them from in front, and only intermittently visible amongst the shadows – so their numbers difficult to make-out – spelt *"Yankee Cavalry!"* In the volley that quickly followed the alerting cry *"General Jackson was shot through the left arm below the shoulder, and in the left wrist."* Also, in the right hand, although Douglas – who was not present – writes that he sustained that wound earlier from Federal fire. Given the plaintive comment of Jackson himself, in the aftermath of the volley by the eighteenth, the claim seems unfounded. Of the small band with the General, his Engineer Officer *"Boswell, gallant, chivalric Boswell, fell from his horse, shot through the heart. Morrison had his horse shot under him. Captain Howard, a staff officer with Hill, was also wounded. Captain Forbes was killed and Sergeant Cunliffe mortally wounded. The courier just behind the General was killed, and another wounded; several horses were killed or wounded. 'Little Sorrel' became frantic with fright, rushed first towards the enemy, then, being turned by the General with his wounded hand, broke again to the rear. The General was struck in the face by a hanging limb, his cap knocked from his head, and when he was reeling from his saddle, his horse was stopped by Captain Wilbourn into whose arms he fell. Suddenly the enemy's artillery opened on the scene and added to the confusion and horror of it."* Having ridden for Dr McGuire, and told him of the wounding, Sandy Pendleton *"at first, overcome by his personal grief and loss, … fell fainting from his horse … but … was soon in the saddle and during the night he remained there. It was a pandemonium of death and confusion, but above it all rose the iron purpose and commands of Jackson."*[471]

A.P. Hill reached the smitten little group whilst it was still between the lines, and almost immediately had to order his escort to *"secure"* a brace of Federal skirmishers who appeared suddenly from the underbrush. Hill *"pulled off Jackson's gauntlets, which were full of blood, and bandaged the shattered arm with a handkerchief. 'Are you much hurt, he asked …* to which Jackson replied … *I think I am, and all my wounds are from my own men."*[472] General Hill ordered two of Jackson's staff officers and one of his own, to help Jackson to the rear. If questioned, he ordered, they were to say only that they were assisting a *"wounded Confederate officer."* No sooner had the four struggled to reach the Turnpike, than batteries of Hooker's Artillery – some fifty guns – deluged the forest in grape and canister, stripping the trees of wood and leaves, and *"striking sparks"* from the surface of the dirt road. The three young

---

471 Douglas.
472 Henderson.

officers laid the General down and tried to shield him with their bodies. After a few minutes the storm of fragments lifted, and the Federal gunners switched to solid shot, their guns searching further into the Confederate rear. Hill's infantry began passing along the Turnpike, and Jackson struggled laboriously aside into the trees, to avoid recognition; but General Pender at the head of his brigade, possibly recognising the Staff Officers, dismounted and expressed concern, adding that so destructive had been the barrage that *"he feared it would be necessary to fall back. … The air seemed to be alive with the shriek of shells and the whistling of bullets; horses riderless and mad with fright dashed in every direction; hundreds left the ranks and hurried to the rear, and the groans of the wounded and dying mingled with the wild shouts of others, to be led again to the assault.*[473] *Almost fainting from loss of blood … desperately wounded … Jackson's heart was unshaken. … Pushing aside those who supported him, he raised himself to his full height, and answered feebly, but distinctly enough to be heard above the din, 'You must hold your ground, General Pender; you must hold out to the last, Sir'.*"[474] The shelling continued, and refusing the exhausted General's request to lie down, a litter was brought and the painful struggle to the rear continued. *"Before they were free of the tangled wood, one of the stretcher-bearers, struck by a shot in the arm, let go of the handle. Jackson fell violently to the ground on his wounded side … in his agony … for the first time he was heard to groan."* To the startled concern of a Staff Officer asking if his wounding was serious, Jackson replied quietly *"No, Mr Smith, don't trouble yourself about me,"* … adding … *some words about winning the battle first and … then … attending to the wounded."* A few hundred yards further on – still to the accompaniment of Federal shelling – they reached Dr McGuire waiting with an ambulance.

"I hope you are not badly hurt, General? … he asked … 'I am badly injured, doctor, Jackson replied, *I fear I am dying.' After a pause he went on 'I am glad you have come. I think the wound in my shoulder*

473 An eye-witness quoted by Henderson.
474 Ibid.

is still bleeding.' ... he was lifted into the ambulance, where Colonel Crutchfield (Jackson's Chief of Artillery) *who had also been seriously wounded, was already lying. Whiskey and morphia were administered, and by the light of pine torches, carried by a few soldiers, he was slowly driven through the fields ... all was done that could ease his sufferings, but some jolting of the ambulance over the rough road was unavoidable; 'And yet, ...* Dr McGuire *wrote to* Henderson, *... his uniform politeness did not forsake him even in these most trying circumstances. His complete control, too, over his mind, enfeebled as it was by loss of blood and pain, was wonderful. His suffering was intense; his hands were cold, his skin clammy. But not a groan escaped him – not a sign of suffering, except the slight corrugation of the brow, the fixed, rigid face, the thin lips, so tightly compressed that the impression of the teeth could be seen through them. Except these, he controlled by his iron will all evidence of emotion, and, more difficult than this even, he controlled that disposition to restlessness which many of us have observed upon the battle-field as attending great loss of blood. Nor was he forgetful of others. He expressed very feelingly his sympathy for Crutchfield, and once, when the latter groaned aloud, he directed the ambulance to stop, and requested me to see if something could be done for his relief.*

"After reaching the hospital, he was carried to a tent, and placed in bed, covered with blankets, and another drink of whiskey and water given him. Two and a half hours elapsed before sufficient reaction took place to warrant an examination, and at two o'clock on Sunday morning I informed him that chloroform would be given him; I told him also that amputation would probably be required, and asked, if it was found necessary, whether it should be done at once. He replied promptly, 'Yes, certainly, Dr McGuire, do for me whatever you think best.'

"Chloroform was then administered, and the left arm amputated about two inches below the shoulder. Throughout the whole operation, and until all the dressings were applied, he continued insensible."

Disruption in the ranks of the Second Army Corps continued. Hill was in a litter, having been wounded by a shell fragment, and command had been devolved on Stuart, who sent Sandy Pendleton to ask Jackson what was to be done. Dr McGuire, at first denied him access; but on Pendleton saying *"the safety of the*

Army and the success of the Cause" depended upon it, McGuire relented. *"Well, Major, I am glad to see you …* Jackson greeted his chief staff officer … *I thought you were killed."* The position outlined and Stuart's request for instructions delivered, *"Jackson was at once interested, and asked in his quick way several questions. When they were answered, he remained silent, evidently trying to think; he contracted his brow, set his mouth, and for some moments lay obviously endeavouring to concentrate his thoughts. For a moment we believed he had succeeded, for his nostrils dilated, and his eye flashed with its old fire, but it was only for a moment: his face relaxed again, and presently he answered, very feebly and sadly: 'I don't know – I can't tell; say to General Stuart he must do what he thinks best.' Soon after this he slept."*[475]

Thereafter, no Confederate General proved capable of rounding out the success which Jackson had begun, and Hooker lacked the creative capability to reverse what Jackson's flank march and surprise attack had already achieved. Although he proved unable, in the all-important, immediate aftermath, to develop the opening which Jackson had created, Lee might have been capable of doing more, had the *"splendid infantry"* both of Pickett, together with Hood's Texans, been available to him, instead of having been diverted away, by Longstreet's failure to comply with the duty of a detached force commander, and stay within recall distance. Lee did plan an attack on Hooker, but nothing had transpired by the third night following Jackson's attack. During daylight on that day – May the fifth – Henderson claims *"it was impossible to push forward, for a violent rain-storm burst upon the Wilderness, and the spongy soil … absolutely precluded all movement across country."* In those same three days, having proved himself unable to achieve anything constructive, Hooker *"who had already made preparations for retreat, took advantage of the weather,"* and withdrew back across the Rappahannock, under cover of darkness. Lee failed to pursue. *'Impossible'* – as will have already been made clear – was simply not in the vocabulary of Stonewall Jackson.

---

475 Henderson quoting Dr McGuire's letter.

Meanwhile, the Commander-in-Chief had had the seriously wounded Lieutenant-General moved back to Guiney's Station, away from the fighting. On learning of Jackson's wounding Lee had written, *"Could I have directed events, I should have chosen for the good of the country to be disabled in your stead. ... I congratulate you upon the victory,* Lee continued, *which is due to your skill and energy."* Jackson himself said in the days before he died *"I simply took advantage of circumstances as they were presented to me in the providence of God. I feel that His hand led me – let us give Him the glory."* To an Aide, shortly afterwards Lee said *Give him my affectionate regards, tell him to make haste and get well ... He has lost his left arm, but I have lost my right,"* and he wrote privately, *"Any victory would be dear at such a price,"*[476]

Jackson remained alive for another five days, following the retreat of the Army of the Potomac, back to its old winter camps around Fredericksburg, when pneumonia finally killed him during the afternoon of Sunday, the tenth of May, 1863. He had remained positive about a recovery, almost to the very end, saying to his distraught wife, Anna, on the Sunday morning *"... 'death is not so near; I may yet get well.' She fell upon the bed, weeping bitterly and told him again there was no hope. ... he asked her to call Dr McGuire. ... 'Doctor, he said, Anna tells me I am to die to-day; is it so?' When he was answered, he remained silent for a moment or two, as if in intense thought, and then quietly replied, 'Very good, very good; it is all right.'"*

Douglas, who claimed that his *"watch stopped at a quarter past three o'clock. At that moment the heart of Stonewall Jackson ceased to beat, and his soul departed for Heaven",* traced the dominance of the pneumonia to Jackson catching a cold on the night before beginning his celebrated flank march. *"The night was clear and cold. ...* he remembered *... The General had neither overcoat nor blanket, for his wagon was far in the rear. Lieutenant J.P. Smith, aide-de-camp* (and one of the three young officers who shielded Jackson from the

---

476 Henderson quoting Lee.

Federal barrage shortly after his wounding) *offered him his cape, which the General at first refused and then, not to appear inconsiderate of Smith's persistent politeness* (surely more than mere cold politeness; consideration, generosity, love even) *accepted. But he did not use it long. Waking up after a short doze, he observed Smith asleep near a tree and went up to him and placed the cape on its owner so quietly that he was not aroused and slept on in comfort. When Smith awoke, the General was asleep in his old position. It was a sad as well as tender incident for the General caught a cold that night, which predisposed his system to the attack of pneumonia which ended in his death."*

In the three days before Hooker withdrew, the Stonewall brigade had attacked fiercely under Stuart to the cry *'Remember Jackson!'* and when the time came to remove to Richmond the body of *"the leader whom they trusted beyond all others,"* they requested, through Douglas, that *"the brigade or part of it"* should provide the escort. With great sensitivity and feeling, Lee turned down the request. *"Those people over the river are again showing signs of movement,* he told Douglas, *and I cannot leave my Headquarters long enough to ride to the depot and pay my dear friend the poor tribute of seeing his body placed upon the cars. ... Tell them,* he concluded, *that deeply as we all lament the death of their General yet, if his spirit remains behind to inspire his Corps and the Army, perhaps in the end, his death may be as great a gain to us as it is to himself."* At Ashland, where the Valley Army had de-trained before the Seven Days Battles, *"a delegation of ladies placed fresh flowers and wreaths upon the coffin."* On reaching the capital, the cortege was given *"a military and civic escort ... to the Executive Mansion – the home of Jackson's staunch friend Governor Letcher. During the night, the body was embalmed and transferred to a neat metallic coffin ... wrapped in the first new Confederate flag that had been made. ... There was an immense military and civic pageant* – the next day – *to convey the body ... to ... the Capitol of the new Republic. ...* The President of the Confederacy and his Cabinet were all present; eight Generals and one Commodore were the pallbearers ... *and with all the pomp and circumstance of a warrior's funeral, the body of our modest and simple chieftain was borne through the crowds which lined the streets. ... There,* in the Capitol, *the throng pressed through in continuous stream for a first and last view of the great General, whom they had learned to honour without seeing, and love without knowing."*

After the lying in state, *"on the fifteenth of May, General Jackson was laid to 'rest in the shade of the trees'*[477]*, at the spot he had chosen, 'at Lexington in the Valley of Virginia.'"*

---

477 The last words of General Thomas J. Jackson have been recorded as;
"Let us cross over the river and rest under the shade of the trees."

42. PATRIOT & REBEL

....

"What is life without honour?
Degradation is worse than death.
We must think of the living and of those
who are to come after us, and see that by
God's Blessing, we transmit to them the
freedom we have ourselves inherited."
Stonewall Jackson

....

JACKSON's death stirred great feeling and emotion in both friend and foe. Not in friend and foe alike, exactly, for in the North, people had to shade sympathy and regret with relief that so formidable a force had been taken out of the reckoning. In the South the regret was untrammelled, and the outpouring of grief, such as is accorded to few. To Lincoln in America – within two years, and in England; to Nelson – nearly sixty years previously. More recently, something akin to that accorded to John F Kennedy, and, nearly half a Century later again, to Princess Diana. The sister of Ellie, Jackson's first wife – Margaret Preston Junkin – wrote in her Diary for the twelfth of May, *"At five this evening the startling confirmation comes, Jackson is indeed dead! ... My heart overflows with sorrow. ... The grief in the community is intense; everybody is in tears. ... Never have I known a holier man ... Never have I seen a human being as thoroughly governed by duty ... He lived only to please God."* Her Diary entry for the burial on the fifteenth of May included the lines, *"The coffin was draped in the* first *Confederate Flag ever made, and presented by President Davis to Mrs Jackson, it was wrapped around the coffin, and on it were laid multitudes of wreaths and flowers which had been piled upon it all along the sad journey to Richmond, and thence to Lexington. The grave too was heaped with flowers. ... Not many better* men have lived and died ... *Sincerer mourning was never manifested for any one, I do think."*[478]

In New York, the *"Daily Chronicle"* published an editorial by Colonel John Forney, headed *"The Death of Stonewall Jackson"*, which included the lines *"... whilst we are only too glad to be rid in any way, of so terrible a foe, our sense of relief is not unmingled with emotions of sorrow and sympathy at the death of so brave a man. ...* More questionably, for Jackson was no proselytiser, Forney linked Jackson, as a fanatic, with *"Mahomet ... Loyola ... Xavier ... as well as ... several of the Popes of Rome."* The Colonel ended his editorial on a rather more rational note, even if he himself tee-tered on the very rim of tub-thumping; *"Let us rather devoutly acknowledge the Providence of God, who, while He smites the accursed land with famine, and the people with madness, takes from their accursed cause its bravest, noblest, and purest defender. Stonewall Jackson was a great General, a brave soldier, a noble Christian, and a pure man. May God throw these great virtues against the sins of the secessionist, the ad-vocate of a great national crime."* Like many, of course, Jackson's ad-vocacy was dedicated to his native Virginia, a sentiment in the era in which he lived that cannot reasonably be termed a nation-al crime. Rather, of all traditional causes in which to do battle, the noblest; the most patriotic.

"The editorial had hardly appeared on the streets of the city of Washington ... wrote Roy Bird Cook, who reproduced the ed-itorial more fully *... until it came to the attention of the President of the United States. With the deep appreciation of the passing of a great American and brave soldier – who wore both the Blue and the Grey – he sent the following note to Editor Forney, from the 'Executive Mansion, Washington, May the thirteenth, 1863. My Dear Sir, I wish to lose not time in thanking you for the excellent and manly article in the 'Chronicle' on Stonewall Jackson. Yours truly, A. Lincoln.'"* While the War con-tinued, the North largely maintained its stance regarding Jackson. A year or so later, when the struggle had become more rabid,

---

478 Quoted by Jackson's nephew, Thomas Jackson Arnold.

Colonel Schoonmaker, commanding the Eighth Pennsylvania Cavalry, on reaching Lexington in the course of the 'Hunter Raid' into Virginia, was ordered to burn the Virginia Military Institute. This he refused to do, on the grounds *"he had not enlisted in the Army for that purpose … the Colonel … formed his command in line at Jackson's grave and fired a salute to his memory."*[479] General Howard, whose Eleventh Corps was shattered by Jackson's flank attack at Chancellorsville, wrote shortly after the War *"… in bold planning, in energy of execution, which he had the power to diffuse, in indefatigable activity and moral ascendency, he stood head and shoulders above his confreres."*

The memory of Stonewall Jackson became world property – 'the whole world his sepulchre,' – from the moment he was buried in Lexington. In the last two years of his life – his only two years as General – he had already attracted a considerable following across the Atlantic, especially in England. Of her husband's great biography, Mrs Henderson wrote *"only about one-fourth of the copies sold every year are sold in America."*[480]

Stonewall Jackson was a traditional style General and leader of armies. He fought by a very exact understanding of first principles, and an equally clear understanding of the type of war in which he was embroiled; by principles which were evolved, tried and proven over centuries, and which were as immutable in his day, as they had been two thousand years earlier, and still are today, a Century and a half or so later. His close inter-relationship with his soldiers, resulting in, what he termed, his 'influence' with them; to their marching and fighting qualities was in the classic mould, from which were fired the very best; the most successful. This was despite the changing style of warfare, which, driven by weapon development, was ushered in by the

---

479 Quoted by Arnold, who noted *the commanding general who so ordered Schoonmaker was a Virginian.* Schoonmaker survived the War to have conferred *"upon him honorary membership in the alumni of the VMI".*
480 Arnold.

Civil War in America. One key to Jackson's outstandingly successful technique, lies in his comprehensive understanding of how the weapons of his day had evolved. Appreciating how the hardware had changed since the turn of the Nineteenth Century, he had the intellect and imagination to translate his understanding into practical action. With this appreciation of the new, went a thorough acceptance of the oldest truisms of all; that battles are won by vigour, cunning, and the speed of movement which enables surprise, and, above all, by shrouding movement in secrecy. He was dismissive of mere numbers, because rarely, if ever, have they been anything more than a secondary advantage, and barely even that in the context of ever-evolving modern weaponry.

Judged by his actions, not even Lee, when he wrote to Jackson that he was right; there should be 'no more Malvern Hills', appreciated what Jackson understood, and fully hoisted-in the implications of Jackson the 'supremest flanker and rearer', nor exactly what he was implying when he said, 'my men never fail to hold a position'. The General who could sanction the enormity of a 'Pickett's Charge', so-called, simply cannot have fully taken the point. In both these revealing glimpses of the incomparable technique, Jackson was working to utilise the advantages of the firearm of his day, whilst at the same time denying those same advantages to his opponent. This is not to disparage other competent Generals of the War; but simply to say that they were in a class – the majority class – below Stonewall Jackson. Neither is it, perhaps, in the least surprising that the majority of Generals have proved below master-class standard, given the complexity of the Art of War, and the vagaries of talent across the spread of human kind. Half a Century later, the years 1914 to 1918 threw-up an entire war-full of Generals; not one of whom showed master-class ability; not one of whom either understood, or had the imagination to creatively exploit, the modern weapon. Many on the Western Front, with their mass slaughtering attacks – from which they remained personally aloof – made them more akin to bureaucratic mass murderers than to true Generals. Especially is this true of Haig's campaign in Flanders between August and

November 1917, which, at least in part, may have prompted H.G. Wells into the un-discerning generalisation: *"the professional military mind is by necessity an inferior and unimaginative mind; no man of high intellectual quality would willingly imprison his gifts in such a calling."* History, and the sheer intellectual complexity inherent in the Art of War, suggest otherwise. Wells continued (of World War One) *"… from first to last it was impossible to get it out of the hands of the regular generals."* Which is an indictment both of the politicians of that time, as well as of the Generals. He might have looked to the American Civil War to appreciate the dangers of direct political intervention in the making of war, and to Jackson, specifically, for a proper spurning of 'impossible', and how best to be rid of an unwanted General. Dismiss instantly and trust to Providence to come up with a better, is the answer.

The next General after Stonewall Jackson to join the exclusive handful which began with Alexander, did not take the stage until the second of the World Wars of the Twentieth Century. He too, interestingly enough, was an American of Irish-Scotch descent.

In the aftermath of the American Civil War, inevitably, comparisons were made, assessments offered, and opinions freely stated. If there really is anything worthwhile to be gained from drawing comparisons between Generals who never confronted one another, other than simply to compare how each went about their business, it is not possible to seriously imagine any other General of the Civil War getting the better of Jackson in a contest of generalship. Including Grant, the ultimate victor. Jackson's fast-moving and vigorous, imaginative and unpredictable boldness would seem more likely to have seduced the Goddess of Victory than the bludgeoning, wearing-down, unimaginative methodology of Grant. It is, perhaps, worth bearing in mind in this connexion, that a feature of the records of all the truly great Generals is that they were able always to resolve whatever situation confronted them, no matter who confronted them. This is no less true of Jackson. There is no reason for believing that his intellect was not up to working out Grant, who does not come across as an especially intellectual winner, and, whatever Napoleon may have said about the big battalions, it is the thinking Generals who are the masters of the battle-field, as Alexander emphatically demonstrated from the earliest times. A clear and precise understanding of the nature of the war being fought, is the first and absolute imperative, which has all too often been lacking in military leaders, including since 1945.

For whatever reason, doubts were expressed about Jackson's capabilities, even whilst he was advancing in rank and out-performing his contempories. In the aftermath of the War, it became something of an academic fad to question whether Jackson would have been capable of supreme command. No unbiased person with the least military understanding can, or could, have any doubt. Relatively brief though the record is, it is sufficiently brilliant, clear and comprehensive to make the question superfluous, especially as the conclusion can never be more than a positive assumption.

Thomas Jackson Arnold, the General's nephew and the son of his beloved sister Laura, was quick to pick up on this negative criticism, and wrote that in his opinion: *"the person never lived who could fathom the depth of General Jackson's mind."*[481] This opinion is true, of course, in the literal sense that the individual human mind can never be completely fathomed by another, and, especially, given that the mind of Tom Jackson was more individual and far less ordinary than most – if, indeed, any human mind can be considered ordinary. *"Notwithstanding the fact that in the war with Mexico,"* Arnold goes on, *"he had received a larger number of promotions than any other of the young officers in the same period of time, yet in the beginning of the Civil War he was not generally regarded as capable of independent command ... when he was commissioned colonel ... that rank was thought to equal his capacity, and there was serious misgiving on the part of many as to the risk of placing him in independent command of as important a post as Harper's Ferry."* As

---

481 Thomas Jackson Arnold, *"Early Life and Letters of General Thomas J. Jackson" ('Stonewall')*. Reprinted 1957 by The Dietz Press Inc., Richmond, Va.

Jackson continued to advance in rank, all the while achieving in the most unforgiving of all crucibles – and in the only true test of generalship – the intellectual and physical confrontation with an enemy *"there were many who each time thought that he had been advanced beyond his capacity."* The 'many' would have included a fair sprinkling of politicians, who would have come to politics via diverse means, including by way of the army or the militia. To get an indication of the flaws in political performance, we need look no further than the example of the two Presidents. Davis, especially, was *"a dictator, and as arbitrary as Lincoln ... starched and egoistic, a man who would neither argue nor listen, and who could not tolerate either assistance or opposition."*[482] And Davis, unlike Lincoln, was West Point trained. He had commanded volunteers in the war with Mexico. Lincoln, on the other hand, did at least try to understand the futile art, however unsuccessfully, and at least, in the end, recognised his own limitations.

Apart from the expression of doubt about his abilities, it has also been said of Jackson that *"He wished to follow, and not to lead."*[483] The man and his record reveal with perfect clarity that the first part of that criticism attempts to impute doubt where no doubt can sensibly exist, whilst the remainder is simply not true. Jackson's sense of duty was too strong, and his instinctive ability too great. Some seventeen months after the Civil War began, when Lee's absence placed Jackson in command of the Army of Northern Virginia, some expressed themselves anxious, despite all that he had achieved, and the unique ability he had demonstrated. If the anxiety was straight forward and genuine, then it indicates a failure, not only to appreciate what Jackson had achieved; but also, to understand the man. In a broader context it displays a complete lack of understanding of the nature and character traits that become and define the greatest Generals. Writing of Alexander, Colonel

482 J.F.C. Fuller, *"The Conduct of War 1789 – 1961",* University Paperback edition, Eyre Methuen Ltd, London, 1977.

483 Henderson.

Dodge[484] observes *"... a great captain must first of all be a great man ... no man can by any possibility blunder into being a great soldier without the most generous virtues of the soul, and the most distinguished powers of the intellect."* Whilst Alexander had to function as both king and statesman, as well as General, and Jackson, obviously, did neither, he nevertheless, unquestionably displayed every trait of the great leader and General, which Dodge – Jackson's contemporary (but in the cause of the North) went on to list: *"Independence, self-reliance, ambition within proper bounds; physical bravery which not only does not know fear, but which is not even conscious that there is such a thing as courage; that greater moral quality which can hold the lives of ... men ... intelligently and unflinchingly in his grasp; powers of endurance which cannot be overtaxed; the unconscious habit of ruling men and of commanding their love and admiration, coupled with the ability to stir their enthusiasm to the yielding of the last ounce of effort.* The latter ... says Dodge ... *comprises business capacity of the very highest order, essential to the care of his troops; keen perceptions which even in extraordinary circumstance or sudden emergencies are not to be led astray; the ability to think as quickly and accurately in the turmoil of battle as in the quiet of the bureau; the power to see to its ultimate conclusion the result of a strategic or tactical manoeuvre; the capacity to gauge the efforts of men and of masses of men; the many-sidedness which can respond to the demands of every detail of the battlefield, while never losing sight of the one object aimed at; the mental strength which weakens not under the tax of hours and days of unequalled strain.* Commenting upon Alexander's Illyrian Campaign in the first year of his reign, Colonel Dodge notes also *"... the rare strategic capacity, the originality of conception, the boldness of resolution, the rapidity of action."* Not one of the mental and physical qualities ascribed to the great Macedonian was not present in the great Virginian.

Understanding of the greatness of Jackson, especially as a soldier, increased as time passed, and the bitterness of internecine war faded. Some fifty years after his death, the *Baltimore Sun*

---

484 Theodore Ayrault Dodge, *"Alexander"* (First published 1890) First De Capo Press edition, New York, 1996.

commented in an editorial on the second of July, 1913: *"Jackson is one of the Civil War figures who grows larger the longer he is studied, and who makes an extraordinary appeal to the popular as well as to the military imagination. He was as strong and singular in character as he was unusual and masterful in genius … What he was in the military sense we know from the almost universal belief that had he not fallen at Chancellorsville the battle of Gettysburg either would never have occurred, or would have had a different termination."*[485] A year and a half after the editorial was published, there appeared in the *Saturday Evening Post* the account of a conversation that took place in England, at the home of Field Marshal Lord Roberts of Kandahar, Pretoria and Wexford, then Britain's Chief of the Imperial General Staff. *"In speaking of the American Civil War Lord Roberts said 'America produced some magnificent soldiers in those four years, and the greatest of them, to my way of thinking, was Stonewall Jackson. In my opinion Stonewall Jackson was one of the greatest natural military geniuses the world ever saw. I will go even further than that – as a campaigner in the field he never had a superior. In some respects, I doubt whether he ever had an equal.*[486]

Others of the select handful of truly great exponents of the Art of War, have been criticised for their achievements, only Stonewall Jackson, it seems, has been doubted for what he did not have the opportunity to attempt. His brilliance was never acknowledged directly with independent command. Promotion to Lieutenant-General was brought about as much as anything by the increasing size of the Army of Northern Virginia requiring a two corps structure. It is hard to envisage Lincoln not recognising and more fully utilising the unique genius of Stonewall Jackson, had his loyalty lain with the Union.

That the Confederate hierarchy chose to overlook their one consistent winner may have stemmed from any number of causes between ignorance and prejudice; but Jackson himself had a strongly developed sense of hierarchy; of submission to the established

---

485 Arnold.

486 Arnold.

military order, coupled to an inflexible, humble dedication to the part played in success by a Supreme Being. He was extremely modest and unassuming. Douglas comments that, *"His worth had a worthy rival in his modesty."* So self-effacing a demeanour may well lead the less discerning – or the less scrupulous; less disinterested – to question ability; but it provides no grounds whatsoever for the assumption that he *wished to follow and not to lead.* Jackson's strong sense of loyalty to Virginia would also have assured his leadership, although he was not of the type to *"wade through slaughter to a throne."* Possibly his lack of interest in politics played a part too in his not pushing for a more prominent role in the military leadership of the South. Had the post of Commander-in-Chief come his way, with his strong sense of duty he would have accepted the task, as being what God wanted him to do. His abilities, clearly, were equal to such a task. Throughout the Valley Campaign he never ceased to take the overall strategic situation into account, while at the same time juggling the complexities of the widely dispersed and numerically superior enemy on his front. Whilst his actions and achievements speak clearly of his exceptional ability, so many of his succinct remarks during the War, are a clear indicator of his comprehensive understanding. Not least that before the Chancellorsville campaign opened, he said, *"We must make this campaign an exceedingly active one, … only thus can a weaker country cope with a stronger; it must make up in activity what it lacks in strength. A defensive campaign can only be made successful by taking the aggressive (step) at the proper time."* A clear mission statement, by one who not only possessed the breadth of vision; but had both the intellectual and physical resources, as well as the patient, unflurried determination to make vision reality. One cannot help wondering if any other General on either side could understand his definition of *"exceedingly active!"* And beneath it all, Jackson had a true understanding too, of that simple reality, which so many either do not fully comprehend, or, even more so today, cower away from; *"War means fighting. The business of the soldier is to fight."*[487]

---

487 Stonewall Jackson.

If the 'Seven Days' battles bear not a trace of the genius of Stonewall Jackson, then the months of Confederate success that followed in 1862 and continued up until the moment of his wounding and subsequent death in April 1863, are hallmarked by little else, unless it be the resolution, stamina and sheer guts of the Rank and File soldiers who were inspired to march and fight under his leadership. Lee's position as commander of the Army of Northern Virginia has, inevitably, meant speculation about the period leading up until Jackson's death, as to whose was the mind behind the winning combinations. On the evidence of what took place, they can only have originated in the brain of one man, just as the physical execution of their ingenuity was driven to triumphant conclusion by the moral and physical strength of that one man. Lee carried out no more great turning and enveloping manoeuvres after Jackson's death because, it has been said, there was no other General in the Confederate Army whom he could trust to carry out such manoeuvres. Partly this may be true. Rather more importantly, Lee did not and could not, because he no longer had access to the mind which could conceive such imaginative, bold, match-winning combinations.

If the Confederate hierarchy failed to appreciate the unique genius of Thomas Jonathan Jackson, like his soldiers; the wider populations of the Southern States, and of those of his fellow-countrymen in opposition, the inmate of a lunatic asylum near Baltimore had no doubts. On being told of Jackson's death, Douglas recorded, *"Deep sadness settled upon his face. Then suddenly a light broke over it and lifting his head and looking up into the sky he exclaimed, "Oh, what a battle must have been raging in Heaven, when the Archangel of the Lord needed the services of Stonewall Jackson!"*

FINIS

SOURCES

....

Page 10 (et seq.) "Stonewall Jackson and the American Civil War" by Lieutenant-Colonel G F R Henderson CB, Longmans, Green & Co, London, New York and Bombay, 1904 edition.

Page 11 (et seq.) "I Rode with Stonewall" by Henry Kyd Douglas, The University of North Carolina Press, Twelfth Printing 1940.

Page 13 (et seq.) "The Family and Early Life of Stonewall Jackson" by Roy Bird Cook (John Esten Cooke).

Page 15 (et seq.) "Early Life and Letters of General Thomas J Jackson" by his nephew Thomas Jackson Arnold, reprinted 1957, by The Dietz Press Inc., Richmond, VA.

Page 37 (et seq.) "Memoirs of Lieutenant-General Scott LLD, Written by himself", Sheldon and Company, Publishers, New York, 1864.

Page 39 "The Influence of Sea Power upon the French Revolution and Empire" by Admiral A T Mahan USN.

Page 41 "The Real Stonewall Jackson" for the February 1894 edition of "Century Magazine", by D H Hill.

Page 60 (et seq.) "Life and Campaigns of Lt-Gen Thomas J. Jackson" by Professor, the Reverend Dr R L Dabney DD.

Page 101 "Oliver Cromwell" by Samuel Rawson Gardiner, published 1901.

Page 106 "New Testament" St Mark's Gospel, Ch.16 v.16.

Page 136 "The Trial and Death of Socrates", Plato

Page 137 "Battles and Leaders of the Civil War", Vol. 2, The Century Company, New York, 1887.

Page 143 (et seq.) "Stonewall Jackson's Campaign in the Shenandoah Valley of Virginia", by Lieutenant-Colonel William Allan CSA, re-issued by Hugh Rees Ltd, London, 1912

Page 152   From the Joint Committee Report on the Conduct of the War.

Page 157   "The Conduct of War 1789–1961" by Major-General J F C Fuller, University Paperback edition, 1975 & 1977.

Page 166   "Nelson" by Carola Oman, Hodder and Stoughton Limited, London, June 1947.

Page 169 (et seq.) "Diary" of Major Jed Hotchkiss CSA.

Page 171 (et seq.) "The Military Maxims of Napoleon" by Lieutenant-General Sir George C Aguiler CB, with a new Introduction and Commentary by David G Chandler, De Capo Press edition, 1995.

Page 189   "From Brook Farm to Cedar Mountain" by General G A Gordon (quoted by Henderson).

Page 222 (et seq.) "Deconstruction and Reconstruction" by General Dick Taylor (quoted by Henderson).

Page 244   From a poem by C. Marshall Barton, (quoted by Douglas).

Page 253   "Military & Naval History of the Rebellion in the United States" by W J Tenney, originally published 1866 (quoted by William Allan).

Page 272   "New York Tribune" of June 7, 1862 (quoted by William Allan).

Page 335 (et seq.) "Letters from Lee's Army" by Captain Charles M. Blackford, compiled by Susan Leigh Blackford, Charles Scribner's Sons, New York and London, 1947.

Page 359   "John Macnab" by John Buchan.

Page 363   "The Army of Northern Virginia" by William Allan (quoted by Henderson).

Page 385   "Our House Divided" by J. B. McMaster (Paperback. edition) original title: "A History of the

People of the United States during Lincoln's Administration" (McMaster quoting General McDowell).

Page 395   "Military Memoirs of Marlborough's Campaigns 1702 – 1712" by Captain Robert Parker, edited by David Chandler, Greenhill Books, London 1998.

Page 396   "Wellington – The Iron Duke" by Richard Holmes (quoting from "Rough Notes on Seven Campaigns" by John Spencer Cooper). Harper Collins Publishers.

Page 409   "Memoirs" by General Bradley T Johnson CSA (quoted by Henderson).

Page 432   "The Times" of June 11, 1863, from a report by The Hon. Francis Lawley (quoted by Henderson)

Page 466   "Alexander" by Theodore Ayrault Dodge (First published 1890) First De Capo Press edition, New York, 1996.

The author

M W Banks divides his time between Malta and Devon, England. He attended the Cathedral School, Chichester, and the Nautical College, Pangbourne, and was commissioned into the Royal Marines direct from school. Four years of Royal Marines and Commando training followed. His specialist qualifications included Shallow Water Diver and, with the Fleet Air Arm, helicopter pilot and Qualified Helicopter Instructor.

On leaving the Royal Marines, he worked in the Scotch Whisky industry, and in management and fund raising in the charitable sector. His leisure and sporting interests include reading, aviation, volunteering with an historic house museum, skiing, swimming, golf and horse riding. He is widowed with one stepson.

The publisher

He who stops getting better stops being good.

This is the motto of novum publishing, and our focus is on finding new manuscripts, publishing them and offering long-term support to the authors.
Our publishing house was founded in 1997, and since then it has become THE expert for new authors and has won numerous awards.

Our editorial team will peruse each manuscript within a few weeks free of charge and without obligation.

You will find more information about novum publishing and our books on the internet:

www.novum-publishing.co.uk